JAMES REDDIE

AN HISTORICAL VIEW OF THE LAW OF MARITIME COMMERCE

Elibron Classics
www.elibron.com

Elibron Classics series.

ISBN 1-4021-3716-8 (paperback)
ISBN 1-4021-1543-1 (hardcover)

This Elibron Classics Replica Edition is an unabridged facsimile of the edition published in 1841 by William Blackwood and Sons, Edinburgh and London.

AN

HISTORICAL VIEW

OF THE

LAW OF MARITIME COMMERCE.

BY JAMES REDDIE, ESQ., ADVOCATE,

AUTHOR OF "INQUIRIES, ELEMENTARY AND HISTORICAL, INTO THE SCIENCE OF LAW."

WILLIAM BLACKWOOD AND SONS,

EDINBURGH AND LONDON.

M.DCCC.XLI.

EDINBURGH:

PRINTED BY PETER BROWN, ST JAMES' SQUARE.

CONTENTS.

PART FIRST.

OF THE LAW OF MARITIME COMMERCE AS A BRANCH OF THE INTERNAL COERCIVE LAW OF NATIONS.

PART SECOND.

HISTORICAL VIEW OF THE LAW OF MARITIME COMMERCE AMONG ANCIENT NATIONS.

PART THIRD.

HISTORICAL VIEW OF THE LAWS AND USAGES OF MARITIME COMMERCE DURING THE MIDDLE AGES.

PART FOURTH.

OF THE MARITIME AND COMMERCIAL LAW OF THE MODERN EUROPEAN NATIONS.

PREFACE.

THE greater part of the following Notes was written, a good many years ago, to serve as an introduction to a contemplated Series of Practical Treatises on the Law of Maritime Commerce; but, from the principal work having been abandoned, the proposed introduction was laid aside until a perusal of the late elaborate work of M. Pardessus, entitled "Collection des Loix Maritimes," suggested to the author the idea of revising and enlarging his Notes.

Having been a pupil of the Scotch Historical School of Law, and early accustomed to peruse the works of the more eminent scientific German lawyers which appeared towards the close of the last and in the course of the present century, of which the doctrines appear, of late years, to have been so generally adopted by the philosophical lawyers of France, the author, perhaps, did not require much farther instruction in the improved mode of studying law as a science. But, in the original compilation of this sketch, he could avail himself only of those works on maritime and commercial law, ancient and modern, whether properly legislative or consuetudinary and judiciary, or the compositions of private individuals, which had been printed, and of which a perusal could be obtained by purchase, or by access to public libraries.

Within these few years, however, M. Pardessus, encouraged apparently by the laudable patronage of the French Government of Louis XVIII. and of Louis Philippe, has nearly completed his collection of the maritime laws now extant, anterior to the eighteenth century, of the different nations, ancient and modern, who have been distinguished by their success in navigation and commerce. In this valuable collection, M. Pardessus has not only, by his indefatigable exertions, brought to light many pieces of maritime and commercial legislation not previously known, and corrected the editions of such as had been previously printed, but has also, in the dissertations which accompany the texts, by his acute and sound criticism, philosophic as well as antiquarian, corrected the erroneous conjectural inferences of many former writers in this department of jurisprudence. And although the author of the following Notes has not had leisure, and has, perhaps, neither talents nor taste for such elaborate antiquarian researches and minute historical criticism, it has occurred to him he might, perhaps, contribute, in some degree, to the diffusion of the knowledge of the law of maritime commerce, by combining with his former historical sketch the results of the investigations here alluded to.

At the outset, therefore, he begs to express his acknowledgments for the assistance he has derived from the learned labours of the author of the "Collection des Loix Maritimes," and to state generally, as he will afterwards do specially, in the course of the sketch, that he has sometimes translated, but generally transfused, and abridged or condensed, such portions of that work as he thought would render more complete the historical view which he had previously prepared.

With the exception of the compilation of the maritime usages generally prevalent during the middle ages, M. Pardessus has, in his Collection, limited himself to the exhibition of authentic copies of what may be called the statutes, or legislative enactments, of the different states which have cultivated navigation and commerce. And, as the Collection thus omits that large portion of the law of maritime commerce, which, although not digested in compilations expressly sanctioned by sovereign authority, has come, in most countries, to be firmly established as common law, by usage and judicial determination, the author has not only continued, as in his original sketch, but amplified his notices of the records of such judicial determinations, and of the works of the individual authors by whom they have been collected and arranged.

GLASGOW, *October*, 1841.

PART FIRST

OF THE LAW OF MARITIME COMMERCE, AS A BRANCH OF THE INTERNAL COERCIVE LAW OF NATIONS.

CHAPTER I.

OF THE LAW OF MARITIME COMMERCE, IN RELATION TO THE OTHER BRANCHES OF COERCIVE LAW.

The law of maritime commerce has been very frequently described as a branch of the law of nations; but, for understanding distinctly what are its proper sphere and limits, and its relation to the other departments of jurisprudence, it may be of use to mark its position under or among the great divisions of human law, primary and subordinate.

As the powers of man, corporeal and mental, are very limited, and adapted to the limited circumstances in which he is placed on earth, and as the habitable parts of this globe are divided and separated by mountains, rivers, and seas, mankind have, from the earliest times, been divided into separate communities, tribes, or nations, forming independent states. And the first grand division of law, therefore, is into national, comprehending the whole internal law of a state, private and public, or constitutional; and into international, formerly more loosely called the law of nations, or, in the modern acceptation of the terms, *Jus gentium*, comprehending the external law of independent states in relation to each other, as regulating the intercourse of these different states in their corporate capacity, and likewise of their respective subjects.

Now, maritime commerce, it is plain, may be carried on, and is, indeed, very frequently carried on, between the subjects of different states; and it may, especially in time of war, involve questions affecting the reciprocal rights and obligations of these independent states and of their subjects: such as the questions, Whether the neutrality of the vessel covers the cargo? and, Whether the hostility of the vessel confiscates the cargo? discussed in one of the oldest of the modern codes of maritime law, denominated the "*Consolato del Mare.*" And, where maritime commerce gives rise to such questions, involving the reciprocal rights and obligations of independent nations, the law determining such questions clearly forms a branch of the law of nations, or rather of what has been recently more correctly denominated international law, and was, for a considerable period previously, distinguished as *Jus maritimum publicum, aut gentium.* But the law of maritime commerce, of which it is now proposed to take an historical view, although it has likewise been described, both in ancient and in modern times, as a branch of the law of nations, does not involve any international questions, or discuss the reciprocal rights and obligations of the governments and subjects of independent states, in relation to each other. It is a branch of the internal law of maritime states; derives its authority and sanction from the supreme power in these states; and has, more recently, and by some jurists, been termed *Jus maritimum privatum,* in contradistinction to *Jus maritimum publicum, aut gentium.*

Still, however, not merely the older continental jurists, such as Stypmannus and Loccenius, but also the more modern, such as Emerigon, Capmany, Jorio, and Piantanida, talk very generally of a *Jus maritimum universale*, of there being something universal in the laws of maritime commerce.

In England too, one of the ablest commercial judges of that or any other country, Lord Mansfield, stated judicially, that "the maritime law is not the law of a particular country, but the general law of nations." And the same view appears to have been entertained by English lawyers generally, such as Molloy, Blackstone, Park, and Marshall. A little further inquiry, therefore, and explanatory discrimination of terms, appear to be requisite.

In the reciprocal exchange of superfluous commodities, whether these commodities be the spontaneous or cultivated produce of the soil, or have been adapted by art to human use and convenience, men, in all countries, are placed in nearly similar or analogous circumstances, and are consequently led to adopt similar or analogous habits of action and rules of conduct. In the tenure by which land is held among different nations, and in the mode by which property of that description is transmitted from generation to generation, we perceive the pervading influence of local customs and peculiar habits; but in the dealings of merchants, there is little room for singularity of institution. The intercourse between the inhabitants of different countries, for the purpose of supplying their mutual wants, is adverse to anything local or peculiar. Expediency obviously requires that, in all countries, commercial transactions should be regulated by the same, or, at least, by similar or analogous rules; and, accordingly, in this department of jurisprudence, we observe a greater similarity of usage and institution than perhaps in any of the other arrangements which are formed in the progress of civil society.

But although, from its general nature, and from its rules being used and observed in common by the inhabitants of different countries, maritime and commercial law has been and may be considered as a branch of the *jus gentium*, in the sense in which that phrase was used by the Roman lawyers, as denoting the system of rules by which men, as rational beings, and as distinguished from the lower animals, regulate, or ought to regulate, their actions, it cannot, with correctness of idea or expression, be held or said on this ground, or in this respect, to form a part of what is now strictly and properly termed the law of nations. The law of nations, properly so called, is that collection of rules by which the reciprocal intercourse of independent states, and of the individuals of whom they are composed, is or ought to be governed. This, in more precise language, has been termed, by that accomplished lawyer Chancellor D'Aguesseau,* *Droit public exterieur*, or *Droit entre les nations*, *jus inter gentes*; and afterwards, by that acute and philosophic jurist Mr Bentham, in his Principles of Morals and Legislation, *International Law*. And to this code, the principles of private, maritime, and mercantile jurisprudence cannot, with propriety, be said to belong. The law of maritime commerce forms a part of the internal law of the state; and may be, and is frequently, enforced by the common-law courts, as well as by the admiralty courts or maritime judicatories of a country. It is established by the governments of different states, to regulate, in that class of transactions, the conduct chiefly of their own subjects, or, at least, of individuals generally, without distinguishing them as natives or foreigners, or to what nation they belong; and it is only when mercantile transactions involve

---

* Œuvres, tome i., p. 444.

questions of right between different states, and between the subjects of different independent governments, considered as such, that the regulation of these transactions becomes a part of international law.

Having thus seen that the law of maritime commerce can be correctly held to form a branch of the law of nations, in the modern, strict, and proper sense of the term, only so far as it involves international relations and questions, corporate or individual, and that when it does not involve such international relations, although not of a peculiar or local, but of a similar and general, if not universal, nature, and used in common by various different nations, it forms properly a part of the Internal law of each separate independent state, we proceed to notice its relative position in the latter character.

Now, the national or Internal law of a state may either regulate the conduct of the individuals of whom the nation is composed, in relation to each other as individuals, or it may regulate the conduct of the individuals of whom the nation is composed, in relation to the community, state, or government, and the conduct of the latter to the former; in other words, the internal law of a nation is composed of private law, or individual jurisprudence, and of public, political, or constitutional law.

The private law of a nation, viewed generally, may be considered with reference to its sources, progress, or mode of formation and accumulation, and may be divided into common or consuetudinary law, and statutory law; or it may be considered with reference to its proper subject-matter, its principles, and detailed regulations, and may be divided into the different classes or descriptions of the private rights and obligations of individuals living in the same community; or it may be considered with reference to the mode of enforcing these rights and obligations, and may be divided into civil and criminal or penal law.

The private law of a nation, again, viewed particularly or in separate parts, may be considered as consisting of or divided into different branches or departments, according to the different descriptions or classes of individuals to whom it is applicable, and according to the occupations of those individuals, and the external material objects and operations with which they are conversant. Thus one great branch of the private law of a nation is applicable to the larger portion of the community, holding substantial interests in land or engaged in agricultural operations. Another great branch is applicable to the portion of the community occupied in modifying external material substances, and adapting them to the use of man; or, in other words, engaged in the various species of manufactures. And another great branch is applicable to that portion of the community occupied in the exchange and conveyance, by land or by sea, of the products of Nature, spontaneous or aided by human industry, or of the products of human industry operating upon matter, from places where such commodities are abundant or superfluous, to places where there is a demand for them; or, in other words, engaged in the various departments of commerce by land and sea.

The law of maritime commerce, it thus appears, is, in a great measure, a branch of the private law of a nation, comprehending the rights and obligations of individuals engaged in such commerce, being composed chiefly of common or consuetudinary law, partly of statutory law, chiefly of civil law, partly of criminal law. And it seems unnecessary here to follow out the subordinate divisions of public or political law into constitutional and administrative, ecclesiastical, military, and financial, provincial and municipal: for the chief if not the only parts of the law of maritime commerce which belong to or are influenced by the public law of a nation, are obviously the navigation laws, enacted by the state for the maintenance of naval power, which regulate the ownership of merchant vessels, and the description of persons by whom they are to be navigated; and the financial laws, for defraying the expenses of government, which impose and regulate the duties to be paid to the state upon exports and imports by sea.

Having thus marked the rank and position of the law of maritime commerce, in relation to the other departments of human law, as chiefly, and to the greatest extent, a branch of the Internal law of nations—and, in that character, as belonging partly to the public law, but chiefly to the private law of a state, as constituting a branch, partly of the statutory, but chiefly of the common or consuetudinary law of a nation—we proceed to take a short view of the leading regulations which may be comprehended under the appellation of the law of maritime commerce, as a branch of the national or Internal law of a state.

In all the different departments of the Internal law of a people, the two great subjects for inquiry obviously are—1*st*, The ascertainment of the rules by which the conduct of individuals is to be regulated in their mutual intercourse in life, in relation to each other, or in relation to the community of which they are members—the state or government; in other words, the legal rights and obligations of individuals in these two relations. 2*dly*, The establishment and enforcement, by suitable means, of these rules, or of these rights and obligations. Accordingly, in the department of law we are now considering, the two great subjects of study are—1*st*, The ascertainment of the rights and obligations of the individuals engaged in maritime traffic, in their intercourse with each other or in relation to the state. *2dly*, The judicial establishments for the enforcement of these rights and obligations.

CHAPTER II.

OF THE COMPONENT PARTS OF THE LAW OF MARITIME COMMERCE, AS A BRANCH OF THE INTERNAL COERCIVE LAW OF STATES.

WITH regard to the legal rights and obligations of individuals engaged in the various branches of maritime commerce, methodical arrangement is certainly of great advantage to the student in facilitating his progress, and in enabling him to retain and apply the information he acquires. But, without now aiming at anything very scientific or profound, (which might be necessary or proper did we now propose to write a treatise or series of treatises on the law of maritime commerce,) we may, in taking a general view of the principal branches of the law of maritime commerce, adopt the following arrangement, which seems to be suggested by the natural order of the subject, and in which the subordinate parts form each a whole of itself; while, as parts of a greater whole, they are linked together by an obvious and intimate connection.*

In maritime commerce, the first grand purpose to be accomplished is the marine conveyance of persons and commodities ; and the first and leading object that now presents itself is the vessel, the instrument by which

* The author has a pride in mentioning that this arrangement met with the approbation of his late inestimable friend, Francis Horner, Esq., M.P., to whose high talents and worth the House of Commons paid so marked and so well-earned a tribute of respect.

that conveyance is effected and that commerce carried on. We may, therefore, begin with the consideration of property in merchant vessels; of the modes by which that species of property is constituted or acquired, is held and exercised, and transferred or extinguished, either as a whole exclusively of others, or partially or jointly along with others, as co-owners; or under limitations in favour of other parties, creating the inferior real rights of lien, hypothec, security, or mortgage; and of the regulations and restrictions to which this species of property is subjected by the navigation laws of particular countries or states, and the privileges thereby attached to particular descriptions of vessels.

After having viewed, in its different legal relations, the instrument of maritime commerce, as an object of property, we naturally proceed to inquire how this instrument may be applied or put in motion; how the vessel is managed and the crew commanded by the master; how the vessel is directed by the pilot and navigated by the seamen. Accordingly, the reciprocal and respective rights and obligations of the owners and of the persons employed in, or incidentally connected with, the navigation of the vessel; the different characters and qualifications of the persons who may be so employed; and the relative legal duties of the parties, not only under their contracts or engagements, express or implied, but also under the various events which frequently take place in the course of the voyage, may form the next subject of discussion.

The vessel having been thus put in motion, the next object of inquiry is, how this instrument of maritime commerce is converted to use, or rendered subservient to the purposes of that commerce, by effecting the marine conveyance of merchandise. There our attention is, of course, directed to the arrangements by which the owner of the vessel undertakes, for a valuable consideration, the conveyance of the commodities of others, according to certain agreed-on destinations; or transfers the possession or use of the vessel, for a time, in whole or in part, for a valuable consideration, to others who have goods for exportation or importation; or engages to convey individuals, who wish accommodation as passengers; in other words, to the relative rights and obligations of the parties engaged in the contract of affreightment, in all its shapes, and to the nature of the documents used by them, under that contract; such as charter parties and bills of lading. And here we have not only to examine the legal duties and responsibility of the owners and the master of the vessel, and the counter-obligations of the freighters, or charterer, or owners of the cargo, resulting from the contract of parties, but also the obligations of these parties to each other, arising from the events which take place in the course of the voyage; particularly the equitable doctrines of salvage and average, or contribution for the reparation of a loss incurred for the common safety.

The means of maritime conveyance being thus secured and discussed, the next point of investigation is obviously the exchange of the commodities so conveyed. And here the domestic or inland contract of sale, or exchange for value, in circulating medium, naturally branches out into different sets of transactions, agreeably to the differences in the situations in which the parties are placed. Instead of the single transaction of purchase and sale concluded by the parties, in the presence of each other, in the same place, and at the same time, we have intermediate agents, and a series of transactions all directed to the accomplishment of the same end. We have a commission or order to furnish and ship, an order to purchase and ship, a consignment for sale, and other different intermediate pieces of business performed by commission merchants, who make advances on the faith of consignments, by mercantile agents, and by brokers.

Having finished the discussion of the principal transactions by which the maritime exchange of commodities is effected, we proceed, in the same natural order, to the consideration of those auxiliary and subservient arrangements by which maritime commerce may be rendered more safe for the individual, by which its extent may be enlarged, and by which its operations may be facilitated.

In the infancy of navigation and maritime commerce, the perils of the winds and waves behoved to be more felt than in the more advanced stages of its improvement. And yet ages passed away before it was perceived that, from this multiplicity of risks, safety and profit might be made to arise; that, by a small contribution or deduction from profit, an individual might secure reparation for loss occasioned by the dangers of the sea; and that, byundertaking to repair a number of such contingent eventual losses, another individual might, upon the average of physical events, reap a profit. This arrangement, indeed, appears to have been preceded, if not introduced, by the practice of lending money on the security of the vessel and cargo, at a high rate of interest, corresponding to the maritime risks to which they were to be exposed in the course of the voyage, and which the lender undertook to bear. But, as soon as the more simple arrangement just alluded to was discovered; its obviously beneficial effects in practice could not fail to hasten its progress; and, accordingly, in none of the maritime contracts have we more reports of cases decided in courts of law than in this highly useful one of maritime insurance.

Even in a comparatively rude age, the scarcity of moveable capital, and the difficulty of mercantile operations on an extended scale, behoved to suggest to individuals that obvious expedient by which the capital, as well as the skill and industry, of several individuals are combined and directed to one common object. The advantage of such an arrangement must have been more sensibly felt as maritime commerce became more extended and multifarious; and, accordingly, the contract of copartnership, or joint trade and adventure, thus forms a very important branch of mercantile jurisprudence.

In the same way, in early times, the scarcity of moveable capital, and the necessity felt by the individual trader of supporting his mercantile credit by the aid of others, onerous or gratuitous, naturally led, not merely to loans of cash on the ship and cargo, at marine risk and at marine interest, or a sort of joint adventure, but also to advances in cash on the mortgage or temporary transferance of the property of the vessel in security at ordinary interest, or on the deposit of merchandise, or on mere personal security, such as the mutual accommodation afforded by mercantile guarantees; all of which arrangements may be ranked along with copartnership, as the other means, though less important, resorted to for the extension of trade.

In the progress of commercial intercourse among individuals of the same country or nation, the utility, or rather the necessity, of an established standard of value, and of one common medium of exchange, could not fail, in time, to lead to the adoption of some natural or artificial production which, from its intrinsic qualities, was well adapted for that purpose. From the use of such a circulating medium, possessing intrinsic value, the advantage of a transition to a less cumbrous and costly instrument of exchange came to be perceived; and, instead of precious metals, there came to be substituted, to a great extent, an artificial representative of value, possessing no intrinsic estimable qualities, and deriving all its worth from conventional arrangement. But if the adoption of such a medium of exchange was advantageous among the inhabitants of one state or country possessing one common coin or current money, a similar plan was still more necessary and expedient between the subjects of different states, and the inhabitants of different countries, who possessed no such common coin or current money. And hence bills of exchange, by which value in the currency of one country is, by the intervention of a written document, set off against value in the currency of another country, and the operations of maritime commerce thereby so greatly facilitated.

In carrying on the various transactions of maritime commerce, thus briefly described, various questions arise; and the reciprocal rights and obligations of parties require to be determined and defined by fixed regulations. For this purpose, and for the enforcement of these rights and obligations, certain courts of law have been established in all countries where commerce has made any considerable progress. In some countries, this power and function have been wholly vested in separate and peculiar courts, such as courts of admiralty, or of maritime jurisdiction, and judges of commerce. In other countries, this power and function have been vested partly in such peculiar courts, partly in the common-law courts of the state; and the constitution and mode of procedure of these judicial establishments thus form the other grand division of this department of law.

CHAPTER III.

OF THE GROWTH OR ACCUMULATION, OR OF THE ORIGIN OR DEVELOPMENT, OF THE LAW OF MARITIME COMMERCE, AND OF ITS GENERAL OR COMMON NATURE, AND PECULIAR SUSCEPTIBILITY OF IMPROVEMENT.

Such seem shortly to be the leading doctrines of the law of maritime commerce, as a branch of the Internal law of a nation; and, before proceeding to trace in detail the history of this interesting department of jurisprudence, we shall first inquire, generally, how it arises and is gradually formed and accumulated, and whether there be anything peculiar in its nature, such as to render it pre-eminently susceptible of improvement from extraneous sources.

The multifarious traffic which individuals and nations maintain with each other, has manifestly its origin and foundation in the physical constitution of man and in the external circumstances in which he is placed. Formed with various wants and capacities of enjoyment, mankind are made dependant on external circumstances for their subsistence and for the various comforts and conveniences of life. And, by the wise arrangement which the Author of the Universe has established on the face of this globe—by the unequal distribution which he has made, not merely in the external means of subsistence and enjoyment, but also in the powers of rendering external objects more subservient to the purposes of life—mankind are likewise made dependant on each other; and, in order to supply their reciprocal wants, are impelled, by necessity and self-interest, not merely to cultivate the earth and to manufacture or adapt to use its various productions, but also to exchange with each other these productions, either in their natural or artificial state. Were there no difference, in point of soil and climate, in the different regions of the globe—did each country afford, in equal abundance, the same substances for the consumption, use, or accommodation of men—there would be no occasion or inducement for the exchange of such commodities, and, of course, no commerce in raw materials or rude produce. In the same manner, were all individuals and nations equal in natural talents, in industry, in the degree of advancement in civilisation, in knowledge and skill in the various useful and ornamental arts, and could these arts be successfully exercised by individuals, as experience shews they cannot without the division of labour, then each nation and individual would be able to supply their own wants, and there would be no occasion for the exchange of manufactured commodities. Through the influence of the physical causes thus shortly alluded to, commerce has been gradually extended from family to tribe, from tribe to people, from country to country, until it has come to embrace all the regions of the habitable globe; and to bind together, by the manifold links of reciprocal interest, almost all the nations of the earth. And thus commerce, although it derives its origin from, is not confined in its operation to, the mere supply of the various animal wants of man. It is the means of connecting all mankind in one great plan of mutual intercourse. It presents an almost irresistible incitement to industry and exertion, and affords a wide and varied field for the exercise of the different intellectual and active powers of our nature. And, in the progress of civilisation, by the gradual distribution and diffusion of wealth and independence among a much larger portion of the community, it creates those middle classes of society which are the great support of a free and enlightened, yet stable, government.

Such commerce, and especially such maritime commerce, between the inhabitants of different countries, it is plain, could not be carried on, even to a very limited extent, without the observance of certain generally understood modes of proceeding or dealing, customs or usages. And, accordingly, like the greater part of the private law of all civilized nations, generally denominated the common or consuetudinary law, the earliest law of maritime commerce appears to have consisted of certain usages observed in practice, but without being reduced into writing, still less prescribed *à priori* by the legislative powers of states. In the infancy of government, like the other reciprocal rights and obligations of private individuals, those of persons engaged in maritime commerce are seldom, if ever, regularly defined, reduced into writing, and established, by the military chiefs or civil rulers of a tribe or people. In such times, it does not appear to be the general understanding that such *à priori* declarations of law are necessary, or fall within the province of the supreme power in the state. In jurisprudence and legislation, as in the other departments of human exertion and attainment, art precedes the elucidation of its rules; and practice is the precursor of theory; customs and usages gradually arise, and make law, long before they are committed to writing. In the generality of cases, the rules thus established by custom are observed; the failure to observe these rules merely constitutes an exception; and it is only in the latter case that compulsion, or recourse to the coercive power of the community, becomes requisite. As soon as, however and wherever, maritime commerce has made any progress, and given rise to business transactions, whether between the inhabitants of the same country or with foreigners, the necessity of insuring the performance and execution of the conventions and agreements, which are the result of it, has been felt and recognised. In the gradual development of the industry of a nation, individuals learn, from experience, modes of dealing conformable to the nature of the different descriptions of business in which they are engaged, and to the respective interests of the contracting parties. When disputes arise, these are determined, at first, generally by arbiters chosen by the parties, who are understood to pronounce their awards agreeably to the established customs; and afterwards, in the progress of government, by judges or tribunals appointed by the state. In time, the judgments of these tribunals form a series "*Rerum perpetuo et similiter judicatarum*"—a body of consuetudinary law or jurisprudence. And it is almost always only after long experience that people have thought of establishing, by legislative enactment, precise rules, the fixed nature of which may preclude, or may render it unnecessary for, judges to have recourse to inquiry into custom and usage.

But not only have custom and usage been the source of, not only do they still constitute, maritime and commercial law in a great part of the world, even in countries distinguished by the flourishing state of their commerce; it is to this department of law, also, that Lord Bacon's observations, "*Lex non sufficit casibus; Angustia prudentiæ humanæ casus omnes, quos tempus reperit, non potest capere*," are peculiarly applicable. For here, however great care may be taken by the persons employed in the composition of digests of positive law, it is next to impossible to foresee and provide for the vast variety of cases that occur. But usages founded on the experience and the interest of those who practise them—who, in a manner, ascertain and establish them, and also rectify them if found hurtful—afford the best data for the decision of new cases, however varied or complicated. And this sort of law, to which individuals are familiarized by habit, and which is thus durably fixed in their minds, has the great advantage of deriving its force from the evidence of the justice and reciprocity which have suggested it, or of the urgent expediency which has led to its adoption. It convinces and persuades, without appearing to command; and conviction secures to it a willing obedience, which mere authority with difficulty obtains.*

Accordingly, in maritime commerce, most nations, and especially modern nations, have, for many centuries, been regulated by usages, which daily acquire additional force from their very antiquity, from their having been established and improved by slow degrees, in proportion as the necessity for them was felt, and from their consequently being always adapted to new occurrences and to existing circumstances. Nor does the growth of such customs and usages appear, as sometimes alleged, to have been the consequence of the ignorance of nations, or of the weakness of governments. Experience has taught, that the individuals interested in maritime and commercial affairs knew best what was necessary to be done; and the interference of governments has repeatedly proved hurtful, from their desire to control and regulate, where they ought to have confined their interposition to affording merely the requisite protection. At the same time, it is not to be inferred, from these facts, that legislative interference in such matters is always useless or hurtful. If usages ought to be respected, for which their long prevalence and their universality have secured the veneration of past ages—if it be true that there is great danger of being misled and deceived by the often vain and illusive appearance of melioration—if we have al-

---

* Pardessus Collection des Lois Maritimes, tome i., chap. prelim., p. 5, 6.

most always seen the ancient usage prevail over the law intended to abrogate it, but passed without good grounds, or at an improper time—it appears, on the other hand, to be generally expedient, and frequently indispensable, that the national authority, or legislative power, should interpose, to ascertain the existence of, and to confirm, such usages and customs, and to confer upon them a positive sanction capable of protecting them, not only against infringement, but also against that licentiousness of opinion, which would terminate in involving everything in doubt and confusion.*

Having thus marked generally the origin and progress of maritime and commercial law, we proceed to consider the nature of this branch of jurisprudence, and to inquire whether there be anything peculiar in it different from the other departments of the internal law of a state, such as to render it pre-eminently susceptible of improvement.

In formerly pointing out the distinction between the law of maritime commerce, as a branch of the internal law of a state, and international maritime and commercial law, we had occasion to remark, as the cause of the former being so generally denominated a branch of the law of nations, that, although the former does not really constitute a branch of the law of nations, in the modern and more correct acceptation of that phrase, in so far as it does not necessarily involve international legal relations and questions, experience, nevertheless, shews that the maritime and commercial regulations adopted by the different nations of the world, in different ages, all bear a very strong resemblance to each other. In their endeavours to trace everything to general principles, philosophers have encountered many obstacles and

---

* Pardessus Collection des Lois Maritimes, tome i., chap. prelim., p. 5, 6.

great difficulties, from the almost incredible variety of civil and criminal laws among different nations, and sometimes in the provinces of the same state; and, although they have so far succeeded in explaining this variety, by the influence of climate and territorial position —by the different modes of obtaining subsistence—by the difference of manners and customs, in the successive stages of civilisation—and by the difference in the forms of government which have been adopted—still the question recurs, How does it happen that, whilst the nature of man is everywhere the same, the laws which regulate the private interests of individuals, and fix the limits of what is just and unjust, have been, and are, so diversified? But, however correct it may be with reference to the other departments of the internal laws of states, this observation is, in a great measure, if not entirely, inapplicable to the usages and laws of maritime commerce; which, although collected and compiled in different states, and at periods very distant from each other, present a singular contrast of similitude. The civil laws which regulate the social state of persons—the relations of families and kindred—the succession to, and the transmission of, lands and moveable effects and funds from the dead to the living—the different modifications and limitations of which the right of property is susceptible—the mode of holding and conveying estates in land, and the forms of judicial procedure—are all intimately connected with the particular nature of the government, and the peculiar and local habits and customs of a nation. But this is not the case with the laws of maritime commerce. In the latter department, the great object was, from the commencement, in every country, to resolve questions originating in, or raised by, the same or similar circumstances. And as the governments of states did not, in early times, interfere in detail with the conventional transactions of individuals, but left the parties interested at liberty to adopt such regulations as they deemed best, the usages of one state readily became those of others, as soon as the latter discovered and recognised their wisdom and excellence. There thus arising among nations whose territories are bounded by the sea, from similar wants, similar perceptions and feelings of necessity, justice, and expediency, the laws of maritime commerce possess, from that very circumstance, a strong character of universality. Embracing, likewise, the interests of the inhabitants of almost all the different countries over the face of the globe, they are, in a manner, independent of national conquests or revolutions: their nature does not change with territorial distribution. As the interests, too, of all commercial nations are physically reciprocal, and each independent state has, in the progress of its commercial intercourse, been, in some measure, forced to be just, in order to obtain reciprocal treatment from foreign nations, their maritime and commercial laws being thus founded upon the same principles, almost necessarily exhibit an essential uniformity, and, with some slight variations, are, in fact, very nearly the same in all countries; and as these laws are almost universally found to be, so they ought obviously to be, everywhere nearly the same: for enlightened views of national self-interest concur with the moral feeling of hospitality in dictating that the provisions of these laws should everywhere hold out and afford the same protection and security to strangers or foreigners as to natives. "The worst civil code," profoundly observes M. Pardessus, "would, beyond contradiction, be one destined for all nations indiscriminately; the worst maritime code, one dictated by the particular habits and customs, and by the peculiar and exclusive interests, of one single people."

The considerations just noticed have not only, as we

have already seen, induced almost all modern jurists to designate maritime and mercantile law as a branch of the law of nations—which was generally held by the earlier jurists of the last century, such as Wolff and Vattel, to be just the principles of the law of nature applied to nations instead of individuals—but have also led to the general belief and doctrine that, distinct from what is called the law of nature, applied either to individuals or nations, there existed, or exists, a sort of positive and practical private maritime and mercantile law—a *jus maritimum privatum universale.* And it may, therefore, be proper to inquire whether, and how far, this doctrine is well founded.

That there exist, between and among the assemblages or societies of men called nations, certain legal relations, distinct from moral relations—that there are certain classes of actions or proceedings, which it is felt to be just, and found and held to be generally expedient, that nations should have the power of preventing or enforcing against each other, by such means as the Author of Nature has placed at their disposal—there appears to be no room for doubt. At the same time, it is manifest that, with the exception of the treaties and conventions into which they may voluntarily enter with each other, and of the usages which they may have actually adopted in their reciprocal intercourse, there is not, in fact, and cannot be, any positive coercive human law which binds generally different independent nations; each of whom observes its own proper laws, either statutory, enacted by the supreme or legislative power of the state, or common and consuetudinary, established by the habits and virtual consent of the individuals composing the nation, and sanctioned by its judicial tribunal.

As there grows up, however, an internal common or customary law in each particular nation, from the very congregation of men living together in society, and having mutual intercourse, for the regulation of their individual affairs and interests, without any *à priori* enactment by the supreme power of the state, there is reason to believe that, in the earlier stages of European maritime commerce, a similar common or customary law grew up, and existed for a considerable time, between or among the mercantile and seafaring inhabitants of different countries. As the internal common law of a people, arising from the connections of family, and of being natives of the same country, and from the intercourse necessary for the supply of mutual wants and the accomplishment of the various purposes of life, if it does not precede the establishment of regular government, at least arrives at considerable maturity, without any active legislation on the part of the supreme power of the state; so a similar common law appears to have been gradually formed and cultivated between or among the inhabitants of different countries engaged in maritime traffic, who, although not united by the bonds of family, nativity, or neighbourhood, are brought into contact, and have frequent intercourse in their mercantile dealings, and thus become connected for the purposes of gain or profit, and interested in the adoption and observance of similar general and uniform modes or rules of proceeding. For the observance or establishment of such a *jus maritimum universale*, an express legislative act of the supreme power of states does not appear to have been necessary, any more than for the establishment of the internal common law of a people. In this comparatively rude and intermediate state of consuetudinary law, which precedes the reduction of law into writing, or the formation of regular codes or digests, if parties do not choose to settle their differences by arbitration, all that is usually expected from, or left to, the supreme power to do, is, that such disputes should be adjudicated under its authority and protection; which does not necessarily embrace the formation of the rules themselves, according to which judgment is to be pronounced. But if we see the internal common law originating in usage, and gradually advancing to maturity in nations, and even in smaller states, such as cities and towns, it seems to follow that laws may also arise and be established in the same manner in other societies, by whatever bond they may be united, although the individuals who are thus connected may not be inhabitants of one and the same native country. Now, no class or description of men, although collected from all the different regions of the globe, more or less distant, maintain so constant a connection, and cultivate so frequent an intercourse, as mercantile and seafaring people. Indeed, in the early times we are now contemplating, they seem, in the prosecution of their business transactions, to have formed a peculiar society separate from others; and it is thus manifest that, while such continued to be the condition of independent states, none of those circumstances were awanting which are requisite to the commencement of a private consuetudinary law among these men, concerning their own mercantile and maritime affairs; so that the modes of proceeding in these matters, which have been once and again observed, should, equally as those which constitute the consuetudinary jurisprudence of a whole people or city, acquire the force of law; and that the disputes which arose among these men should, in the judicial tribunals of all maritime states, be decided agreeably to that law.*

The great influence of this common or consuetudinary *jus maritimum universale*, is conspicuous in the internal maritime and commercial laws of all the differ-

* See "Gildemeister, Dissertatio Sitne aliquod, Fueritve, Jus Maritimum Universale? 1803."

ent European states at this day. But, from the time these nations began to improve their own internal law by statutes and ordinances, and to commit it to writing in digests general or particular, this maritime universal consuetudinary law, however valuable as a model for imitation, however rich in materials for the construction of new national codes, cannot be said to have existed as a general compulsory or coercive body of law: for, as already observed, there can be no *jus privatum scriptum commune*, in the learned acceptation of these terms, or proper, positive, or statutory law, among different independent nations, unless a treaty, or convention, or long usage, have intervened. While, however, various points in the law of maritime commerce have been fixed by treaties between particular states, the mode in which the *jus maritimum universale non scriptum*, or the common consuetudinary law of maritime commerce, which appears to have formerly existed in an indirect compulsory shape, now exerts its influence, and still operates powerfully among modern nations, is, by the wise adoption of its rules, which are comparatively susceptible of common, uniform, and universal application, into the statutory, and particularly into the common consuetudinary and judiciary internal law of these several nations. And, in this way, it may still be correctly said, in the language of the erudite Baldasseroni, quoting Montesquieu—"*I mercanti di tutte le nazioni, e di tutti i paesi, formano una sola societa, ed un solo linguaggio, commune a tutti*;" and that the law of maritime commerce consists mainly—"*Delle regole, che in forza dell' uso, e della scambievole utilita, hanno fra loro fissate i mercanti.*"*—Farther, although the consuetudinary law of maritime commerce may thus have

---

* Delle Assecurazioni Maritime, tome i., p. 17.

ceased to have any compulsory force in modern Europe, except as adopted by, and through the medium of, the different independent states, still the similarity, uniformity, and universality of its principles, render this interesting branch of the internal jurisprudence of each people, in an eminent degree susceptible of improvement from external sources. It is, indeed, in this department chiefly that one people can profit by the legislative and judicial experience of another; it is in this department that the laws of ancient nations, and of the middle ages, afford the most valuable suggestions; it is in this department that the legislators and judges of a nation, especially of a nation which comparatively has not advanced so far in the career of commercial improvement, may, with the greatest safety and with the greatest advantage, take lessons of practical wisdom from the institutions, usages, and judicial precedents, of its predecessors or contemporaries. Accordingly, in this department of jurisprudence, the judges and lawyers, both of England and Scotland, have, when any difficulty occurred, been accustomed to look abroad for illustration in point of legal principle, if not for direct authority. And, from the operation of the causes we have just been contemplating, the maritime and commercial systems of the different European nations may, to a certain extent, and in many material points, be traced to one common origin.

PART SECOND.

HISTORICAL VIEW OF THE LAW OF MARITIME COMMERCE AMONG ANCIENT NATIONS.

CHAPTER I.

OF THE MARITIME AND COMMERCIAL LAW OF THE PHŒNICIANS AND CARTHAGINIANS.

HAVING noticed generally the leading doctrines of the law of maritime commerce, investigated its origin and development generally, in the shape of usages and customs, and marked the similar, uniform, and universal nature of its rules, and its consequent pre-eminent susceptibility of improvement, we proceed to trace the history of this branch of jurisprudence in ancient, and particularly in modern times, and to mark the steps by which it has arrived at its present state of comparative perfection.

The progress of the law of maritime commerce is obviously dependent upon, and must necessarily, to a certain extent, keep pace with, the advancement and extension of maritime commerce itself, and with the improvement of the art of navigation. But, however interesting the subject, it is not proposed in the present sketch to enter into any long details on the origin and progress of commerce in general, or on the wonderful attainments of mankind in nautical skill and enterprise. The history of commerce and navigation will be noticed only so far as may appear necessary for giving a distinct view of the progress of maritime and commercial jurisprudence and legislation.

We, of course, commence our inquiries with the jurisprudence of the ancient nations, who are represented as having devoted themselves to, and as having succeeded and excelled in, maritime commerce. And here it may be noticed, at the outset, how much it is to be regretted that the information contained in the works of the ancient historians, and other writers which have reached us, should be so scanty, meagre, and defective. More anxious or ambitious to narrate and describe the political destinies, the conquests, and the revolutions of the nations whose memory they transmitted to posterity, than to record their internal administration, these writers talk at length of the power and the riches which such nations owed to their commerce and navigation; of the pretensions which they made to the dominion of the seas, and of the wars occasioned by such pretensions; but they leave us in almost complete ignorance with regard to the laws by which the transactions to which maritime commerce behoved necessarily to give rise, were regulated.

It would be contrary, however, to the ordinary rules of evidence, to suppose that these nations never had any positive laws, or at least recognised customs and usages, for the direction of their maritime and commercial intercourse; for later experience proves that the more commercial a state is, the greater necessity is there for laws to direct the efforts and promote the progress of industry, and especially for the determination of the contests and disputes which are multiplied in proportion to the business, dealings, and transactions of which commerce is the cause.

For obvious reasons, maritime commerce could not make great advances in early times. The indispensable requisite of vicinity to the sea is enjoyed, to any extent, only by a portion of mankind. And, although a considerable part of the territory of a large nation be washed by the ocean, it is only after a free and easy intercourse has been introduced in the progress of civilisation, that the people of the interior feel the benefit of their local situation. Mankind are naturally disposed, so far as practicable, to earn their subsistence in the country possessed by them by means of agriculture and manufacture, however rude and imperfect, before they think of embarking on a dangerous element in search of other regions. And they have the less inducement to do so, in proportion to the fertility of their native land. The art of navigation, too, presupposes a considerable degree of improvement in most of the other mechanical arts; and, without the aid of the mariner's compass, the perils attending voyages in distant and unknown seas must have been comparatively very great.

Among the early nations of antiquity, accordingly, whom history represents as the first that formed themselves into large states, such as the Assyrians, whose empire was broken down into the kingdoms of Babylon, of Nineveh, and of the Medes, and which territories the Persians afterwards united into one empire, enlarging it by great conquests, we find little or no traces of maritime traffic, no regulations but what relate to inland commerce.

Among the Indians, indeed, early attempts at navigation might have been expected, from the structure of the country, as intersected by large rivers, as to a certain extent surrounded by an ocean, and as indented with large bays. The ancient monuments, too, of their literature, discovered in the course of last century, appear to establish that loan upon marine risk or adventure was not unknown in the legislation of Menu.* But, so far as appears from ancient history, the Indians do not seem to have made much progress in navigation;

* Hindu Law, by Sir William Jones, chap. viii., § 136-137. Colebroke, Digest of Hindu Law, book v., § 173.

whether from their early legislators having dissuaded them from embarking on the ocean; from the fixed and almost invariable habits of the race, by which the usages of the ancestors are found, after the lapse of ages, to be those of their posterity; or from their enjoying at home a fertile territory, affording the necessaries and many of the conveniences and luxuries of life, and from their thus having had little occasion to look abroad for the supply of their wants. Whatever may have been the cause, the Indians appear, in this respect, to have followed the example of, or at least to have acted in the same manner as the inhabitants of the other fertile portions of Asia, on the west, bordering upon the Mediterranean, or on the east, by carrying on their commercial communication by land, across the barren deserts by which the fertile regions of that vast continent are separated.

It was reserved for the Phœnicians, so celebrated in antiquity, to be, if not the inventors, at least the first great cultivators of navigation and commerce. Inhabiting merely a narrow and barren territory, situated between Mount Lebanon on the east, and the Mediterranean on the west, the Phœnicians soon became industrious, because they felt the necessity of being so. Deriving but a scanty supply of food from their soil, they naturally had recourse to fishing for subsistence; the neighbouring mountains afforded timber for the construction of vessels, and convenient harbours seemed to open the sea to them as their appropriate element. Finding they must go abroad in quest of resources, which they had not at home, they applied themselves to navigation, and more easily became powerful by sea, because there they had no competitors. When they had provided for the supply of their more urgent wants, there gradually arose a taste and a demand for those articles which administer to the enjoyment of life; and the industry which indigence had at first excited, persevering in its exertions, led, in time, not merely to the extension of commerce, but to the attainment of great skill in arts and manufactures. At first, their commerce appears to have consisted chiefly in taking from one people its superfluous rude produce in barter for other rude produce which they had received from other nations: but, in time, they learned to employ the precious metals as a convenient medium of exchange; and, by the value which their manufactures added to the raw materials they procured from abroad, to render their commerce still more profitable. The result of industry thus employed in trade and manufacture was, of course, the accumulation of wealth; and this wealth the Phœnicians carried with them from their ancient capital, Sidon, to Tyre. The riches of Tyre at last excited the jealousy or attracted the rapacity of the neighbouring nations of the East; and, although they excelled the surrounding states in the art of fortification, because they had more to lose and more to protect against invasion, the Tyrians, after a long and bloody siege, were obliged to yield to numbers: but, with a spirit worthy of imitation, they resolved not to sink under the ruins of their city; and they built a new city, which soon surpassed the former in strength and magnificence. New Tyre became, in fact, for a time, the mistress of the Mediterranean, and the fleets which sailed from its ports traversed all the seas then known. It has even been alleged that the Tyrian navigators knew, and several times doubled, the Cape of Good Hope; and, although there be great reason to doubt this statement, it seems probable that they carried on an extensive traffic by the way of the Red Sea, and frequented the sea on the east of Africa, if not the Indian Ocean: in short, no ancient nation, except the Greeks in the most flourishing period of their history, appears to have surpassed the Tyrians in the degree of improvement to which they carried the arts and manufactures; and the commercial greatness of Tyre yielded only to the victorious arms of Alexander.

That a nation so civilized, so commercial, and so skilful in navigation, as the Phœnicians appear to have been, must have had a collection of regulations for their mercantile as well as for their military marine—the former originating probably in consuetude, but recognised and enforced by their tribunals, if not specially enacted by the supreme power—there cannot be a doubt. But whether it has been owing to the lapse of time and the ravages of war, or to the rivalship and envy of other nations, no account has reached us of the maritime laws of the Phœnicians: even the historians of the Greeks, who seem to have been indebted for their letters and the rudiments of almost all the arts to the Phœnicians, give us no information on the subject; and we are merely left to conjecture, from the vicinity of their island to the coast of Asia Minor, that, in forming their collection of maritime laws, the Rhodians may have profited by the experience and practical wisdom of the Tyrians.

Nor were the Phœnicians less celebrated for the extent and variety of their voyages and maritime traffic than for the colonies which they founded in Asia, Europe, and Africa. Of all these, the most distinguished was Carthage, whose history, so far as handed down to us, forms an interesting branch of the annals of mankind. With habits of industry and activity, formed by education and recommended by the example of their forefathers, the Carthaginians devoted themselves to navigation and commerce with the greater success that they had only to follow the footsteps of the Tyrians. Everything, indeed, concurred to render them a commercial people. Their local situation was favourable for nautical and mercantile enterprise ; and, to render their establishment on the continent of Africa stable, and sufficiently extensive to be secure, it was necessary they should make themselves powerful by sea. Their commerce, in time, appears to have embraced not only the western part of the Mediterranean, the western coast of Africa, and the East Indies, by the ordinary route of the Red Sea, but also the west coast of Spain, the Gauls, and even the British isles; and there is reason to believe that the accumulation of mercantile and manufacturing capital was greater in Carthage than in any other state of antiquity. Indeed, it appears they had made such advances in the machinery of commerce as to have had a representative circulating medium, resembling modern bank-notes. Some unknown substance, sealed up in small bags and guaranteed by the state, passed current among the merchants for a fixed value.*

Upon their extensive mercantile marine, the Carthaginians founded a great military marine, which was formidable for ages, and which not only secured them the empire of the sea, but enabled them to push their foreign conquests to a great extent. In Africa, they possessed a large territory, crowded with populous towns. Beside Spain, of which, after great efforts, they made themselves masters, they had many establishments in Italy, Sardinia, and Sicily; and what might have been the extent and the direction of their commercial and maritime greatness, it is not easy to conjecture, had they not, in the enlargement of their empire, encountered a fierce and ambitious people, who set at nought the peaceful arts of civilized life—whose trade was warfare—and who cared for no profits but what were earned by the plunder of mankind.

That the commercial institutions and regulations of such a nation as the Carthaginians would have been

* De Pauw. Rech. Phil. sur les Grecs, vol. i., § 5.

valuable, if handed down to us, as lessons of practical wisdom and models for imitation, is universally acknowledged; and that they had jurists and historians to record their laws, usages, and institutions, there is as little room for doubt. But the Romans, when they destroyed Carthage, seem to have wished that that state should be known merely as one of their conquests;—with a vindictive and an illiberal jealousy, they seem to have destroyed all the monuments which could tell posterity what Carthage had been; and we have not at this day a fragment of the maritime legislation of this once ingenious and enterprising people, except a few international treaties, collected by Barbeyrac, and commented on by Professor Heyne, of which the chief object was to establish reciprocal restrictions on the plunder of vessels at sea.

CHAPTER II.

OF THE MARITIME AND COMMERCIAL LAW OF THE GREEKS, AND PARTICULARLY OF THE ATHENIANS.

In following historically the progress of commerce and navigation, we pass to that part of Europe which is situated on the north-east of the Mediterranean. And here the Peninsula of Greece presents, for a country of narrow limits, a vast extent of sea coast. Notwithstanding this local advantage, however, the inhabitants of this celebrated region, whose posterity excelled so much in almost all the arts of civilized life, appear, from the obstacles to improvement presented by the interior structure of the country, from intestine quarrels and incessant warfare, or from other causes, into which this is not the place to inquire, to have remained for ages almost in a state of barbarism, until they received the first rudiments of the arts of life from bands of foreigners, who came from the opposite coasts of Asia and Africa. But the knowledge possessed by these strangers appears to have been very imperfect and limited; and they seem to have been, not regular colonies from Egypt or Phœnicia, such as the latter country spread over Africa and Spain, but merely bands of adventurers, who, possessing little consideration or influence in their native country, went in search of establishments in less frequented regions. Indeed, nothing could be more opposite to the spirit of the ancient Egyptians than to think of carrying their arts, by colonisation, among other nations; and Greece was then too poor a country to attract the attention of a commercial state like the Phœnicians, who, in sending out colonies, seemed to have had scarcely any other object than that of extending their trade.

In time, however, from the operation of those general laws upon which the progress of mankind in society depends, aided by their advantageous maritime situation, and by external instruction, the Greeks commenced that career of improvement in all the useful and elegant arts of life in which they have never perhaps been surpassed. Although, in all probability, not very skilful instructors, the strangers from the south, who settled among them, taught them, at least, the rudiments of agriculture, made them acquainted with the sea, and extended their views to other nations. As agriculture advanced, and the means of subsistence increased, the population of the Peninsula increased in proportion. A number of the petty tribes were gradually united into one people and reduced under one government; and the occasions and consequent evils of intestine warfare were thus diminished. Even their religious ceremonies and superstitions tended to soften and polish the people, by removing the obstacles which kept the different tribes separate from each other, by leading them to meet together at Delphi or Dodona, by thus promoting communication of thought and social intercourse, and by giving rise to the Amphictyonic Council, by which the different states, having a common interest, if not confederated for grand political purposes, were, at least, put in a situation to give each other the reciprocal assistance, of which they might stand in need. And if the public games of the Greeks, at which such crowds assembled at stated intervals, are not to be traced entirely to a commercial origin, like the fairs of the middle ages, and even of more modern times, it is certain that, on these occasions, a great and varied traffic was carried on.

In the progress of national advancement, we find the different states of Greece uniting, under their kings or chieftains, in different warlike enterprises and foreign expeditions; and we observe a marine, sufficient at least to transport numbers of warriors to the adjacent coast of Asia. At a more advanced stage, we find great bodies of the inhabitants of the Peninsula, partly impelled by the want of subsistence for an increasing population, partly driven away by internal dissensions, and partly urged on by a restless desire for new establishments, migrating from their country, spreading themselves over not only the coast of Asia, but the different isles of the Archipelago, and founding new communities or cities. About the same period, we find the inhabitants of the different states of Greece beginning to feel their own independence; making vigorous and successful efforts to throw off the yoke of their rulers or tyrants, as they were called; and, from an over-jealous and not sufficiently enlightened love of liberty, passing into the disorders of anarchy. We next find the different states, wearied of the struggles of popular faction, anxious for a more settled government; willing, for the attainment of this object, to sacrifice a part of what they had erroneously supposed to be liberty; and requesting laws to repress the abuse of popular power.* And, at last, we find them establishing governments in which, although the great body of the people could not be considered as in any better condition than that of slaves, a considerable proportion of the inhabitants enjoyed as high a degree of civil and political liberty as men seem capable of attaining.

Under such governments, each free member of the community was left, in the pursuits of commerce and of manufacture, to follow that course which his own individual interest pointed out to him as best; and the steady step of self-interest was quickened by the spirit of political enterprise which animated the nation. In such circumstances, the useful and ornamental arts could scarcely fail to flourish: and the commerce of the small but free states of Greece embraced not only all the islands of the Archipelago and all the countries around the eastern part of the Mediterranean, but also most of the countries bordering on the Euxine. The empire of the sea, indeed, which Athens and Sparta successively claimed, these states were compelled to yield to Philip and Alexander. But Alexander was an enlightened, not a barbarous conqueror: if he destroyed Tyre, he founded Alexandria. By the foundation of that city, by the conquest of Egypt and India, and by the complete discovery of the ocean to the south of the latter country, he gave an extension and a direction to maritime commerce which it retained for ages.

Among a nation like the Greeks, who carried almost

* Condillac, Cours d'Etude, tome iv., pages 91-108.

every branch of art and science to such a high degree of perfection, we naturally look for a corresponding improvement in maritime jurisprudence and legislation; and, although neither the Athenians nor the Corinthians—the two chief commercial states of Greece—have transmitted to us any digest or collection of maritime laws, it is certain that they must have had regulations for their multifarious internal and foreign traffic, as well as for the conveyance of, and succession to, their land estates. Dr Adam Smith's observation, that law was never cultivated in Greece as a science, is unquestionably too general and unqualified. From the speeches of their orators, independently of their historians and philosophic writers, it appears they had made great progress in various branches of commercial jurisprudence; and, although the trading states of continental Greece have left us no code of sea laws for our study, it may be worth while, before investigating at greater length the celebrated nautical laws of the Rhodians, briefly to inquire what were the usages of trade, and the practical rules of maritime commerce, observed and enforced at Athens, the most civilized state of that civilized nation.

CHAPTER III.

MARITIME AND COMMERCIAL LAW OF THE ATHENIANS.

THE inquiry here proposed is greatly facilitated, not only by the "*Themis Attica*" of Meursius, and by the collection of Samuel Petitus, in 1635, entitled, "*Leges Atticæ commentario illustratæ*," but still more by the recent historical and more philosophic labours of Barthelemy and Pardessus. To these authors, and particularly to the latter, we are indebted for well-arranged accounts, not only of the maritime commerce of the Athenians, but likewise of the laws by which that commerce was regulated; extracted, with great skill and discernment, from the works which have reached us of the orators, historians, and philosophers of Greece.* And, in the present sketch, we cannot do better than present an abridged view of the result of the erudite researches of these authors.

The Athenians combined the characters of a commercial and of a manufacturing people. The increase of their population compelled them to look abroad for subsistence; and a great part of their import trade consisted of grain, brought from Egypt and Sicily, but chiefly from the Tauric Chersonesus, or Crimea. From the coasts of the Euxine they imported wood for the building of vessels, salt, wax, coarse wool, and hides; from the coasts of Thrace and Macedonia, salted fish; from Phrygia, fine wools for the manufacture of cloths; and from the islands of the Ægean Sea, wines and fruits.

In exchange for such a variety of commodities, the Athenians exported oil—the only vegetable product which Solon allowed to be carried out of the country; the silver produced from the valuable mines of Attica, either coined or in a rude state; and their different manufactures, such as arms, fine cloths, and articles of furniture; for which, owing to the superior skill and taste displayed in the workmanship, there was everywhere a demand. And when they could not effect a direct traffic, they adopted a circuitous mode, and gave the wines which, with the produce of their silver mines, they purchased in the isles of the Ægean Sea, or on the coasts of Thrace,

* Chiefly from Demosthenes, in his various speeches; but also from Thucydides and Xenophon; from Lysias, Isæus, and Isocrates; from Æschines and Aristophanes; from Theophrastus, Plutarch, Diogenes Laertius, Athenæus Deipnosophist, and Pollux Onomasticon.

in exchange for the commodities which the nations round the Euxine had to furnish.

Among the Athenians, the merchant and manufacturer were not only protected by the laws—they were respected and held in considerable estimation. The state gave encouragement to all the different branches of industry, as the sources of its power. Great facility was afforded to the settlement of strangers and to intercourse with foreigners. The number of merchant ships which traded to and from the port of Athens was great: in the flourishing times of the Republic, the naval force of the Athenians amounted to about four hundred vessels. Their ships of war, however, were very small, not being equal in size to our sloops, and were navigated chiefly with oars. Their merchant ships, also, were not only very small, when compared with those of modern times, but were likewise inferior in dimensions to those of the Phœnicians; and the value of the cargo embarked in one bottom was, of course, comparatively small.

From the extent of their foreign commerce, and the variety of their exports and imports, it is manifest the Athenians must have practised and been well acquainted with the different transactions by which the exchange of commodities is effected. And, accordingly, we find that the Grecian merchants were not only in the habit of undertaking distant journeys and voyages, for the purpose of disposing of their commodities and of procuring others in demand at home, but, where the trade was constant, had permanent establishments of factors and clerks in foreign countries, for the purpose of collecting and preparing, during winter, the cargoes which were sent home in summer; and likewise came, in the natural progress of commerce, to have regular correspondents in all the places to which the hope of gain attracted them. Their mines of silver supplied them, from an early period, with an excellent medium of exchange; and silver continued long their principal coin, as copper was despised for that purpose, and gold was scarce in Greece till the days of Philip of Macedon.

At Athens, as formerly in this country, almost all retail trade appears to have been carried on in public sheds or booths allotted to the different kinds of merchandise, and to have been much encouraged by the government. And, as already noticed, the greatest part of the internal commerce of the different Grecian states, both wholesale and retail, appears to have been transacted at the fairs, which were held at stated times, under the protecting auspices of religion. Indeed, the earliest bankers of Greece appear to have been the priests of Olympus and Delos, who, it is alleged, found means to give currency to a part, at least, of the metallic offerings consecrated to Jupiter and Apollo.

As commerce flourishes, laws are necessarily multiplied. The questions and disputes to which the multifarious transactions of an extensive traffic give rise, are an almost inexhaustible source of litigation. The Athenians, accordingly, appear to have had a variety of regulations applicable to maritime commerce; and we shall notice them in the order in which we have placed the general doctrines of that branch of jurisprudence.*

The voyages of the Athenians, we have seen, were chiefly, if not entirely, confined to the Mediterranean and the Euxine; and, comparatively, the art of navigation had made little progress. The owner of the vessel was, in many cases, likewise the master or captain, the same expression being frequently used to designate both. The same word, too, (Επιβατης,) was used to denote, in-

* See Pardessus Collection de Lois Maritimes, tome i., chap. vi., and the ancient authorities there quoted or referred to.

discriminately, the mere passengers, and the proprietors of the goods with which the vessel was loaded, who frequently themselves accompanied and took charge of these goods. The reach or capacity of vessels was expressed by the quantity or numbers of bales which they could carry.

The agreements of affreightment, for the conveyance of merchandise by sea, were subjected to the common rule, which prescribes that every contract shall be faithfully fulfilled; and penalties were enacted against those who, having engaged to sail for a particular port of destination, did not exactly repair thither. The state deemed it its duty, likewise, to take precautions, by a public enactment, against the consequences of the unskilfulness of those who offered themselves for the command or pilotage of vessels. The law against the mariners of Salamis, which Æschines mentions in one of his orations,* ordered that he who lost the vessel under his command or direction, though without any fault on his part, should be no longer employed. Measures were also adopted for the protection of seafaring people, by the state maintaining a naval force, to defend them against enemies and pirates.

The desertion of mariners engaged for the service of vessels appears to have been punished with great severity; but the excessive punishments of which some authors speak, were probably only directed against deserters from vessels employed in the public service. On the other hand, the owners, or fitters-out, or charterers, and the masters of vessels, were held bound, on their part, faithfully to fulfil towards the mariners the agreements into which they had entered for the payment of wages.

The rules which fixed the reciprocal obligations of

---

* Æschines in Ctesiphon, iii., 545.

the owners of the cargo of a vessel to contribute towards the reparation of sacrifices made for the common safety in a storm, have not been handed down to us; but they appear to have been the same as those which were afterwards borrowed by the Romans from the laws of the Rhodians.* The laws, also, imposed the same obligation when it had become necessary to ransom the vessel captured by the enemy or pirates; and there does not appear to be any sufficient ground for believing that the public treasury had any right to shipwrecked goods, except when the owners or other persons interested therein did not appear or could not be found.

With regard to the maritime exchange of commodities, the citizens, or even strangers or foreigners, enjoyed an almost unlimited liberty of commerce; and the chief, if not the only exceptions to this freedom, originated in political considerations, and were, *first*, the restrictions imposed on foreigners, in the exercise of retail trade in the public market-place; which, however, in no respect otherwise diminished the protection afforded them by the laws; *secondly*, the often-renewed prohibition, under the pain of death, against Athenian merchants purchasing grain destined for the supply of other cities than Athens, or carrying it elsewhere than to an Athenian market; and, *thirdly*, the prohibition against individual citizens amassing beyond a certain quantity of grain for their support. The taxes, too, which were imposed by the state, do not appear to have pressed severely on commerce: they secured the country against the exportation of commodities which it did not produce beyond its wants; and they were levied chiefly upon foreign productions, of which the importation was not manifestly necessary.

The holding at stated times, and the police, of mar-

* Demosthenes in Lacritum, ii., 327.

kets, the superintendence of the correctness of weights and measures, and the enforcement of regulations regarding the quality of things sold, and sometimes even regarding the price and the excessive quantity of purchases, were confided to special magistrates; and severe laws punished the monopoly of the necessaries of life or the manœuvres practised to raise or sink the price of them; and likewise all alterations of the coinage.

The manufacturing branch of national industry was likewise prosecuted with great activity, not merely in articles of the first necessity, but in various articles of luxury. Artisans were permitted to form companies or corporations among themselves, provided they were in no respect repugnant to law and public order; and the working of the silver mines of Attica, considered as one of the sources and instruments of commercial wealth, was subjected to regulations, of which the object was to encourage it, and thereby secure a revenue to the state in the tax levied on the produce of these mines.

The great advantages of proof by writing, in commercial transactions, was felt and recognised. The document which contained the evidence of the contract was deposited in the hands of a third party, when the contracting parties did not judge it proper to leave it in the hands of either of themselves; and the deposit was proved by witnesses, or by the declaration of the depositary. Unless, however, the law expressly required the reduction of a contract into writing, the obligations undertaken, and particularly the discharge of these obligations, by delivery, payment, or otherwise, might be proved by witnesses, who were bound to depose not to what was merely hear-say, but to what fell within their own personal knowledge.

The laws enforced faithful performance on the part of the vendor, both in the fixing of the price and in the punctual delivery of what was either expressly or by necessary implication comprehended in the sale. Commission or mercantile agency, such as we know the contract, formed an important branch of commercial business. The correspondent, who resided in one country, intimated to the correspondent resident in another country, the current prices of merchandise; and it was thus known when a profit might be expected to be realized, by shipping or transmitting goods, or by ordering the purchase and shipment of goods.

Merchants undertook, also, to receive or to pay money for behoof of each other; and it is in this chiefly that the profession of bankers consisted. Independently of what they realized by lending to others the funds which individuals deposited with them, with or without the stipulation of interest, they devoted themselves to the exchange of different species of money. They served as intermediate agents for the recovery of debts, for verifying and ascertaining reciprocal borrowings and discharges, and for making payments; and, to prevent frauds being practised upon them, they were in the habit of causing to be certified to them, by known witnesses, the identity of the persons who appeared before them.

Bankers were particularly, and more than other merchants, held bound to keep books or registers, in which they behoved to inscribe daily what they received and what they paid, from whom they had borrowed and to whom they had to repay; and these books served as evidence not only in the disputes which were personal to themselves, but also in those between or among third parties, to whom loans, payments, or any other kinds of exchanges of funds had been made, through their intervention or in their presence.

From finding the Athenians so skilful in the department of banking business, we are led to suppose that they might have been acquainted with bills of exchange; and the ingenious M. de Pauw thinks he has discovered evidence of the existence of these useful commercial documents among the Athenians in a passage in one of the orations of Isocrates, (Trapezeticos,) in which it is noticed that a stranger, who had brought grain to Athens, delivered a draft to one Stratocles, for money due to him in some place situated on the coast of the Euxine. M. de Pauw adds that the receiver of the bill found it very advantageous, because his property was thereby saved from exposure on a sea covered with enemies and pirates; but, at the same time, took care to have a banker of Athens made responsible, in case the bill should be dishonoured. Further, referring to the same passage, M. Pardessus observes—"The Athenian merchants and bankers engaged in negotiations, of which the object was to make payment of sums of money in one place for value received in another, which is, properly speaking, our contract of exchange." But this insulated passage, even supposing it to have been more clear and explicit than it is, would afford very unsatisfactory proof of the general use of bills of exchange among the Grecian merchants, and no proof at all that such written documents, as the one therein alluded to, were invested with the privileges which belong to bills of exchange in modern practice. Had bills of exchange been used, to almost any extent, by the Greeks, some account of them, or at least occasional allusions to them, would unquestionably have occurred in the writings of their different historians, orators, or philosophers; and the sounder opinion seems to be, that this expedient for setting off the reciprocal exports and imports of different countries against each other, without the intervention of a medium of exchange possessing intrinsic value, was unknown to this highly civilized peonle.

The great advantages of commercial associations or companies for establishments at home, or in countries with which the state was in alliance, or even in foreign countries with which no such alliance existed, had been felt and were duly appreciated; and the union of individuals in such copartnerships promoted both the extension and the activity of domestic and foreign commerce. Loans on security were frequent; but it does not appear there was any standard rate of interest established by law, or that any precautions were taken against the abuses, real or imaginary, of usurious loans. The Athenians, and their legislator, appear to have seen no good reason why the commerce of money should be placed on a footing different from that of other commodities. The lenderhad a right to cause the subject which had been given him in pledge to be sold, when the debtor did not discharge the debt on the day appointed for payment. It appears even that, until repayment of the capital lent, he had a right to use or employ, or let in lease, the subjects impledged, if they were susceptible of such application; and neither the debtor nor his heirs could exact restitution of the pledge, as long as they had not paid the debt in full. Vessels were not exempted from such conveyance in security; and when one had been thus impignorated for payment of a debt, the creditor might, on the arrival of the term of payment, prevent the vessel's departure, put watchmen on board, and cause it to be arrested and sold.

Mercantile guarantee, or suretyship, was also a mode of security which the law admitted and favoured; the right of action, however, against the surety or guarantee for a merchant, lasting only for a year.

In order to insure fidelity in the fulfilment of mercantile contracts, a compulsory and almost a penal sanction was found necessary to constrain those in whom a sense of justice and the dread of public opinion, which has so great an influence on the credit of a merchant, was not sufficiently strong. The greatest rigour was exercised against the debtor who did not fulfil or satisfy his engagements. His creditors might cause his effects to be seized, or imprison him; and the only resource which remained to him, was to conceal himself, or to surrender to his creditors the remainder of his estate. Such was the conviction of the necessity, for the promotion of commerce, of affording the strongest guarantees or securities to lenders of money, without whose assistance it was, in those times, impossible to accomplish any considerable mercantile enterprises, that they even went the length of punishing with death the merchant who had contracted debts beyond his means, and could not point out the articles of property upon the faith of which he had borrowed or obtained credit.

Notwithstanding these great advances, however, in the practical cultivation of maritime and commercial law, that ingenious but simple arrangement, by which the owner of a large investment, in a single bottom, divides his risk among a number of wealthy individuals—the highly useful contract of marine insurance, of which it is difficult to find even faint traces in Roman jurisprudence—appears to have been entirely unknown to the Athenians and other Greeks, as well as to the Phœnicians and Carthaginians. Of this the principal causes may have been the limited extent of their navigation, and the care which was taken in practice not to keep the sea during the six months of the year when it presents the greatest and most frequent dangers; and, in his excellent treatise on marine insurance, Mr Marshall endeavours to account for this circumstance from the maritime commerce of these nations being not only less extensive, but also less perilous, than that of the moderns. But, although the range of navigation was comparatively limited, the maritime intercourse was great. The Athenians, too, in their principal voyages, were exposed to the shoals of the Propontis, as well as to the storms of the Euxine. Nay, it has been supposed they used small trading vessels in preference to large ones, to avoid the risk of embarking a very considerable or valuable cargo in a single bottom. Indeed, there seems to be reason to believe that the navigation of the ancients was, from the operation of physical causes, and from the want of the mariner's compass, independently of the risk of capture by national enemies or pirates, at least as dangerous as that of the moderns; while the quantity and value of the commodities which they conveyed by sea from one country to another were such as to render a division of the risk highly expedient, if not indispensably necessary. The most probable conclusion therefore is, that they were unacquainted with marine insurance, not solely because their ships and cargoes were less exposed to the perils of the sea, to hostile attack, or to piratical depredation—not solely because their ships and cargoes were of too inconsiderable value to be worth insuring—but also, if not chiefly, because there was no great accumulation of moveable capital in the hands of individual shipowners and merchants. On the one hand, from the want of such accumulation, the vessel, though small, was usually divided into a number of shares; the part-owners frequently sailed with the vessel; the investments of the different merchants, whose goods composed the cargo, were individually small; and the merchant himself frequently accompanied his goods. On the other hand, from the same cause, there were few individuals possessed of such extensive capital as to enable or induce them to undertake that variety of maritime risks, in which the safety and profit of the underwriter consists.

But whether the non-existence among the Greeks of marine insurance, as a business or trade, can be satisfactorily explained from these causes or not, it is very probable that to the want of accumulated capital in the hands of individual shipowners and merchants, combined with the perils to which their maritime commerce was exposed, we are chiefly to trace the prevalence among them of the contract of *fœnus nauticum*, marine usury, as it is called, or of bottomry and *respondentia*. In the practical exercise of this contract, the theory of maritime risks came to be pretty extensively unfolded, as it was a species of investment or adventure very frequently resorted to by fathers of families, who had thereby the chance of reaping large profits.

By this contract or agreement, a person borrowed a sum to enable him to carry on maritime operations, and bound himself to restore it, with nautical interest or profit, of which the rate was arbitrary or optional, to the parties; which might, according to some writers, be stipulated at so much per month or day, but which, most frequently, was fixed at a particular sum or rate, more or less considerable according to the port or place where the voyage was to terminate. The borrower subjected to this debt either the vessel and her rigging, tackle, and appurtenances, as accessories, or the rigging and tackle separately; or the merchandise or cargo which he proved he had loaded, or which he bound himself to put on board; or, finally, the vessel and cargo together. There might, also, be subjected to this debt precious articles not destined for sale.

The essential condition was, that the borrower should be bound to repay the capital, with marine interest, only if the subjects burdened with it arrived in safety at the destined port. The lender often took the precaution of causing the other effects of the borrower to be hypothecated to him, in security of the rights which he might have to exercise, when, upon the vessel having arrived in safety, his loan would be freed from all risks.

This mode of borrowing did not take place in the case in which the vessel experienced necessities in the course of her voyage and it became a matter of urgency to supply them. People borrowed money in this way prior to the adventure, either to procure the merchandise which they wished to ship, or that they might take it to a foreign country, there to purchase merchandise destined to be brought home to Athens, or even to be sold in another country, and replaced by goods which were ultimately to be brought to the Athenian market. This last case is that of the contract, of which the formal deed is preserved in the pleading of Demosthenes against Lacritus.*

The lender usually stipulated that the value of the things burdened with the debt should be double the amount of the capital lent; and the borrower behoved to declare whether or not he had already borrowed any money on the faith of the article proposed to be assigned in security.

The loan was evidenced by a written deed, which was afterwards torn in pieces when the debtor was completely discharged. The result was, that he who made a formal judicial demand, not supported by such a title, was met by an exception, and was nonsuited. The deed remained in the hands of the lender, or was deposited with a third party, as in the other cases where contracts were reduced into writing. Most frequently, the owner, or ship's husband, or the master of the vessel, received intimation of the transaction, and he thereby became entitled to require the borrower to put on board the vessel goods of sufficient value to cover the loan.

The loading of the cargo was proved by the registers

* Reiske, vol. ii., p. 925, 6, 7.

of the public comptrollers, or by witnesses, in presence of whom the borrower certified what goods he put to sea at the risk of the lender. The borrower could not, without the consent of the latter, borrow from others upon the faith of the goods already burthened with the loan, unless he increased the quantity in proportion to the new debt incurred, or unless the articles burthened with the first loan were clearly sufficient to cover both; and, even in this last case, he had not the right to do so if he had renounced it by the deed of loan.

The borrower bound himself to restore, at the place appointed, the capital, with the nautical interest, and frequently even to pay a fine, which was sometimes double what was lent, in the case of the infringement of the contract, either by failing to employ the funds borrowed for the purposes held out, or by not loading the stipulated merchandise, or by the non-arrival of the vessel at the port agreed upon in consequence of his fault or omission, or by a violation of the prohibition to borrow twice upon the same goods, or in case of a false declaration that the goods burthened with the loan were free; and these infringements might be proved by witnesses.

The lender had often no other security or guarantee against pretended losses or shipwrecks brought about by a borrower, who might have loaded nothing on board the vessel, than the honesty of the person with whom he had contracted, and the severity of the laws; but he could communicate to his correspondent the amount and conditions of the loan, and the goods burthened with it; cause the loading of the vessel to be watched; satisfy himself whether the goods were really put on board; and follow the sale or disposal of them.

The loan was made either for going merely to a place agreed upon, or for going and returning; and the contract or usage determined within what time the voyage behoved to be accomplished, according to the destination of the vessel. The borrower might sell the merchandise burdened with the loan, and replace it by merchandise shipped on the homeward voyage, which was substituted for the former in point of risk; and the agent of the lender took care that he did not abuse this power. Sometimes the possibility was foreseen of the voyage terminating in a place where the Athenians did not enjoy the right of causing the effects of their debtors to be seized; and the lender, in that case, stipulated what he deemed suitable for the protection of his interest.

On the arrival of the vessel at the port fixed by the contract, the lender had a right to exact his payment from whatever was impledged to him; and this demand might be enforced by seizure and sale. The owner, or charterer, or master of the vessel, was frequently authorized by the contract to receive payment on behalf of the lender. For this purpose, the latter sometimes took the precaution of causing the deed to be extended in duplicate, and of sending one of the duplicates with the vessel; and parole proof of the payment liberated the borrower, although the contract had remained in the hands of the lender. But if, in consequence of goods being thrown overboard, for the safety of the vessel, or of ransom money being paid to pirates, or of any other event beyond the power of man, the goods impledged for the loan had been diminished, or had been subjected to a contribution, the lender bore this loss, to the relief or discharge of the borrower.

Sometimes it was stipulated that the borrower should enjoy, in accounting, upon the return voyage, a certain delay, to enable him to discharge the debt; and that, for his safety, the creditor should be secured in all the goods on board the vessel, until he obtained complete payment. If it happened that the borrower could only pay in part, or to account, the creditor was not bound to give up or destroy his written title or document; but was bound to appear before a banker, who received and certified his acknowledgment that a part of the debt was discharged.

The borrower was entirely relieved if the vessel or goods burdened with the loan had been lost; and the rights of the lender were reduced to the value of the things saved, without his having the power to avail himself, for the balance, of the other effects which might have been hypothecated for his debt; reserving always to the lender to prove, by way of exception, that the loading of the goods had not taken place, or that the vessel, having been preserved, had unloaded her cargo elsewhere than at the port agreed upon. The borrower, therefore, it was held, could not be punished with too great severity, who, having had the bad faith to secrete, or put out of the way, the merchandise liable for his debt, caused the vessel to be wrecked, that he might avoid payment of the sum borrowed.

From these detailed regulations, as collected by M. Pardessus, relative to loans, in which the lender, for a suitable consideration, undertook the risks and perils not only of the winds and waves, but of capture by enemies or pirates, it is plain that such transactions were very frequent at Athens. The owners of a vessel who were unable to procure a cargo, or the merchant who was skilled in traffic, but who had not sufficient capital to commence or complete his proposed investment, applied to the monied man for a loan of cash, to be laid out in the purchase of goods, which were to be conveyed to a distant port, and there to be disposed of with profit, either for cash, or in exchange for other commodities, purchased at that foreign port, which were to be brought home to Athens. And this advance the monied man agreed to make, and to take the risk of losing the advance, by the perils of the sea or by captures, upon condition of receiving a per centage or interest upon the sum advanced, corresponding to the accommodation which he thereby gave, and to the risk which he thereby incurred.

As the risk incurred was various, the interest on the advance was not and could not be fixed by law. It behoved to depend on the agreement of parties, which was generally expressed in a deed, deposited in the hands of a banker or common friend. In this deed, the time of the departure of the vessel, the port or ports of destination, the kind of commodities to be conveyed thither, the manner in which they were to be disposed of there, and the goods which were to be brought back to Athens, were all specified. And, as the duration of the voyage was generally uncertain, some people agreed that the interest should not be exigible till the return of the vessel; while others, more timid, and content with a less profit, stipulated that the money advanced should be repaid at the port of destination, after the sale of the merchandise; and others followed their money themselves, or sent some confidential person to the port of destination, with power there to receive payment of the capital and marine interest. The lender in such transactions had a security either upon the merchandise shipped or upon the separate estate of the borrower; and as the former, to a certain extent, run the risk of the sea, beside the accommodation afforded by theadvance, while the profit of the latter might be very considerable, the interest of the money thus lent amounted generally to a high per centage, varying according to the length and dangers of the voyage. In short, the law of maritime usury or bottomry and *respondentia* appears to have attained maturity among the Athenians; and the operations of this arrangement, although very limited in effect when compared with that of the contract of insurance, appears, upon the whole, to have been found very beneficial in a commercial point of view.

Nor did the Athenians merely establish excellent laws for the regulation of maritime commerce, defining the legal rights of individuals engaged in that trade; they established also particular tribunals, with comparatively simple forms of procedure, adapted for the speedy decision of such questions, and took many wise precautions to insure the correct and prompt distribution of justice.

The determination of lawsuits relative to contracts concluded at Athens or in foreign countries, for a voyage which was to terminate at Athens, was remitted by the magistrates to a judicatory nearly similar to those which exist in most modern states, under the appellation of Judges of Commerce, or Courts of Admiralty. Those judges called Ναυλοδικαι, and chosen each year, pronounced without appeal; and when treaties contained a stipulation to that effect, foreigners were in these courts judged conformably to the laws of their own country. The heirs of a deceased merchant were subjected to this jurisdiction, with reference to the deeds to which he had consented or been a party; but the defendant, against whom it was not proved by written evidence that the transaction had been concluded at Athens, or for that port, might decline the competency of the court.

These judges held their sittings during the six months when navigation was interdicted: namely, from the month of October to the month of April, that seafaring people might depart without being stopped by the necessity of appearing in a court of justice. The decision was almost always pronounced in the course of a month from the time the action was brought into court; and it appears that, in general, the pursuer or plaintiff was held bound to institute his action within a very short period, under the penalty of it being dismissed as incompetent.

A reference might be made by the one party to the oath of the opposite party; and when he to whom the reference was made accepted of the proposal, a sum was agreed upon, which he behoved to pay, if he did not give his oath, beside the refusal involving the loss of the suit. The heir of a deceased merchant, prosecuted for fulfilment of a verbal obligation by his ancestor, might offer to affirm that he did not believe the deceased had undertaken the alleged engagement.

Disputes, even when already depending before the court of law, often gave place to voluntary arbitration, which must not be confounded with the remit to public arbiters pronounced by the judges in certain cases. The law was thus expressed :—The citizens are, in their individual disputes, entitled to take such arbiters as they choose. When they shall have chosen one or more arbiters in concert, they must abide by what he or they shall have decided, and shall not have the power of carrying their demand before any tribunal, the award of the arbiters having the force of an irrevocable *res judicata.* A writing deposited in the hands of a third party, or of one of the arbiters, and sometimes even presented to a magistrate, that it might be invested with a more solemn power, evidenced this submission or reference to arbiters; and the parties gave each other security, respectively, to answer for the due fulfilment of the sentence or orders which might be pronounced. The parties most frequently agreed upon three arbiters, whose decision was not required to be unanimous.

Arbiters, before taking the oath to render justice faithfully, sometimes endeavoured to reconcile the parties; and could, when they had not succeeded, remit the cause to the ordinary judges. This refusal to decide did not expose them to be prosecuted, as the public arbiters were in a similar situation; but, like them, they might be found guilty of having failed in the discharge of their duties. The day fixed for the decision having arrived, and the preliminary formalities having been gone through, if one of the parties did not appear, and if the other declined a remit, the arbiters, after having waited till the close of the day, gave a decision by default against the party not appearing, which, however, might be afterwards opened up.

Such seems to be the substance of what we know of the commercial and maritime usages and regulations of the Athenians. And we have detailed them at such length, as recently elucidated by M. Pardessus, because the collection thus exhibited, although it cannot be viewed as a bequest to posterity of a systematic code of maritime laws, constitutes the earliest monument of maritime jurisprudence which the ancients have transmitted to us, and the only ancient monument of the kind which has reached us, except those parts of the maritime laws of the Rhodians which the Romans adopted and have preserved, as incorporated in the writings of their classical lawyers, and in the Digest of Justinian.

For, upon inquiry, we shall find reason to believe that the maritime laws of the Rhodians, so celebrated in antiquity, were not collected, compiled, or enacted by that people till after the Republic of Greece had yielded to the arms of Philip and Alexander; and that the Greek work published in modern times, under the title of "Jus Navale Rhodiorum," is not a true record of the maritime laws of the ancient Rhodians, but a crude compilation made during the less enlightened ages of the decline of the Roman Empire in the East.

CHAPTER III.

OF THE MARITIME AND COMMERCIAL LAW OF THE RHODIANS.

No writer of antiquity treats expressly of the Rhodians. What we know of them must be collected in fragments, or detached articles, from various different sources. But, owing to their extensive connections, and the active part which, for so long a period, they took in the affairs of the Greeks and Romans, our information respecting them is by no means so scanty as might otherwise have been expected. Some authors, such as Selden,* Fournier,† and even M. de Pastoret,‡ apparently influenced by the desire of shewing the high antiquity of the object of their admiration, rather than guided by historical evidence, place the existence of the maritime laws of the Rhodians so far back as about 900 years before the Christian era, and thus make them contemporary with Homer, and scarcely 150 years posterior to the Trojan war. But these writers do not adduce any proof of this, or any presumption deduced from the testimony of ancient authors. On the contrary, there are opposed to their opinions the testimonies of the historians Diodorus Siculus§ and Strabo,|| who fix the foundation of the city of Rhodes in the year 408 before the Christian era.

* Mare Clausum, lib. i., cap. v., § 5.

† Hydrographie, lib. v., chap. iv.

‡ Des Lois Maritimes des Rhodiens, p. 59.

§ Lib. xiii., § 75.

|| Lib. xiv., cap. ii., § 4.

The island bearing this name, indeed, was known much more anciently. Homer and Pindar speak of it as a flourishing community; and Strabo informs us that, before the institution of the Olympic games, the Rhodians had undertaken long voyages, and founded colonies on the distant coasts of the Mediterranean, even at the foot of the Pyrenees. It is, therefore, not improbable that, in such a position, experience, the frequent recurrence of similar cases, the necessity of determining disputes, resolving difficulties, and of repressing hurtful practices, might have taught the Rhodians the expediency of having fixed laws. But, on the other hand, it is still more probable that the building of the city of Rhodes by the inhabitants of the ancient towns or villages, who abandoned their former homes to unite themselves in one great metropolis, was the principal cause of the Rhodians acquiring that high degree of commercial power which placed them among the rulers of the sea; and that it was about or after this period, also, they compiled or digested their maritime laws. And this probability is greatly increased by the fact that the historical testimonies relative to their laws, namely, the writings of Livy, Cicero, Strabo, Aulus Gellius, are all posterior to that epoch; while the authors who have mentioned the Rhodians before the foundation of the city of Rhodes, have said nothing of their maritime legislation.

The Rhodians appear to have enjoyed from nature a fertile territory, combined with the maritime and commercial advantages of insular situation and safe harbours. And, at a very early period, they seem to have applied themselves to navigation and merchandise, and to have been an industrious and enterprising people. But the period of their greatest maritime and mercantile power and prosperity appears to have been the fourth and third centuries before the Christian era, after they had built their metropolitan city, after continental

Greece, fallen from its ancient greatness, had sunk under the dominion of the successors of Alexander. Indeed, the great maritime power of the Rhodians appears to have succeeded that of the Athenians; and the decline of the latter may be dated from the time of their disputes with Philip of Macedon.

During these ages, the magnificence of their chief city, its harbours, its arsenals, its massy walls, and towers, its store-houses, its temples, its theatres; and their colossus—one of the wonders of the world;—all announce them a people who had a taste for the arts, and opulence adequate to the execution of great designs. Their island was a kind of road-stead and place of anchorage, and an intermediate port for the vessels trading between Egypt and continental Greece. The celerity of their vessels, their naval discipline, and the skill of their commanders and pilots, were unrivalled. They navigated, without fear, to all the coasts of the Mediterranean; and they established colonies in many of the countries to which commerce attracted them. In the midst of their national opulence, however, they retained the simple manners of their forefathers. Their general deportment was grave; and they were extremely observant of external order and decorum. Their sailors were distinguished for courage and intrepidity, and their government for its consummate prudence. Their alliance was courted by other states; but, as long as they could, they maintained an armed neutrality. And their greatest national objects are stated to have been, to have fleets always prepared for the protection of their commerce; to have commerce sufficiently extensive for amassing wealth; and to have wealth sufficient to enable them to maintain their fleets.

By pursuing this prudent line of policy, the Rhodians arrived at such a degree of wealth and naval power, as to have had great influence, for a long period, among the different states of antiquity. Their alliance was held in high estimation by the Athenians; and they afforded assistance, in time of need, to Greece itself. They were able successfully to resist the different attacks of the powerful and ambitious princes of the continents of Asia and Europe. They materially aided the Romans, by harassing and checking the naval armaments of the Carthaginians; and, by their prudence, and the essential services they rendered, they succeeded in maintaining a long friendly alliance and intercourse with that all-conquering people; which lasted, with little interruption, until their island, along with the different countries bordering on the Mediterranean, became a part of the Roman Empire.

The conclusion to which we are thus historically led is, that the Rhodian laws were not compiled and digested till a period after Athens had enjoyed its greatest prosperity, and after the very extent and the wants and necessities of her commerce had required and given birth to the laws, of which a pretty detailed account has been given. And the great similarity to the latter of those parts of the Rhodian laws which have been preserved to us by the Romans, affords reason to believe that the Rhodians were indebted for part, at least, of the excellence of their system to the Greeks of the continent. But, from whatever sources derived, there seems to be sufficient reason for holding that the maritime laws of the Rhodians were not mere vague, indefinite, variable, unwritten, and unauthoritative customs and usages, as appears to have been the opinion not only of M. Boucher, the editor of the *Consulat de la Mer*, but also of those able jurists, Dr Gildemeister (1803) and Dr Meyer, (1824,) both of Bremen, but were compiled, digested, recorded in writing, and enacted by the supreme power of the state, so as to form a body of positive and authoritative law, so far as regarded the citizens or subjects of that state and its colonies.

For, with reference to the argument of M. Boucher, it by no means follows, from the use of the word Πραξεις, in the Greek preface to the collection, entitled, "Jus Navale Rhodiorum," to be afterwards noticed, which Terrasson has translated "Usages," that the laws of the Rhodians were mere unwritten and variable customs; the proper signification of this Greek word being not so much customs and usages as regulations and institutions. And from the term Νομος not being employed in this preface, all that can be legitimately concluded is, that the maritime laws of the Rhodians may not have been established with the same formality as the constitutional laws of the state, which, in the Grecian republics, were enacted by the assembled people. As little is it to be inferred, as M. Boucher does, that the maritime laws of the Rhodians had not previously been committed to writing, from the Emperor Tiberius, or rather Augustus, having been obliged to send commissioners to Rhodes, for effecting the introduction of their laws into the Roman legislation. That copies of these laws must previously have found their way to Rome, there scarcely can exist a doubt: but, in all probability, they had not a sufficient character of authenticity; and, before presenting them for the sanction of the senate, it was proper that persons invested with a public character should collect them with fidelity, and ascertain their advantages by studying their application to practice in the very places where they had their origin.

With regard, again, to the more ingenious arguments of Dr Gildemeister and Dr Meyer, the object and tendency of them seems to be not so much to prove that the maritime laws of the Rhodians were never committed by that people to writing, as that these laws, like the greatest part of the common or consuetudinary laws of other nations, grew up in the shape of customs and usages, from feelings of necessity and considerations of convenience, and came to be recognised and enforced by their courts of justice, more from a general tacit consent, than from any express or special legislative enactment. And, in all probability, the Rhodians merely adopted and improved the usages of the sea observed or established by their predecessors, both with regard to the navigation and management of vessels, and also with regard to the rules to be observed in the determination of the disputes which arose among merchants. But a community which advances in civilisation, and especially a people that has come to possess a considerable mercantile marine, feels the necessity of having the rules by which the conduct of individuals is to be regulated recorded in writing. Unwritten and traditionary usages are found to be too easily eluded and evaded; and the rules which have been found equitable and convenient in practice, come to be committed to writing, if not by express statutes passed by the legislative power, at least by the recorded determinations of the supreme judicial power of the state; and the most probable conclusion, therefore, is, that the usages of the Rhodians must have, in time, ultimately assumed the form of positive laws. Succeeding to the maritime power formerly enjoyed by the Phœnicians, Athenians, and Carthaginians, there is every reason to believe they also availed themselves of the maritime and commercial experience of these nations, and collected the rules of practice which they had followed, and compiled and digested the practical rules which they themselves had previously adopted, about the time when the progress of their increasing manufacturing industry, and the extension and greater frequency of their voyages, made them feel more sensibly the necessity and expediency of such a code. But, independently of these grounds of probable inference, several texts of the Roman Digest establish the fact of the Rhodian law having been recorded in writing, by express reference to it as existing law; such as, *Lege Rhodia Cavetur;* and the celebrated response of the Emperor Antoninus, *Lege Rhodia Judicetur.* Indeed, it cannot be supposed that the Roman lawyers, Servius, Labeo, Ofilius, &c., would have taken, for the basis and subject of their commentaries, mere unwritten foreign customs and usages, resting on tradition, and having no other place of deposit than the memory of men.

Nor are the historical proofs of the fact less strong. Strabo,* ascribes to the Rhodians an admirable legislation in nautical matters, Ευνομια Θαυμαστη προς τα ναυτικα; and Cicero,† observes, "*Rhodiorum, usque ad nostram memoriam, Disciplinæ Navalis gloria remansit;*" the word *Disciplina,* in the sense in which it is used by the orator in other passages, signifying not merely customs and usages, but the institutions of a state in general, and a written or recorded legislation.

At the same time, it is plain that, although they had not merely been recorded in writing, but enacted by the legislative power of the people, the maritime laws of the Rhodians could only bind their own citizens or subjects, colonies, and dependencies, and could have no obligatory force upon the inhabitants of other independent countries, continental or insular. But, whatever may have been the precise age in which the Rhodian code of maritime laws was composed—whether its authority rested upon recorded usage, legislative enactment, or judicial determination—its excellence was universally admitted, and it for ages possessed a great though indirect influence among many of the foreign nations inhabiting the coasts and islands of the Mediterranean, from the wisdom, equity, and practical convenience of its regulations, and from the natural tendency,

* Lib. xiv., c. 11, § 4.

† Pro lege Manilia.

which we have already explained, of maritime and commercial laws to become almost universal, until Rhodes became a part, and its maritime laws were adopted, to a great extent, if not entirely, as the positive law of the Roman Empire.

From the acknowledged superior excellence of the Rhodian sea laws, curiosity is naturally excited to ascertain whether any genuine fragments of the original text have survived the lapse of ages, and been transmitted to modern times. How and to what extent these laws were adopted by the Romans, and engrafted into their system of jurisprudence, we shall afterwards have occasion to inquire, when we come to consider the maritime and commercial law of that people. At present, the object of investigation is, whether the whole or any part of the Rhodian code, either the original Greek text in the Ionic or Doric dialect, or even a Latin literal translation, have been preserved. For upwards of a century, it seems to have been the opinion of most of the eminent jurists of the Continent and of this island, that, if not the whole, the most material part of the original Greek text of the Rhodian code had survived the decline of civilisation and the eruption of the barbarous nations, and was actually in preservation; being the collection of Greek maritime regulations known by the title of "Jus Navale Rhodiorum." But the result of subsequent historical research, and of more accurate critical examination, is, that the opinion, so long entertained by many of the learned on this subject of literary juridical curiosity, is erroneous.

The collection of naval regulations here alluded to, under the denomination of the Rhodian Laws, was first published at Basle, in 1591, by Simon Schardius, apparently from a manuscript communicated to him by the jurisconsult, Antonius Augustinus; and was afterwards republished at Frankfort, in 1596, by Leunclavius, in the collection entitled, "Jus Græco-Romanum," from a manuscript in the possession of the celebrated Pithon. These laws were presented to the public by the editors without any discussion of their authenticity. The learned and acute Cujacius appears to have died before the date of thesepublications; and, in the articles of this collection, which he cites from the "Basilica," he does not appear to have recognised the ancient Rhodian law. But Mornac seems to have considered this compilation as the genuine Rhodian code. Selden, when pronouncing an eulogium, in his work, "De Dominio Maris," on the nautical laws of the Rhodians, cites this very collection. The able Gothofred, in his treatise, "De Imperio Maris," 1637, dwells on the merits of this compilation. Vinnius thought he rendered an important service to the public when, in 1647, he subjoined this Greek collection to his commentary on the work of Peckins, containing those titles of the Pandects which treat of maritime affairs. And Giannone, in his "History of Naples," adopts the same opinion.* Nay, even Valin himself, it is to be regretted, has not, in this matter, displayed his usual critical acumen; and, in his "Commentaire sur l'Ordonnance de 1681," speaks of the compilation as if its authenticity were neither doubtful nor controverted. And M. de Pastoret, the very learned author of the "History of Legislation," in his juvenile dissertation on the "Influence of the Rhodian Laws," which gained the prize of the Academy of Inscriptions and Belles Lettres, in 1784, while, in a note, he almost admits the true and genuine laws have not reached us, yet appears to have yielded to the authority of those who ascribe to the ancient Rhodians the compilation which now bears their name; and has devoted a considerable portion of his work to an analysis

* Lib. i, c. 3.

of that compilation, in which he very ingeniously endeavours to reconcile the inconsistencies it contains.

On the other hand, however, several civilians, in the course of the sixteenth century, such as Franciscus Balduinus and Antonius Augustinus, before referred to, appear to have doubted the genuineness of the collection of laws we are now considering; and, at last, about the beginning of the eighteenth century, (1703,) the acute Cornelius Van Bynkershoek, who contributed so much to the improvement of general jurisprudence, proved the spurious nature of this collection, in his learned dissertation, " Ad Legem Rhodiam de Jactu." Almost all the later civilians, such as Heineccius, in his " Historia Juris Civilis ;" Gravina, in his " Origines Juris Civilis;" Emerigon, in his " Traité des Assurances ;" Bouchaud, in his " Théorie des Traités de Commerce ;" Jorio, in his valuable but very scarce work, entitled, " Codice Ferdinando," of a considerable part of which, M. Pardessus informs us, Azuni has, without acknowledgment, given a literal translation, in his " Droit Maritime de l'Europe ;" Meyer, in his dissertation " De Historia Legum Maritimarum Medii Ævi"—and Pardessus himself, in his collection, " De Lois Maritimes ;"—have adopted the opinion of Bynkershoek. And the following considerations appear more than sufficient to convince us that the collection of laws, published since the revival of learning, under the appellation of " Jus Navale Rhodiorum," is by no means entitled to be held as the true and genuine maritime code of the Rhodians, so celebrated in antiquity.

In the *first* place, the title of this compilation bears, that the laws have been taken, in some editions, from the eleventh, and, in other editions, from the fourteenth book of the Digest; but, if by Digest be here meant the Roman Pandects, or Digest by Justinian, the fact is, that the eleventh book of that work does not treat of nautical affairs at all; and the fourteenth book, although it contains different titles relative to such matters, is obviously, and upon the slightest examination, by no means the original from which the collection in question has been extracted or compiled. At any rate, how the ancient Rhodian laws could be extracted from the Digest of Justinian, is a difficulty which does not admit of any possible solution. If, on the other hand, we understand by Digest the code of Rhodian laws in general, and hold the meaning to be, that the collection under consideration was taken from the eleventh or fourteenth book of this general code, we are by no means relieved from the embarrassment; for what was this general Rhodian code, of which the ancients have not given us the slightest notice?

In the *second* place, the preface prefixed to this collection contains several inconsistencies, anachronisms, and statements contrary to historical truth, which Bynkershoek and Pardessus have pointed out, and which it is unnecessary here to repeat, but which clearly shew that it is the production of a comparatively ignorant age. And the style and manner, also, in which this collection is composed, as well as the matter which it contains, afford strong evidence against its authenticity. To those who are sufficiently acquainted with the Greek language, to distinguish the changes which it has undergone in different ages, it is obvious that these laws are written in the Greek language, such as it was spoken during the decline of the Roman Empire, not in the pure Ionic or Doric dialect of the Rhodians, at the time the Romans borrowed from them their maritime jurisprudence. Nay, in this collection we find Latin words written in Greek characters; we find a reference made in one passage to the Rhodian law; and we find a direction, that the person who fits out a vessel, or sends her to sea, as well as the person intrusted with the navigation and management of the vessel; shall be obliged to take an oath upon the Gospel;—all circumstances necessarily leading to the inference, that these laws are not really the genuine laws of the ancient Rhodians, but the production of later ages.

In the *third* place, the legal principles recognised in this collection are, in several important instances, different from, and less enlightened than, those of the ancient Rhodian laws, as borrowed from them by the Romans. It is placed beyond dispute, as matter of fact, by title ii., book xiv. of the Digest, that the Romans borrowed from the Rhodians, if not the whole of their maritime legislation, at least that which relates to jetson and contribution; that, in the time of Cicero, the Roman lawyers had decided questions on jetson and contribution, conformably to the Rhodian law; and that the Emperor Augustus had authorized that practice. If, therefore, the compilation published by Schardius and Leunclavius contained the true and genuine Rhodian laws, they ought to have been conformable to those of which the import and, so far, even the expression are found preserved in the Digest; it might, no doubt, present more laws, but it could not well contain less, nor other and different laws. Now, important rules which, agreeably to the fragments in the Digest, behoved necessarily to exist in the Rhodian laws then known, are not found in the compilation we are considering; and, what is still more remarkable, it exhibits regulations entirely opposite. Thus the Digest "De Lege Rhodia de Jactu" prescribes that, if the vessel receive any damage in its masts or in its rigging, from the violence of the winds or from lightning, the owner or fitter-out of the vessel has no right to demand any contribution from the owners of the cargo; and that the contribution takes place only so far as the damage or loss has been the result of a deliberate determination that the sacrifice was necessary to save the vessel, and for the preservation of the merchandise on board, and of the lives of the passengers. On the other hand, the compilation, entitled, "Jus Navale Rhodiorum," decides the question in the directly opposite manner: it establishes between the ship and cargo, and even among the owners of the cargo, respectively, a sort of communion of all risks; thus rejecting the distinction of averages into common or general and particular, which forms the basis of this title of the Digest, and which is thus expressed by a text of the genuine Rhodian law preserved in this title, "*Lege Rhodia cavetur, Si, levandæ navis gratiâ, jactus mercium factus est, omnium contributione sarciatur, quod pro omnibus datum est.*"

Again, the Digest decides that goods saved from shipwreck do not contribute to the reparation of losses sustained by the owners of the other parts of the cargo in that event. And the reason given for this by the Roman jurisconsults is, that the contribution ought only to take place in cases where the goods have been sacrificed with a view to common safety, and the vessel has been saved in consequence of that sacrifice. On the contrary, the compilation establishes a contribution between the vessel which has perished and the goods which their owners have succeeded in saving from the shipwreck.

Again, the Digest decides, according to the opinion of Servius, Ofilius, and Labeo, who lived in the time of Augustus, that, in the case of pirates carrying off anything from an owner of a part of the cargo, or from a passenger, the loss must fall on him alone. On the contrary, the compilation places this loss to the common account, and directs it to be repaired by contribution.

It would be superfluous to push this contrast any farther; and there cannot be a stronger proof than this opposition between the principles of the Roman law and those of the compilation which now bears the title of "Jus Navale Rhodiorum," that the latter does not contain the genuine Rhodian laws, which existed in the days of the classic Roman jurisconsults, and upon which these lawyers wrote treatises.

At the same time, there does not appear to be sufficient ground for holding, as Bynkershoek seems to have done, that the "Jus Navale Rhodiorum," republished by Peckius, was absolutely a forgery, or an attempt to deceive succeeding ages into the belief that this compilation was either the original or a copy of the ancient Rhodian maritime code. The greater part, and the more important articles of this compilation, appear to be contained in the title on the Rhodian laws of the Basilica, or general legal code, commenced by the Emperor Basilius, the Macedonian, and completed and promulgated, in the year 886 of the Christian era, by his son Leo IV., surnamed the Philosopher. The Emperor Constantine Porphyrogenitus likewise published, in the year 909, a new edition of the collection by Leo, under the title of "*Ανακαθαρσις*," or Repurgatio, which is said, at this day, to be observed as law by the Greek subjects of the Ottoman Empire;* and we seem, therefore, warranted to conclude, that the collection of laws published in modern times, under the appellation of "Jus Navale Rhodiorum," was a compilation of the ninth or tenth century.

Having thus ascertained that this Greek compilation has no title to be considered either as the original or as a copy of the ancient Rhodian maritime code, and it being admitted, on all hands, that there is no other Greek work extant in modern times which has the slightest pretension to be held as the production of that intelligent trading people, it only remains to inquire whether any

* Isambert sur les Lois des Rhodiens. Themis i. p. 401, 117; also p. 201.

Latin translation of the original Rhodian laws has been preserved; and, in particular, whether the compilations made under the authority of Justinian contain such a translation. And here, again, we find that some modern lawyers have supposed the title of the Digest, "Ad Legem Rhodiam de Jactu," to be a Latin translation of part of the nautical laws of Rhodes; but for this opinion there does not seem to be any good foundation, beyond the text before quoted from the Digest, lib. xiv., tit. ii., after the words *lege Rhodia cavetur;* for, on examining the other fragments of which this title of the Digest is composed, we find them ascribed to the lawyers Servius, Ofilius, Labeo, Alfenus Varus, Paulus, Julianus, Hermogenianus, and others, who lived in different ages. The division of the Digest, too, in which these fragments are contained, does not bear the title of the Rhodian laws, which it would, in all probability, have done, had it consisted of the original text, but is entitled, "Ad Legem Rhodiam de Jactu." From these circumstances, the fair inference is, that, with the preceding exception, this division or title of the Digest consists of nothing but commentaries, composed by certain Roman lawyers, upon the Rhodian code, and contains merely the more important opinions and decisions of these lawyers, founded upon that more ancient system of maritime jurisprudence. Nor is there anything extraordinary or surprising in the conduct of the lawyers here alluded to. They merely did, in this instance, what they would have done with respect to any other laws which they were called upon to discuss, or upon which they had occasion to argue and reason. In committing these discussions, opinions, or decisions to writing, they did not deem it necessary to recite, or even to give a translation of, the original text; and, accordingly, we are not indebted to them for its preservation.

CHAPTER IV.

OF THE MARITIME AND COMMERCIAL LAW OF THE ROMANS.

In thus tracing the history of the Rhodian maritime code, we have been led, from the curious and interesting nature of the subject, into a pretty long investigation. We proceed, in the order of time, to take a short historical view of the maritime and commercial law of the Romans; and, in doing so, we shall have an opportunity of inquiring how and to what extent the Romans adopted the laws of the Rhodians into their system of jurisprudence, and, of course, of ascertaining to what extent the nations of modern Europe are indirectly indebted to those industrious and skilful islanders for the basis and leading rules of their maritime legislation.

It is admitted, on all hands, that, from the infancy of their state, the great aim and object of the Romans was to aggrandise themselves, not by their industry, not by the peaceful operations of commerce and manufacture, but by conquest, by the subjugation and plunder of mankind. They scorned to procure, by the exercise of their own art and ingenuity, or by the exchange of value for value, those articles of comfort and convenience which, by superiority of military skill and prowess, they could wrest from other nations; and, agreeably to this spirit, they employed the naval power which, though late, they at last attained, not so much for the protection and promotion of commerce, as for the purposes of conquest and the extension of their empire.

For a series of ages from the foundation of their city, agriculture was deemed the only honourable occupation except that of arms. Mercantile pursuits were discouraged not only by public opinion, but also by the laws; trade of every description was expressly forbidden to men of noble or illustrious families; seafaring people were held in low estimation; the merchant and mechanic were not allowed to enjoy any dignity, or to exercise any office in the state. Military skill and valour opened the only certain road to honours.. The warlike were preferred to the peaceful arts. The formation of a people of soldiers was the grand political scheme, to which were sacrificed all the advantages of those varied pursuits and occupations which constitute the delight and embellishment of civilized life.

But, however warlike, however adverse to commerce and manufactures, the political constitution and the habits and customs of the Romans may have been, in the earlier periods of their history, it is manifest there could not fail to exist among them, even in these times, those rude descriptions of manufacture, and those frequent exchanges of commodities, which are indispensable for the supply of the necessary wants and comforts of a people; and, in the more advanced ages of the Republic, the peculiar views, feelings, customs, and institutions, to which allusion has just been made, appear to have gradually yielded to the influence of those general physical laws by which the progress of civil society appears to be regulated, or which, at least, have operated among all nations which have made any considerable advances in civilisation—a change which could scarcely fail to be the consequence of the introduction of the extraneous wealth amassed by their victories and conquests.

A people who had founded a city, and occupied considerable adjacent territory, however little disposed to industry, could not well exist without a great number of articles, of which the manufacture must necessarily become the habitual occupation of a corresponding number of individuals; and the number of the workmen employed in such manufactures, and of the dealers in the produce of their labours, behoved to increase in Rome, in proportion as the population increased, and their wants and desires expanded. For a long time, however, their commercial transactions appear to have been limited to barter, or the exchange of commodities. Money, that necessary instrument of commerce, did not, we are told, begin to be known at Rome till the reign of Servius Tullius, and even then consisted only of pieces of copper. Silver, so common among the states who then had the dominion of the sea, was not used by the Romans for money till five years before the first Punic war; and gold not till near a century afterwards.*

But, in proportion as their conquests introduced riches, and riches a taste for articles of luxury, commercial transactions, at first confined to objects of primary necessity, gradually extended to and embraced everything that could gratify the new wants which sprung up and increased, according to Sallust, with an almost incredibly rapid and lamentable progression. Commerce thus received a development, which the frugality and, perhaps, the virtue of the earlier ages of the Republic had precluded. Agriculture ceased to be considered as the only reputable and honourable profession, when the fields of Latium, in the expressive language of Pliny, so long proud of being cultivated by hands which had earned triumphs, and tilled with ploughs adorned with laurels, were abandoned to the mercenary labour of disreputable men, and of slaves accustomed to work under the lash. The idea of a fortune gained by trade

* Plin. Hist. Nat., lib. xxxiii. cap. 13.

ceased to offend the austerity or pride of patrician manners. The citizens of Rome, even of the higher ranks, came to apply themselves with avidity to a branch of industry which appeared likely to prove a source of abundant profit. Pride took refuge behind the magnitude of such commercial operations. Commerce, according to Cicero, came to be held in more or less estimation, according as it was more or less extensive and important. What pride or the ancient laws still did not permit to be done directly, came to be performed by slaves, for the behoof of their masters; and, at this period, M. Pardessus supposes, with a high degree of probability, the Roman judges, called upon to decide cases for which the more ancient laws had not made any provision, found themselves under the necessity of introducing the actions called *Institoria* and *Tributoria*, in order to give persons who had dealt with a slave, authorized by his master to carry on trade, the power of compelling the latter to fulfil the engagements of the *præpositus*, agent or factor, or at least to prevent him from reaping the profits of the business of which he refused to discharge the burdens.

This great change in the views and habits of the Romans, which took place during the latter ages of the Republic, could not fail to be accompanied with a corresponding extension of the old *jus civile*, and improvement in commercial law. Even while their commerce was still merely inland, the rules of the contract of sale, fixing the qualities and risks of things sold, and repressing the frauds of vendors, admitted of easy application to purchases and sales made for the purpose of mercantile adventure and profit, as well as to those of which the object was merely individual consumption, or possession and use. The same was the case with the contracts of pledge or security, or of conveyance from one place to another. And there is reason to believe the circumstance of being a stranger or foreigner did not form any obstacle to the right of carrying on commerce, as the transactions of which it is composed were denominated by the Roman lawyers contracts *juris gentium.*

In the natural progress of inland commerce, too, the *jus civile* and *jus gentium* appear to have recognised and enforced the contracts of *mandate* and *locatio operarum,* mercantile agency and mercantile copartnership. The almost incredible severity of the ancient laws against insolvent debtors, was softened and relaxed into imprisonment and *cessio bonorum.* And provision was made for repressing the frauds of bankrupts, and for the due distribution of their funds among their creditors, according to the respective rights of preference which the latter might have obtained.

But it was the extension of their conquests beyond Italy, the attention at last paid by them to navigation, and the multifarious traffic with the countries surrounding the Mediterranean, which (from the causes before alluded to) arose during the latter ages of the Republic, that chiefly led to the development and great improvement of the law of maritime commerce among the Romans. The wars in which, for the first five centuries of their history, they were so incessantly involved with their neighbours, may, in some measure, account for their paying so little attention to naval affairs, while many of the other small states of Italy, such as the Tarentines, the Tyrhenians, and Liburnians, carried on considerable trade for these early times, and made improvements in navigation of which the Romans afterwards availed themselves. At last, however, the increasing power and haughtiness of Carthage roused the jealousy of the Romans, and taught them the necessity of maintaining a marine force, if they wished to extend their conquests beyond the peninsula of Italy. The success which attended their first great exertions in this department, encouraged them to persevere; and, in a short period, they constructed such fleets, and formed such a powerful marine, as enabled them not only to triumph over their more skilful rival, but also to maintain afterwards a superiority at sea. This naval power they continued to employ, as one of the indispensable instruments for the extension and maintenance of their dominion over the various nations with whom the Mediterranean was the chief medium of communication. And after their conquered provinces had, towards the close of the Republic, almost encircled that inland sea, they, in one grand expedition, directed the whole naval strength of the nation against the formidable piratical confederacy which had long infested the ports of Italy and Sicily; and, with a fleet of upwards of five hundred sail, scoured the Mediterranean from the Pillars of Hercules to the Thracian Bosphorus. At the same time, the Romans appear to have all along employed the naval power at which they at last arrived, not so much for the purposes of trade as of conquest, and to have entertained but limited or narrow views as to commercial intercourse. Their fleets were seldom dispatched to open new communications or to discover distant and unknown regions. Their object was to subject mankind to the same common yoke, not to unite them by the ties of reciprocal interest. But, as observed by M. Pardessus, if the desire of aggrandizing their state by conquests was the first or chief motive which induced the Romans to construct ships and fleets; if the maintenance of such fleets was continued chiefly for securing the obedience of the transmarine nations whom they had subjected to their sway; if the supply of their overgrown capital with provisions, for which the produce of Italy, transformed almost entirely into mansion-houses and villas, pleasure-grounds and gardens, for the residence and enjoyment of the noble and wealthy citizens, was no longer sufficient, gave rise to the first or principal maritime adventures and speculations, and became the cause of the various encouragements granted by the government to those who devoted themselves to that trade; still, on the other hand, the variety of enjoyments which commerce in general afforded to the wealthy, the livelihood and comfortable subsistence which it insured to others, could not fail to multiply its operation; while the great advantages which the state derived from it, in time procured for it a comparatively high degree of favour. The remains of ancient manners, and considerations of public order and propriety, it is true, deprived men, in situations of dignity and power, of the right of being owners of, or of employing, vessels in traffic. But there is reason to believe that even their citizens managed to evade the more ancient laws, by employing their slaves in maritime adventure for their account and profit.

These great changes in the circumstances and habits of the Roman people, in the later or more advanced ages of the Republic, as was to be expected, were attended with corresponding changes in their commercial and maritime law. The new positions of parties, the new dealings or transactions and events which occur in maritime, so different from those of inland commerce, while they attracted the attention of the lawyers, called for the interposition and corresponding exertions of the magistrates intrusted with the administration of justice, and with the maintenance of peace and order, in the different parts of the Roman dominions; and it was in these times, and in the progress of their conquests eastward, that the Romans appear to have become more intimately acquainted with the Rhodians and their institutions.

When they had resolved upon, and prepared for, the conquest of the East, the Romans at once perceived of what importance the aid of the marine force of the

Rhodians would be for the accomplishment of their designs, and made amicable advances to these islanders. The latter, again, dreading the victorious arms of that enterprising and insatiable Republic, abandoned their connection with the kings of Macedonia and Pontus, and entered into a close alliance with the Romans. The result of this alliance was unfavourable to the Rhodians, inasmuch as it terminated in the loss of their independence as a separate people, and in their being obliged, along with the countries to the east of the Mediterranean, to acknowledge the sovereignty of Rome. But, in other respects, the Romans all along treated them with great attention and regard; partly, no doubt, on account of the services they had rendered, but chiefly from respect for their institutions, of which the wisdom and beneficial influence had long been generally appreciated and extensively felt.

From this intimate connection and intercourse with the Rhodians, the magistrates or judges and jurisconsults of Rome, when called upon to regulate or determine the transactions and disputes arising in the progress of their now rapidly encreasing maritime commerce, appear to have thought they could not do better than adopt the rules of which the experience of that people had proved the excellence. In these times there appeared the Prætorian Edicts, which obliged the owner or charterer of a vessel to fulfil the engagements entered into by the master whom he had appointed, and rendered the former responsible for thefts committed by the crew of the vessel, or even for the mere negligence of the master.* The principal Roman lawyers, contemporaries of Cicero, such as Servius, Labeo, Ofilius, and Alfenus Varus, impressed with the wisdom of the Rho-

* Dig., lib. xiv., tit. i., de Exercitoria Actione. Dig., lib. iv., tit. ix., Nautæ Caupones, &c.

dian laws, appear to have made them a particular object of study, and to have gradually assumed their principles, adapting them, however, to the wants and habits of the Romans, as well as to the forms of their judicial procedure; and, in this way, even during the Republic, the maritime and commercial law of the Romans appears to have been gradually unfolded, and to have received various additions and improvements from the decisions of the jurisconsults, and from their establishing rules for the application of the contract of *locatio conductio* to the conveyance of commodities by sea, for the reparation of damage occasioned by the collision of vessels, for the loan of money subject to sea risks, called *fœnus nauticum*, for jetson, and the cases in which contribution takes place, and for a number of other similar questions.

Still, however, the laws of the Rhodians had not, during the Republic, received any proper legislative sanction, and had not the form of positive statutory law. They had not been received, at first, like the other laws borrowed from the Greeks at an earlier period, engraved on tables, and ratified and rendered Roman by a solemn act of the people; they were merely held in high estimation as written reason, (*ratio scripta,*) as a code of equity and natural justice. They received effect only so far as the prætor adopted them in his edicts, or the jurisconsults were guided by them in delivering their opinions and decisions in particular cases. It was reserved for the Emperor Augustus to give to these laws a direct and positive legislative sanction, in consequence of which the judges were no longer permitted to deviate from them in their decisions. This appears from a rescript of the Emperor Antonine, preserved by the jurisconsult Volusius Mæcianus, and forming Fragment IX. of the Digest "De Lege Rhodia de Jactu;" and whatever diversity of interpretation this rescript may admit of in other respects, it places beyond doubt that Augustus, or at least Tiberius, according to some commentators, recognised the Rhodian laws as Roman, and gave them, instead of a precarious and voluntary, a stable and binding authority, so far as they were not inconsistent with the pre-established national laws of the empire. It further appears, that the Rhodian laws, in general, were afterwards, at intervals, approved of and confirmed by successive emperors; and although there is only one title in the Digest of the Emperor Justinian which expressly bears to be a commentary on a branch of the Rhodian laws, the doctrine of contribution towards reparation of a loss voluntarily incurred for the preservation of the vessel or cargo, there is great reason to believe that not merely this branch, but the whole, or at least the greater part of the Rhodian regulations, relative to maritime transactions and events, were transferred, if not in the exact language, at least in spirit and substance, into the jurisprudence of Rome. Indeed, this very title contains other matters than jetson; such as, the rights and obligations of the master of a vessel who has undertaken the conveyance of goods, and questions as to shipwreck. The very special terms of the rescript of Antonine, just referred to, afford strong evidence that the other numerous maritime laws, which Tribonian collected and scattered throughout the Pandects, must also have been of Rhodian origin, though probably modified to suit the views and habits of the Romans; and this conclusion is confirmed by the circumstance remarked by Cujacius and Pardessus, that, in different manuscripts of the "Receptæ Sententiæ" of Paulus the jurisconsult, the title containing regulations, exactly similar to those in the Digest, is entitled "Ad Legem Rhodiam de Nauticis."

The text of the Rhodian laws, as already noticed, has not been preserved by the Romans; and it is to be regretted, as a literary as well as a juridical loss, that so valuable a system of maritime legislation has not survived in its original form and language. In fact, the Romans, in adopting the Rhodian laws, appear to have been more anxious to avail themselves of the practical excellence of the precepts than to preserve them in their original, ancient, and, so far, foreign form. And accordingly, although, as we have already seen, the greater part of the Rhodian regulations appear to have been recognised and adopted by the classic jurisconsults, and also substantially incorporated into the Digest of Justinian, they are so promiscuously scattered over that immense compilation, and are so involved in the discussions and interpretations of the jurisconsults, that, not being specified by name when they occur, they cannot with any certainty be selected from the body of maritime and commercial law which was gradually accumulated during the later ages of the Republic, and under the Emperors.

But although we have no longer the form, and cannot even accurately distinguish the substance of the Rhodian legislation in the compilations of Roman jurisprudence which have been handed down to us, we have at least the satisfaction of possessing in these authentic compilations the combined legislative and judicial experience, the united practical wisdom, of Rhodes and Rome; and we shall now, therefore, take a cursory view of the detached laws in the Pandects, relative to mercantile and maritime matters, nearly in the order formerly adopted, availing ourselves of the subordinate arrangement of Pothier in his "Pandectæ in Novum Ordinem Digestæ," and of the scientific analysis of Pardessus.*

---

* See Excerpta Juris Romani ad Rem Nauticam Spectantia. Pardessus, Collection, vol. i., 85-132.

In the Roman law, we find the different descriptions of trading vessels enumerated, and the right of property in such vessels clearly defined and enforced. The general rules previously established were found sufficient for regulating the acquisition of vessels by construction, and the transference of them by sale; and many of the special questions, to which this description of property gives rise, the Roman jurisconsults did not fail to resolve. When once built, the vessel, possessing a sort of individuality, was always considered as one and the same body, whatever repairs it might have undergone. Accordingly, the person who, after bequeathing a vessel, had repaired it of new, was not held to have revoked his legacy; but if, after bequeathing a vessel, one had broken it up, the detached pieces of timber resulting from this demolition could not be legally claimed by the legatee. On the other hand, if any one had bequeathed timber or other materials, and had, after making this bequest, employed them in building a vessel, the legatee of these materials could not claim the vessel. The rule, that the accessory follows the condition of the principal, being applicable to vessels as well as to all other objects of property, if the owner of a vessel had repaired it with timber belonging to others, he continued to be the exclusive proprietor of the vessel, under reservation of an action of indemnity to the person to whom the materials belonged; but when a person had built a vessel wholly with timber belonging to another, the jurisconsults appear to have been divided on the question who was the proprietor, whether the builder or the owner of the materials. A vessel, considered as a whole, was held to comprehend whatever was destined and applied to its use; but this did not prevent the articles of rigging and other appurtenances from being considered distinct objects, or from being seized for debts, or separately sold or reclaimed without the vessel;

and the combination of these principles rendered the question sufficiently puzzling, whether the purchaser of a vessel, with its rigging and appurtenances, could maintain that the boat was comprehended in the sale.

Every free person, without distinction of sex, might be proprietor of a vessel; even a minor might be so, but with the provision that he did not bind himself, in what concerned his vessel, without the authority of his tutor. Vessels frequently belonged to several individuals; and we find the rights and obligations of co-owners of vessels, both in relation to each other and in relation to third parties contracting with them, pretty distinctly unfolded. Indeed, in a comparatively little advanced state of maritime traffic and naval enterprise, owing to the little accumulation of capital in the hands of individuals, a number of persons must concur and combine their means, in order to accomplish the then difficult undertaking of building and fitting out a vessel of any magnitude. It thus appears that the branch of the law which relates to co-ownership in vessels, and which involves questions of considerable nicety, is cultivated and brought to maturity at an earlier period than would otherwise be the case; and, accordingly, although the spirit of the Romans was, as we have seen, for a long period, certainly rather anti-commercial, their lawyers perceived the expediency of the rule which, while it determines the reciprocal obligations of the part-owners or co-owners of a vessel, in proportion to their respective shares, holds them each jointly liable to the public, *singuli in solidum,* in all matters connected with the voyage and trade in which the vessel is engaged. When a vessel belonged in common to several individuals, the property was held to form a sort of copartnership. The part-owners, indeed, were not held liable *singuli in solidum* for the fulfilment of the engagements undertaken by each of them severally, because they were not presumed, without special stipulation to that effect, to have constituted themselves *præpositi* factors or managers for each other; but when they had, in common, intrusted the management of the vessel to the master, they might be prosecuted *in solidum* for his engagements, or for the delinquency of the sailors or crew..

Vessels were not less liable than the other effects of a debtor to be attached for his debts; but the nature of some of these debts secured them a privilege or a preference; such as the claim of a creditor who had lent money to build, purchase, or equip, the vessel, or to procure necessary articles in the course of the voyage. And priority in time did not, as in ordinary cases, give preference in point of right; for the privilege of the person who had lent money to fit out or repair the vessel, or for the subsistence of the crew, or for other similar purposes, was preferred even to the privilege of the vendor; because, in fact, such advance alone preserved to the previous creditors a fund for their payment, which would otherwise, in all probability, have perished.

The care and government of the vessel was intrusted to a *præpositus*, *patronus*, *magister*, or master; sometimes even to several; among whom the functions were divided, or who were obliged to act in common. And this master, and, under his orders, the crew of mariners of different classes, employed in piloting and navigating the vessel, had an action for their wages against the owner of the vessel, or *exercitor navis*. The name of *exercitor navis* was given to the person who had the use of a vessel and reaped the profits arising from its employment, whether as owner or as usufructuary, or as hirer or charterer for a longer or shorter period. If it happened that a vessel had been possessed and employed by a person who had no right to such possession, the rules of the common law were followed; the heir, in general, was held bound to restore to the special legatee the hire or freight which he had thus received; and the *mala fide* possessor to account to the owners for the freight which the latter would have earned, if he had not been unjustly deprived of possession.

With the contract of affreightment the Romans appear to have been quite familiar. The distinction between the contract by which the whole ship is freighted for a particular voyage or for a definite period, and the case of a general ship conveying, at a certain rate of freight, the goods and merchandise of a variety of individuals, is clearly recognised. And the necessary rule of law, by which the engagement of the master binds the owners in all matters relating to the vessel and the voyage, was firmly established. Indeed, the different cases of the responsibility of the owners for advances made to the master abroad for refitting the vessel, and other such purposes, were so accurately defined and decided, that the rules laid down coincide very nearly with those observed in practice at the present day.

The freighting of the vessel most frequently consisted in giving a right to ship or load a certain number of persons, or quantity of merchandise, and in the obligation to convey such persons and merchandise to a destined port; forming a contract compounded of the *locatio rei* and *locatio operarum*. In this case, the contract of affreightment was usually entered into by the master; but under the ordinary limitations of his powers, in consequence of express instructions, or implied from the known and usual description and destination of the vessel. The reach or burden of the vessel was determined by the number of casks it could contain. Sometimes a penal clause was inserted in the contract, to provide for the master not fulfilling his obligation at the appointed time; but he was released from this by *vis major*, irresistible event; as when he had fallen sick, or when the vessel was arrested by public authority, or was unable to keep the sea, without any negligence or fault on his part.

If the contract gave a right to occupy the entire ship, the whole freight was due, however small the quantity of goods actually loaded. If the contract was by weight or measure, freight was paid only in proportion to what was loaded;—and even if a woman was delivered of a child during the voyage, no freight was due for the infant, because it did not increase the weight of the cargo, and did not use the provisions destined for the passengers.

No freight was payable for what perished through inevitable accident; and if it had been paid in advance, it behoved to be restored; but if the goods perished through the fault of the party shipping them, as by confiscation from their being contraband, freight was nevertheless due. And the same rule was observed when the loss of goods was occasioned by their own inherent defect, as in the case of slaves, unless the agreement was only to pay freight for those who should arrive at their destination. The owner or master of the vessel had a privilege, or preferable right, upon or over the cargo or goods conveyed, for payment of the freight; and the same privilege was extended to the person who had advanced money for that purpose.

The master was responsible for such goods as were delivered to him personally, on the quay or in the vessel: the delivery of goods to one of the mariners or crew, bound the master only so far as the mariner had received them with the consent of the master, express or presumed. This responsibility extended to every loss or damage happening through any fault whatever; as when, having entered the mouth of a river without a pilot on board, the vessel was lost; or as when, having undertaken to convey goods by a particular vessel, he put them, without the consent of the shipper, on board another vessel, less seaworthy, which had perished, while the vessel which ought to have carried the goods arrived safe. But, on the other hand, if necessity had compelled the master to tranship the goods—for instance, if it was not possible to enter the port of destination without putting the goods on board another vessel which drew less water, and this second vessel perished with the goods—the master was not responsible, unless he had made the transhipment against the will of the shipper, or without necessity, or had acted imprudently, or *mala fide.* In general, irresistible force, by which goods had been destroyed, or had been carried off, as by pirates, was recognised as an exception or defence pleadable by the master.

The master was also obliged to watch over the preservation of the goods which he had taken on board for the purpose of being conveyed, and was held responsible for all damage which was not the consequence of irresistible force. He was not released from this responsibility by proving that the damage, theft, or robbery had been committed by the sailors, or even by passengers, whether on board the ship or in the port, from the moment the charge of the goods had been intrusted to him, unless, by a precaution which was not prohibited, he had intimated to the shippers he was not to incur such responsibility, and they had not insisted on his doing so.

The right of claiming the goods with which the vessel was loaded, or of pursuing for reparation of damage or loss, might be exercised by the person who had delivered them for conveyance by sea, on condition of the payment of freight, or gratuitously, whether they belonged to him or whether he had only charge of them; the latter circumstance giving him an interest in their preservation.

The owners, or *exercitores*, of the vessel were bound, by the engagements of the master, in a more extensive manner than their constituents were by the acts of the *institores*, *præpositi*, or factors, in inland commerce; because, in the latter case, third parties contracting with the *præpositus* might ascertain the extent of his powers; whereas, in the course of navigation, and distant voyages, there was seldom an opportunity of procuring such information. Parties contracting with the master might, consequently, and independently of their direct action against him, pursue the owner or exercitor; and, if the master had been appointed by several part owners, the action might conclude against them *in solidum.*

The owner or exercitor was equally bound by the person whom the master had substituted in his place, even although the power of doing so had been withheld, or such substitution had been prohibited.

The master, however, bound the owner or exercitor only for what he did within the limits of his office, *præpositura;* and this was, in general, held to embrace only authority to purchase such provisions and other articles as were necessary for the use of the vessel, to let the vessel out on freight, to undertake the conveyance of goods, to engage mariners, and to borrow money indispensably requisite for the payment of these expenses. In such cases, the dishonesty or fraud of the master, who might divert from its destination what was so purchased or borrowed, did not liberate the owner or exercitor in relation to the *bona fide* creditors. But a special authority would have been necessary to purchase or sell the cargo of goods in port. Sometimes the owner prohibited certain acts, which fell within the ordinary limits of the master's power; or, if there were several masters, required their concurrence; and then such persons as knew these restrictions had themselves to blame if they treated with a person who exceeded his powers. Although the owner was held bound by the acts of the master, he was not presumed or understood to be so by the legal acts of the mariners, unless by his consent, express or tacit, to agreements made by them. But he was held responsible for their delinquencies, even when there was no participation or accession on his part. He might, consequently, be prosecuted by one whose goods had been stolen or carried off by force; and might, in his turn, prosecute the thieves or robbers.

Among the maritime laws of Rome, as well as of Rhodes, the regulations relative to shipwreck and distress at sea occur very frequently, and form a large portion of the maritime code. Nor is it difficult to account for this fact. Of all others, perhaps, the art of navigation most requires the accumulated labour, experience, and ingenuity of ages, to bring it to any degree of perfection. And, although we cannot but admire the nautical skill and enterprise displayed by many nations of antiquity, and the boldness and extent of their naval expeditions, when we consider the great and various obstacles which these early mariners had to encounter, we must, at the same time, bear in mind that their efforts and attainments were very inferior indeed to the more skilful exertions and enterprises of modern times. The arts of shipbuilding and of navigation, though zealously cultivated by many ancient nations, were, if compared with their present state, extremely rude and imperfect. The external form and structure of their vessels was ill contrived for security or expedition, even in the most prosperous weather, and rendered them, in tempests, almost totally unmanageable. Nor was this defect remedied by the shape or disposition of the sails and rigging. The mariners, too, were, for the most part, confined to particular coasts; and, as their experience was so limited, their nautical skill behoved to be proportionally moderate. They were ignorant of the scientific principles of their art, and they had not the aid of the compass, that almost infallible guide of modern navigators. In such circumstances, we cannot be surprised at the caution with which they ventured upon a voyage, or at the multiplicity of regulations adopted for determining the respective rights of those whose properties and interests were exposed to such a variety of accidents and adverse events.

As already noticed, the only title in the Roman Digest which expressly bears to be a commentary on the Rhodian law, is that which relates to the subject we are now considering—general average or contribution towards reparation of losses sustained at sea; and in that title the principles of this equitable doctrine are so clearly and so fully unfolded, that they have been almost universally adopted, and form, at this day, the basis of this branch of the maritime jurisprudence of almost all the nations of modern Europe.

The first point of inquiry in this title is, what kind of loss gives rise to the contribution? The general rule is laid down, that the loss must be incurred for the purpose of warding off a common danger; and this rule is illustrated by instances of its application, and by cases which do not fall under it. It is then established, that all were bound to contribute who had an interest in the loss not being incurred—the owners of the vessel as well as of the cargo. The next object of inquiry was, how far those goods were liable to the contribution which had been saved through the loss voluntarily incurred, but have sustained some damage. It is then laid down, that the amount of the loss was to be distributed according to the price paid for the goods lost, and according to the price obtained at the port of destination for the goods saved.

Imminent danger, and the necessity of escaping from it, impose on all parties interested the obligation to make sacrifices calculated to avoid it. This principle was carried so far as, when the provisions belonging to the vessel were exhausted, to compel those who had them to give them for the common use. On the other hand, all those for whose behoof a sacrifice had been made were bound to repair, by a contribution, the loss which it had occasioned.

The most frequent cases were those of jetson of parts of the rigging or appurtenances of the vessel, or of goods or portions of the cargo thrown overboard into the sea to lighten the vessel, or of the application of such articles to ransom the vessel when captured by enemies or pirates. As this rule of law was founded on necessity, there was no action of damages against the person who thus disposed of the property of others; but such a measure required an adequate cause to justify it, and the dread of an imaginary danger was not sustained as an excuse.

A similar case to that of jetson was, when the master was obliged, in order to lighten the vessel, which could not otherwise enter a port or river, from drawing too much water, to unload goods into a lighter, and these goods were lost. The goods which remained in the vessel, and arrived safe at their port of destination, behoved to contribute to repair this loss which had operated their preservation. But the converse did not hold if the vessel was lost, although the lighter was saved; the goods which had been put on board the latter did not contribute towards reparation of the loss of the goods which had remained in the vessel, because this loss could not possibly be considered as a sacrifice made to save them.

For all goods thrown overboard, or sacrificed in the view of the common safety, the contribution was due to those whose property had been so sacrificed, whether ordered in consequence of a deliberate resolution, or the imminence of the danger had not permitted any previous consultation. But this was not the rule in the case of damage happening accidentally to the vessel or rigging in the course of navigation, although occasioned by events extraordinary and unforeseen, however considerable the damage might be. In the same way, when pirates took possession by force, or pillaged goods belonging to the shippers, or when, in consequence of a tempest, their merchandise perished, they were not admitted to claim any contribution in reparation of such losses. In short, no sacrifice which had not been made with a view to the common safety, and which had not procured the expected result, afforded any ground for a contribution. As soon, however, as the vessel had escaped from the danger with which it was threatened, the right of indemnity was acquired; and hence, therefore, a subsequent shipwreck from accident did not liberate, from the contribution already due by them, the goods saved from this new disaster. On the other hand, if, when goods had been thrown overboard on the first accident, there afterwards occurred another which required a jetson, these goods, even when they were afterwards recovered, owed no contribution for the new jetson, because it had not served to save them.

To apportion the contribution justly between the goods lost and the goods saved, the quantity and the value of the losses were ascertained, and there was comprehended therein the damage caused by the jetson to the merchandise that remained in the vessel. The valuation of the goods lost was made only according to what they had cost, because the object in view was solely to indemnify, and not to procure or bestow a benefit. The goods saved, upon which alone the contribution behoved to fall, were estimated at the price for which they could be sold; and, consequently, those which had sustained damage were estimated only in their deteriorated condition.

The owner or exercitor behoved to contribute in proportion to the value of his vessel, but not for the victuals or provisions on board: each shipper contributed for his merchandise or goods, of whatever kind they might be; but the passengers contributed nothing for their persons, because a freeman was not susceptible of valuation—they were bound only for their clothes and jewels.

Jetson being a forced loss, which, far from supposing, in the individual who bears it, any intention of abandoning the property of the goods sacrificed, presumes, on the contrary, the desire to recover them if he can, no one, it was held, could lawfully appropriate them on the plea of having found them; the possession of him who had found them was not even a title which could enable him to acquire the property by prescription; but the proprietor who recovered them behoved to restore the indemnification which he had received, after deduction of the deterioration of the goods, to be divided proportionally among those who had contributed.

The owner or exercitor might be prosecuted by those whose effects had been sacrificed, to pay them the price or value; and, in his turn, he might prosecute those who were bound to bear a share in the contribution, and even exercise a right of retention over their effects or merchandise in security of this debt; but he was not responsible for their solvency.

The collisions of vessels, so frequent in navigation, the damage which one vessel might cause to another by running foul of it, or by cutting its cables, were also provided for. If the force of the winds or waves, or the necessity of self-preservation, had caused the unfortunate event, there was no room for any responsibility.

Such appear to have been the leading doctrines of the Roman law relative to property in vessels, the navigation of vessels, the employment of vessels on freight in the conveyance of commodities, and the reciprocal rights and obligations of the owners of the vessel and cargo, arising from contract, the perils of the sea, or other events. With regard to the maritime exchange of commodities, the Romans, in the later ages of the Republic, and under the Emperors, as already noticed, from various causes became more commercial than during the earlier part of their history. And although the nobles were prohibited by law from engaging in the pursuits of commerce and manufacture, such dealings, transactions, and operations, were multiplied and extended among the middle orders of the people. The principles of the contracts of barter, and of purchase and sale, came to be fully developed and clearly established. By the *actio institoria* and the *actio exercitoria*, the wholesale merchant, as well as the retail dealer, and likewise shipowners, were made responsible for the conduct of the persons intrusted with their business, or employed in their warehouse or shop, or in their vessels. And although the Roman contract of *mandate*, being gratuitous, without any commission or remuneration, was obviously more adapted to the purposes of friendship than of commercial intercourse, yet, by means of the contracts of *locatio et conductio rei et operarum*, and of *mandate*, combined with the equitable doctrine of *negotiorum gestio*, transactions not merely of manufacture, but of distant maritime and colonial, if not foreign, commerce were carried on with facility and to a very considerable extent.

Incorporations of tradesmen or craftsmen, and also of inconsiderable merchants or dealers, for the ordinary purposes of life, appear to have existed in Rome from an early period; and were afterwards greatly increased, both in the number of separate bodies, and in the number of members, of whom they were composed. While, under the Emperors, these corporations were subjected to such special regulations as the preservation of order and the interest of the public required, they were, at the same time, protected and encouraged; and the disputes relative to the engagements of these merchants and retail dealers, and of these manufacturers or craftsmen, among themselves individually, or with the persons employed by them, were determined agreeably to the principles of the common law, and produced a variety of decisions, still extant.

As commerce was extended, the necessity for intermediate agents, to prepare and conduct its various operations, increased; and the general principles applicable to the powers, rights, and obligations of these agents, called *proxenetæ*, and to the effect also of the agreements or bargains made through their intervention, were gradually unfolded, without the intervention of any new special rules.

As commerce was extended, too, the individuals engaged in its speculations and undertakings could not fail to perceive, and feel more strongly than formerly, the advantages to be derived from the formation of private companies or copartnerships, by which several persons united, in one common interest, their capitals and their industry. Indeed, in earlier times, from the comparatively little accumulation of mercantile and manufacturing capital among the Romans, individuals were naturally, or rather necessarily, led to unite their means, their skill, and their exertions, for the accomplishment of mercantile enterprises of any magnitude. Accordingly, we find that the contract of *societas*, or copartnership, which, while it is necessary in a limited, continues to be advantageous in an extended, state of commerce, was well known at Rome and in the provinces; and its leading rules so distinctly unfolded, and so accurately ascertained, as to have been adopted, with little variation, by almost all the modern European nations.

The intervention of bankers, to pay money and to prove payments, was likewise usual, in their ordinary transactions, among the citizens of Rome. These bankers filled a sort of public office, or exercised a sort of public function: they had particular places of assembling, called *basilicæ;* they were severely punished when they misapplied the deposits intrusted to them; they were bound to keep books in the order of dates, and to produce them in judgment, even when the dispute was between third parties, under certification of being subjected in damages to those to whom such production might be useful. In proportion as mercantile transactions were enlarged and multiplied, the employment of the services of bankers became, of course, more frequent, and almost indispensable. And, without requiring any new special regulations, the principles of the common law came to be more fully unfolded, and applied to this new direction and extension of banking operations.

The extreme rigour which creditors exercised towards their debtors, in the early ages of the Republic, is well known; if the former had not the disposal of the lives of the latter, they might at least reduce them to slavery. This severity was afterwards considerably relaxed. But besides insolvency exposing the debtor to certain political incapacities, and attaching to him a sort of infamy, the coercion of imprisonment, and of a *cessio omnium bonorum*, appears to have continued during the Empire.

For the different cases to which the insolvency of debtors might give rise, the advancement of commerce rendered it still more necessary to provide than formerly; and provision was accordingly made for annulling the acts of the bankrupt debtor, done in defraud of his creditors; for securing to the creditors the goods abandoned by the debtor, or of which the judge had given possession; and for ranking the different classes of creditors *pari passu*, or according to their respective order of preference. But while the doctrines of *emptio venditio;* of *locatio conductio, rei vel operarum;* of *mutuum* and *commodatum;* of pledge or guarantee; of agency, gratuitous or for remuneration; of reimbursement in the case of unauthorized agency; of salvage, and contribution in reparation of a loss incurred for the common safety or benefit; of mercantile copartnership in all its details; of banking operations to a considerable extent; and of bankruptcy, and the ranking of creditors according to their preference—were so familiar to the Romans, it appears rather singular that the other two contracts, so prevalent in modern times, letters or bills of exchange and marine insurance, by which maritime commerce is so protected, facilitated, and extended, should have been, if not entirely unknown to them, at least never introduced into actual, or at all extensive, practice.

For bills of exchange—the modern arrangement by which the metallic coins, or specie, of one country is, by means of a paper document, set off against, or exchanged for, the specie of another country, by which the reciprocal debits and credits arising from the exported and imported surplus produce, natural or artificial, of different countries, are, by means of a medium possessing no intrinsic value, and without the expense and risk attending the conveyance of metal, or any other valuable substance, balanced and adjusted—we look in vain in the Roman jurisprudence. Had that people been acquainted with the negotiable documents now known by the name of bills of exchange, some distinct notice of them would have been found in the numerous writings of their lawyers still extant. But instead of finding in their works any such lucid exposition of bills of exchange as of the other legal doctrines before alluded to, we are left to presume, from the state of maritime commerce which the establishment of these other legal doctrines, as positive law, proves to have existed, that some expedient equivalent to bills of exchange must to some extent have been adopted, so as to save the expense and risk of all mercantile exchanges of commodities, however distant, being accomplished solely by the transportation of the precious metals; and, in aid of this presumption, we are referred by certain modern ingenious jurists, in addition to the brief title in the Digest, "De eo quod certo loco," to the frequent use of the terms, *Argentarii*, *Trapezitæ*, *Nummullarii*, *Collybus*, or *Collybium*, and *Collybistæ*, and to a few passages in classical Roman authors not strictly juridical.* These passages are chiefly selected from the Epistles of Cicero to Atticus and his other friends, and from his oration against Verres. Two of the former relate to the supply of his son with money for his expenses while prosecuting his studies at Athens. "De Cicerone, tempus esse jam videtur; sed quæro, quod illi opus erit Athenis, permutarine possit, an ipsi ferendum sit:"† and "Quare velim cures, (nec tibi essem molestus, si per alium hoc agere possem,) ut permutetur Athenas; quod sit in annuum sumtum, ei scilicet Eros numerabit, ejus rei causa Tironem (Romam) misi."‡ Another passage regards his proceedings at Laodicea:—"Quæris, quid hic agam? ita vivam, ut maximos sumtus facio. Mirifice delector hoc instituto. Admirabilis abstinentia ex præceptis tuis; ut verear, ne illud, quod tecum permutavi, versura mihi solvendum sit."§ Another letter mentions when he was to be at Laodicea, and adds:—"Ibi, perpaucos dies, dum pecunia accipitur, quæ mihi ex publica permutatione debetur, commorabor."|| In another letter to Atticus, he writes:—"De Cœlio, vide, quæso,

---

* Ayrer, De Cambialis Instituti Vestigiis apud Romanos, 1746.
† Cic. ad Att., lib. xii., ep. 24.
‡ Cic. ad Att., lib. xv., ep. 15.
§ Cic. ad Att., lib. v., ep. 15.
|| Cic. ad Div., lib. iii., ep. 5.

ne qua lacuna sit in auro, ego ista non novi; sed certe in collubo est detrimenti satis, huc aurum si accedit."* In his oration against Verres there occurs this passage:—"Nam Collybus esse qui potest, cum utantur omnes uno genere nummorum?"† And referring to the return of Crispus Sallustius from Africa, Cicero says:—"Unde tantum hic exhausit, quantum potuit aut fide nominum trajici, aut in naves contrudi."‡ And these passages certainly, combined with the title in the Digest, "De eo quod certo loco," and the use of the terms before referred to, appear to shew that the Romans knew and practised, not only immediate exchanges, in the same place, of money of different values, and of the coinage of different sovereign states or nations, called *cambia realia*, but also those transactions called *cambia trajectitia*, of which the object was to pay, or deposit, or advance, money in one place, that an equal value might be furnished, paid, or received in another place. But no distinct evidence is thereby afforded that the contract of exchange, such as it exists in our days, and still less the admirable invention of bills of exchange, and of the safe and rapid mode in which they are now negotiated, so highly useful in promoting and accelerating the operations of commerce, were in actual and frequent use among the Romans.

As little do we find in the Roman law any distinct evidence of the existence, or, at least, of the actual use, of marine insurance, as practised in modern times—that most useful contract, by which the risk of loss, by being divided among a number of persons, is so much diminished to the individual trader. We find, indeed, from certain passages in the histories of Livy and Suetonius,

---

* Cic. ad Att., lib. xii., ep. 6.

† Cic. in Ver., act. ii., lib. iii., § 78.

‡ In Crispum Sallustium Responsio, § 7.

that, in the times of the Republic as well as under the Emperors, it was usual for the government, in the case of warlike stores and provisions being conveyed by sea, to relieve the contractors, and to take upon itself the risk of loss arising from the perils of the sea, or from capture by enemies or pirates. Thus we find in Livy—"Ut quæ in naves imposuissent, ab hostium tempestatisque vi, publico periculo essent:"* and, "Publicum periculum erat a vi tempestatis in iis, quæ portarentur ad exercitus."† And the Emperor Claudius, Suetonius informs us, accelerated the importation of grain into Italy during a famine—"Suscepto in se damno, si cui per tempestatem accidisset."‡ But these passages do not amount to evidence of a separate and independent contract of marine insurance; they merely indicate a contract of purchase and sale, *emptio venditio*, with a particular stipulation as to the party who was to bear the risk of the commodity sold, or a *locatio conductio, transvehendi causâ*—a contract for the conveyance solely of commodities, with a special stipulation as to risk. And although, from these passages, it appears the Roman government agreed to bear the risk of the perils of the sea, it must be admitted that, in these and some other analogous cases in the Digest, the contract or agreement to undertake the risk was merely an accessory to another principal contract, which implied an exchange of commodities for other value, or the conveyance of commodities for hire or freight. The object of the principal contract between the government and the furnishers, or contractors, was, that the latter should deliver stores or provisions at a particular place; and as, by this agreement, these contractors had not sold any

* Lib. xxiii., cap. 49.
† Lib. xxv., cap. 3.
‡ Vita Claudii, cap. xviii.

particular or individual article, which would, in that case, have been conveyed at the risk of the government as purchaser, the common law left them at the risk of the sellers; and it was only by a deviation from the ordinary rule that the state consented to undertake the risk. This was just the reverse of the case provided for in some texts of the Digest, in which the seller of a particular article takes the burden of fortuitous events, by the operation of which it may perish, although, according to the common law, the risk is with the purchaser. There are numerous examples, also, in the Digest, in which a party who is not legally responsible for the risk of a thing consents to take it upon himself; thus, the workman who undertook to set precious stones might burden himself with the loss of the articles intrusted to him, through fortuitous accidents. And thus, although an individual article, deposited, lent, or impledged, was, by the Roman law, at the risk of the party who had deposited, or lent, or impledged the article, the depository, the borrower, and the person receiving the pledge, might take upon themselves the responsibility of fortuitous events. But here, too, there had previously intervened a principal contract, of which the ordinary legal effects were, that one of the parties should run the risk of the loss, through inevitable accident, of the things which formed the subject of the contract; and it was only by a clause which the judge had declared legal that the other party took these risks upon himself.

This was, no doubt, approaching very near to the contract of insurance; yet it must be acknowledged that none of these texts mention a principal contract, by which one of the contracting parties, in consideration of a premium, *pretium periculi*, which is given him, or promised, by the other contracting party, binds himself to repair the damage which irresistible or inevitable events may occasion to the property of the latter. A passage, however, in one of the letters of Cicero, it has been maintained, proves that the stipulation of insurance as a principal contract, not a mere accessory, as in the cases before noticed, was known at Rome. Cicero, having gained in Cilicia a victory which he hoped would procure him the honour of a Triumph, wrote as follows: "Laodiceæ me prædes accepturum, arbitror, omnis pecuniæ publicæ, ut et mihi, et populo cautum sit, sine vecturæ periculo."* And, certainly, the word *prædes* is occasionally used to signify sureties, or guarantees, given to private individuals, as well as to the state; and the terms *sine vecturæ periculo*, appear to imply the dangers of conveyance by sea, rather than those of land carriage, and to be in conformity with the expressions relative to sea risk before quoted from Livy and Suetonius; but Heineccius,† Ayrer,‡ and Hugo,§ have all considered the passage just quoted, like the others before quoted, to be applicable rather to the contract of exchange, than to that of insurance. This view is supported by the word *prædes*, which, in its general acceptation, was used to denote suretyship for the public money; and also by the word *pecunia*, which, though sometimes used to denote any description of property, generally signified money or current coin; and the meaning of the passage is held to be, that the *prædes*, whom Cicero expected to obtain, were not insurers against sea risk, but sureties or guarantees either that the money which he paid in Laodicea should be repaid to him in Rome, or that the price of the things which he sold and made over in Laodicea should be paid in Rome; the principal contract being, in the for-

---

* Ad Divers., lib. ii., ep. 17.

† Elem. Jur. Camb. cap. i.

‡ Dissertatio de Cambialis Instituti vestigiis apud Romanos.

§ Civilistisches Magazin, B. 11, p. 125.

mer case, *mutuum*, in the latter, *emptio venditio*, and the *prædes* being merely an accessory.

Other attempts have been made to shew, from certain Fragments in the Digest, that marine insurance was known to the Romans as a principal contract; such as, "Illa Stipulatio, Decem Millia salva fore, promittis? Valet."* But the agreement here mentioned as valid, appears, like the obligation of the tutor, *rem pupilli salvam fore*, to be merely suretyship, or a guarantee for the solvency or proper conduct of other individuals. And, as Hugo observes, an insurance might, perhaps, be sooner or more easily discovered in the frequent stipulations, *si navis venit*, and *si navis non venit*—for every insurance consists of the combination of these two; the proprietor stipulates the worth or value, *si navis non venit*, and the underwriter stipulates his premium, *si navis venit.*

But really the important question here is, not whether insurance might not naturally arise among the Romans, and a suitable form for it be found in their law, or even whether a few passages occur in the classics which may seem to indicate historically its existence, but whether this kind of arrangement was, in any measure, in actual and frequent practice among the Romans. And the last is, at least, highly improbable, were it only for this reason, that they had no particular name for the transaction; *fœnus nauticum* being very different from a simple insurance. And even supposing the contract of insurance, as a principal convention, to have been known to the Romans, we do not find, in the whole body of their laws, any examples of its application to navigation and maritime expeditions; which proves that this kind of transaction must, at least, have been very rare and infrequent.

---

* Digest, De Verborum Obligationibus. lib. xlv., fr. 67.

We formerly endeavoured to account for the beneficial contract of insurance having been unknown to the Athenians, and other Greek communities. The same causes, to all appearance, operated to prevent its introduction into practice among the Romans; and these causes it would be superfluous here to recapitulate at length. Notwithstanding the immense wealth acquired by an unexampled series of conquests for ages, and accumulated in Italy by the military and subsequent civil spoliation of the subjugated provinces, there do not appear to have existed, even under the Emperors, that general diffusion of moveable and mercantile capital among the middle class of the nation, or conquered nations, that advanced state of commercial dealing and intercourse, which the practice of insurance, as a trade or profession, necessarily presupposes. Even in the now so commercial, and manufacturing, and maritime country of Great Britain, the universal or extensive practice of marine insurance is not of a very old date.

But, although they thus appear to have been ignorant of the practical utility of marine insurance, the Romans were familiarly acquainted with the contracts of *bottomry* and *respondentia*, under the appellations of *fœnus nauticum* and *pecunia trajectitia*. This contract, indeed,—by which, on the one hand, money is advanced, with a view to a maritime adventure, upon the condition that, if the money or the goods purchased with it are lost through the perils of the sea, the risk shall be with the creditor, who, in that event, shall receive nothing; and by which, on the other hand, the creditor is allowed to stipulate an indefinite interest on the sum advanced, as a consideration for the risk he incurs,—appears to have been known during the first ages of the Roman Empire, or rather during the later ages of the Republic. It was, in all probability, borrowed from the Athenians, or rather, perhaps, from the Rhodians. It is treated of by several of the most eminent Roman lawyers, such as Papinian, Ulpian, and Paulus, and a distinct title is assigned to it in the Digest.

That the Romans should have been so well acquainted with a contract so nearly allied to marine insurance, and yet should not have practised the latter contract itself, is rather difficult to be accounted for. The cause, however, of this rather singular fact may, perhaps, be traced in circumstances already briefly alluded to. Marine insurance evidently supposes a great number of individuals capable of insuring, that is, a great accumulation and diffusion of mercantile capital; and it also supposes a great number of risks, that is, an extended state of commerce and navigation. But the contract of *respondentia* and *bottomry*, or *fœnus nauticum*, which was practised by the Romans, does not necessarily suppose any of these things. It is adapted to a limited state of commerce, and, indeed, arises from the scantiness of mercantile capital. It is because persons engaged in trade have not a sufficient capital to carry on their foreign commerce, that they are induced to apply to those individuals who are unskilled in such traffic, but who have some moveable property acquired by their own exertions, or by inheritance, and to tempt them to embark their money in commercial undertakings, by giving them a large share of the profits. The foreign and maritime trader, finding his own stock inadequate to the enterprise, and finding it difficult to obtain a large sum from any single individual, because few single individuals have such sums to lend, contrives, by borrowing small sums from a number of different persons, to raise what may be requisite for the investment. A sort of partnership is thus formed between the lenders and the borrowers; the former supply the capital, the latter the activity, skill, and experience; the former take upon themselves the perils of the sea, and the latter, by the payment of high interest, in fact, gives them a share in the profits of the adventure. In an early state of society, and in a comparatively poor country, such an arrangement is highly beneficial. But in proportion as large capitals are accumulated, in the different branches of manufacture and commerce, the arrangement under consideration becomes, in a great measure, unnecessary, and comparatively of little use. And accordingly, in Great Britain, while the business of insurance is carried on to a greater extent than ever, the contract of *bottomry* and *respondentia* is now but seldom resorted to.

With regard to the details of the last-mentioned contract, the rules relative to the loan of money on marine risk were precisely the same as those we have seen in the account formerly given of the maritime law of the Athenians. It consisted in the delivery of a sum by the lender to the borrower, either in order to purchase merchandise destined to be loaded on board a vessel, or in order to employ the money at the port or place for which the vessel was fitted out, with the security of the vessel, or of the merchandise purchased at the place of departure, and in the replacing either of the money or of the goods transported to the place of destination, or, sometimes, of the vessel and of the cargo; but under the condition that the lender should not be repaid, except in the event of the safe arrival of the vessel and goods. The sum thus lent was denominated *pecunia trajectitia*, or *nautica*.

The loan might be made either to go from one place to another, or to go to a place and return to that of departure, or for a certain duration of voyages. The contract determined the period at which the vessel was to sail; sometimes, also, the period at which the borrower, when arrived at the port of destination, was to depart with the return cargo, after which the debt due to the lender should become exigible.

The lender undertook merely the maritime risks, and might exact the capital and interest, provided the goods burdened with the loan were preserved, or arrived safe, although they should have suffered a depreciation, or have procured no profit to the borrower; of course, any loss sustained through the fault or act of the latter—for instance, confiscation for contravention of the law—did not fall upon the lender.

There thus resulted, in favour of the borrower, an exception from the principle that the loss of his estate does not liberate the debtor; and the creditor might also legitimately stipulate and exact, under the name of *nauticum fœnus*, a much higher rate of interest than that payable for an ordinary loan.

It was this condition of risk which formed the distinction and essential characteristic of the loan on *bottomry* or *respondentia*, and did not admit of any assimilation to it of any other conditional loan whatever, not involving such risk.

Sometimes the creditor required other securities than the ship or the goods burdened with the loan by the contract; but this circumstance did not change the nature of the agreement; and if the goods principally burdened perished, the debtor was liberated, the condition of safe arrival, upon which depended the obligation to pay the debt, not having been fulfilled.

The exigibility and the cessation of risks, on the part of the creditor, took place, *ipso jure*, by the lapse solely of the term agreed upon for the duration of the risks. A new agreement between the lender and borrower would have been necessary to prolong the original conditions of the contract. Indeed, the creditor often stipulated interest, in case of delay in payment. He might reserve the right of placing a slave on board the vessel of the borrower, to take care that what was impledged to him should not be diverted to other purposes, or that frauds should not be committed to his prejudice, or to exact payment at the time agreed upon; he often even stipulated an indemnity for the wages of the slave, if he was obliged to wait some time for payment. But this (penal) stipulation had nothing in common with the principal convention, and was not subjected to the same rules. It had, however, its effect, although at the time the debt became due the debtor had not been summoned to pay; unless it was proved that the creditor had it in his power to receive, without the debtor having thrown any obstacle in the way.

It is thus manifest that, although not practically acquainted with the benefits of insurance, the Roman jurisconsults were by no means ignorant of the principles, or omitted to lay down rules on the theory, of maritime risks. In unravelling the doctrines of the *fœnus nauticum*, or bottomry, they were necessarily led to the study of these risks; which are obviously the essential basis of insurance, as well as of that contract. And to the aid afforded by the principles unfolded by them in this delicate branch of their jurisprudence, modern lawyers are much indebted for the highly improved state at which the law of insurance has now arrived throughout the different European nations.

Although the object of the present historical inquiry is merely the private law of maritime commerce, it may be proper, before concluding this brief account of the maritime law of the Romans, to notice shortly some matters which may, perhaps, be viewed as strictly belonging to the public law of the state, or to international law, but which materially affect the private interests of individuals.

According to the principles of the Roman law, which have, with a few modifications, been recognised in modern times, the sea was considered as common to all mankind; and its shores—the sand, or *solum*, which the highest tides cover in winter—were placed among the things which belong to nobody. Every individual had the liberty of landing on the sea-beach—of gathering there the things which the sea produces or the tide casts on shore—of fishing, and, for that purpose, of constructing a hut to dry his nets, and even of there establishing a fishery, if in conformity with the conditions imposed by the laws of the state.

The practice of plundering shipwrecked goods appears, even from the laws passed against it, to have been but too frequent in the times of the Romans; and the fisc, or public treasury, has been accused of taking advantage of such disasters to add to its revenue. But this claim of the fisc appears to have embraced only goods cast on shore, to which nobody pretended any right of property, to the effect merely of abolishing acquisition of them by occupancy. And it does not appear the Roman law ever gave the fisc the right of acquiring shipwrecked goods which were capable of being vindicated by their owners, whom the storm had merely deprived of the possession, but not of the property.

In the compilations of Justinian, there are very few traces of the state having exercised any public superintendence of navigation in point of maritime police. Indeed, the chief, if not the only regulations of this description, appear to have been the general prohibition against vessels putting to sea during a certain period of the year; the apparent appointment of local pilots for the guidance of mariners at the mouths of rivers or on dangerous coasts; and the encouragement given to seafaring people to form associations, to be incorporated by the state.

The Roman government, however, it is well known, exhibited much more care and energy in the measures which it adopted for the protection of navigators and of seafaring people against the attacks of pirates.

History records the excesses to which the audacity of these plunderers was carried, in consequence of the civil wars. The genius of Pompey, and the whole maritime force of the Republic, placed at his disposal, were found requisite to restore security to navigation. And "*mare pacavit a prædonibus*" has been deemed one of the fairest eulogies of the first Augustus. The law placed the depredations of pirates among the number of cases of *vis major*, or irresistible event, which furnished the owner or charterer of a vessel with a legitimate defence against the demand of the proprietors of the cargo for the goods which had been intrusted to him; and, among sacrifices made for the common safety, the sums or value given for the ransom of vessels captured by pirates. In short, it viewed the pirate less as a public or national enemy than as a robber, who could not acquire, by any lapse of time whatever, the property of what he had seized, or legally transfer it to others, or transmit it to his heirs.

In the decline of the Empire, and in the course of the fifth century, Honorius and Theodosius prohibited their subjects, under the pain of death, from teaching the enemy the art of ship-building, as they had been long previously interdicted, under the like penalty, from selling to the enemy iron, corn, and other such commodities. And the measures which were adopted in those times, for the double purpose of protecting the integrity of the Empire and of securing an adequate supply of provisions for the capital, may probably, as observed by M. Pardessus, have suggested the ideas of licenses, passports, and bills of lading, which the vessels behoved to have on board; of the visitation and inspection of vessels, to ascertain if they were sea-worthy or otherwise in good condition; of the obligation of ship-masters not to deviate from the route of their destined voyage; of the reports or protests which they were bound to make;

and of the verification of these reports by the examination and testimony of the crew.

Such were the leading doctrines of maritime and commercial law among the Romans; and they seem to have been expounded and enforced by the ordinary magistrates or judges who administered justice according to the common and statute law of the Republic or Empire. Several important equitable doctrines in maritime and commercial law, we have seen, were introduced or established by the edicts of the Prætor; and there existed, also at Rome a Prætor Peregrinus, charged with the administration of justice among strangers or foreigners; and he may have judged foreigners according to their own laws, or, more likely, according to the general principles of the *jus gentium*. But it does not appear that the special cognizance of maritime and commercial questions and disputes was exclusively committed, at Rome, to any particular set of judges.

CHAPTER V.

OF THE MARITIME AND COMMERCIAL LAW OF THE EASTERN OR GRÆCO-ROMAN EMPIRE.

In the preceding view of the maritime and commercial law of the Romans, we have considered that law generally as composed of the *leges* or statutes, properly so called, of the *Plebiscita et Senatus Consulta*; of the edicts of the Roman magistrates; of the constitutions of the Emperors; and of the authoritative writings of the great jurisconsults, particularly the writings of Papinian. Paulus, Gaius, Ulpian, and Modestinus, all as pre served, partly in the Gregorian and Hermogenian, and in the Theodosian codes or collections of imperial constitutions, but chiefly in the subsequent more general compilations made by direction of Justinian, and also in other ancient manuscripts discovered since the revival of learning, and particularly in very recent times. And such may be correctly held to have been the constituent parts of the Roman law, so far as embodied or recorded, from the later ages of the Republic, or near the Christian era, down to the invasions by the northern nations, towards the close of the fifth century, and the subversion of the Roman Empire in the West. From this period, in tracing the progress, advancement, or decline of maritime and commercial law, we have to direct our views separately to the eastern and to the western nations; and we shall first advert to the state of that law in the remnant of the Roman Empire in the East.

Constantinople, as it had been from its foundation, still continued to be a place of immense trade. The subjects of the Oriental or Greek Empire continued still to be the most civilized of mankind. They imported the valuable products of more eastern countries, they carried on a variety of fine manufactures, and their vessels traded to most of the countries bordering on the Black Sea and the eastern part of the Mediterranean. The example set by Justinian as a legislator, was followed by succeeding Emperors; and although the declining agesof the Empire seemed to have ceased to be capable of producing much new or valuable in legislation, the memory of the old Latin law was preserved by a new large compilation in Greek, and by practical epitomes or abridgments.

Section I.

Of the Basilica, &c.

A desire to complete the compilations made by the order of Justinian, which he himself had never ceased to modify, and which commentaries and abridgments had rendered rather obscure; the urgent expediency of furnishing an authentic text of the law to nations who did not speak the language in which the Digest and Code had been composed; the necessity of remedying the inconveniences of a prevalent arbitrary administration of justice by the tribunals; and, according to some writers, a desire and design to cause the work of Justinian to be forgotten,—appear all to have concurred in producing the body of law called the Basilica;* and the most probable opinion is, that this compilation was undertaken by the Emperor Basilius, called the Macedonian, and was finished and promulgated towards the end of the ninth century, by his son Leo, surnamed the Philosopher. But whether it was afterwards revised by Constantine Porphyrogenitus, the son of Leo, seems very doubtful.

That independently of a number of regulations in the department of maritime law, scattered through different books, the author of the Basilica allotted a particular book to that subject, and that this book was the LIII., is established by the circumstance, that the greater part of the Fragments of the Digest and Code of Justinian, relative alike to inland and maritime commerce, have been transcribed into the analogous titles of the Basilica, but with the suppression of what concerned the latter, and by two manuscripts, still extant in the Royal Library of France, which contain the first nine books of the "Basilica," a general table of all the books and titles

* Pardessus Coll. tome i., chap. v.

of the whole work, and particularly summaries of eight different titles of the LIII. Book, relative to the different subjects of maritime law, as published by M. Pardessus in 1828. That learned jurist discovered similar indications of the contents of the LIII. Book of the Basilica, in a document but little known, bearing the appellation of the Paratitla of Tipucitus; and being obliged, in his researches, to give up the hope of finding the text of this LIII. Book, he has endeavoured, with considerable success, to supply it by the aid of other documents, of which the lapse of time has not deprived us. The chief of these auxiliary documents bears the title of Synopsis Major, exists in manuscript in several of the public libraries in Europe, particularly in the Royal Library of France, and was published by Leunclavius in 1596. The author of this work is not known, and the time when it was composed has not been ascertained, farther than that it existed during the latter half of the twelfth century. But it is a collection of texts, copied from the Basilica, under titles placed, by an awkward arrangement, in alphabetic order; and it contains a pretty full statement of the rules of maritime law recognised in the imperial compilation.

The next auxiliary document resorted to by M. Pardessus, for supplying the text of the LIII. Book of the Basilica, is the code of the Greek inhabitants of the isle of Cyprus under the Latin kings, which is of the thirteenth century, and exists in manuscript in the Royal Library of France. It was the code which the inhabitants observed before the conquest of that island by King Richard I. of England. A number of passages of this work shew they were extracted from the Basilica; and this was quite natural, as, while Cyprus was subject to the Greek Emperors, the Basilica behoved to be the law of that island as of the other parts of the Empire. A third auxiliary work resorted to by M.

Pardessus for supplying the LIII. Book of the Basilica, is the Synopsis Minor, which is still unpublished, but is to be found in manuscript in the libraries of Vienna, of the Vatican, and of Florence. The author, and the exact period of its composition, are not known; but it is an abridgment of the law of the Basilica, in the same alphabetic form as the Synopsis Major, with this difference, that while the Synopsis Major is a literal abridgment, or compilation of texts, copied from the Basilica, the Synopsis Minor gives the sense and spirit of the law without the texts—the former an extract, the latter an analysis. The other documents resorted to by M. Pardessus, are the abridgment of Attaliata, composed by direction of the Emperor Ducas, in 1073; and the Procheiron of Harmenopolus, published in Vol. VII. of the Thesaurus of Meerman.

In his erudite endeavours thus to supply, from subsidiary sources, the LIII. Book of the Basilica on maritime law, M. Pardessus finds considerable difficulty in ascertaining the genuine text, from these auxiliary manuscript documents having had added to them, asconnected therewith, a part, if not the whole, of the compilation which we formerly considered, as known by the appellation of Jus Navale Rhodiorum. The Synopsis Major of the Basilica contains fourteen chapters literally conformable to fourteen chapters of the third part of that compilation; and, in publishing the manuscript of the latter, Fabrotus, assuming that it must have been a part of the Basilica, has transcribed in whole the fifty-one chapters of which it is composed, in the usual editions. One of the manuscripts, too, in the Royal Library of France, before referred to, designates, as among the number of titles of which the LIII. Book of the Basilica was composed, two titles relative to the Rhodian laws; and the Paratitla of Tipucitus contains a similar summary indication. On the other hand, so far as the mere contents or texts of these auxiliary documents go, the Synopsis Minor and the code of Cyprus present no regulations but what are conformable to the texts of the third title of the LIII. Book still extant; and the other manuscript in the Royal Library of France, that of Coislin, makes no reference in its summary to the Rhodian laws. And what is more decisive, and seems to place it beyond doubt that the Jus Navale Rhodiorum formed no part of the Basilica, is, that the legal doctrine of the former, relative to jetson and contribution, making no distinction between general and particular averages, is quite different from the legal doctrine, on these very matters, contained in the other remaining texts of the Basilica still extant, or as ascertained from the Synopsis Major and Minor; for it cannot be believed that the Emperors Basilius and Leo, or the lawyers employed by them to draw up the Basilica, would have included in the same digest doctrines so completely adverse to, and subversive of, each other.

Having, upon these and other grounds, for the detail of which reference must be made to his learned work itself, detached from the genuine Basilica the additions of later times, M. Pardessus is enabled, from the manuscript documents before referred to, principal and subsidiary, to make out a very distinct view of the doctrines of maritime and commercial law contained in that compilation; but of this view it seems unnecessary to give even an abridgment in this historical sketch, as the doctrines of the genuine Basilica, in that department, although composed after an interval of between three and four centuries, appear to be identical with those of the classical Roman jurisconsults, and of the Digest and Code of Justinian, as already detailed at some length, with a few exceptions, which it will be sufficient briefly to notice.

Several rules are mentioned in the Synopsis Minor of the Basilica, which do not appear in the Roman digest, but may probably have been contained in the texts of the Basilica which have not reached us. When the passengers, and the master and crew, agreed to sail without a pilot, they were held liable to the owner for the loss of the vessel; because they were all in fault. Whoever caused, or was accessory to, the retarding of the departure of the vessel, was held responsible for accidental losses or damage; and when, of different parcels or quantities of goods, mixed and confounded, probably in consequence of their being of the same kind, a part had been thrown overboard for the safety of the vessel, and the rest preserved, it was determined that what was saved should be divided between the proprietors, in proportion to their shares and interests in these goods. Farther, with regard to shipwrecked goods recovered from the sea, the Basilica, or the interpreters of that code, appear, from the Synopsis Minor, to have made rather a singular distinction between the case of the person who had saved the goods, having done so without risk or danger, and that of his having actually incurred such risk or danger; requiring him, in the former case, to restore them to the previous owner, on receiving remuneration or salvage; and allowing him, in the latter case, to appropriate them to his own use.

The doctrines of the classical lawyers of Rome, as contained in the compilations of Justinian, thus appear, when translated into Greek, to have continued, with little variation, to be the only genuine and authentic maritime and commercial law of the Eastern Empire, not merely during the reign of the Emperor Leo, who promulgated the Basilica towards the close of the ninth century, but for centuries afterwards, whether with or without the revisal by the Emperor Constantine Porphyrogenitus, and probably down to the extinction of that Empire by the Turks. But in the lapse of ages between the reign of Justinian and the final subjugation of the Eastern Empire, it is very probable there may have grown up among the subjects of that Empire, trading in the eastern parts of the Mediterranean, certain practical maritime usages, extending or narrowing, departing from or modifying, the established maritime and commercial law of the Empire. It is also very probable that these usages may have been collected and embodied in writing, and mixed with the known established law, by private individuals, for the use of seafaring people.

Section II.

Of the Compilation entitled, Jus Navale Rhodiorum.

Such seems to be the most probable view we can take of the origin of the compilation to which we have so often alluded, the Jus Navale Rhodiorum. And this seems to be the proper place and time for its consideration, as concluding our view of the Roman law in the Eastern Empire, and as intervening between that law and the maritime customs and usages of the middle ages, in which the private maritime and commercial law of the modern European nations appears to have, to a certain extent, originated.

That this Greek collection was made during the decline of the Eastern Empire, there seems to be no room for doubt, and, to all appearance, without the sanction of any public, or, at least, imperial authority. It consists, as originally edited by Leunclavius, and afterwards by Peckius and Vinnius, of three parts; the first, a preface, narrating that a compilation of the maritime usages of Rhodes had been directed and approved of by successive Roman Emperors; the second, entitled, Jus Navale, consisting of twenty-one chapters; the third, entitled, Jus Navale Rhodiorum ex Libro undecimo Digestorum excerptum, consisting of fifty-one chapters. From the minute description given by M. Pardessus of the four manuscripts of this compilation, still extant in the Royal Library of France, it is evident that the three parts of which it appears to be composed, in the printed editions, do not form a whole, and have never been considered as one sole and entire whole.

The first part, or introduction, Pardessus, after Bynkershoek, demonstrates, by sound historical and critical investigation, to have no claim to authenticity, and to be, in all probability, one of the apocryphal fabrications so frequent in the middle ages, and even during the period which immediately succeeded the revival of letters.

Of the second piece of this collection, the first thirteen chapters record local usages relative to the division among the crew of the portion of freight allowed them as wages, and to the maintenance of internal order on board vessels, which are scarcely of a nature to form the subject of law, properly so called. The other chapters contain an abridgment, frequently obscure, of the rules of law relative to *bottomry* and *respondentia*, and the responsibility of shipowners for the acts of the crew as contained in the Digest of Justinian and in the Basilica. But the occurrence of purely Latin words with a Greek orthography, the requisition to take an oath upon the Gospel, and the style of Greek so different from what was spoken in the times of the Roman Emperors mentioned in the preface or introduction, inferior even to that of the Basilica, clearly shew that these chapters were not compiled under any of these Emperors, but during the later ages of the Byzantine Empire.

Indeed, this second piece appears to be a collection

of nautical usages merely, drawn up probably for the use of seafaring people, such as exists in almost all maritime countries, even when provided with a comparatively complete body of maritime law; because the legislature cannot enter into the multitude of petty details of mere practice, but must confine itself to the exposition of principles fertile in consequential deductions; and the most probable conclusion is, that this series of chapters, without belonging to, or forming a part of, any positive legislation, was merely attached to it, as a book of practice is attached to the law of which it offers the development, and presupposes the existence of a general system of maritime law.

With regard to the third piece contained in this collection, entitled Jus Navale Rhodiorum, more difficulties occur. Beside a certain number of chapters, which are little else than a repetition of the common law of the Empire, this piece, as we have already seen, established a system of average and contribution quite opposed to that of the Digest and Basilica. It rejects the fundamental distinction between the averages which are called general or common, *Removendi communis periculi causa*, and those which are called particular, *Cum cœteris, in communi periculo, non est consultum;* and prescribes contribution in both cases. While these considerations appear sufficient to have determined M. Pardessus not to include this collection among the documents of the maritime law of the Eastern Empire, we agree with him it is worth while to endeavour to ascertain the origin of this new doctrine, and the object in thus recording it; and we shall notice the ingenious manner in which he accounts for it.

In the decline of the Eastern Empire, the natural perils of navigation in the Mediterranean, augmented by the invasions of the northern nations and of the Saracens, and other similar events recorded in history, appear to have created a necessity for combination in resisting, or at least in bearing, the common danger, and to have in this respect led individuals interested in maritime navigation to form associations, which ultimately suggested the idea of maritime insurance. Before insurance for a premium—the result of experience, and of the calculation of chances—could have been devised; before its advantages could have been perceived and appreciated; before that mutual confidence, without which it is impossible that contracts of that description can take place, could have been established; and before the great number of maritime enterprises and adventures could have offered opportunities for speculations of risk—mutual insurances, still some times practised at this day, may have been in use.

Early in the middle ages, in point of fact, as we shall afterwards see, individuals interested in navigation entered into contracts, known in Italy by the appellation of *Gernimamento*, from the entire vessel and cargo being considered as one whole, *unum Germen*, of which each part was liable *in solidum* for the losses which the others might experience from adverse accidents. And in certain isles or coasts of the Greek Archipelago, or certain parts of the coasts of the Adriatic, this mode of mutual insurance may have become so well known and so frequent, as to have led to the attempt to digest its rules, whether for the instruction of the judges and arbiters who decided the differences arising in its execution, or to guide and enlighten seafaring people in this new and extraordinary transaction. This supposition M. Pardessus confirms, by an extract from the Synopsis Minor—*Est autem alia contributio, quæ gratis fit;* and submits that the author of this doctrinal work, who sought to make known the state of jurisprudence and of actual practice, rather than to copy texts, like the author of the Synopsis Major, probably alluded in this passage to the mutual assurance just mentioned, in which the contribution results from the free will of the contracting parties, *quæ gratis fit*, and not from the law, which enforces it only for sacrifices made with a view to the common safety And, to account for the other chapter of the third piece of the collection under consideration, M. Pardessus submits, as also highly probable, that, after having compiled the usages upon partnerships of risk, there may have been joined with them rules respecting the police of mariners, upon the repression of robbery and barratry—which crimes the unfortunate state of society had multiplied; and even some regulations regarding maritime conventions in general, extracted from the existing imperial code of laws, which it might be convenient to bring more immediately under the view of seafaring people, as in a sort of manual.

With regard to the author or authors of this collection, or of the third and most important piece of which it consists, there are nothing but vague and unsatisfactory conjectures; and, as to the periods at which the different pieces were compiled, we know merely the time at which the third part was extant. The Synopsis Major, which has extracted fifteen chapters from it, was anterior to the year 1167, since the Vatican manuscript bears to have been written during that year. And the code of the Greeks of Cyprus under the Latin kings, in which this third part is found inserted, was compiled during the twelfth century.

With respect, again, to the value of the rules which this collection contains, the first part, or preface, is clearly a crude and stupid fabrication; but the second and third pieces—while the former details many matters of little consequence, or of mere mercantile practice—contain also various regulations of importance, chiefly with regard to the usages of mariners, their duties, and their delinquencies; the affreightment of vessels, and the respective obligations of the owners, charterers, freighters, and shippers; the collisions of vessels, and consequent damages; voyages of mutual protection, averages, jetson, and contribution; shipwrecks and salvage; and loans on maritime risk. In particular, the third piece, although we cannot consider it as an integral part of the Basilica, or ascribe to it any public authoritative character, records, as we have seen, maritime usages introduced in some localities, in consequence of new wants, to which the increased and more frequent dangers of navigation had apparently given rise; especially a new kind of convention, which several modern codes of law have sanctioned—a mutual insurance between or among the owners of the vessel and the owners or shippers of the cargo. And, in this point of view, M. Pardessus ingeniously observes—This compilation, although it be difficult to determine with precision its character, or the period or the place where it was made, and even although it cannot be denied that certain passages are very obscure, and that others are contradictory, yet merits the attention of lawyers, inasmuch as it marks a great step in the march of maritime commerce, and may be viewed as the dawn of insurance for a premium, and must have been of assistance down to the time when the latter contract, so astonishing in its theory and results, caused the former, its precursor, to disappear, and to be almost forgotten.

PART THIRD.

HISTORICAL VIEW OF THE LAWS AND USAGES OF MARITIME COMMERCE DURING THE MIDDLE AGES.

CHAPTER I.

STATE OF THE LAW OF MARITIME COMMERCE AMONG THE NORTHERN NATIONS, ON THEIR SETTLEMENT IN THE PROVINCES OF THE ROMAN EMPIRE.—PROGRESS OF CIVILISATION IN MODERN EUROPE.

Having, in the preceding observations, traced the history of the law of maritime commerce among the ancients, through the flourishing ages of Greece and Rome to the decline of the Byzantine Empire, we now turn our view westward to the European nations, and propose to trace the history of this branch of jurisprudence and legislation during what have been called the Middle Ages, and in more modern times.

"The natural progress of a people in civilisation and improvement," as observed by Dr Adam Smith, "is from the country to towns. Some of the lands of a people must have been cultivated before any considerable towns could be established; and some sort of coarse industry of the manufacturing kind must have been carried on in these towns before they could well think of employing themselves in foreign commerce."

"But," continues Dr Smith, "though this natural order of things must have taken place, in some degree, in every such society, it has in all the modern states of Europe been, in many respects, entirely inverted. The foreign commerce of some of their cities has introduced all their finer manufacture, or such as were fit for distant sale; and manufactures and foreign commerce together have given birth to the principal improvements of agriculture. The manners and customs which the nature of their original government introduced, and which remained after that government was greatly altered, forced them into this unnatural and retrograde order."

Into the causes of this inverted order, this is not the place to inquire at length; but a short notice of them appears to be proper, in so far as they have affected the progress of maritime and commercial law.

One of the obvious effects of the successive invasions and inundations of barbarians, who overran, and afterwards settled in, the different western or European provinces of the Roman Empire, was, if not the extinction, at least the reduction and, in a great measure, the cessation of distant commercial intercourse and maritime enterprise. The moveable wealth which, from the date of the Roman Conquest, had been gradually accumulating in the western provinces, through the exercise of agricultural and manufacturing industry, was consumed or wasted by the barbarians, who had neither the habits nor the skill requisite to repair the losses they had thus occasioned. Amid the incessant wars, first between the invaders and the ancient inhabitants, and afterwards among the different tribes or nations of barbarian settlers, there was of course a great waste of human life; and a great proportion of those individuals perished who had either the capital or the skill requisite for carrying on any nice or fine manufacture, or any extensive or complicated commercial adventure. The customs, habits, and views of the barbarians were all adverse to commerce. It appeared weak and contemptible to earn by patient industry what could be at once accomplished by the sword. The only maritime enterprises were piratical expeditions to plunder the coast towns of what had once been comparatively civilized nations; and in the inland parts of Europe, the small independent territories into which the different conquering tribes divided the country, combined with the incessant state of hostility, and the want of any great head or bond sufficiently strong to afford protection or security to individuals, either in the enjoyment of the fruits of their industry or in their intercourse with the members of the same or other tribes and nations, could not fail to impede and depress, if not to extinguish, manufacturing industry and commercial dealings. Trade was reduced, in a great measure, to the simple exchange of commodities in kind; and although the use of the precious metals, as money, did not cease, these metals were seldom found, except in the hands of the higher members of the state. In short, commerce, as has been remarked, passed from manhood and old age to infancy, and the career of improvement behoved in a great measure to be run anew.

But, on the other hand, the extinction of the former inhabitants was by no means, as has sometimes been supposed, the consequence of the conquests of the barbarous nations who ultimately settled in the European provinces of Rome. Along with the defeated Roman armies, many of the resident inhabitants of these provinces must have fallen in battle; many of them appear to have been massacred in the heat and abuse of victory; many of them appear to have been reduced into slavery;—but such was never the fate of any one entire nation. After the completion of their conquests, the invaders had no interest or inducement to put their new subjects to death. They occupied the greatest part of the lands, and seized any moveable wealth in the towns, or where it could be found; but after the conquerors had seized, and so far exhausted, the accumulated wealth of the subjugated countries, agricultural and coarse manufacturing industry became necessary for their subsistence and the ordinary comforts of life. They thus had a strong inducement not to destroy but to profit by the labour and superior skill of their subjects; and that the ancient inhabitants of the southern countries of Europe, at least, continued, after the invasions and conquests, to form the largest portion of the population of these countries, is manifest from the very great preponderance of Latin vocables, roots, derivatives, and idiom, in the constitution of the Italian, French, and Spanish languages.

As little does it appear to have been an object with the northern invading nations, or to have been practicable for them, although so disposed, to transform their new Roman subjects into Goths, Franks, Burgundians, or Lombards, or to compel the former to embrace, all at once, their manners, institutions, and laws. The remains of Roman population of Italy and the provinces, though subjected by conquest, continued to exist, and to live beside their conquerors on the same territory, frequently in the same city or town. They were allowed to retain, in a great measure, their customs and laws, sometimes by tacit acquiescence, sometimes by express authority; and this gave rise to a peculiar organization of the private or civil laws of the country, and to the division of these laws into personal and territorial; the conquering race living according to the laws of their fathers, and the ancient inhabitants according to the Roman law, until the different races of population became completely amalgamated.

But although a people may have been subjected by conquest, yet, if it has ever possessed civil laws for the regulation of the private interests of individuals, these laws continue to exist and prevail in the country until they have been supplanted and replaced by other laws; and experience proves how difficult such a substitution is, how the attachment of nations to their private civil laws is often stronger than to their public or judicial institutions. Conquest may change the forms of government, and produce violent and great alterations in property, particularly in the tenure of landed property, and in the legal or conventional order of its transference, or transmission from generation to generation; but while a people is not entirely destroyed, and civilisation is not annihilated, transactions among individuals necessarily take place, and disputes may be, and are invariably, the consequence; and laws, at least rules, are found requisite to instruct the contracting parties, and to direct the functionaries intrusted with the administration of justice. If the law of the conquerors establishes or enacts nothing in that behalf, the law which has ruled the country, before the conquest, remains in the memories, habits of thinking, and ordinary practice of the former population, and exercises a powerful influence over the whole nation, if not as a positive law, at least as necessary rules, or customs of manifest utility.

Accordingly, in his learned and laborious researches,* M. Savigny has distinctly proved that the Roman laws, and particularly the Roman civil and judicial institutions, all along had a great influence throughout the continental territories of the Empire in which the northern nations settled; and, what is more immediately connected with our present inquiry, he has also shewn that the Roman law, and civil and judicial institutions, were, in a peculiar manner, preserved, and excited a peculiar influence in the municipal cities and towns not only of Italy, but of the provinces adjacent to the Mediterranean. In these cities and towns, the ancient population greatly preponderated; the ancient free municipal institutions were, to a certain extent, maintained; the middle classes of the community enjoyed more liberty, and were more intelligent, than the rural inhabitants of the provinces; they were not so immediately under the dominion of the chiefs or kings of the con-

* Geschichte des Römischen Rechts im Mittelalter, 1816.

quering tribes or nations who occupied the extensive adjacent territories; and their internal strength enabled them to render themselves respected by, and to obtain privileges from, these sovereigns.

Now, the circumstances just noticed appear sufficient, without further detail, which would be foreign to our purpose, to account for the inverted order, in the progress of civilisation, to which Dr Smith has alluded. They seem sufficient to shew why we were not to look for the origin and early advancement, or early revival, of manufactures and commerce in the great European kingdoms formed on the ruins of the Roman Empire, or for the early advancement of maritime law, in the legislative codes of the monarchs or feudal aristocracies of these kingdoms; for the comparative degree of civilisation which was prematurely and forcibly accomplished by the superior genius of Charlemagne, expired with its author. And these circumstances seem sufficient also to explain why we should find, as we actually do find, in the history of the small but comparatively free and independent cities and states situated on the sea-coast of Italy, and of the other countries in which the great feudal kingdoms were formed, the first dawning of commerce and manufacture, and of commercial and maritime legislation.

The order, therefore, which the actual series of events seems to prescribe, and which we propose to follow, is, *first*, shortly to mark the rise and progress of the commercial greatness of these maritime states which arose on the sea-coast of the Europeankingdoms, all the way from the Adriatic to the Baltic, and to consider, at some length, the several maritime codes which these different small states established or adopted for the regulation of their commercial intercourse; *next*, to notice, shortly, the gradual progress of Inland as well as maritime commerce in modern Europe, the rise of interior towns, the establishment of regular markets or fairs, the fall of the feudal aristocracy, and the consolidation of the different detached and independent component parts of the European kingdoms, under regular and comparatively strong governments; *lastly*, to consider, at some length, the different systems of maritime and commercial law which the great modern European governments have established, and the works of the authors who have illustrated this branch of jurisprudence.

Before directing our attention to the state of maritime law in the Eastern Empire, we had occasion to specify the sources and recorded component parts of the Roman law at the commencement of the invasions of the northern nations; and, from the specification, as given in detail by Professor Savigny, it is plain that the great Montesquieu, and several other modern writers, have erred in supposing that, at the period we are contemplating, the sole source and whole extent of the Roman law were comprised in the Theodosian code; which, in fact, was never intended to be a whole and complete code, but was merely a collection of the more important imperial constitutions from the time of Constantine. The Perpetual Edict, digested by direction of the Emperor Adrian about the year 131 of the Christian era, the commentaries on that edict, and the works of the classic jurisconsults, of which the Digest of Justinian was destined to preserve the Fragments—but, perhaps, also to accelerate the loss—formed, at that time, the foundation and substance of Roman legislation and jurisprudence. A large portion of this general body of law was, we have seen, devoted to maritime and commercial affairs; and the maritime and commercial law which had been thus established by the Romans was not confined to Italy, but embraced and was observed throughout the western as well as the eastern provinces of the Empire.

Now, however disastrous the invasions of the northern nations, in the destruction of life and property, such a body of positive laws, which had grown up with, and been recorded in, the memories, and fixed in the habits and customs of the people for centuries, could not be all at once extinguished, except by the total extirpation of the ancient inhabitants. But no such extirpation took place; a large portion of the ancient inhabitants remained; and such remaining population continued to observe, and to be regulated by, the laws to which they had been so long accustomed, and were either expressly or tacitly, in general, allowed by their conquerors to do so. It is chiefly those laws of a civil nature which relate to the power and rank of persons, the public institutions, the state of family, and the acquisition, tenure, and transmission of property in land, that are affected by the conquest of a nation; because these are more immediately connected with the political constitution of the state. Commercial transactions, and particularly maritime trade, are compartively little liable to such influence. Indeed, the northern conquerors, when called upon to legislate, even in matters of government, or with regard to the distribution, or tenure, or possession of the territory they had seized, generally resorted to the aid of their more educated and skilful subjects; and, having little or no knowledge themselves of maritime and commercial law, allowed the portion of the community engaged in such occupations to be guided by the Roman law, so long as it continued to be preserved in writing, or by tradition.

Accordingly we find the codes of the barbarians, such as the edict of Theodoric, King of the Ostrogoths, in the year 500; the Breviarium of Alaric, King of the Visigoths, in the year 506; and the *Lex Romana* (Papianus) of the Burgundians, about the same time, are almost entirely silent on the subject of maritime and commercial law. And from these different codes being thus all silent with regard to maritime commerce, it is manifest that another law must have existed, and been recognised, which, whether it receive the appellation of statute, custom, or usage, could be no other than what had hitherto been practised and observed, namely, the Roman law.

The subversion of the Western Empire could not fail to give a severe blow to commerce, not so much because Rome had been so long the centre of commerce, and that the destinies of the two were, in all respects, inseparable, but because that great event had introduced disorder, anarchy, and individual insecurity, and had, in a manner, dissolved the bonds of civil society, so as to reduce commercial business to the mere supply of indispensable wants. External commerce had no longer almost any object, and was deprived of almost all protection from government. The nations, hitherto united by one common tie, protected by one united power, all at once found themselves completely separated from each other, often even subjected to conquerors who were enemies of each other. Navigation came to be directed chiefly towards piracy. The dread of such attacks from the sea, and the barbarous habits of the invaders, introduced the practice of plundering shipwrecked goods and materials—a resource, in some measure, for men who had neither agricultural nor manufacturing industry. But if, in these times of ignorance and misery, commercial transactions were few in number, and took place only at distant intervals, during the moments of repose which the lassitude of the barbarians, their compassion, or their private interest, allowed the subjugated population, certain legal rules for the conduct of parties were indispensable, and the laws to which they and their predecessors had been so long accustomed were, in all probability, resorted to as their guide in such matters.

The more, no doubt, the successive invasions of the northern tribes, by accumulating calamities, almost ruined commerce, the more apt, consequently, were the former population to lose sight of, and almost forget, the Roman law, which had regulated their commercial transactions; but when the victorious tribes, desirous of forming a settlement, gave to their usurpation a legitimate form, and held out the prospect of protection being afforded to individuals by the government, commerce, and, with it, the principles of the Roman law, revived.* The subjugation and misery of the nations might obstruct the development of industry; piracies might suspend navigation, and frighten and discourage seafaring people; but these circumstances and events did not change the nature of the small number of contracts which were entered into, nor that of the principles to which it was necessary to conform in order to secure their fulfilment and execution. Nay, more, these extraordinary circumstances might become, and did, in fact, become, as we shall afterwards see, the occasion of contracts till then little known, such as bills of exchange and marine insurances; invented for the purpose of preventing or repairing the losses with which individuals were threatened, and which then so frequently occurred. These new contracts called for and required laws equally new; and the earliest usages and customs relative to exchange and insurance, shew that the Roman jurisprudence still furnished the fundamental basis of these new laws.

With these explanatory observations on the general state of maritime and commercial law among the different European nations, formed by the conquests and set-

---

* Pardessus, vol. i, p. 138-9.

tlements of the various northern tribes, who occupied extensive portions of the western provinces of the Empire—such as the Ostrogoths, the Visigoths, the Franks, the Burgundians, the Lombards—we pass from the crude codes enacted by these comparatively barbarous nations, at intervals after their settlement, to the investigation of the state of maritime and commercial law in the cities and towns, or small municipal communities, which arose, during the period we are considering, on the sea-coasts of Italy, and of the western provinces.

CHAPTER II.

OF THE MARITIME LAWS OF THE COMMERCIAL REPUBLICS OF THE MIDDLE AGES.

SECTION I.

Venice.

OF the different commercial Republics which arose after the ruin of the Roman Empire in the West, Venice appears to have been the earliest. From the invasion of the Goths under Alaric, about the beginning of the fifth century of the Christian era, and from the still more ferocious ravages of the Huns under Attila, about the middle of the same century, some of the inhabitants of the fallen towns and ruined country sought an obscure shelter in the small islands situated at the northern extremity of the Adriatic. Amidst the marshes formed by the sea, and occupying islands hitherto uninhabited, this little people, inaccessible to conquest, was driven by indigence to labour. They had no occasion, like the barbarian conquerors of the continent, to build castles to secure the obedience of the subjugated population. Their insular soil did not even furnish them with the bare means of subsistence. To obtain that subsistence, maritime commerce, and skill in shipbuilding and navigation, were indispensably necessary. The habits of industry, however, thus generated and confirmed by local situation, led in time to the usual result and reward of labour; and the refugees from the continental ravages of the barbarians, secure and independent in their insular retreat, gradually rose into a maritime and commercial Republic.

As soon as the population of Venice had so increased as to enable its inhabitants to undertake distant commerce, they commenced, and carried on for centuries, an advantageous traffic with the luxurious capital and maritime provinces of the Eastern Empire. When the Greek Emperors came to be stripped of almost all their possessions in Asia Minor, towards the Danube and the Black Sea; and the ports of the Empire, and of these conquered countries, were reciprocally shut against each other; the Venetians interposed their services, thereby not merely maintaining, but extending their mercantile operations. And, by the ninth and tenth centuries, a considerable time before the commencement of the crusades, the activity produced by want, the ambition of a young people, and the skill of a vigilant government, had enabled them to accumulate a great deal of wealth, and to attain a decided superiority in navigation and commerce.

Into the nature of the motives in which the crusades originated, this is not the place to inquire; but there can be no doubt, that these expeditions, while they wasted a vast deal of blood and treasure, exerted a powerful influence on the progress and civilisation of the different European kingdoms formed by the invaders of the Roman Empire and their descendants; and, in particular, contributed greatly to the commercial prosperity of Venice, and of the other maritime states on the coasts of the Mediterranean, such as Amalfi, Pisa, Genoa, Marseilles, and even Barcelona. Nor were the advantages arising to these maritime states from the Crusades confined to the transportation by their vessels of the persons and property of the warriors and pilgrims who hastened in crowds to the Holy Land; they were of a more permanent nature, having lasted for nearly two centuries, in the increased intercourse of these states with the Christian kingdom established in Palestine. But to inquire minutely into the political constitution, the naval power, or the commercial greatness of Venice, or of the other maritime states we are now contemplating, would be foreign to this sketch; our plan being limited to the progress of the private law of maritime commerce in these Republics of the middle ages.

That the families who took refuge in Venice, from Italy and the adjacent provinces, carried with them the practice of the maritime and commercial law of the Romans, as then known, is highly probable; and that a people who had made such advances as the Venetians had done by the ninth century, must have had regulations, at least, in the shape of established usages, there seems to be no room for doubt; but none of the maritime and commercial regulations which had been established by the Venetians prior to the Crusades, or, indeed, prior to the year 1255, have been preserved. In that year, a statute was enacted, and is still extant, consisting of 129 chapters, entitled, Statuta et Ordinamenta super Navibus. This statute appears, from its preamble, to have been merely a revision of anterior regulations; and, in its turn, appears to have undergone corrections and improvements in the years 1281 and 1302. And these later laws are collected at the end of the Sixth Book of the Statuta Civilia Veneta, compiled in 1347, by order of the Doge André Dandolo, under the title, Additiones et Correctiones super Statutis Navium et Navigantium.

But the statute of 1255, and the subsequent additions thus recorded and preserved, are far from forming a body of maritime law. They consist almost entirely of local regulations of maritime police; and in those parts which belong to private maritime law, properly so called, they are rather modifications on particular points of the Roman laws, which had continued to regulate such matters in Italy and the provinces after their conquest by the northern nations, or a supplement for the cases which these laws had not resolved or decided in a manner sufficiently precise or explicit, than an actual digest or code, viewed as a whole. In fact, there appears to have existed at Venice, as in all the other states formed out of the fragments of the Roman Empire, an ancient maritime and commercial law, as well as general, civil, common, or consuetudinary law, independent of the special statutes made at different successive periods—a common law which had preceded these statutes, and which continued to be observed in all cases in which it had not been expressly modified.

Even after the Venetian commerce came to be greatly extended and unfolded, the disputes and judicial processes to which it gave rise appear to have been judged of according to this traditionary common law, derived from the Perpetual Edict and the writings of the great Roman lawyers, or from the subsequent compilations of the Eastern Emperors, Justinian, Basilius, and Leo. Inheriting this common law, as contained in these original works or subsequent compilations, or as abridged at later times in the Synopsis Major and Minor of the Basilica, or as transmitted in the shape merely of usages, by oral tradition, the Venetians do not appear to have made any new laws for the regulation of their maritime commerce, except when occasion required, and only to the effect of providing for new wants, and for cases which the common law did not afford the means of resolving and deciding, or in which it had been found necessary or expedient to modify that law. Thus the Roman maritime law had not provided for a number of questions relative to the police of navigation, to the measures proper for the prevention of accidents and losses occasioned by the bad construction of vessels, the insufficiency of the rigging, or the inadequacy of the crews, to the overloading of vessels, to their internal order and discipline, to the reciprocal obligations of ship-owners and seafaring people. And still less did the Roman law present rules for the superintendence of sea-ports and of naval expeditions, because, from their nature and object, such rules are necessarily local and variable. Accordingly the Venetians, and, as we shall afterwards see, the other commercial states of the Mediterranean, appear to have been much occupied with the important objects just alluded to. With regard, again, to the modifications of the ancient or Roman traditionary maritime law, the chief alterations sanctioned by the Venetian statutes appear to have related to the distinction between general and particular averages, and to have extended the obligation of contribution from cases of loss voluntarily incurred for the prevention of common danger, to cases of loss or damage to the vessel or cargo arising directly from the perils of the sea, or from capture or depredation by the enemy or pirates. In the progress, however, of time and experience, it became requisite or convenient to unite these additions and modifications into one collection, not so much in the view of forming an entire and sole code of Venetian maritime and commercial legislation, but that the judges, while conforming to the common law, might know exactly in what, and how, it had been derogated from or supplied. And in this way, and for these purposes, it appears the Venetians continued at intervals to enact similar statutes during the fourteenth, fifteenth, sixteenth, and seventeenth centuries, as contained in the Novissima Veneta Statuta of 1729, in the Biblioteca di Gius Nautico of 1786, and as reprinted by M. Pardessus, without having composed any complete and properly digested code. Indeed, the place of such an authoritative digest appears in later times to have been very much supplied in Venice, as well as in the other maritime cities of the Mediterranean, by the adoption in practice of the equitable doctrines of the Consolato del Mare, without any formal or positive legislative recognition or enactment, or any other sanction than the approbation of the judicial tribunals, of the lawyers who practised before them, and of the mercantile and seafaring part of the community. Into the history of this valuable work we shall inquire in the due order of time; it was probably introduced into Venice in the course of the fifteenth century, if not before, soon after the invention of printing, in the latter part of that century, had so greatly facilitated communication among nations, and multiplied copies of useful works. The Italian translation of the Consolato appears to have been first printed at Venice in the year 1539. It was then held in great repute and of great authority, from the comprehensive and equitable nature of its doctrines; and we shall afterwards see, when we come to consider the present state of maritime law in Europe, it was, in the eighteenth century, edited, revised, and commented upon by the great Genoese jurisconsult Casaregis.

SECTION II.

Amalfi.

After Venice, the small city of Amalfi, situated on the south side of the Italian peninsula, not far from where Naples now stands, appears to have been the next earliest maritime state distinguished for trade and navigation. The foundation of Amalfi, probably in the course of the fifth or sixth century, appears to have had the same origin as that of Venice—a refuge for families who fled from their own countries, suffering under the horrors of invasion, tyranny, and anarchy. Possessed of a territory narrow but open and accessible to the sea, the Amalfitans seem to have been among the first who, after the settlement of the northern nations, thought of supplying the west of Europe with the produce and manufactures of the countries situated to the east and south of the Mediterranean. In the prosecution of this traffic they rose, in the course of the ninth, tenth, and eleventh centuries, to opulence, and to such power as to be able to contend with the Saracens. The town of Amalfi is said to have contained 50,000 citizens; the government, under the supremacy of the Greek Emperors, was popular, though less free than that of Venice. And having ultimately delivered themselves from the incursions and domination of the Saracens, by placing themselves under the authority of the Norman princes, the Amalfitans appear to have been the first Europeans who obtained access to the countries which had been conquered by the Mohammedans, for the purposes of trade, and to have thereby indemnified themselves for their exclusion from Constantinople by the Venetians.

That, after such progress in maritime commerce, the Amalfitans had regulations for such transactions, in the shape either of statutes or usages, and magistrates to decide the disputes to which such commerce naturally gives rise, is highly probable; but the allegation of M. Azuni that the Amalfitans had a court of admiralty, to which all the commercial states of the Mediterranean, and even Constantinople itself, voluntarily resorted or appealed, is most improbable, and not supported by any historical authority. And although it appears, from a grant by the city of Naples, in May 1190, to the merchants of Amalfi, to nominate consuls to judge in their disputes with each other, that the latter must have had some body of laws, we are left in complete ignorance when it was compiled, and what regulations it contained. Indeed our only information respecting it rests upon the assertion of Marino Freccia, who lived after the middle of the sixteenth century, (1570,) and who refers to a body of maritime jurisprudence, called Tabula Amalfitana, and assures us that it served for the decision of all maritime questions in the kingdom of Naples, and was in vigour in his time. "In regno, non lege Rhodia, maritima decernuntur, sed tabula quam Amalfitanam, vocant; omnes controversiæ, omnes lites, ac omnia maris discrimina, ea lege, ac sanctione, usque ad hæc tempora, finiuntur."* Brencman, Giannone, Jorio, Azuni, who copies the latter, and Sismondi, all repeat the words of Freccia without further investigation, or adducing any proofs of his assertion, which he himself did not prove, and which, besides the vagueness of the expression, is so very unlike the truth. For if, as Freccia states, the Tabula Amalfitana was still in vigour in the kingdom of Naples in the year 1570, it is most surprising that it should have been all at once so completely forgotten, that no remembrance or vestige of it has remained, while maritime laws much more ancient, and enjoying a reputa-

* De Subfeudis, lib. i., c. vii., De officio admirati maris, No. 8.

tion much inferior to what Freccia ascribes to the Tabula Amalfitana, have reached our times; and it is equally unaccountable that a body of law in such habitual and extensive observance, in an age when the art of printing had been discovered, and had multiplied all works of generally recognised utility, should not only not have been printed, but that it should have left no trace behind it except this brief passage of Freccia. And we are, therefore, disposed to conclude, with M. Pardessus,* that Freccia has written at random, or given the appellation of Tabula Amalfitana to the maritime statute of Trani, a city of the kingdom of Naples, situated upon the coast of the Adriatic, which appears to have been promulgated in the year 1063, and is entitled Ordo et Consuetudo Maris.

Section III.

Pisa.

Next to the Venetians and Amalfitans, the Pisans and the Genoese rose to eminence as mercantile and manufacturing, as well as seafaring communities.† From their geographical position, they could more easily than Venice carry on trade with the southern coast of France, and the south and east coast of Spain, the eastern parts of Italy, Sicily, and the north of Africa. Their vessels also frequented Venice, the coast of Syria, and the adjacent isles. For the protection of their merchant vessels they had to construct ships of war; and their successful expeditions against the Saracens roused and strengthened their courage in the pursuit of riches. The

---

* Vol. i., p. 145-6.

† Muratori Antiquitates Italicæ Dissert., 30.

wealth and power thus acquired by commercial, manufacturing, and naval industry, enabled them gradually to withdraw themselves from any subjection to the German Emperors, and ultimately to establish their absolute political independence. The Crusades, too, as we have already seen, which, in the course of the eleventh, twelfth, and thirteenth centuries, were so ruinous to Europe in general, and wasted so much of the blood and treasure of the kings, great nobles, and inferior vassals of the feudal kingdoms, tended only to aggrandise the commercial Republics of Italy. The merchants of Pisa and Genoa, as well as of Venice, furnished the crusaders with vessels to transport them to Palestine, shared in the booty, availed themselves of the conquests to form commercial establishments on the coasts of Asia, and enlarged the sphere of their commerce and manufacture, by communicating to the more northern and less civilized inhabitants of Europe new wants, and a relish for those commodities which administer to the comforts and conveniences of life.

Whether, as a maritime community, Pisa had adopted that common maritime law which has been designated in ancient times as the law of the Rhodians, or whether it had by conquest been subjected to the jurisprudence of the Romans, who had themselves adopted that of the Rhodians, it seems beyond dispute that Pisa must have preserved its ancient law during the revolutions by which it was subjected, in succession, to the domination of the Goths, the Lombards, the Carlovingian race, and the Emperors of Germany, until it attained its independence as a state. There no longer, however, exist any statutes enacted at Pisa prior to the twelfth century; for there is no foundation, as we shall afterwards see, for the opinion of Gaetano, who ascribes to the Pisans the composition, in 1070, of a body of maritime usages, in his description of which it is impossible not to recognise the celebrated compilation called Consolato del Mare. But there are still extant two statutes enacted by the Republic of Pisa, in 1156 and 1160, called Constitutum Legis et Constitutum Usus; which last contains important rules in maritime law. This document ascertains that the civil law of the Pisans was composed, first, of the Lex Romana, whether it consisted solely of the Theodosian code and of the authoritative writings of the jurisconsults, or whether the compilations of Justinian had, in a great measure at least, never ceased to be known in Italy, especially in Pisa; and, in the second place, of some regulations of the Lex Longobarda, of which the practice had been preserved; "vivendo lege Romana; retentis quibusdam de lege Longobarda."

But the intercourse of the Pisans with other nations, the extension of maritime commerce, and the occurrence of different and new kinds of transactions and mercantile operations, upon which the Lombard, and even the remaining Roman law would have been consulted in vain, in time gave rise to another branch of private law. The questions which these new transactions raised, could be resolved only by an appeal to the principles of natural justice and general expediency, and to usages generally admitted in the different countries with which Pisa was in commercial relations; and recourse appears to have been had to a method, highly worthy of being remarked, of providing for the inconveniences which the silence of the positive laws occasioned. They were not unaware of the dangers of legislation *a priori;* they were convinced it was necessary, for a long time, to consult experience before applying the interposition of public authority; and they created an annual magistracy, under the name of Provisores, or Prævisores, charged with the duty of pronouncing upon questions, "ex æquitate, pro salute justitiæ, tam civibus quam advenis, et peregrinis." It was, in some measure, a mixed magistracy, invested with the legislative power of investigating usage, and of declaring and establishing it, and with the judicial power of applying the general principle to the contested point which it was requisite to resolve and determine.

The jurisprudence which resulted from the decisions of these magistrates gradually unfolded itself, in the progress of time; oral tradition and, subsequently, judicial records, though rude, preserved the remembrance of it—and Pisa had thus its Constitutiones non Scriptas.

On the other hand, the changes introduced in the constitution of the state, particularly in the organization of the judicial power—others, not less important in the status of persons and relations of family, in the forms of procedure and the means of proof—also insensibly occasioned a necessity for modifications being made in the Roman and Lombard laws. But as these modifications related to laws which still continued to be in force, the judgments pronounced, even according to this modifying jurisprudence, preserved the character and the name of Judicia Legis.*

There were thus at Pisa two classes of lawsuits, or contested questions, quite distinct; the one called *quæstiones legis,* which behoved to be judged according to the Roman and Lombard laws, regard being had to the modifications introduced by jurisprudence, perhaps also by some legislative acts; the other, which could be judged only according to usage, and were called *quæstiones consuetudinum,* or *usus.* The precaution even was taken to determine individually, and by detailed and precise edicts, the questions which belonged *ad leges,* and those which belonged *ad usum.*

The time arrived when, after a sufficiently long experience, it appeared useful to put in writing, and to clothe with legislative authority, what had hitherto been

---

* Pardessus Coll. tome iv., p. 545, &c.

only traditional jurisprudence; and, agreeably to the division before indicated, there were compiled a Constitutum Legis and a Constitutum Usus, which the manuscripts present, the one after the other. The Constitutum Legis appears to have been composed so early as 1156, and it is probable its regulations were observed for a considerable time previous, although not expressly sanctioned by the legislative power. The Constitutum Usus, again, appears to have been compiled in 1161. The motives which led to the composition of the Constitutum Usus, were manifestly stronger than those which had led to the composition of the Constitutum Legis. The disputes susceptible of being regulated by the *usus*, or *consuetudines*, rarely found their solution in the Lex Romana et Longobarda. The rules in these matters flowed from natural justice or equity, from universal custom and expediency, from the reciprocity indispensable between commercial nations. It was not merely an additional law, or a law in modification of others, which it was requisite to make in this case; it was a body of usages as complete as circumstances would permit.

If it is generally expedient that public authority should respect usages—that it should not substitute an arbitrary will and a spirit of system, strict and local, for what is required by the common interest of all those who, to whatsoever nation they may belong, must desire to find everywhere the same jurisprudence—it seems not less so that, after a certain time, when usages have become fixed, the sovereign authority should ascertain them, and, after having recognised their universality and utility, should impose upon the judges of its territory the obligation of conforming to them.*

In doing so, however, the Pisans do not appear to have wished to legislate *a priori*, any more than in the

---

* Pardessus, vol. iv., ch. 23.

composition of the Constitutum Legis. They were not legislating for a new people, who, till then, had neither civil laws nor the jurisprudence of judicial tribunals, nor customs observed in business transactions among individuals. They ascertained what had been practised for a long time preceding, and if some new regulations were adopted, it was only or chiefly to rectify an usage which appeared to have been attended with some inconveniences, or to make a choice in those cases of great doubt, in which the preamble informs us the judges had decided some in one way, and others in a way diametrically opposite; and the duty of the compilers, therefore, was to arrange the rules in a consistent and uniform manner.

In ordinary matters, justice was administered, conformably to these statutes, by two tribunals, *curia legis* and *curia usus*; and some causes were competent in either court, without distinction. There were, besides, tribunals or courts of commerce, *curia mercatorum, curia maris, curia artium*, who behoved to judge all the causes within their jurisdiction, either according to the Constitutum Legis or according to the Constitutum Usus, "prout causa fuerit legis vel usus;" and even in the case of the laws and Constituta being silent, according to the *bonum usum mercantiæ*, or equity.

There can be no doubt that the rules established by the Constituta were followed before they were reduced into writing; for a charter granted to the Pisans in 1081 contains these expressions: "Constitutiones, quas habent de mari, sic iis observabimus, sicut illorum est consuetudo;" and the preamble to the Constituta of 1160 shews clearly that no previous compilation of such customs had been made: "In scriptis, statuerunt redigere, consuetudines suas, quas hucusque in memoria retinuerunt." At the same time, it is probable there were in circulation written statements or narratives of these usages, composed by practical men of business, (*practicians*,) before the public authority was interposed to ascertain and establish them.

It is also highly probable that the two Constituta of Pisa we have been considering, present, in the actual state of the manuscripts now extant, additional regulations, perhaps even some interpolations, belonging to periods posterior to 1160, which appears to be the true date of their compilation. For it was a prevalent practice during the middle ages, upon the first composition of a statute, to leave, either at the end of the general work or at the end of some of its parts, blank leaves, for the purpose of receiving additions; and, accordingly, there very frequently occur the words "addentes, huic addimus constituto."

It was the Constitutum Usus, chiefly, which contained the regulations applicable to mercantile commerce, as recently published from authentic manuscripts by M. Pardessus, and it continued in vigour even after that Republic had been subjected to the domination of the Republic of Florence, in the fifteenth century; but the regulations of the Constitutum Usus underwent, in time, various extensions and modifications. Of these the greatest part are unknown; but some of them are preserved in the document called Breve Consulum Maris, which is still extant.

As in all countries whose existence and power depend on maritime commerce, the Pisans, we have seen, at a very early period recognised the necessity of a magistracy to watch over navigation, and to administer justice in the contested matters connected with it; and, in the twelfth century, had actually established such a magistracy. It was also an early practice at Pisa to have a sort of manual prepared for each magistracy, called Breve, containing, under the form of an oath, all the obligations which the laws or the duties of their stations imposed upon its members; such as, Breve Potestatis, or manual of the principal magistrate, Breve Pisani Communis. There was also compiled, for the magistrates intrusted with the administration of the maritime jurisdiction, a manual called Breve Consulum Maris, in which were minutely explained the rules and the forms which they were to observe in the exercise of their functions; and a manual of this description existed in the middle of the thirteenth century.

This Breve Consulum Maris necessarily received successive modifications, from two obvious causes; 1*st*, Because, in terms of their obligations and oath, at entering on their office, the consuls were bound to add to the Breve the administrative regulations which their experience might suggest, so as to render it more and more comprehensive and complete; 2*dly*, Because the Republic, having at intervals found it necessary to enact laws posterior to the statute of 1160, on matters for which this statute had not provided, or which it had not well enough regulated, it became requisite that the consuls charged with insuring the execution of them should embrace, in their Breve or manual, the laws regarding their jurisdiction and functions; and several compilations of this description were made in the Latin language, of different dates, from 1294 to 1306, are still extant, and have been so far published by M. Pardessus; such as, Breve Consulum Curiæ Mercatorum, Breve Curiæ Maris, and Breve Curiæ Artium. The Breve Curiæ maris contains 126 chapters; of these the greatest part relate to the constitution of the court and its officers—to the administrative police which it exercised at home, and in the Pisan establishments in foreign countries—the preparation of causes—and the execution of judgments; some of them are the further exposition and development of different regulations contained in the Constitutum Usus; and others, copies of subsequent laws enacted by the legislative councils of the Republic for the improvement or completion of that statute. And, from the Breve Curiæ Mercatorum and the Breve Curiæ Maris, it appears that, in the maritime court, as in the commercial court, the judges were constantly occupied with the amelioration of their regulations; that the Constitutum Legis and the Constitutum Usus were the rule for their judgments; that there was preserved in these courts a copy of these Constituta, for the instruction of all those who wished to consult them, and that the consuls were charged to watch over the correctness of this copy.

Such appear to be the authentic documents of the maritime and commercial law of Pisa, while it remained an independent state. For the Italian manuscripts referred to by Valsechi and Azuni, as compiled in the years 1323 and 1337, M. Pardessus has shewn to be merely Italian translations of the Latin Breve Curiæ Mercatorum and Breve Consulum Maris, which we have just been considering; the first translation having been made in 1323, transcribed in 1333, and again corrected in 1337 and 1345, but without any change in maritime legislation.

About the beginning of the fifteenth century, Pisa fell under the dominion of Florence, whose maritime laws we shall in the sequel trace down to the present time. It may only be here remarked, that we do not find, either in the Pisan statutes of 1160 or in the Breve Consulum Maris of 1298, any regulation upon marine insurance, although the Constitutum Usus contains principles applicable to the risks of things sold and exposed to the dangers of the sea; and this absence of positive enactments, relative to insurance, probably arose from a cause which indicates the prudence of the magistrates of Pisa; for, in all matters of a nature to be regulated by universal usage and the principles of commercial reciprocity, they allowed a long period to elapse between the time when the usages had their origin and the time when it was deemed expedient to enact them as positive law.

It rather appears, however, that the practice of insurance existed at Pisa and Florence about the commencement of the fourteenth century, from an unpublished document mentioned by M. Pardessus, entitled Breve Portus Calleritani, (Cagliari,) compiled in 1318 by the commissioners of the Republic of Pisa, which had then long had establishments in Sardinia. In this document, cap. 48, on the duties of brokers, there occur the words "per quello ligno naulegare u sigurare," which M. Pardessus holds to denote the contracts of affreightment and insurance; and, in confirmation, refers to the work of Pegoletti on the commerce of Florence, composed in the early part of the fourteenth century, which, in treating of the rights of brokers at Florence, mentions contracts a "rischio di mare et di genti." Uzzano also, it appears, in his treatise on commerce, composed in 1400, mentions insurances made at Florence for London and Bruges. And it may fairly be concluded that the practice of insurance prevailed at a still earlier period, as these documents presuppose a state of things then in existence and well known.

Section IV.

Genoa.

The antiquity of the commerce of Genoa, and the maritime power which it had acquired, even before the revolutions which the invasions of the barbarians occasioned in Italy, and before the destruction of the Western Empire, are attested by the historians of these times. And as Genoa was not less commercial nor less powerful by its marine than Venice, Pisa, and the other maritime cities of the Mediterranean, there can be no doubt it had laws, at an early period, for the regulation of its merchants and seafaring people. Semini, in his manuscript memoirs, M. Pardessus informs us, cites a Genoese code of 1143, of which there was then a copy in the library of Philip Durazzo. From the Annals of Genoa, of Foglietta, Capmany cites this passage:—"Jam seculum alterum transierat, (ann. 1250,) cum, præter consules in causis forensibus, quatuor cives socii et consiliarii dati, quorum cura quam maxime ad res maritimas pertineret; ideo, vulgo consules maris appellati sunt." And the statute printed at Bologna in 1498, and which appears to have been enacted prior to 1408, contains a chapter having for rubric, "De potestate et bailia officii mercantiæ;" and contains this passage:—"Sit etiam dictum officium, judex competens de et super omnibus et singulis causis et quæstionibus, quæ coram eis movebuntur, occasione assecurationum, quamvis de ipsis esset confectum publicum instrumentum vel scriptura privata. Item de quæstionibus quæ vertuntur inter patronos et eorum participes." The Officium Mercantiæ of the fifteenth century, called, in the fourteenth century, Tractatores Mercantiæ, thus appears to have succeeded to the functions of the Consules Maris of the thirteenth century; and this last-mentioned statute also shews that the tribunals behoved to conform to the common law and to the statutes of the city—the Jus Commune implying the Roman law, as affected by subsequent usages and customs.

But it appears, from the learned researches of M. Pardessus, that of the Genoese maritime and commercial laws which have reached us, the most ancient is to be found in the collection of statutes made by a magistracy formed at the commencement of the fourteenth century, under the name of Officium Gazariæ.

In the twelfth century, the three cities of Italy which prosecuted maritime commerce with the greatest success, Venice, Pisa, and Genoa, had directed their navigation to Constantinople, and thence to the Black Sea. Each of these cities, according to the importance and necessity of its position, had deemed it indispensable to make special regulations for that commerce, and for the administration of the mercantile factories which they had there established; and Genoa, in particular, in consequence of the aid it afforded the Greek Emperor in expelling the Franks, who had invaded the Empire in 1204, had obtained a power and right to possess and to fortify a suburb of Constantinople, known under the double name of Galata and Pera. This colony of Pera was to the Genoese a sort of intermediate fulcrum, by means of which they extended their establishments on the coasts of the Black Sea; from which sea they ultimately succeeded in entirely excluding the Pisans, while they at the same time acquired a decided preponderance over the Venetians. To this country, which was then occupied by the people called Chazares, distinguished among the pastoral tribes of higher Asia, the Genoese gave the name of Gazaria; and Caffa was the principal seat of their establishment in the course of the thirteenth century. The importance of this establishment, and the necessity of having there a steady system of administration and superintendence, came in time to be more and more felt. The government of the Republic, therefore, appointed a commission of eight distinguished citizens to carry its views on this subject into effect; and the new magistracy, thus constituted, promulgated a series of statutes, commenced in 1313, and continued till 1344, contained in a manuscript, for a long time preserved in the Bank of St George. These statutes appear to have been revised in 1403, and, to a certainty, in 1441. The result of this last revisal was a work entitled "Officium Gazariæ," containing one hundred and four chapters, still extant, and recently published by

M. Pardessus; and, in this last work, the object of the author appears to have been the compilation of a body of law, general and common, for the navigation and maritime commerce of Genoa, to whatever quarter directed.

It thus appears that, in 1441, the Republic of Genoa had not yet included in its code of civil laws the rules of maritime jurisprudence, which existed solely in the statutes of the Officium Gazariæ—a judicatory which, although originally created for the superintendence of the commerce and colonies of the Black Sea, soon acquired the inspection and direction of the general navigation of the Republic, and came to exercise an exclusive jurisdiction, without appeal, in all maritime disputes.

But a change in this state of matters took place a few years afterwards. The Greek Empire could no longer resist the victorious progress of the Turks: the Republic of Genoa, consequently, lost its establishment in the Black Sea: the Officium Gazariæ ceased to exist, because the original and principal object of its creation no longer existed. The magistrates, known under the name of Tractatores Mercantiæ, or Officium Mercantiæ, resumed the cognizance of maritime affairs, as had been provided by the statute of 1339; and it is also probable that, at this time, the police of navigation and of seafaring people was separated from the jurisdiction in the affairs of maritime commerce.

Section V.

Marseilles.

In tracing the progressive rise of the small maritime and commercial states of Europe, Marseilles next presents itself. Even in ancient times, this city had risen to such eminence as a commercial Republic, that Aristotle is said to have composed a work on its constitution, which has not reached us; and, in the course of a long and prosperous period of independence, it formed for itself laws which Cicero eulogises.* It suffered greatly, indeed, from the war of Cæsar against Pompey, between whom it endeavoured in vain to remain neutral. But it did not cease to be governed by its own laws, which, in regard to maritime commerce, are said to have resembled those of the Rhodians, as is highly probable, from the origin of Marseilles, and its commercial relations with Greece.

After the fall of the Roman Empire, the territory in which Marseilles is situated, peculiarly denominated the Roman province, and known in modern times by the appellation of Provence, underwent various revolutions. It passed successively under the dominion of the Visigoths, of the Ostrogoths, and of the Franks. But the conquest of Marseilles by the Franks, in the fifth century, did not substitute any new system of maritime law in place of, or different from, that which had been previously observed. Provence was afterwards ravaged by the Saracens, who established themselves for a time on many of the northern coasts of the Mediterranean. But, in the tenth century, the Saracens were expelled; and the maritime cities, resuming their commerce, in time repaired the losses they had sustained. Like the other parts of the French territory, Marseilles was subjected to certain Counts or over-lords, whose supremacy, however, was in fact in a great measure nominal, and consisted chiefly in the exaction of certain taxes, and the performance of certain feudal services. And having, by the commencement of the thirteenth century, acquired, by treaties and pecuniary compositions from those who shared the sovereignty of the city, a complete exemption

---

* Pro Flacco, chap. xxvi.

from such feudal superiority, Marseilles might be considered as again an independent Republic. And to such a height of prosperity did it then arise, that it not only carried on an extensive trade with Italy and Spain, and with the eastern and southern coasts of the Mediterranean, but had a military navy, which signalized itself in warlike expeditions. The first use made by Marseilles of its entire liberty, was the promulgation of a statute, in 1228, abolishing certain taxes burdensome to the inhabitants and to commerce. But the chief piece of legislation of this Republic is a statute, divided into five books, promulgated in 1253 and 1255, still extant in manuscript, and of which M. Pardessus has published the chapters relative to maritime commerce. This statute, however, appears to have been a compilation and revisal of laws still more ancient: and it is especially distinguished from the other codes published during the thirteenth century, inasmuch as it is not servilely copied from the Roman law, but has features of its own, recording, no doubt, the ancient and traditionary customs and usages of that maritime people.

Section VI.

Barcelona.

In Spain, too, as well as in Italy and in the south of France, the small maritime states outstripped the rest of the country in the march of civilisation. The eastern and southern districts of Spain were one of the most important conquests of the Roman Republic; and, under the Empire, Barcelona was a place of trade, populous and opulent. On the fall of the Western Empire, these districts passed, like the remainder of the Peninsula, under the dominion of the Visigoths, who, after their settlement, promulgated the celebrated Codex Visigothorum, still held in estimation in Spain under the denomination of Fuero Juzgo. In this code we find nothing relative to maritime commerce, except the earliest testimony, during the middle ages, of the right granted to seafaring strangers, or foreigners, of being judged by the magistrates and arbiters of their own nation, and according to their own laws. But from this we may infer, as M. Pardessus remarks, that the countries from which these foreign navigators came, which could be no other than the south of Gaul, Italy, and the Greek Empire, had maritime laws or usages formed from the remembrances and traditions, if not from the documentary records, of the Roman law; and that, as the code of the Visigoths preserved the most complete silence as to all matters connected with maritime commerce, similar traditionary, if not recorded, laws and usages, must also have been observed by that portion of the population of Catalonia who applied themselves to navigation.

The ravages and depredations of the Moors, and their conquest and temporary occupation of the eastern and southern districts of Spain must have greatly depressed, and been so far destructive of, the growing industry and commercial prosperity of the former inhabitants of these countries, scarcely yet amalgamated into one people. As soon, however, as it was delivered from the Saracen yoke, Barcelona was in a great measure repeopled with its ancient inhabitants, and manufacturing industry and commercial enterprise revived. According to Capmany, the progress of the people of Barcelona, in trade and manufactures, may be traced back to the tenth and eleventh centuries. Under their Counts they appear to have enjoyed many privileges, and a comparatively free government. Their system of municipal polity, composed of a mercantile magistracy, and of various subordinate incorporated societies of merchants and tradesmen, appears to have been as complete, if not more so, than that of any of the other states of the Mediterranean. The wise maxim of not excluding foreigners from their trade, appears to have been early adopted at Barcelona; and, from the twelfth century, it was a free port for all the then trading nations. In the course of the thirteenth and fourteenth centuries, their merchant vessels traded not only to the ports of the Levant, but also to those situated on the western and northern coasts of Europe, particularly to those of the Netherlands. The enlargement of their mercantile, led in time to the establishment of a military navy; and the Barcelonese became not only able to lend great naval assistance to the small kingdoms into which Spain was then divided, but rose to be the maritime rivals of the Venetians and Genoese.

In proportion as industry and commerce were thus unfolded, the usages necessary for supplying the defects or inconveniences of the ancient laws acquired greater extension and fixedness; the urgent expediency of recording them in writing came to be more strongly felt. And from the very active trade and navigation which the learned researches of Capmany prove Barcelona to have carried on, during the tenth and eleventh centuries, there is every reason to believe that local usages, analogous to those which the statutes of Pisa and Marseilles prove to have previously existed in these cities, were already adopted and followed at Barcelona, for the determination of the obligations of owners and masters of vessels, and mariners. But if these usages were reduced into writing, they have not been preserved; and the earliest document in which we find regulations on maritime trade, is a work by the discreet men (*prud'hommes*) of Barcelona, in the course of the thirteenth century. In 1238, King James had reconquered Valencia from the Moors; and, in 1250, promulgated an extensive body of laws, under the title of the Costumbres de Valencia. Of all the monuments of legislation of the thirteenth century, M. Pardessus observes, this body of laws is that which the most deserves to be remarked, from the influence which jurists, and civilians versed in the study of the Roman law, must have exercised in its compilation. For, although written in the vulgar language of the time, its regulations are free translations of the texts of the Digest and Code of Justinian, among which are frequently interspersed different and new rules. This work of 1250, printed at Valencia in 1527, under the title of Forum Regni Valenciæ, with additions and posterior laws interspersed or appended, contains a pretty large number of regulations on maritime law. But these were far from responding to all the wants of the times and, in 1258, King James adopted and confirmed the ordinance on navigation before alluded to, prepared and propounded by the discreet men of Barcelona. The discreet men who composed this work do not appear to have had any contentious jurisdiction; they probably decided disputes by arbitration, and served as a council to the judge appointed by the King; but the establishment of special judges for commerce did not take place in Catalonia till the end of the fourteenth century.

As navigation and commerce extended, new questions still arose; the insubordination and want of discipline amongst sailors, the frauds of shipmasters, required more coercive laws; the ordinance of 1258 was found insufficient, and the result was a new ordinance, compiled by Bernard Cabrera, and promulgated by King Peter IV. about the year 1340 or 1343. In the course of that century, too, the decision of maritime disputes was separated from the ordinary jurisdiction; the jurisdiction of the consuls of the sea was instituted, and this institution was completed by the establishment of a court of appeal from the sentences pronounced by the consuls. This last ordinance refers, in several chapters, to "Les Costumes Scrites de la Mar;" but, by a learned investigation, M. Pardessus has shewn that the written customs here alluded to are not the collection of usages which has been handed down to us under the title of Consolato del Mare. Besides laying down the forms of procedure with great exactness, the ordinance of 1343 contains provisions of importance upon the privileges which creditors may exercise over vessels; in particular, recognises a distinction between a vessel recently built, which has not yet been put to sea, and a vessel which has already performed a voyage; and makes this the basis of a difference in the rights of creditors—a distinction followed in the more modern legislation of some countries.

Subsequent to the ordinance of 1343, which we have just considered, and in the course of the remainder of the fourteenth century, or early in the fifteenth century, the celebrated work to which we have before alluded, and which we shall afterwards consider in detail, the Consolato del Mare, appears to have been composed; for, in November 1435, the magistrates of Barcelona promulgated an ordinance on maritime expeditions, and on the obligations of the owners, masters, freighters, and crews of vessels, evidently intended to complete the jurisprudence ascertained by the Consolato, of which it makes express mention, while it secures to it a sort of legislative sanction.

About the same time, (1435,) the magistrates of Barcelona enacted and promulgated an ordinance upon marine insurances, of which the practice had then become prevalent among the merchants and shipowners of the Mediterranean, but of which the Consolato does not contain a word. This ordinance was successively corrected and enlarged in the years of 1436, 1458, and 1461; and the whole of these statutes being experimental drafts, were finally recast, in an ordinance promulgated in 1484. Farther, while the original ordinance of 1435 is the most ancient known in Europe on that branch of law, it contains, in itself, incontestible proofs of the existence of anterior laws; for several of its articles announce that their object is to remedy abuses, and to decide certain controverted points.

Section VII.

Cyprus.

We have thus taken a short view of the maritime and commercial laws and usages of the principal trading Republics which arose on the coasts of the Mediterranean after the destruction of the Western Empire; and particularly of their maritime statutes But this brief account would be very defective, particularly with regard to the maritime and commercial common or consuetudinary laws of these Republics in later times, subsequent to the thirteenth century, did we not also endeavour to trace the history, and notice generally the doctrines of the work known by the name of the Consolato del Mare; and, before proceeding to do so, we shall merely stop to notice, as belonging to the Mediterranean and the middle ages, the maritime law of the kingdom which the Crusaders established for a time in Palestine and Cyprus.

About the close of the eleventh century, Godfrey de Bouillon, and his followers, established a body of laws for the kingdom of Jerusalem, which they had conquered from the Infidels, under the denominations of the Assise de la Court des Barons and the Assise de la Court des Borges, viz., des Bourgeois or Burgesses; the former of these codes appears to have been revived or remodelled, and both of them to have been preserved in the island of Cyprus. But, as was to be expected, the Assise des Bourgeois only contained any laws regarding maritime commerce, and these far from numerous, relating chiefly to jurisdiction, the shipping of cargoes for sale, with a view to joint profit between the shippers and owner or master of the vessel, the valuation of goods in jetson, at the price they had cost, not at the price they might have brought, and the fulfilment of their engagements by sailors hired at stipulated wages. It is probable, however, that the usages of France, as contained in the ancient statutes of Marseilles, the Roman law, which had never been forgotten, and the Basilica, which had ruled the territories conquered by the Crusaders from the Mussulmans, before the latter had wrested them from the Greek Emperors, formed the general body of the common law. And the sole object of the few positive regulations inserted in the Assise des Bourgeois, appears to have been to settle some controverted points, and to make certain modifications which had become necessary from change of circumstances, not to digest any complete code of maritime jurisprudence.

CHAPTER II.

OF THE CONSOLATO DEL MARE.

THE compilation which bears the title of Consolato del Mare, or Consulado del Mar, is usually admitted to be the earliest General Code of maritime law in modern Europe that is now in preservation. It contains a pretty complete collection of maxims and usages for the regulation of maritime trade, adapted to the state of society and to the circumstances of the times in which it was composed; and from its intrinsic excellence, and the equitable nature of its principles, it has been voluntarily adopted almost wholly by some, and to a certain extent by others, of the different European nations who have cultivated navigation and commerce.

Nor is the Consolato del Mare merely a work of importance to the professional lawyer, as the source or basis of modern maritime jurisprudence. It is an object of curiosity, also, to the general scholar, as a monument of the learning of the middle ages, prior to the revival and general diffusion of the classic literature of Greece and Rome. And to the philosopher it is interesting, as presenting a picture of the manners and customs of the times, and as a branch of civil arrangement formed in an intermediate state of society, arising in the natural course of advancement from rudeness to civilisation.

That it is not a mere copy, or translation, or compilation, from any ancient classic code, is obvious upon the slightest perusal. But by what particular modern nation, or in what particular age, it was composed, it is not so easy to ascertain with accuracy. As all its regulations are entirely of a practical nature, the probability is that it was formed gradually, and grew up rather in the shape of customs or usages than of positive enactments, and kept pace with the progressive advancement of navigation and commerce. The influence of Roman legislation, though by no means extinguished by the ravages of the barbarians in the provinces they overran, must have been greatly enfeebled and contracted. And the maritime and commercial cities of the Mediterranean, which gradually arose out of the ruins of the Roman Empire, as we have seen, either adopted and followed the maritime and commercial law of the Romans, while it continued to be recorded in the Perpetual Edict and the writings of the classical jurisconsults, or was merely transmitted, from habit and custom, from generation to generation, by oral tradition; or they enacted statutes for their own particular government in new cases, for which this traditionary common law had not provided, and also in cases in which greater experience, or an alteration of circumstances, required a modification of its rules.

But the authority of these statutes was very much confined to the territories of the small states which enacted them; and they appear to have been rather supplementary of a recognised traditionary common law, than to have formed of themselves a complete digest of this branch of jurisprudence. And, after the subversion of the Western Empire, there was no single Continental sovereign either sufficiently enlightened to form, or sufficiently powerful to enforce, a general code of law among the different maritime states of the Mediterranean. The usages, however, which had been transmitted, either by written record or by custom and oral tradition, from their Roman ancestors, or which feelings of justice, or considerations of particular convenience or general expediency, had suggested, a more enlightened experience confirmed and improved. In their commercial intercourse, one maritime state was naturally led to profit by the wisdom of another. And as, in the maritime conveyance and reciprocal exchange of commodities, men in all countries are placed nearly in similar circumstances, and are, therefore, led to follow similar rules of conduct, the same maritime customs and usages came, in time, from considerations of convenience, and without any compulsion, to be observed by a great number of different independent states in common, and thus acquired a generality of adoption which does not take place in any other branch of internal national jurisprudence.

Nor is it merely probable that such was the origin of the Consolato del Mare from the nature of its regulations, and from what we know, from other sources, was the state of Europe during the ages in the course of which it must have been framed;—the probability is increased and confirmed by the contents of the work itself, and by different facts respecting it, which, notwithstanding the obscurity in which the early part of its history is involved, have been distinctly ascertained.

The character of this document, in point of authority, its date, and the place of its composition, are uncertain, and the name of its author unknown; but, in our inquiries respecting it, we are fortunately illuminated by the recent learned and acute researches of Capmany, Jorio, Meyer, and Pardessus; and the first point obviously is, to ascertain what is the *real* and *genuine* compilation known by the Italian appellation of Consolato del Mare, or by the Spanish appellation of Consulado del Mar.

The printed editions of the Consolato now extant commence with a series of forty-two chapters relative to the judges consuls of Valencia, and the procedure before them. But this series of chapters, which may be viewed as a genuine code of procedure in maritime matters, was compiled for the use of the city of Valencia, to which King Peter III. of Arragon had, in the year 1283, granted a special jurisdiction in maritime commerce.

At the end of these forty-two chapters, the XLIII. is a statute of King James I., who died in 1275, relative to the tribunals of the island of Majorca; and Nos. XLIV. and XLV. relate to the reach of vessels despatched from Alexandria. It was once believed that these forty-four or forty-five chapters formed part of the Consolato; but this opinion is now abandoned. It is indeed refuted by the bare inspection of all the editions, in which chapter XLVI. is preceded by the words, "Aci commencen les bones costumes de la mar;" and this forms the first chapter of the collection of maritime usages. In all these editions, likewise, chapter CCXCVII. is followed by the words, "Fins aci havem parlat de les leys e ordinacions de actes maritims mercanticals;" evidently announcing the end of the Consolato.

Afterwards, however, and in successive numbers, these editions add a pretty long collection of chapters, forming an ordinance relative to *armemens en course*, privateering expeditions commencing with No. CCXCVIII. and ending with No. CCCXXXIV. These chapters again are followed by a number of different documents, chiefly ordinances, or grants of privileges, by the Kings of Arragon, and ordinances or regulations by the magistrates of Barcelona, all in the language called Romana, vulgarly Catalan; and the annexation of these pieces to the the real Consolato has led some authors, and particularly Castillo, to say that they formed a part of it. But the opinion of Castillo, which would be of importance chiefly in an historical point of view, as postponing the composition of the Consolato till after the statutory recognition of marine insurance in the south of Europe, is controverted and refuted by Roccus and Cardinal de Luca; and besides, the preface of the editor of the Consolato, in 1494, expressly bears that, after having corrected the text of the Consolato, with the advice of experienced persons, it had been agreed with them that he should add some ordinances and privileges relative to such matters. And we may, therefore, hold it as certain, that the genuine Consolato del Mare consists only of the chapters which, in the printed editions, commence with No. XLVI. and end with No. CCXCVII.

With regard to the title and general origin of the

work, the appellation of Consolato del Mare, as it is termed by the Italians, or of Consulado del Mar, as it is termed by the Spaniards, is obviously derived from the words Consules Maris, which, in the Latinity of the middle ages, as we have seen, came to be used to denote the magistrates or practical judges of those commercial and maritime tribunals which were established in the trading states of the Mediterranean, such as Venice, Pisa, Genoa, Barcelona, for the easy and expeditious distribution of justice in such matters. Even at this day, we, as well as the French, apply the term consul to those public personages who are stationed in the great commercial towns of foreign countries, for the protection of the rights of the merchants and seafaring people of their respective nations trading to these countries. And the consular tribunals and jurisdictions, for the determination of all questions of right among merchants and seafaring people, still exist in the Italian states, in France, and in Spain. From the name of the judge, the court or tribunal came to be denominated Consolato, or Consulado. From the compilation being generally known by the name of Libro del Consolato del Mare, there is reason to believe not only that it was the code by which these mercantile and maritime courts regulated their decisions, but that, originating in unwritten usage, it was afterwards amplified and improved by the adoption of the leading decisions of the courts, which experience had sanctioned as equitable. And that it is the production of one or more of the modern commercial states which arose on the coasts of the Mediterranean, and which so far outstripped, in the career of improvement, the continental mass of European population, is beyond dispute. From the early maritime and commercial greatness of the Venetians, the Pisans, and the Genoese, it might have been supposed that one or other of these states was the author of the first modern code of sea laws; and that each of these states contributed largely, though indirectly, towards the formation of the code, by communicating and handing down those practical maxims which, in the course of their extensive maritime commerce, experience had suggested, there is, from their respective statutes, which we have seen to be still extant, great reason to believe. But, so far as appears from the general histories, from their detailed annals, or from their public national records, now in preservation, none of these states have a title to be considered as the original framers or promulgators of the code which, in time, came, in a great measure, to regulate the commerce not only of the south, but of the north, of Europe. And in asserting the title of their country to modern juridical pre-eminence, the Italians, Jorio and Azuni, confine themselves exclusively to the Pisans, without, however, as we shall immediately see, any sufficient grounds.

In investigating more minutely the origin and date of the compilation we are considering, it seems unnecessary to go into the inconclusive and almost absurd arguments by which M. Boucher, who published an edition of the Consolato in 1808, attempts to shew that it was composed at Barcelona in the year 900. And we shall, with greater advantage, accompany M. Pardessus in following out the critical examination of this point, previously commenced by Capmany and Jorio.

In a sort of preface to, or chronological list inserted in, the printed editions and translations of the Consolato hitherto in circulation, it seems to be announced that this body of law was approved, adopted, and sanctioned by a great number of sovereigns and trading Republics during a period which commenced in 1075 and continued to 1270—viz., at Rome in 1075; at Acre, by King Louis and the Count of Thoulouse, in 1102; by the Pisans in Majorca in 1102; at Pisa in 1118; at

Marseilles in 1162; by the Count of Barcelona in 1175; at Genoa in 1186; by the Venetians at Constantinople in 1215; and at Paris in 1250. And, if this document be correct, the compilation of the Consolato behoved to be fixed about the middle of the eleventh century; for it bears that the Romans adopted it in 1075, and the other adoptions are all posterior.

But is this document entitled to any credit? Most of those who have written on the Consolato have not, on this point, raised any doubt. Whether historians or jurisconsults, they all speak of this unanimous agreement among sovereigns—of this alleged event, unique in the annals of mankind—as of an ascertained fact; and do not appear to have remarked how much out of the ordinary course of events such an occurrence would have been. Capmany was the first who shewed this document to be a fabrication, in his work, published in 1779, under the title of "Memorias Historicas sobre la Marina, Comercio y Artes di Barcelona." Jorio, who probably knew Capmany's work, unfolded at length the view of that author in his work entitled "Codice Fernando." Azuni, in his "Droit Maritime," it appears, literally copied Jorio And Pardessus, following out the views of Capmany and Jorio, has, with great critical acuteness, proved that no reliance can be placed upon the statement in this document. To enter into all his arguments in detail would be inconsistent with the brevity of this sketch, and we shall merely give an abridged view of them.

In the *first* place, Supposing the document to be otherwise free from suspicion, it is by no means clear, and no sufficient reasons are assigned for holding, that this document is applicable to the Consolato. The editor of 1494, and those who have copied him, place it at the end of the chapters on privateering expeditions, giving it a title, from which it is plain they considered it as relating to the Consolato, as well as to these chapters. But this title is merely the work of the editor; it is not found in the manuscript copy of the Consolato in the Royal Library of France; the document is there placed among the additional pieces appended to the Consolato, with a title which does not refer either to the piece which precedes or to that which follows the document. But, *secondly*, Even supposing it to have been the intention of the framer of this narrative to speak of the Consolato, Capmany, Jorio, and Pardessus have incontestably proved that, in itself, it is not entitled to any credit. The manuscript copy in the Royal Library of France does not contain all the announcements of ratification which appear in the printed editions: it presents several variations; and the order is altogether different. A great number of the assertions which the document contains are not susceptible of discussion, because they are so vague, that all means of verification and of historical investigation are impracticable. But the falsehood of many of them is so evidently demonstrated by history, as to afford sufficient reason to reject the others. And in a perspicuous review of the different pretended adoptions and ratifications of the Consolato, from 1075 to 1270, one by one, M. Pardessus, upon irrefragable grounds, which we cannot here stop to detail, establishes that they are all most improbable, if not incredible, or are actually contradicted and proved to be false by the authentically recorded facts of history.

After demonstrating, negatively, that no credit is due to the document containing a narrative of the pretended various formal adoptions and ratifications of the Consolato, M. Pardessus proceeds to shew that there is as little foundation for the statement, on which Azuni relies, of the Abbé Gaetano, in his notes upon the life of Pope Gelasius II., that the Consolato was composed by the

Pisans in the year 1075. Gaetano lived in the seventeenth century, more than four centuries after the date of the event he narrates, and yet cites no authority for his assertion, and makes no reference to any chronicle or writer contemporary or anterior. No trace of a fact so remarkable is to be found in the archives of Pisa, although documents more ancient and much less important are there preserved. If the Pisans had composed the Consolato in the year 1075, it would have been in Latin, which was at that time, and long afterwards, particularly at Pisa, the language of the law; or it would have been, at least, in Italian. But there exists no manuscript of the Consolato in Latin; and the Italian editions, of which the earliest appears to have been published at Venice in 1549, are everywhere considered as mere translations. If the Pisans had composed the Consolato in 1075, would they have inserted regulations less numerous and less complete in the statute which they actually promulgated in 1161? Would they have said, in the preamble of that statute, that hitherto Pisa, governed by the Roman law, had had no written law? Would not this statute, on the contrary, have referred to the maritime code which, according to Gaetano, had been so solemnly approved by the Pisans in 1075, and afterwards in 1115 and 1118? In short, this assertion of Gaetano appears to have been entirely gratuitous, or to have had no better foundation than the fabricated narrative in the printed editions of the Consolato. And, of course, the statements of the authors who have relied upon the faith of Gaetano, such as Valsechi, Bettinelli, Jorio, Azuni, and Pompeio Baldasseroni, are not, in this matter, entitled to greater regard. Indeed the argument of Azuni establishes no more than that the Pisans had, as we have seen, a more ancient, but less complete, collection of maritime laws in Latin, of which a good many were adopted into the Consolato.

But it is not enough to shew, negatively, that the chronological account, in the printed editions of the Consolato, of its adoption and ratification by a variety of sovereign princes and commercial republics, in different countries, between the years 1075 and 1270, is contradicted by historical facts, and is a fabrication; and also, negatively, that it was not composed by the Pisans in 1075: it is desirable to make a nearer approximation, positively, to the nation by whom, or among whom, and to the period when, this work was digested; and M. Pardessus proceeds to do so with sound criticism, and in a satisfactory manner.

It is, in the *first* place, of importance to ascertain in what language the manuscripts or more ancient editions of this work are composed; for, although this does not always amount to a proof, it often, at least, affords the means of removing doubts. If there were found anywhere a Latin manuscript or printed copy of the Consolato, or if the copies in other languages were announced as translations from the Latin, there would arise a very strong presumption of its high antiquity. Until the thirteenth century, almost all the laws, as we have already seen, were composed in Latin: such as the statute of Pisa of 1161, those of Marseilles of 1228 and 1254, containing rules of maritime law; the Capitulare Nauticum of Venice in 1255; and the maritime Ordinance of King James I. of Arragon in 1258. But the result of the indefatigable researches of M. Pardessus, aided by the influence of the French government, is, that there never existed an original Latin manuscript of the Consolato.

The jurisconsults, who earliest refer to the Consolato, have quoted from the Italian; and those of the north of Europe (such as Marquardus, Grotius, and Loccenius) appear to have entertained the opinion that the Consolato was originally composed in Italian, until Westerveen published his Flemish or Dutch translation from the Italian, acknowledging, at the same time, the latter language was not the language of the original. Cleirac often transcribed chapters, and portions of chapters, of the Consolato; but he never quoted from a French translation. Valin does not appear to have taken any trouble to ascertain the original text, representing it as a mixture of Spanish, Catalan, and Italian, and quoting from the Italian editions of 1576 and 1599. Emerigon appears to have known the existence of a text, which he calls Catalan; but considers it as a translation from an original, of which he indicates neither the language nor the country. And Azuni, apparently from national partiality, borrowing the opinion of his countryman Jorio that the Pisans were the authors of the Consolato, has hazarded the groundless assertion that there never existed a Catalan original.

But from the citations by the jurisconsults being from the Italian, no farther conclusion can be legitimately drawn than that the Italian edition was in more extensive circulation. And all these opinions and authorities must yield to the decisive fact that the Consolato exists, in manuscript and in print, in a language which is not Italian; and that these manuscripts, as well as several editions, such as that of 1494, are anterior to the Italian translation. Now this language, which has been called, by Gaetano, Narbonnese, Provençal, and Catalan, is neither more nor less than a dialect of the Romance, out of which are formed the French, Italian, and Spanish—a dialect which is preserved in several southern countries, and particularly in Catalonia, with less alteration than in any other. It is, therefore, in a country where the Romance language was in use, or was the vernacular language, that we must seek for the origin of the Consolato; and this country can be no other than the south of France, or the south and east of Spain.

But, before considering the circumstantial presumptive grounds for ascribing the Consolato to Spain or to France, it may be proper to examine more particularly the question of the character of this composition; whether it was an act of public authority, supreme or local and subordinate, or whether it was merely a private work.

The first of these opinions has been embraced by most of those who have believed that the Consolato was composed in Spain. Some of them ascribe it specially to the magistrates of Barcelona, and cite the work as the Barcelonese laws; thus falling into the error before pointed out, and confounding the Consolato, properly so called, with the Ordinances which have been prefixed or appended to it, and considering the whole as an entire and one and the same code. Other authors ascribe this composition to the Kings of Arragon; but, besides their producing no proof of this, it may be asked for what singular reason should these princes, who promulgated a large enough number of laws on maritime commerce both before 1300 and also in the course of the fourteenth century, not have put their name to a code much more extensive than these laws? How should this code be found composed in a style different from all the statutes or legislative acts, and even from the simple subordinate regulations of these times—in a style which announces a work of doctrines of practice, rather than a positive law or statute? How should there be found no vestiges of it in the archives of Barcelona, where we see, from the documents published by Capmany, the laws and regulations were registered with the greatest exactness? The same observations, too, apply to the theory which would ascribe the Consolato to the government of France. In that country, it was not till the thirteenth century that the vulgar or vernacular language came to be generally substituted for Latin in the composition of laws.

Besides, the mere perusal of this compilation is sufficient to convince any one that it cannot be considered as positive law, properly so called, in any country in which it may have been held to have been composed. It does not exhibit any characteristic of command; everything, on the contrary, demonstrates in it the intention to instruct, by conveying doctrine, by recalling to remembrance and recording usages, by giving the reasons which have introduced or modified them.

It is also evident, from perusal, that the Consolato, in the state in which we possess it, is not a work executed at one effort, or all at once. We remark in it chapters belonging to a primitive compilation, and others which serve as developments. In reading the different chapters of this compilation in succession, one is repeatedly tempted to believe he is beginning a new work, the subsequent chapters often repeating in substance, and sometimes in identical terms, the doctrines of the preceding chapters.

If we cannot but admit that the Consolato is not a positive law or statute, or even a custom or ordinance, promulgated by sovereign authority, or composed under its directions, perhaps we may, with some probability, suppose that it was made for the use of a body of men charged with the duty of deciding commercial disputes, for the double purpose of maintaining uniformity in jurisprudence, and of ascertaining the law which was to serve as a rule for the judges. And it may very easily be conceived that a work of this kind must have been executed by little and little, and must have increased in proportion as new questions presented themselves. But as there is no proof to serve as a foundation for this hypothesis, we may equally suppose that the Consolato was composed by private individuals.

The causes, however, which led to the compilation of such a work are sufficiently obvious. The barbarous practice introduced by the northern nations who settled in the Western Empire, of deciding causes by single combat, or other modes of trial, by which the result was made to depend on force, chance, or contingent events, very frequently to the subversion of justice and legal right, does not appear to have ever been admitted, or to have had any influence in the determination of maritime and commercial disputes. The judges in such matters, whether denominated discreet men or *prud'hommes*, or arbiters, consuls of the sea, or courts of admiralty, appear all along to have admitted only proof by witnesses or by writing; and to have been guided in their decisions by principles of natural justice, and especially by the traditionary rules of the Roman law, with such modifications as experience, new wants, and new kinds of transactions, had introduced. There was, therefore, a necessity for judges or arbiters knowing the rules according to which they were to decide the suits, of which the fate was to depend upon reason and legal right, and not upon force or superstitious practice. Experience, and the repetition of decisions upon cases which frequently occurred, naturally furnished the first materials for a manual, destined not only for the judges who were to decide, but also for parties, that they might know their rights and their obligations. By the time, too, the Consolato appears to have been composed, not only Venice, Pisa, and Genoa, but also Marseilles, Barcelona, and Valencia, possessed, under the title of customs or statutes, bodies of legislation on maritime commerce—the chief element of the prosperity of those cities. These statutes contained, independently of a number of rules of local police, many general principles, of which it was necessary that practice should develope the mode of application. Besides, the greater part of these statutes were written in Latin, which language, though still familiar to lawyers, was already no longer that of the community; and, consequently, the merchants, or judges and arbiters, whom they chose from among themselves, had a great interest in possessing a kind of manual which might guide them in their own business transactions, or in the judgment of disputes which were referred to them.

It must not, however, be imagined that the Consolato is a complete maritime code. It contains no rules on the loan of money at maritime risk, of which several chapters indicate and presuppose the use, and with which the statute of Marseilles is occupied in detail. The authors of the Consolato doubtless referred, in this respect, to the common law, viz., the Roman law, pretty extensively diffused at the period when it appears to have been composed, and from which they have derived a number of general maxims and rules, without, however, any one being able to say that they have exactly adopted the decisions in matters of maritime law.

Whatever may have been the causes which gave rise to the compilation of the Consolato, the authors were, assuredly, well instructed in the principles of the Roman law, of the Basilica, and of the legislation of the cities of France and Spain which carried on the commerce of the Mediterranean, and of the coasts of Asia and Africa. This may have led Grotius to say that the Consolato was formed of different legislations of the Greek Emperors, of Germany, of the kingdoms of France, Spain, Syria, Cyprus, of Majorca, and of the Republics of Venice and Genoa. And this is, perhaps, the most reasonable interpretation which can be given of the narrative of the acts of approbation and confirmation by so many sovereign princes and states, of which M. Pardessus has demonstrated the fallacy.

At a period when lawyers were little occupied with writing commentaries on maritime and commercial law, when all the scientific talent of the times was directed to the exposition of the Roman and of the canon law, and still more to scholastic study than to practice, a book composed in the vulgar or vernacular tongue, easy to be understood by mercantile seafaring people, without the parade of science, was calculated to acquire, and did actually acquire, a great reputation. Presenting to the seafaring people of the Mediterranean an abridgment of the laws which each of them practised in his own country, more complete than any of these laws, since it borrowed from each of them what was awanting in the others, and formed of them one whole, it could not fail to be appreciated and in demand; and, by the sole authority of good sense, to serve as a guide in the tribunals of commerce. And this explains the eagerness with which editions of it were multiplied very soon after the art of printing was discovered.

At the same time it is to be observed, that the Consolato sometimes presents decisions entirely different from the legislation anterior to or contemporaneous with its compilation. Of this, average contribution in jetson furnishes a striking example, both with regard to the kind of sacrifices which give rise to average contribution, and with regard to the mode of valuing the articles which are to contribute. The Roman law, the Basilica, the law of the Crusaders, admitted contribution only when the jetson had saved the ship: and the same rule was adopted at Pisa in 1161; at Marseilles in 1224 and 1228; at Barcelona in 1240. The Greek compilation called Jus Navale Rhodiorum, and the Capitulare Nauticum of Venice, had extended the contribution to shipwreck and to capture by pirates. The Consolato has admitted both systems; the first as legal, the second as conventional, viz., as taking place only so far as the parties interested had entered into an agreement, called Germanimento, by which all losses, from any accident whatever, gave rise to contribution, even when the law did not otherwise require or enforce it.* And the Consolato thus madea sort of compromise between the ancient law, preserved in most maritime countries during the middle ages, and the law more recently introduced into others of these countries during those ages. But for the mode of valuation of the articles sacrificed, and of those which behoved to bear the contribution, the Consolato adopted a system not to be found in any anterior or contemporaneous legislation. The Roman law and the Basilica caused the things sacrificed to be valued at their prime cost; and the things saved, according to what they were worth at the place where the contribution was made. The maritime states of the Mediterranean, such as Pisa and Marseilles, and the Ordinance of Arragon, substituted for this imperfect system a more just rule, directing that the valuation of the things lost and of the things preserved should be made according to their worth at the time of contribution. But, instead of choosing between these two systems, the Consolato directs that the goods shall be valued at the prime cost, if the jetson has been made during the first part of the voyage; and if during the second part of the voyage, at the price at the port of arrival. And the authors of the work, although they have borrowed much from the legislations existing or known at the time of the compilation, have thus also sometimes presented their own peculiar views; which circumstance is certainly adverse to the supposi-

* Targa Ponderaz. Marit, cap. lxxvi.

tion of the work having been composed for the use and by the order of any maritime tribunal of Catalonia.

But, leaving to future inquirers to ascertain more exactly what were the causes, and who the authors, whether public or private, of this—notwithstanding its imperfections—truly remarkable work, we proceed with M. Pardessus to investigate more narrowly what was the place of its compilation. This place, we have already seen, was a country where the people spoke the Romance language; and this country must have been engaged in maritime commerce, and have had connections with Armenia, Syria, Egypt, and the north coast of Africa, all mentioned in the body of the work. Now, in the countries in which the Romance language has most anciently prevailed, and has remained for the longest period the vernacular language, two cities only appear to combine the conditions which can render it probable that the Consolato was compiled in them—the cities of Barcelona and of Marseilles. It is a fact, that neither in the archives of Marseilles nor in those of Barcelona do there exist any traces or indications which can warrant even a conjecture that the Consolato was composed in either of these cities. It is equally certain, in point of fact, that the usages, the moneys, the measures spoken of in the Consolato, were common to the two countries.

If this question were to be decided solely by commercial antiquity, the Consolato might undoubtedly be ascribed to Marseilles, for that city had extensive commercial connections with the countries mentioned in the Consolato, and, as admitted by the learned Capmany, its commerce clearly preceded that of Barcelona.

It may also be remarked, that in the Consolato, in which the relations with Spain and other countries are frequently mentioned, not a word is said of France or of Marseilles. This silence would not be surprising if

Marseilles were the native country of the Consolato; but it seems extraordinary if the compilation be ascribed to Barcelona, for the latter city must have had frequent intercourse with Marseilles, not only in consequence of the vicinity, but because the inhabitants of the two cities spoke the same language, and all the maritime commerce of France, with the east and south of Spain, could be carried on only by means of the ports of Marseilles or Arles.

On the other hand, the greater part of the considerations which militate in favour of Marseilles, are available in favour of Barcelona. Although the commercial greatness of Barcelona was less ancient, its navigation and maritime trade had made great advances in the middle ages. In the course of the twelfth and thirteenth centuries, the maritime cities of Barcelona and Valentia, and, indeed, the whole province of Catalonia, protected by several enlightened princes, and roused to activity by their favourable situation, made great progress in navigation, manufactures, and commerce. Their vessels traded from the Levant to Flanders. From the Memorias Historicas de Barcelona, published by Capmany in 1779, and supported by authentic documents subjoined in his Colleccion Diplomatica, it appears that the Barcelonese and Valencians in these ages carried on a maritime traffic sufficiently extensive and multifarious to require, and were sufficiently enlightened to compose, a code of nautical law.

It does not, indeed, appear that Barcelona had fixed or positive maritime laws before the Ordinance of King James I., of 1258; for M. Meyer, and some other writers, have erred in citing the Usatici, since they do not contain a word on mercantile transactions or maritime contracts—the chapters Quoniam periniquum, and Omnes quippe naves, relating merely to public law, and to grants by the sovereign in favour of navigation. At the period, nevertheless, at which we can fix the composition of the Consolato, the Ordinance of 1258 existed, and is by no means a work without merit. The seafaring people of Barcelona had abundant opportunity, also, of becoming acquainted with the laws of the other cities situated on the coasts of the Mediterranean; particularly with the rules of maritime law contained in the Ordinance which, in 1258, King James I. gave to the kingdom of Valencia, and with the usages of Marseilles, of which a number of chapters on maritime law are transcribed into the Consolato, sometimes literally, and sometimes with farther expositions.

The Romance dialect, also, in which we possess this work, is, by the confession of the most erudite persons, that which was spoken in the thirteenth and fourteenth centuries, and which is still preserved, almost without change or modification, in Catalonia; while the Romance Provençale, spoken at Marseilles before the alterations which it underwent under the dominion of the princes of the house of Anjou, has less resemblance to the idiom of the Consolato.

The common and general opinion, too, has always considered this composition as having had its origin in Catalonia: the first known printed editions of the work have been published at Barcelona: the manuscript in the Royal Library of France, more ancient than these editions, has probably been written there, since it contains the Catalan translation of a custom of that city: finally, no historical evidence, no opinion of any author whatever, indicate Marseilles or Provence as the place in which the Consolato might have been compiled; while all the authors whó have cited it, during the times nearest that when it was rendered better known by means of the press, have unanimously ascribed it to Barcelona. And, upon these grounds, so impartially stated by M. Pardessus, although otherwise naturally inclined, as a Frenchman, to give the preference to Marseilles, we concur in the opinion so candidly expressed by him, that the probabilities are decidedly in favour of Barcelona.

It remains to investigate, by conjectural inference, at what precise period the composition of the Consolato may be fixed; and, we may rest assured, it was not posterior to the year 1400. Indeed, it was at the commencement of the fifteenth century that the first known laws on marine assurance in Europe made their appearance. The most ancient of these laws, we have seen, is the Ordinance of the magistrates of Barcelona in 1435; and, as there exists no indication of this contract in the Consolato, we may presume it to have been of anterior date: for, if that contract had been in practice when the Consolato was compiled, there is every reason to believe that work would have noticed it, seeing almost all the usages of maritime commerce are there so carefully collected and recorded.

Whether the compilation of the Consolato was much anterior to the fifteenth century, is a more difficult question. The document appended to the printed edition, narrating the acceptance of the Consolato by a great number of sovereigns and states, from 1075 to 1270, we have already seen, is a fabrication, and entitled to no credit whatever; and the grounds for decision must, therefore, be sought in less suspicious sources.

In the interval between 1228 and 1254, Marseilles undertook the compilation and definitive revision of its civil statutes, of which the fourth book was dedicated to maritime law. Barcelona, then subject to the Kings of Arragon, and rendered still more flourishing by the attention which these able princes paid to maritime commerce, received from King James I., in 1258, the statute before referred to. Now, if the Consolato had existed in 1228, 1254, or 1258, such existence, certainly, would not have afforded any sufficient reason for preventing the legislators of Marseilles or Barcelona from digesting and establishing maritime laws or regulations, obligatory upon their judges and individual citizens. But it is to be presumed that, in the case supposed, these laws would have been more comprehensive than they are—that these legislators would have profited by the labours of the compilers of the Consolato to provide for and decide many important questions treated in that work, upon which these laws are entirely silent.

Mornac, Giballinus, Vinnius, and Giannone all say that the Consolato was composed in the time of St Louis, whose reign commenced in 1226, and ended in 1270. And, although they do not support their opinion by any evidence, this opinion, of different writers, in different places, and at different times, may be considered as the result of a sort of tradition, if it has not originated in the false document before mentioned. This opinion, too, receives some support from the following circumstances:—Peter III., the successor of James I., having, in 1283, created the consular jurisdiction of Valencia, authorized these judges to pronounce "inter homines maris et mercatores, juxta consuetudinem maris, prout est in Barchinona, fieri consuetum." And the regulation for the procedure of the consuls of Valencia, which certainly existed in 1343, bears that the consuls shall judge after the written rules in the customs of the sea. And, if these expressions apply to the Consolato, we might infer it was known and followed at Barcelona in 1283. This was the opinion of Capmany. But the inference is not quite conclusive; for the expressions in the Diploma of 1283 may more probably refer to the institution of consular judges, recently introduced, in 1279, at Barcelona; and the expressions in the regulation may, perhaps, apply to the ordinance of James I. in 1258.

On the same side, Fischer, in his "History of German Commerce," finding, in a treaty between the cities of Arles and Pisa in 1221, a clause relative to the capture of hostile goods in neutral vessels, has inferred that this treaty confirmed the chapter of the Consolato which treats of prizes; and that the Consolato existed, and served as a rule in maritime law, in the thirteenth century. But this treaty, which is to be found in Muratori, does not quote or refer to the Consolato; and the resemblance of some chapters to the principles contained in this treaty proves nothing, because it is plain the Consolato, at whatever period compiled, has collected the usages in vigour in the different maritime countries.

M. Meyer, also, believes that this work was not composed after 1267, because there is no notice in it of the jurisdiction of the consuls, which a royal grant of that year authorized the magistrates of Barcelona to establish in foreign countries. But this argument is not decisive, since the ordinance of 1340, long posterior to that of 1267, makes as little mention of these consuls. And the reason is easily perceived. The right of jurisdiction of the consuls of a country, in a foreign territory, is derogatory to or an exception from the principle of territorial sovereignty. It was not enough that the King of Arragon had authorized the municipal magistrates of Barcelona to establish consuls in foreign countries; it was still necessary that the jurisdiction of these functionaries should be consented to and recognised by the sovereigns of the places where they were stationed. But nothing proves that, at the date of the ordinance of 1340, or at the time of the composition of the Consolato, the jurisdiction of the consuls of Barcelona was actually and indisputably in exercise.

On the other hand, there are considerations which lead to the belief that the Consolato, such at least as we possess it, is posterior to 1340. In that year, King Peter IV. promulgated at Barcelona a statute, in thirty-three articles, printed in all the editions of the Consolato, under the title of Capitolo del Rey en Pere. The substance of these articles, except two relative to the local police of the port of Barcelona, is found in the Consolato, with explanations, which prove it to be a commentary on an anterior text. The Consolato, besides, contains a great number of important rules not to be found in this ordinance. Now, would the compilers of that ordinance, who in the preamble announce their intention of completing the legislation, have omitted to insert these rules, if then in existence and included in the Consolato, in their work, and to fortify them by the public sanction? The same observation applies to an ordinance of 1343, by the councillors and discreet men of Barcelona, upon maritime transactions. And these reflections lead to the conclusion that the Consolato was not compiled till the fourteenth century; which appears to be the opinion of M. Josè Salat, a learned Catalonian of the present day, as it was of the late Mr Justice Park and of Mr Sergeant Marshall. Upon the whole, however, it cannot be denied that the question is attended with great uncertainty; for the first incontestable document in which the Consolato is named, is an ordinance of the magistrates of Barcelona, in 1435, of which chapters third and fifth designate this work by the title which it now bears, and cite exactly its text.

For detailed information respecting the original text, and manuscript copies, the different printed editions, and the translations of the Consolato, we must refer to the learned researches of Capmany and Pardessus. The latter gives an account of a manuscript of the Consolato still extant in the Royal Library of France, which does not bear a date, but appears from the writing to have been executed about the end of the fourteenth century. And having been compiled, at the latest, in the second half of that century, or, at the soonest, in the thirteenth century, the Consolato must have been circulated in manuscript for a considerable time before it was printed. This appears from a passage in the description of Barcelona by Jerome Paul, composed about the year 1491.* "Sunt et mercatoriæ leges; per has, judicium ex bono et æquo et sub compendio redditur ab duumviris, qui Consules appellantur; unde consulares leges dictæ sunt; quarum, hac tempestate, non in ea urbe, modo, usus viget, sed per cunctas fermè maritimas civitates, nauticæ, et mercatorum controversiæ, hujus modi legibus, vel ex his depromptis, summa cum auctoritate terminantur; utque Rhodias olim, ita plerique nunc, per orbem, Barcinonias leges appellant." And the preface itself of the printed edition of the Consolato of 1494, the most ancient of those to be now found in the libraries or other places of public deposit, proves that it was made with the aid of a number of manuscripts, compared with each other:—"Whereas, in consequence of there being found in the book of the Consolato many alterations, both in the expression and in the decisions, and many errors, to remedy that, I, Francis Cercelles, from charity merely, and with a great deal of labour, after having compared and consulted with persons of skill and experience, shipowners as well as merchants, mariners, and others—after having examined many manuscripts—have exerted myself to correct the present book as far as has been possible for me."

At the same time, it does not appear clear that, before the invention of printing, the work was extensively circulated, or in distant countries. And what Jerome Paul says of the conformity of the laws of a great num-

* Schot. Hispania Illustrata, tome ii., p. 845.

ber of maritime cities with the Consolato, may probably result rather from the compilers of the work having borrowed laws from all the cities with which their experience had made them acquainted, than from the Consolato having served as a model for the legislation of these cities. But after the printed edition of the Consolato in 1494, of which a copy is extant in the Royal Library of France, and which seems to have been preceded by an earlier edition, which Capmany perused and describes, the value of the work appears to have become much more extensively known: and new editions were published in 1502, 1517, 1523, and 1592; those of 1502 and 1592 by order of the consuls of Barcelona.

With regard to translations, the most ancient appears to have been into Italian, by Pedrezano, published in 1549, at Venice. It has been very often reprinted; but it presents many obscurities, whether from the defects of the text from which the translation was made, or from the translator not understanding the original language. Casaregis has endeavoured to introduce corrections in the edition which he has given, with a paraphrase of each chapter; but, as he frankly admits, he has not cleared up all the obscurities.

Prior to the collection by M. Pardessus, published in 1831, there were two French translations: that of Mayssoni, at Marseilles, in 1577, and at Aix, in 1635; and that of Boucher, in 1808; the former of which, according to Valin and Pardessus, are full of imperfections and contradictions. Cleirac never translated the Consolato into French. Emerigon undertook a translation of it from the Italian version, but abandoned it in consequence of the difficulty he experienced from the obscurity of the Italian.

Lange mentions that David Fischer, consul at Rostock, translated the Consolato into Latin; but this translation is not generally known; and the book has never been translated into English, as Boucher alleges, although it is believed Lord Mansfield, Lord Stowell, and other profound English lawyers, were well acquainted with the work.

Westerveen made a translation of the Consolato into Dutch, from the Italian version, which was printed at Leyden in 1704, and at Amsterdam in 1726; and refers to a Catalan edition. And, in 1790, Engelbrecht published, in his Corpus Juris Nautici, a German translation of what Westerveen had translated into Dutch; but, according to M. Meyer, the translation is inaccurate.

The Consolato has been translated into Spanish three different times: *first*, by Francisco Diaz de Roman, printed at Valencia in 1539; *secondly*, by Cayetan de Palleya, in 1732; and, *lastly*, by Capmany, in 1791, in his Codigo de las Costumbres Maritimas. The last author has separated the Consolato from the pieces attached to it in the former printed editions, which, we have seen, are quite extraneous to it; and he has arranged the chapters in a new order, under fourteen titles, to which he has given rubrics of his own composition. The distribution thus adopted by Capmany is, undoubtedly, more methodical than the original text; and it might have been rendered more perfect, either by arranging the chapters better, or by dissecting them, since many of them contain subjects quite distinct from each other. And, while we agree with M. Pardessus that this is no longer, strictly speaking, a publication of the primitive work, and that that work was known for much too long a period, both from the printed editions of the original text and from the translations, to admit of its being reproduced under a new form without being attended with many inconveniences, we are inclined to consider the juridical public as much indebted to Capmany for the improved arrangement he has suggested; and that his only error consisted in his not giving first a literal copy or translation of the primitive work, as it existed in the original text, and then adding, as a separate work, his improved arrângement.

The latest and best edition of the Consolato is that published in 1831 by M. Pardessus, from the Princeps edition of 1494, extant in the Royal Library of France, compared with the manuscript of the work, also extant in the same library; and to the original, M. Pardessus has, with the aid of M. Llobet, a merchant of Barcelona, added a translation into French, in which, intentionally avoiding all change in the original, and all attempts at greater elegance of diction, M. Pardessus has exhibited a mere copy and exact picture of the original, as actually composed by its authors.

Having thus considered the probable origin of the Consolato del Mare; ascertained what are its genuine component parts; investigated, both negatively and positively, by or among what nation it was composed; inquired into the nature of the compilation, whether it was composed by public authority, sovereign, or local and subordinate; and made an approximation to the time when it appears to have been compiled, by a comparison with other authentic documents and recorded events; we proceed to inquire what are its contents and its doctrines generally, and what the state of private maritime law which it exhibits.

Of the mere contents, the arrangement by Capmany, before alluded to, of the 252 genuine chapters under fourteen titles, affords a concentrated view. These titles treat in succession—1*st*, Of the obligations between the captain or master, generally a part owner, the builder, or shipwright, and the persons who agree to become part owners, relative to the construction and sale of the vessel; 2*d*, Of the obligations of the mate of the vessel, of the clerk and keeper of the register or log-book, of the pilot, and of the crew of the vessel, or common mariners; *3d,* Of the reciprocal obligations of the master and of the mariners or crew; *4th,* Of the acts, contracts, and stipulations relative to affreightment, between the master and the shippers of the goods or cargo; *5th,* Of the loading, stowage, and discharge of the goods or merchandise, and of the damage which may be occasioned to them by these operations; *6th,* Of the contracts by which vessels were intrusted and given in use, or chartered for a particular voyage, or by which goods were intrusted and delivered for a particular voyage, or for conveyance to a particular port of destination; *7th,* Of the regulations for the anchorage and moorage of vessels in a roadstead, on the sea-shore, or in port; *8th,* Of the mutual obligations between the owner or part owners and the master, the shippers of the goods or cargo, and the passengers embarked; *9th,* Of the obstacles which may occur to the master, or the merchant shipper of goods, commencing or continuing a voyage; *10th,* Of voyages of mutual preservation, and agreements by the owners and masters of different vessels to afford each other aid and protection on particular voyages; *11th,* Of shipwreck, of the running aground, or stranding of vessels, and of the other accidents and damage which occur at sea; *12th,* Of damage caused to a merchant vessel by the attack of hostile vessels or pirates; *13th,* Of the mutual obligations of the master, of the part owners, or persons interested in the vessel; *14th,* Of the observance of contracts, and of good faith in the sale and purchase of commodities.

But, in addition to this skeleton of the Consolato, it may be worth while to take a view of the body of the work, and, so far as not already done, of its doctrines generally. To give a detailed account of all its particular regulations would much exceed the limits of this sketch; we may, however, endeavour, in a few remarks, to convey some idea of what was the state of the law of maritime commerce during the ages in which it was in general observance.

The genuine Libro del Consolato del Mare which was sanctioned by a general and almost universal voluntary adoption by the Mediterranean states, detached from the municipal and other regulations peculiar to different countries which have been added to it in the printed editions, consists, we have seen, of 252 chapters. It contains various repetitions, almost every chapter forming a sort of whole of itself. The different subjects of which it treats are not digested or methodically arranged; and it is evidently a monument of practical wisdom, not of taste or genius.

In the work itself, it is stated that the customs of which it is composed were collected by wise and skilful men, during voyages and travels to various countries and places. From a perusal, too, it is manifest that, in compiling the code, the object of the authors was to combine the practical wisdom of former times, and of all the different states of the Mediterranean; and, unquestionably, whoever they were, these authors, in thus collecting from all quarters, and in selecting what was most equitable and expedient, display a liberality and a skill highly honourable to an age which we are accustomed to consider as barbarous.

In the ages in which the Consolato was composed, the construction of the vessel, or instrument of maritime commerce, appears to have been comparatively an undertaking of great difficulty. The accumulation of moveable capital by individuals was comparatively inconsiderable. For building even those small vessels which then navigated the Mediterranean, several individuals behoved to combine their stocks, or it was found requisite to borrow on the credit of the ship. Hence the multiplicity of regulations in the Consolato for determining the reciprocal rights and obligations of the master, the shipbuilder, and the parties who were to become part owners of the vessel. From the minute details respecting their various duties, privileges, and accommodations, the common mariners appear, in those days, to have been persons of comparatively greater consequence than at present. They appear frequently to have possessed capital to a considerable extent, and to have had shares either in the vessel which they navigated or in the mercantile adventures which formed the object of the voyage. For this circumstance it does not seem easy to account, unless it arose from the ability to navigate safely, prior to the invention of the compass, requiring a greater degree of experience and skill, which was only to be found in a class considerably above the lower orders in society.

Prior to the invention of the compass, the perils of navigation, even in an inland sea like the Mediterranean, must have been much greater than since that important discovery. Accordingly we find in the Consolato a great body of legislation on the reparation of damage at sea, and on salvages and averages, that is, on due remuneration for the recovery of goods which have been in danger, or so far lost, and in the equitable arrangement by which a partial loss, voluntarily incurred for the safety of the whole, is laid upon and divided among the persons who are thereby benefited.

In the Consolato we, of course, find the leading principles of the contract of affreightment, by which the instrument of maritime commerce is converted to use; and likewise the rudiments of those marine documents now known by the name of charter-party and bill of lading; and, among the different officers of the vessel, the secretary or clerk, whose business it was to keep an accurate list of the passengers and cargo, and to record the adventures of the voyage, makes a conspicuous figure. But, instead of the simple transactions of order, or commission and consignment, by which the exchange of commodities is now effected between the domestic and foreign merchant, we find, in the Consolato, a very different state of matters. Commercial capital and credit were yet in their infancy: it was seldom that a merchant had such a quantity of goods to export or import as required that he should freight the whole of a vessel: the cargo was usually made up of the investments of eight or ten different merchants; and instead of intrusting the goods to the care of the master, and the management to the foreign merchant or consignee, as at present, the owner of the goods, or his partner, or, at least, a skilful supercargo, went along with them, to make the bargain in the foreign country, and to purchase and bring home other goods in exchange. In this way the people in the vessel consisted not merely, as at present, of the crew or persons employed in the navigation of the vessel, but also of a pretty large assemblage of merchants or dealers, who each required accommodation for himself and his stock of commodities; and the picture presented by a mercantile voyage in these days resembles that of a modern German or Russian waggon, or caravan, destined for one of the great fairs, with this difference, that, instead of being dragged by animals, the marine dealers of the Mediterranean were wafted over the waves. For the decision of the disputes likely to arise in this intermediate state of maritime commerce, the Consolato contains an ample collection of rules and maxims.

Nor is the Consolato del Mare a less curious or interesting historical monument in tracing the gradual development of the other branches of the law of maritime commerce—of those auxiliary, but most important arrangements, by which maritime commerce is rendered more safe for the individual, by which its extent is enlarged, and by which its operations are facilitated. In the infancy of navigation, the perils of the winds and waves behoved to be more felt than in the advanced stages of its improvement; and yet ages passed away before it was perceived that from the multiplicity of risks safety and profit might be made to arise; that by a small contribution, or deduction from the profit, one individual might secure reparation for loss occasioned by the dangers of the sea; and that, by undertaking to repair, to a limited extent, a number of such contingent losses, another individual might, upon the average of physical events, reap a profit. As soon as it was discovered, the obviously beneficial effects of such an arrangement behoved to hasten its progress; and, accordingly, in none of the maritime contracts have we more decided cases than in the highly useful one of marine insurance. Yet of this so useful arrangement, which, we formerly saw, was unknown to the ancients, there is still not a vestige in the Consolato. That this contract must have been known in practice for some time before it became the subject of legislation, is obvious; but that, when once introduced into practice, it would soon become the subject of discussion in the maritime and commercial tribunals of the age, is highly probable. And laying aside the fanciful conjectures of men whose zeal for antiquity, or whose national vanity, has impeded the sound exercise of their judgment, we cannot correctly state the introduction, or at least the general practice of marine insurance as earlier than the commencement of the fifteenth century, since, as formerly shewn, the first authentic document we have on the subject is the ordinance of 1435, by the municipal magistrates of Barcelona. The late introduction of so useful an institution is, no doubt, rather a singular phenomenon; but the causes may be traced in the slow accumulation of mercantile capital, in the requisite extensive and continued observation of physical events, and in the calculations of risks, and the combination of abstract and yet complex ideas, which the contract of insurance presupposes.

Even in a comparatively rude age, the scarcity of moveable capital, and the difficulty of mercantile operations on an extended scale, behoved to suggest that obvious expedient by which the capitals, as well as the skill and industry of several individuals, are combined and directed to one common object. And, accordingly, in the Consolato del Mare we find a great many regulations for determining the reciprocal rights and obligations of persons connected by copartnership and joint adventure, either in a vessel or in the commodities which it is employed in transporting.

In the progress of commercial intercourse among individuals of the same country or nation, the utility, or rather the necessity, of an established standard of value, and of one common medium of exchange, could not fail, in time, to lead to the adoption of some natural or artificial production which, from its intrinsic qualities, was well adapted for such a purpose. From the adoption of such a circulating medium, possessing intrinsic value, the advantage of a transition to a less cumbrous instrument of exchange came to be perceived; and, instead of precious metals, there came to be substituted, to a great extent, an artificial representative of value, possessing no intrinsic estimable qualities, and deriving all its worth from conventional arrangement. But, if the adoption of such a medium of exchange was advantageous among the inhabitants of one state or country possessing one common coin, a similar plan was still more necessary among the subjects of different states, and the inhabitants of different countries, who possessed no such common coin or current money. And hence bills of exchange, by which the exports and imports of different countries and places are set off against each other, and the merchant is enabled to obtain value for his commodityin that shape which is most convenient for him. But such an enlightened and beneficial arrangement could not be expected to arise in the infancy of commerce. It presupposes a pretty extensive and varied interchange of commodities, so as to create that reciprocity of claims and interests among different individuals, in different countries, on which the contract is founded: it presupposes the existence of mercantile credit to a considerable extent, which can only grow up in a state of comparative security: it presupposes the existence of banks, and some skill in banking operations: and it presupposes the establishment of regular tribunals, to give to the conventional documents, by means of summary legal compulsion, that effect or value which is not inherent in themselves.

That bills of exchange, as now in use, viz., as negotiable documents between individuals of the same state, or of different independent states, were unknown to the ancients, we have seen there can be little doubt; and, as was to be expected from the causes just alluded to, there is not a trace of any such contract or of any such document in the Consolato del Mare. Nay, not only does this early maritime and commercial code contain no notice of bills of exchange, it rather affords evidence that they were not then in use. It affords evidence of the existence of a less convenient mode of dealing, which, in the natural progress of improvement, behoved to precede the introduction of bills of exchange. It contains various regulations relative to *comanda en diners*, or *comandita in denari*, or what may be called factorage in money, and prescribes rules for the conduct of the person who is employed by the home merchant to go with the vessel and purchase commodities in a foreign port, and who is for that purpose intrusted with cash or specie. And that between this mode of dealing and the use of bills of exchange there may have been some intermediate steps, is highly probable. But the history of bills of exchange has by no means as yet been so carefully investigated or clearly elucidated as could be wished. The story of these documents having been invented by the Jews, when banished from France, for the purpose of concealing their effects, or of secretly removing the effects they had concealed—a story originally told by Cleirac, in the edition of the Us et Coutumes de la Mer, which he published at Bordeaux in 1661, adopted without reflection, and sanctioned, in his epigrammatic style, by the great Montesquieu, and, of course, repeated by every inferior writer—is highly improbable, vague, and unsatisfactory, if not absurd. And, although bills of exchange are not treated of or mentioned in the Consolato, there is reason to believe they came into mercantile practice, if not before, at least soon after the date of that compilation; for in the Colleccion Diplomatica of Capmany, and in the middle of a public authentic document, there is to be found a copy of a bill of exchange, drawn by a merchant in Bruges upon a mercantile company in Barcelona, somewhat in the present form, dated the 28th April, 1404, commencing with the salutation, "*Al nome di Dio,*" and ending with the prayer, "*Christo vi guardi.*"

CHAPTER III.

OF THE ROLES D'OLERON.

Having thus taken a short view of the maritime and commercial law, statutory and also consuetudinary, of the trading Republics which arose in the middle ages on the European side of the Mediterranean, from Venice to Barcelona, and having also considered, at some length, the compilation of maritime usages and customs which latterly came to be recognised as common law in these different states, and in their intercourse with each other, we proceed to trace the progress of the law of maritime commerce, advancing northward, round by the Bay of Biscay and the British Channel, to the Baltic, in the laws of Oleron, the laws of Wisby, and in the code which, at Lubec, received the public sanction of the Hanseatic League.

The best known and most generally cited text of the Roles d'Oleron is that published by Cleirac, in his collection, entitled, Us et Coutumes de la Mer, first printed in 1647; and this text Cleirac took from a book composed by Garcie de Ferrande, under the title of Grand Routier de la Mer, first printed in 1542, dividing it into forty-seven articles. But this is not the state in which the Roles are found in the manuscripts and in the ancient prints.

Two manuscripts, still extant in England, the one at Oxford, in the Bodleian Library, and the other at London, in the Cottonian Library, contain twenty-four articles, corresponding to the first twenty-two of Garcie and Cleirac. A third manuscript, also extant at Oxford, in the Bodleian Library, in a collection commonly known by the name of the Black Book of the Admiralty, contains, with the intercalation of eight unpublished articles, the twenty-four articles of the manuscripts just mentioned, and two articles corresponding to the twenty-third and twenty-fourth of Cleirac. These twenty-five or twenty-six articles, and, besides them, two articles which none of the manuscripts of England contain, being No. 27 and No. 28 in the edition of Cleirac, compose the compilation found in the editions of the ancient Coutumes de Bretagne, published in 1485 and 1501, in the Coutumier de Normandie, edited in 1539, and in a French manuscript in the Histoire de Bretagne de Morice. The Flemish and Castilian translations, the last about 1266, likewise contain only the twenty-four articles in the Oxford and London manuscripts.

From this exposition, we are led to conclude that the whole of the Roles d'Oleron, in the state in which the editions of Garcie and Cleirac present them, have not been composed at one and the same time; yet these editors have made no distinction, and evidently had no idea of doing so, having clothed the primitive articles in a more modern style, similar to that of the latest. Besides this, Cleirac has suppressed, at the end of the primitive articles, the final formula—*Tel est le jugement en ce cas*—which we find in all the manuscripts and printed editions before mentioned, and yet terminates the whole by a certificate of 1266, which accompanies only the first twenty seven articles in the manuscripts, and in the ancient editions of France.

This confusion has not only the inconvenience of not permitting us to distinguish and recognise the ancient text, but also that of presenting the whole of the publication as made at one and the same period, which we might believe very recent, according to the language, although the date of the certificate be long anterior, and of thus exhibiting improbabilities which have, more than once, embarrassed historians, and furnished arms to criticism for contesting the antiquity of the compilation. But, from the unimpeachable documents before referred to, we are clearly warranted in separating what has reached us under the name of the Roles d'Oleron into three or even four distinct parts.

The first part is composed of twenty-five articles, which may be called primitive or original, because they are the only ones of which the manuscripts of England, and the Castilian and Flemish versions, attest the existence, and of these there is subjoined a summary analysis: 1*st*, Prohibition against the master selling the vessel, and the case in which he may borrow money; 2*d*, Prohibition against the master setting sail without consulting the crew; 3*d*, Of the salvage due for the recovery of a shipwrecked vessel; 4*th*, Of the case of the vessel becoming unnavigable; 5*th*, Obligation of the crew not to quit the vessel; 6*th*, Of the police of the vessel, and of a mariner hurt or wounded in the service; 7*th*, Of the sailor who falls sick in the vessel; 8*th*, Of jetson to save the vessel; 9*th*, Of the mast or anchors sacrificed for the common safety; 10*th*, Of the obligation of the master and crew to discharge the cargo in a proper manner; 11*th*, Of losses occasioned by bad stowage; 12*th*, Of the disputes of the mariners among themselves, and between them and the master; 13*th*, Of the expense of loading the cargo; 14*th*, Of the right of the master to dismiss and cashier a sailor; 15*th*, Of the damage caused by one vessel to another at anchor; 16*th*, Of the damage caused by the anchors of one vessel to another; 17*th*, Of the hiring of mariners upon the reach of the vessel, or voyage, or upon freight; 18*th*, Of the maintenance or subsistence of the mariners; 19*th*, Of the obligation of mariners to continue on the return voyage; 20*th*, Of the rights of the mariners in the case of the prolongation or shortening of the voyage; 21*st*, When the sailors may go on shore; 22*d*, Of the indemnity due by the shipper of the cargo in the case of delay; 23*d*, Of the captain who has need of money on the voyage; 24*th*, Of the obligations of the seaman or pilot who conducts a vessel to the place of discharge; 25*th*, Of the punishment of the seaman or pilot who causes the loss of the vessel.

The second part consists of two articles which, not being contained in the manuscripts and early versions before mentioned, are probably less ancient than the preceding: the one regarding damage done to goods at the time of their discharge from the vessel; and, the other, joint adventures in shipping.

The third part is composed of eight articles, for the first time only lately published by M. Pardessus, added to the first class in the Black Book of the Admiralty. Their objects are, 1*st*, The obligation imposed on the master, who has undertaken the conveyance of commodities, to load them without delay; 2*d*, The prohibition against the master, who has let his entire vessel on freight, putting on board of it anything else than victuals or provisions; 3*d*, The quantity of loading which he who has freighted an entire vessel has a right to put on board; 4*th*, The mode of payment of the sailors who go on the voyage on freight, and the right of the master to exact the freight of goods thrown overboard for safety; 5*th*, The prohibition against the sailors exacting anything from the shippers of the cargo; 6*th*, The obligations of the master for the maintenance of the merchants, and the superintendents of the wines on board; 7*th*, The delay or period (lay days) within which the merchandise must be discharged, and the right of the master to retain the cargo in security of his freight; 8*th*, The rules as to what goods ought to contribute in the case of jetson. The old style of these articles, the fact that they are contained in a book which everything leads us to believe was composed in the fourteenth century, and which has evidently the language of that age, afford decisive grounds for placing them before those which are found solely in the editions of Garcie and Cleirac, and which are of a less ancient style.

The fourth part consists of twenty articles, which treat exclusively of shipwrecks, shipwrecked goods, and marine waifs.

Such being the state of the compilation, we proceed

to examine to what country and to what period we are to attribute the different parts, particularly the first and third, as being the most important.

The glory of having compiled this code is disputed by the English and the French, both equally anxious for the glory of their country. In his celebrated treatise, De Dominio Maris, the learned Selden maintains that a number of regulations relative to maritime affairs had been previously established, and were corrected and published anew, in the island of Oleron, by Richard I., on his return from the Holy Land; and adduces this circumstance as one of the proofs of the dominion claimed by the kings of England over the adjacent seas. Sir Edward Coke repeats this statement. In his charge to the Cinque Ports,* Sir Leoline Jenkins observes:—"The western world received them (the Roles d'Oleron) from the English, by way of deference to the sovereignty of our kings in the British ocean, and to the judgment of our countrymen in sea affairs." And Mr Justice Blackstone, in his Commentaries,† informs us "that Richard, when abroad, composed a body of laws at the isle of Oleron, which are still extant, and of high authority."

If, however, we investigate the historical fact more accurately, and divest ourselves of all national bias, we shall find that the glory of composing this code, whatever it may be, does not belong either to the kings of England or to the English nation. In making the preceding statement, Selden, and the other English writers who have copied it, found upon a document which has not been inserted in the collection of Rymer, but was then extant, and appears to be still extant in the Tower of London, and to be dated in the twelfth year of the reign of Edward III. This document, however, does

---

* Page 87. † Vol. iv., p. 423.

not appear to be by any means sufficient to support the claim made in behalf of the kings of England as original authors or compilers of the Roles d'Oleron. According to the account of Mr Luders, the document itself has but little of the appearance of a public act of state; and its narrative is so far contradicted by the well-ascertained historical fact that Richard was not at Oleron on his return from Palestine, but returned from his unfortunate shipwreck and captivity by Flanders. But, supposing the document to be authentic, and quite entitled to credence, it is by no means clear that it refers to the ancient Roles d'Oleron; for the subject of the Consultation of the Judges, therein mentioned, was matter of public law, the sovereignty of the sea of England, and the jurisdiction of the admiralty for the punishment of offences against the safety of navigation; whereas the Roles d'Oleron contain nothing on that subject, but relate to the reciprocal private civil rights and obligations of mercantile and seafaring people.

It is admitted, on all hands, that the original code was compiled prior to the time of Richard I., who, according to this document, (if it refers to it at all,) merely corrected and enlarged it. But it was not till the marriage of Richard's mother, Eleanor Duchess of Aquitaine or Guyenne, one of the grand fiefs held in vassalage of the crown of France, with his father, then Duke of Normandy, and afterwards King of England, under the name of Henry II., that the English nation, or their monarchs, came to have any connection with, or power over, the duchy of Guyenne, or the isle of Oleron, which is attached to and forms a part of it, or could possibly frame laws either in or for the use of that island. As the duchy was not acquired by conquest, it is plain that any maritime laws which Richard could there establish must have been in the character of Duke of Aquitaine, not in that of King of England. Accordingly, when the duchy, as one of the grand fiefs of France, finally reverted to the crown, in virtue of the sovereignty, Charles V., by the ordinance of 1364, admitted the Castilians to the commerce of the ports of the Loire, and granted them the privilege of having their causes adjudicated *par les loix de Leyron*, recognising them as the laws of France. Besides, the most ancient laws of Oleron relate exclusively to the navigation of the Sea of Gascony, from Bourdeaux to Rouen, and do not mention either the Channel or any of those other seas which England, even then, considered as peculiarly her own. The language, too, in which the primitive part of this nautical code is composed is old French, and has no mixture of the English idiom.

The fact, therefore, seems to be, that, like the inhabitants of the coasts of the Mediterranean, those of the west coast of France, bordering on the Atlantic Ocean, from their favourable situation, and in the natural course of events, early addicted themselves to navigation, and made some progress in maritime commerce. In the course of their own experience, and in consequence, probably, of their intercourse with the more civilized maritime states in the south, they were naturally led, from views of general convenience, to observe certain usages, and to adopt certain rules of trade. And these usages and rules appear to have been at last collected and confirmed by the sovereign of the duchy or province of Aquitaine.

Although, however, the laws of Oleron must thus be considered as more properly a provincial French than as an English work, the great wisdom and equity of the regulations appear to have recommended them to both nations. The early writers, indeed, on the law and antiquities of England, such as Bracton, Britton, and the authors of Fleta, say nothing of the Roles d'Oleron, and there does not appear to have been any early act of the English Parliament expressly and legislatively adopting them as a part of the statute law of the realm. But an ordinance of King John appears, as Prynne observes, to be grounded on the laws of Oleron; and the celebrated statute of the forty-third year of the reign of Edward III., known by the appellation of the Inquest of Queenborough, appears to recognise them as common law: in short, these laws may be viewed as forming the basis of the English, as well as of the western and northern French maritime jurisprudence. Their influence, indeed, seems to have extended over the western seas of Europe, from the Straits of Gibraltar to the coast of Norway; and, as Molloy observes, (Introduction,) they obtained the same force as those of Rhodes formerly did—"they were esteemed for the reason and equity found in them, and were applied to the case emergent."

With regard to the period at which the Roles d'Oleron were composed, it appears certain the compilation existed, and had been translated into Castilian, about the middle of the thirteenth century, and that it is referred to in the laws of England and of France in the fourteenth century; and it is not surprising there should be difficulty in ascertaining precisely its more ancient date, seeing it is merely a collection of usages, not a legislative act. As it contains nothing on the contract of insurance, it may be inferred that the compilation took place before the introduction of that arrangement; but, as this is merely negative, we may shortly notice the argument urged by M. Pardessus for the greater antiquity of the compilation. And we quite agree with that learned jurisconsult that it is proved by the Ordinance of 1364 that, in the fourteenth century, the Roles d'Oleron served in France to regulate maritime disputes; that Oleron was then under the dominion of France, and that it is highly improbable the name of Oleron would have been given to usages not compiled in France, or that a law would then be generally adopted which was made by a foreign and hostile prince. But we do not think the latter reasons afford sufficient ground for fixing the date of the compilation at a time anterior to 1152, the year of the marriage of Eleanor of Guyenne with Henry II. of England, and still less for referring it to the end of the eleventh century. There can be no doubt the Roles d'Oleron are a compilation of the usages of the people inhabiting the western coasts of France, which then formed feudal provinces holding of the French Crown; and whether the compilation was sanctioned by a native prince, or by a foreign prince in virtue of marriage, the usages were French, and there is no improbability in their being afterwards formally recognised and enforced by the French King; especially when the duchy in which the compilation was originally made had come to be completely united to the French Crown.

But we think M. Pardessus has succeeded in carrying back the date of the primitive part of the compilation at least to the year 1266; and, of course, the existence oft heusages, as transmitted by oral tradition, to an earlier period. For, besides the year 1266 being the date of the certificate which terminates the Roles d'Oleron in the ancient manuscripts and editions of France, it appears from the manuscript translation of the Roles, which, as attested by Capmany, existed in the library of the Escurial in 1791, that in 1266 Alphonso X. approved of *il Fuero de Layron*, and caused these maritime laws to be inserted in the fifth part of the compilation known under the name of Partidas.

With regard to the style of the Roles d'Oleron, if we believe Cleirac, followed by Valin, and even by M. de Pastoret, the text is in the old French language, with some Gascon expressions, but (as formerly stated) without any mixture of Norman or English idiom. But, as M. Pardessus, with great candour, remarks, it would have been desirable that Cleirac had pointed out in what place of deposit, public or private, the original manuscript existed; for, assuredly, the text which he has published does not deserve or warrant such a description; being, as Mr Luders observes, of the age of Francis I., precisely the time when the Routier of Garcie was published, of which Cleirac copied and modernized the text. The manuscripts and the ancient printed editions in France, and the manuscripts in England, although in French greatly more ancient, do not contain Gascon expressions; and the style, in point of orthography and the disuse of certain words, M. Pardessus informs us, rather has some relation or resemblance to the Norman idiom. But what was the language of the primitive compilation? What alterations did it undergo in its transition from Aquitaine to Bretagne, from Bretagne to Normandy, and from these provinces to England? This Cleirac has not explained; and his assertion seems to be one of those rashly hazarded opinions, successively copied, until they became a sort of tradition, for which we can find no solid foundation when we attempt to verify its exactness and ascertain its origin. We have, of course, no direct proof that the primitive compilation was of an older style than that which we possess; and, seeing the French manuscript copies and printed editions were likely to undergo changes in style, to adapt them to the living language, whereas, from the abolition of French in England, it became there in a manner a dead language, we may conclude the two manuscripts of Oxford and London, if not the genuine text of the original compilation, are at least the most ancient.

With regard to the proper character of the Roles d'Oleron, it is not easy to discover in them an act emanating from sovereign authority—such acts have always borne the name of the prince, of the magistrates, of the public body by whom they were promulgated. It is this which, in France, distinguishes laws from customs. The denomination of Roles or Rooles, too, by which this compilation is designated in all the ancient manuscripts and editions, has been, for a very long period, given in France to the acts or judgments of courts or tribunals written on parchment or rolls.

With regard to the true place of composition, we, of course, are led to fix upon the Isle of Oleron, from the undisputed tradition to that effect, from the manuscripts of England and France bearing the title of Roles d'Oleron, and from several of these manuscripts, and all the ancient French editions, bearing for their finale "Temoin le Scel de l'isle d'Oleron." But, with the exception of this title, and the indication dated 1266, after the usages had probably been some time in traditionary observance, there is not in the ancient articles a word designating Oleron; the ports of Bordeaux and Rochelles, the coasts of Bretagne and Normandy, are there alone named; and it is, therefore, probable these usages belong not specially to Oleron. Indeed, they contain rules essential to maritime commerce generally, wherever it may be carried on. Even the regulations which relate to localities are not special for the isle of Oleron; they regard the extensive maritime territory of France, from Bordeaux to the coast of Flanders, and the sea of England and Scotland; and, from all this, M. Pardessus, with much plausibility, infers that the Roles belong not peculiarly to Oleron, but were there known and followed as throughout the duchy of Aquitaine, of which this isle was a dependency; as in Bretagne, Normandy, and the western coast of France, of which they formed the common maritime law; as in England, whose kings, having become dukes of Aquitaine, finally adopted the Roles in their own proper kingdom; and as in Spain, where Alphonso X. gave them the force of law.

In the preceding remarks we have considered the first and most ancient and genuine part of the Roles d'Oleron, as before described. The two articles composing the second part are clearly a French production entirely, and are not of much importance. The third part, consisting of the till lately unpublished eight articles in the Black Book of the English Admiralty, inserted after the twenty-four original articles, obviously belong to England. They appear to have been compiled in the reigns of Richard I. or Henry III.; and the French is thought, by M. Pardessus, to have a resemblance to that of two statutes of the 12th and 49th years of the reign of Edward III.

The fourth part, consisting of twenty-one articles, is found only in the editions of Garcie and Cleirac—no other country than France claims them. They had never been printed till Garcie published them in his Routier de la Mer; and they appear to be written in the language of the sixteenth century.

They treat exclusively of shipwrecks and waifs; they do not contain a single regulation applicable to contracts, or the other transactions of private individuals; and their object is, obviously, quite different from that which gave rise to the compilation not only of the first two parts, but even of the eight articles added in England.

With regard to the doctrines of the primitive articles of this compilation, they are obviously adapted to an early and limited state of maritime commerce; and many of its rules are no longer applicable to the more extended dealings and more enlarged views of later times.

With regard to property in merchant vessels, we find, from the Roles d'Oleron, that part ownership, or joint ownership, was then very frequent; arising, of course, from the scantiness of commercial capital in the hands of single individuals; and we find it laid down as a rule, that, although he could not sell the vessel in a foreign port, without the express authority of the owners, the master might, with the advice of the mariners, impledge the appurtenances of the vessel, in order to raise money for defraying necessary expenses.

With regard, again, to the relative rights and obligations of the owners, and of the persons employed in and connected with the navigation of vessels, we find various regulations and provisions in the laws of Oleron. The powers and duties of the master are detailed at considerable length. The rights and obligations of the owners and master, in relation to third parties, with whom an occasional intercourse takes place during the voyage, are also expounded. The rights of the mariners as to subsistence and wages are explained; and their various duties in loading and unloading the vessel, in the event of shipwreck, and on other similar occasions and emergencies, are pointed out. The duties of pilots, too, are defined; it appears, indeed, that in those early days it had not been unusual for pilots to enter into compacts with the proprietors of the adjacent coasts to share in the profits of shipwrecks which they wilfully occasioned; and to repress this horrible offence, the laws of Oleron enacted a severe and exemplary punishment.

In the Roles d'Oleron the leading principles of the contract of affreightment, or charter party, are likewise distinctly unfolded. The owners and master were held bound to fit out the vessel with sufficient sails, cables, cordage, and other appurtenances. The master and crew were held bound to manage the sails, and to navigate the vessel with skill; and they were held liable for damage sustained through improper stowage, or through negligence in loading or unloading the cargo. If the voyage was interrupted through accidental damage, the owners were held entitled to freight, in proportion to the part of the voyage which had been accomplished. And, if the master either got the vessel soon refitted, or procured another vessel to carry forward the goods to the place of destination, he was held entitled to the full freight. If the vessel was detained through any delay on the part of the merchant, the master was entitled to demand demurrage or compensation for the detention. And, if the master was obliged, from necessity, to borrow money in a foreign port, or to dispose of part of the merchandise on board, the vessel became hypothecated to that extent.

In the Roles d'Oleron the principles of the legal obligation of salvage, or of remuneration for the labour bestowed in saving or recovering goods from the perils of the sea, are likewise distinctly explained. And even the equitable principles by which general average is regulated, and the loss voluntarily incurred for the benefit of the whole, divided among all the parties benefited, appear to have been pretty well understood.

In the Roles d'Oleron we also find traces of the contract of copartnership and joint adventure in the fishing trade. But no mention is made of the contract of marine insurance. There is even nothing explicit on loan on maritime risk, or bottomry and respondentia. At the date of this compilation these beneficial contracts do not appear to have been known, or at least much in use, in the west of Europe. And of bills of exchange we find in this collection no trace whatever.

CHAPTER IV.

OF THE JUDGMENTS OF DAMME, OR LAWS OF WEST CAPELLE, AND OF THE CUSTOMS OF AMSTERDAM.

SECTION I.

Flanders.

IN following, historically and geographically, the progress of maritime law in modern Europe, we proceed from the western and northern coasts of France, and the southern coast of England, to the southern part of the Netherlands, or Low Countries, namely, to Flanders or Belgium.

The fertility of the soil, and the facility of interior communication by navigation, led at an early period —about the tenth century—to the establishment of great fairs in Flanders, and to the cultivation of internal commerce; and in the thirteenth and fourteenth centuries the cities of Bruges and Damme, situated near each other, carried on, from their common sea-port, Sluys, an active and extensive maritime traffic; Flanders thus becoming and serving as an intermediate station and depôt for the southern and the northern countries of Europe.

Such a state of maritime commerce, of course, required regulation, and, like the other nations of Europe, the Flemings or Belgians, before establishing regular digests of laws, appear to have been guided by customs and usages, which several writers have published from manuscripts, under the appellation of Judgments of Damme, or Laws of West Capelle. But, in establishing or recognising these usages, the Flemings appear not to have aimed at anything new, but to have been satisfied with adopting the usages of the neighbouring nations, who had had longer experience in maritime affairs; for these usages are almost a literal copy of the first twenty-four articles of the Roles d'Oleron, the most ancient and best authenticated of that compilation.

Verwer, indeed, a Dutch merchant, in his work entitled, Nederlants See-rechten, published in 1711, and reprinted in 1736, from a mistaken zeal for the glory of his native country, pretends that the Judgments or Decisions of Damme are the more ancient and original compilation, and that the Roles d'Oleron are merely a copy. But for this patriotic pretension there is no foundation; and as no preceding writer had put forth this claim, so it appears to be discountenanced by all subsequent intelligent jurisconsults or historians, such as Van Hall, Meyer, and Schlegel; and M. Pardessus places the matter beyond dispute.

It is a matter of historical fact, that the maritime commerce of Guyenne, Bretagne, and Normandy, whose ports, products, customs, and navigation are indicated in the Roles d'Oleron, was more ancient than that of Flanders, which is admitted by Verwer himself to have flourished only at a later period. He thought, indeed, he had discovered in the manuscript of the Judgments of Damme an article not to be found in the Roles d'Oleron; but even that article exists in the manuscripts of France and England, and in the Castilian translation; and there is in the two compilations not merely a resemblance of ideas, but such a conformity of expression, with the sole difference that, in the Judgments of Damme, the name of Sluys is added to the names of the French ports mentioned in the Roles d'Oleron, and such a literal and complete similitude, that the one must necessarily be held to be the translation of the other. Besides, the compilation itself proves that it could only be made in France, and for the coasts of France. Verwer himself remarks that all the articles relate to the navigation of the west, that is, of the sea beyond the English Channel. Indeed, the chief commerce mentioned in the compilation is in wines, which were not the produce of Flanders; and the sole measure of capacity there referred to is that of *tonneaux*, an expression originally peculiar to the coasts of France, and from which, as Valin observes, has been derived the practice of reckoning the burden of a vessel by tons; whereas the Flemish and Dutch reckon by the *lest* or *last*. Another article, the eighteenth, regulates the subsistence or victualling of mariners, and fixes it differently according as they belong to Bretagne or Normandy; but such a regulation could not be necessary for mariners in the Netherlands or Low Countries; and why insert, in a law made for these countries, rules solely applicable to the coasts of France, and be quite silent as to what should be done in Flanders?

It being thus clear that the Flemings borrowed the Judgments of Damme from the original twenty-four articles of the Roles d'Oleron, it remains to be inquired whether these articles were communicated to Flanders through England, or whether they were taken and received directly from France; and, from the description of the commodities, and the nature of the trade between the countries, as described in the Roles d'Oleron, it rather appears the Flemings derived them directly from France; but at what precise time the introduction took place it is not easy to determine. From the connection between the countries, it may probably have occurred soon after the Roles d'Oleron were committed to writing, in the thirteenth century, and, at all events, during the fourteenth.

The usages of Damme, whether they reached Flanders by way of England or directly from France, could not fail easily to find their way into the neighbouring countries with which the relations of language and commerce placed that city in habitual correspondence; and it is, therefore, not surprising they should have been adopted in Zealand, where they assumed the name of the Laws of West Capelle, and were afterwards published as such by Boxhorn and Van Leuwen; and, accordingly, these articles, with the exception of one, are a literal copy of the Judgments of Damme, and consequently conformable to the Roles d'Oleron.

The knowledge of the articles of the Roles d'Oleron, thus adopted in Flanders and Zealand, was in time extended successively to the different cities on the shores of the Baltic; and they were translated into what was then the language of that country, the Low-German, which, besides, differed little from the Dutch of that time. One of those translations exists in the Dreyerian Museum of Lubec, under the title Van See-rechte. Other translations into Low German are to be found in three manuscripts extant at Hamburgh; one dated 1469, and the others apparently of the writing of the fifteenth century. There is also a Danish translation of these twenty-four articles, combined, as in the Hamburgh manuscripts, with the maritime usages of the northern Low Countries, ascribed by the Danish historians to their kings, John, or Christian II., or Christian III. But to whichever of these princes this compilation be ascribed, it can be held to belong to him only in form, or rather in the subdivision of the articles; for, in fact, it is a literal translation, with the omission of the names of the cities, of the twenty-four articles we have been considering, and of the thirty-four articles we are next to consider.

Section II.

Holland.

From Flanders we proceed to the northern part of the Low Countries, or Holland, and there we find a collection of maritime usages, designated in the different manuscripts as the Customs of Amsterdam, of Enchuysen, of Stavern. Of the series of articles which compose this collection, a number are literal translations, or contain the substance, of those of the Roles d'Oleron, obviously communicated to Holland through Flanders. The greater part contain either general rules, mostly borrowed from the usages of the cities of the Baltic, or merely local regulations. The text almost exclusively designates Amsterdam and the ports of Holland; and while the articles adopted in Flanders referred principally to the navigation of the coasts of England and France, those we are now considering relate to the navigation of the Baltic and Norway.

It is not easy to determine at what precise period these usages were compiled in the state in which we now possess them; but if, according to Verwer, the compilation is to be ascribed to Holland, it is not likely to have taken place earlier than towards the middle of the fifteenth century; for Holland was much behind Flanders in commercial advancement. Indeed, the first attempts at such trade in Holland appear to have been made by the merchants of the Hanse Towns, who perceived the advantage of Holland being made an intermediate station for commerce between the north and south of Europe, in times when navigation had made so little progress, and enjoyed so little security, that people dared not sail directly from the ports of Spain or France to the North Sea. And the Dutch did not attain any extensive commercial prosperity till the sea had opened the passage of the Marsdiep, towards the close of the fourteenth century, so as to admit the large vessels of the west to Amsterdam, and till the wars between France and Flanders, and the northern nations, and the long struggle between Austria and Flanders, had given the Dutch all the advantages of neutral trade, and proved so ruinous to that of their neighbours. Accordingly, it seems only to have been at this time that the Dutch felt it requisite to commit to writing, and adapt to their localities, the maritime usages with which their intercourse with foreigners, particularly the Flemings and Zealanders, and the traders of Lubeck and Hamburgh, had made them acquainted.

But the question still remains, whether the articles we are now considering were originally compiled in the maritime cities of Holland, or belong to a more ancient foreign legislation; and whether, instead of being originals, they are not simply translations? Now, besides several of these articles being literal copies of the Judgments of Damme and the Laws of West Capelle, a superficial perusal shews these maritime usages to be identically the same with the compilation of Wisby, from article thirty-seven to article seventy. And although, in the law of maritime commerce, for the reasons already explained, a mere general resemblance in substance of the regulations would by no means afford a decisive proof of one country having borrowed from another, yet, when a body of maritime laws, containing both general rules and also special arrangements exclusively applicable to one country, is found to have been established in another country, to which these local arrangements are not applicable, there arises a very strong presumption that this body of laws and usages belongs to the country of which the special articles indicate the localities.

The circumstance of the title of Amsterdam, or Enchuysen, being prefixed to the articles, may be equally the result of these articles having been really composed in Holland, or of its maritime towns having borrowed and appropriated them; and, as the articles before specified exist in both compilations, and as in such a parity of conditions the antiquity of possession is naturally a pretty decisive authority, the commercial importance of Wisby being anterior by several centuries to that of Holland, appears to give the preference, in point of originality, to the former. At the same time, without here questioning the very high antiquity hitherto almost universally ascribed, particularly by the northern jurists and historians, to the laws of Wisby, it may be observed that these articles do not (as M. Schlegel supposes) mention Amsterdam and the other ports of Holland as foreign places, but have for their object the special interests of Amsterdam, in providing against accidents which may happen in the harbour of that city, or in the course of navigation to vessels departing from that port; while it is the localities of Norway, and other parts adjacent to Wisby, which receive that designation, since vessels are there spoken of as coming from these countries to Amsterdam. Nay, one of the articles provides that, if the master shall have set sail from the place where he loaded, outward into the Vlie or the Marsdiep, the sailor shall have the whole of his wages—a provision totally inapplicable to Wisby.

M. Schlegel is, no doubt, right in objecting to Verwer that the indication of the localities of Holland is not a completely decisive proof; because, in the middle ages, the countries which borrowed the laws or usages of another substituted in them the names which its own localities required. This kind of argument was employed when it was shewn that the Roles d'Oleron had been borrowed from France by the cities of Damme and West Capelle; but, in the present case, this reasoning would be valid only if in the manuscripts or editions of the compilation of Wisby there should be found, instead of the names of the ports and localities of Holland, names peculiar to Wisby and the Isle of Gothland, of which it was the capital. On that supposition, reasoning by analogy, and taking into consideration that Wisby was a very important commercial entrepôt long before the rise of Holland, we might have some ground for ascribing to Wisby the articles in question. But, in fact, these articles bear solely the names of Amsterdam, Amelande, Vlie, and Marsdiep, not only in the Dutch text, but even in the manuscripts and texts of the compilation of Wisby, and particularly in the most ancient edition, of 1505.

Again, various articles in the compilation of Wisby make provision for vessels entering the Vlie or Marsdiep drawing too much water, (a provision which could never occur to the magistrates of Wisby,) and refer to Amsterdam as the centre city to which the regulations applied.

On the other hand, there was a sort of general assent of the lawyers and writers of Holland in not raising any claim to the articles under consideration, till Verwer did so in 1711; and there is a declaration of the magistrates of Amsterdam, in 1570, that part of the law observed by them was the maritime law of Wisby. But this declaration probably referred to the other articles contained in the compilation of Wisby, viz., to the thirty-six articles which precede, and the two last which follow, those contained in the Dutch compilation.

CHAPTER V.

OF THE MARITIME AND COMMERCIAL LAWS OF WISBY.

THE compilation known under the title Hogheste Water-Recht de Wisby, (the Supreme Maritime Law of Wisby,) has been represented, by the greatest part of the jurisconsults and historians of the north, as the most ancient monument of maritime law of the middle ages, and as the source of the primitive or earliest part of the Roles d'Oleron. But M. Pardessus has shewn, by a very learned and elaborate train of critical argument, that this long and generally entertained opinion has but a very slender foundation in historical fact: and it may be worth while shortly to notice his argument.

He begins with shewing that the maritime laws of Wisby, to which Leibnitz refers and erroneously ascribes an old date, the reign of the Emperor Lotharius, about the twelfth century, is not the Hogheste Water-Recht we are now considering, but a compilation entitled Wisby Stadt-Lag pa Gotland, (the Laws of the City of Wisby, in Gothland,) published by Hadorph in 1676-1687; which appears to have been compiled and promulgated under the authority of Magnus, the son of Erick, in the early part of the fourteenth century, and which contains, in the third part of Book III., a considerable number of regulations in maritime law. And having established this point, M. Pardessus proceeds to inquire whether, prior or subsequent to the code just described, the city of Wisby had any maritime legislation, the same as we possess under the title of Hogheste Water-Recht.

In the priority, in point of antiquity, claimed for the

laws of Wisby over all the other maritime laws which have succeeded the Roman law in Europe, Grotius, Kuricke, Loccenius, Arpe, Bynkershoek, Langenbeck, all concurred; Westerveen alone raised any doubts, until Verwer appeared, who maintains that all the articles, except the first twelve, are nothing but the Judgments of Damme and the maritime usages of Holland. The later writers, Fischer, in his History of German Commerce, and Benecke, in his Treatise on Insurance, likewise recognise the high antiquity of the laws of Wisby as an incontestible fact: nay, even royal and legislative documents, such as the charter to the town of Husum, and the maritime code of Sweden, of 1667, sanction the same opinion. But the framers of laws are not, in matters of historical fact, and in assertions upon a point of literary antiquity, more exempt from error than private individual writers. Whatever be the number of authorities, they must yield to the evidence of facts; and M. Pardessus ventures to affirm that no historical monument, no manuscript, no print of the compilation, either by its own date or by connection with or reference to more ancient manuscripts, furnishes the slightest indication which can (proof being out of the question) even afford a presumption of the antiquity which the writers before mentioned assume and take for granted: in short, all those writers who maintain this high antiquity confine themselves to allegations successively copied, so that each avails himself of, and founds his assertion upon, that of his predecessor; and the first, who is thus the source of the subsequent opinions, has no other authority than his own.

The very existence of the code entitled Wisby Stadt-Lag, which, we have seen, was promulgated under sovereign authority in the course of the fourteenth century, and which proves the existence of previous legislation, affords a strong argument against the great antiquity assigned to the compilation we are now considering: for it is highly probable that all that this code contains of rules in maritime law, previously existed in the shape either of positive enactment or of usages practised for a long period. But if the maritime law observed in the city of Wisby, before the composition of the Stadt-Lag, had consisted of what, at this day, composes the compilation known by the title of the Laws of Wisby, how does it happen that this authoritative code should differ from that compilation in a manner so remarkable? How should more than three-fourths of the regulations contained in this alleged more ancient compilation not be found in the code, nor be even therein referred to? Such an omission would form a singular contrast with the desire of improvement manifested to so great an extent even in this very code.

But passing over, as not quite decisive, the argument urged by Selden against the theory which would ascribe to the compilation of Wisby a greater antiquity than the Roles d'Oleron—namely, that before 1266 Wisby was of too little importance to have a peculiar legislation of its own, having been only then erected into a city and surrounded with walls—an attentive examination and critical discussion of the different articles of the compilation itself appear sufficient to refute the erroneous opinion so long entertained. The articles, from thirteen to thirty-six inclusive, are literally conform to the twenty-four primitive articles in the Roles d'Oleron, or Judgments of Damme. But it was not till the fourteenth century that commercial relations were formed between France and the inhabitants of the shores of the Baltic, in consequence of which the latter were known under the name of Ostirlings, not only in historical monuments but in those of legislation. The thirty-seventh and following articles indicate the commerce of Holland and Amsterdam, which, as we have seen, was not anterior to the fourteenth century; and in particular designate the Marsdiep, which was not formed till about the year 1400.

Nor can the difficulty be solved or eluded by supposing that the places, of which the designation carries us necessarily to the fourteenth or even fifteenth century, may have been added as an after-work in the countries which might have borrowed the maritime legislation of Wisby; for there does not exist one single solitary Low-German copy of the compilation, whether in print or manuscript, in which the same names are not found. And there thence results a degree of probability, equivalent to the only attainable certainty in such matters, that the compilation called Hogheste Water-Recht, whoever may have been its authors, is not anterior to the fourteenth century.

Such was the opinion of M. Schlegel:—"The march of commerce," says he, "proves, if I am not mistaken, that the Laws of Wisby are more modern than the other two codes of maritime law, the Consolato del Mare and the Roles d'Oleron." "It is pretended that the city of Wisby was founded and began to flourish after Jonsberg was destroyed by the King of Denmark, Waldemar I., surnamed the Great, in 1158: but it is probable that its commerce was not very extensive before the Hanse Towns had there formed establishments. If the body of laws was originally in Low-German, as cannot be doubted, and not in the language of the country, it is thereby proved that the Hanseatic merchants and seafaring people had the greatest share in its compilation."

Although, however, this compilation should have no claim to the high antiquity ascribed to it by the authors before mentioned—although, in particular, it is not probable that it is anterior to the code composed under the authority of Magnus Ericksen, at the commencement of the fourteenth century—it would not necessarily follow that there was not composed at Wisby a code at a more recent date. It is not unreasonable, or out of the circle of probabilities, that some legislative or high administrative authority in the city of Wisby may have recognised the necessity of farther unfolding the maritime regulations contained in the Stadt-Lag, and that the feeling of this necessity may have given birth to the compilation known under the title of Hogheste Water-Recht. The insufficiency of the former may have been supplied by the latter, as the Hanse Towns substituted for their maritime law of 1591 that of 1614. There is nothing impossible in this: but a possibility is not a fact; and since the question is a point of historical research, it is with facts, or at least with the monuments by which they are ascertained, that we have to do, and by them we must abide. And no historical testimony informs us, directly or indirectly, at what period or by whom such a new maritime law was or might have been compiled at Wisby.

But not only does this compilation belong to other times than those conjecturally supposed—it may also be proved that it has had its origin in other places, and that we cannot, without a violation of the rules of evidence, consider it as made at Wisby, or for that city.

All the manuscripts and editions present, under the general title Hogheste Water-Recht, two distinct pieces, designated each by a peculiar rubric. The first, composed of thirty-six articles, bears the title, "Here begins the supreme, or very excellent maritime law." After article thirty-six, and at the head of the remainder of the compilation, there is another rubric:—"Here the ordinances which the mariners and the shipmasters have made among themselves;" and after this second rubric there are the words, "In the first place."

Upon inspection, then, there are exhibited as a whole,

announced as an unique and entire composition, two distinct parts; and this circumstance alone is sufficient, of itself, to raise well-founded doubts with regard to the legislative character wished to be attributed to the whole compilation. For if it was a law, a regulation, or even usage, composed under the auspices of public authority, there would not have been inserted, or allowed to exist, a division into two fragments, each under its peculiar title, each treating of the same matters in terms sometimes identical in phraseology, and almost always so in the sense.

If we examine these two divisions separately, we find the first, in its turn, composed of two series of articles, of which the features are quite different. In the first twelve articles there is no mention of any port of Wisby, or of the country of which it was a dependency. All the places named in these articles are those of the opposite coast of the Baltic; and even these places belong exclusively to the territory of Lubeck. In the thirteenth and following articles, as little mention is made of the port of Wisby, or of the country of which it is a part; almost all the ports and places mentioned belong to France; two or three times the name of Sluys, and once the name of Lisbon, are added.

No one can deny that there is in this something very strange and odd, of which it is necessary to search for and explain the cause; for it would be supposing great credulity indeed in readers to ascribe this singularity to chance, or the inadvertence of the authors. It is evident that, if the first half were one sole and entire composition, the ports mentioned in the first twelve articles would also be those mentioned in the others. The events provided for in most of these articles are not special or peculiar to such and such ports; they may occur in any navigation whatever, and whatever may be the destination of the vessel.

But while it is difficult to comprehend and explain this strange and extraordinary fact according to the theory which would consider the first half, and still more the whole, of the compilation as one sole and entire work, everything is easily explained when we recognise sources foreign to Wisby, from which have been derived the articles of the first part.

Now, the first twelve articles of the compilation we are considering are literally identical with an equal number of articles in the most ancient codes of Lubeck. Verwer, indeed, pretends that these twelve articles are the primitive and genuine law of Wisby, and Schlegel seems favourable to that opinion; but what was formerly said of the real and genuine law of Wisby, such as it is found in the Stadt-Lag, seems sufficient to refute that opinion, and the comparison of these articles with the codes of Lubeck will remove all doubt. For if it be pretended that Lubeck borrowed these articles from Wisby, merely changing the names of the places, it is plain that those who drew up the compilation of Wisby, if it was really the law of that city, would never have adopted these changes; they had, and could have, no reason or inducement for substituting for their own proper localities those of another country; and yet all the manuscript copies, all the prints, even the Princeps edition of 1505, indicate merely the localities of Lubeck.

Besides, by what strange singularity would these articles, if they had been originally composed at Wisby, contain rules for the police of the harbour and port of Lubeck, without saying a single word of Wisby, while the code Stadt-Lag contains such rules precisely for the port and shores of that city? To suppose the articles in question to have been originally framed at Wisby, would be a violation of the most simple rules of legislation.

Let the same mode of discussion be now applied to

the thirteenth and following articles, which form the remainder of what has been called the first fragment. Upon a careful perusal it will be found that, with the exception of some names of cities, of which none belong to the country in which Wisby is situated, these articles literally correspond with as many articles of the Roles d'Oleron; and the conclusion is, that they have not been, and could not be, originally composed at Wisby.

If we suppose France borrowed these articles from Wisby, we must assume frequent and extensive commercial intercourse to have existed at the same time between the north of the Baltic Sea and the west of France, by means of which that kingdom might have received the maritime laws in question, and transmitted them to England and Spain—which is contradicted by the history of commerce. It is, besides, quite incredible that the framers of a law made at Wisby should be exclusively occupied with what passed at Bordeaux or Rochelle to such a degree that the names of the places referred to should be those of the coasts of France, not places peculiar to, or immediately adjacent to or connected with, Wisby. Upon these grounds we may therefore conclude that the first of the two principal divisions, of which it is evident the Hogheste Water-Recht is composed, does not belong to Wisby.

The examination of the second division furnishes the same arguments. Like the first, it presents two parts. The one is composed of the articles from thirty-seven to seventy, which are identical with the laws or customs of Amsterdam, of Enchuysen, of Stavern, or maritime usages of the northern Netherlands, which we have already considered, and which, from a discussion of the terms of the articles themselves, as well as from the text of two manuscripts of Lubeck, we ascertained were composed in and for Holland, and could not have been framed elsewhere, or for any other country. The second part is composed of two articles, of which we find the text in the ancient codes of Lubeck; and not only are the city of Wisby and the ports and seas bordering upon it not once named in these two articles, they also carry with them the demonstration that they could not have been framed at Wisby, but, on the contrary, must have been composed in a country situated diametrically opposite to Wisby.

From what precedes, we must conclude that the compilation, Hogheste Water-Recht, is not so ancient as the authors before mentioned pretend; and, secondly, that it does not constitute the proper maritime law of Wisby, which is to be found in the third book of Wisby Stadt-Lag. Nevertheless, for more than three centuries this compilation has existed in the state in which we possess it, and under the title which it bears at this day. It is, therefore, of itself an ancient monument, and consequently it may be worth while to inquire where, when, and how it has been compiled.

In the *first* place, it appears, we must reject the hypothesis which would consider this compilation as made under any sovereign or public authority. The rubrics, initial, intermediate, and final, which it bears, announce nothing of the kind, and even prove the reverse, since we find in it the words "Laws or Regulations made by the Mariners, Shipowners, and Shipmasters." A legislator, or even a magistrate, who establishes a law or regulation, uniformly gives it a title from his own name or official character; he never employs, at the commencement or end, expressions which are appropriate only to an historian who narrates, or to a copyist who transcribes.

In the *second* place, among the hypotheses which may be formed, two only appear to have any probability, and both may be founded upon incontestible facts, namely, that Wisby was a port to which resorted the seafaring people of all the northern and western countries of Europe, particularly from the coasts of the Baltic, of Holland, of Flanders, of England and Scotland, of France, and even of Spain, as historians attest; and that these strangers had there obtained the privilege of observing their own proper laws, as several historical documents prove.

Now it may be supposed that the merchants and traders of these different nations, whose maritime laws rested upon the same principles, may have compiled a body of common law, for the composition of which each had in a manner furnished his contingent—namely, the different collections of articles we have last considered in succession, beginning with the Roles d'Oleron; and that this joint compilation may have formed the maritime law of the foreigners resorting to Wisby, and may have been ultimately followed, as written reason and as a supplement to their local law, by the magistrates of Wisby when they decided such disputes among their fellow-citizens or subjects. But this hypothesis is scarcely admissible; for, first, it has been established that this compilation could not have been anterior to the fifteenth century, and it cannot be denied that by that time the great prosperity of Wisby had disappeared, and its commerce had passed to Dantzic and the other Hanseatic cities, which had their proper laws, forming the common law of almost all the towns admitted into the confederacy. Again, such an agreement among the merchants of the north, centre, and west of Europe, to establish for themselves a common law, could not fail to be attended with great difficulty. Such a compilation, too, although made by skilful persons, from usages, being without any public character, would not have afforded any actual sanction, or such binding force, as could alone impart to the work the utility which must have been expected from it—an agreement among the different governments could alone attain this object: and such an agreement, which the more civilized condition of Europe does not permit us to hope even at this day to see realized, was manifestly impracticable during the times to which we must refer it.

Farther, a perusal of the compilation itself renders the supposition before made still less probable. A compilation made by an assemblage of delegates of merchants and seafaring people would have had, at least, some of the characteristics of unity. We should not have found out one series of articles indicating exclusively certain localities, another indicating different localities, a third repeating neither the first nor the second indications. Although compiled by the concurrence of a number of men of experience, it might not have exhibited a methodical arrangement or a high degree of perfection, which our more modern laws themselves have not always attained; but the imperfections in it would not have been so gross as to introduce regulations absolutely opposed to the state and condition of the places, and often contradictory; as to repeat two or even three times the same regulations, sometimes in the same terms, sometimes with a slight variation; or as to exhibit under one title, and a common conclusion, two fragments, which have each their proper title, and which we are obliged to recognise as two separate and distinct compositions. Upon these grounds we must rather adopt the alternative hypothesis, and believe that the compilation was the work of private individuals. And it is not difficult to perceive how, in this way, such a compilation may have come to be made. The usages followed in the southern Netherlands under the name of Judgments of Damme and West Capelle, whatever may have been their origin, and those followed in the northern Netherlands under the name of the usages of Amsterdam, were evidently known to the navigators of the Baltic. From the thirteenth century, Lubeck and Hamburgh had mercantile establishments in Flanders. At the outset they there enjoyed a jurisdiction over their own countrymen, as a charter of 1349, of which Dreyer has published the text, attests. Subsequently, the sovereigns of that country, in granting different immunities to German merchants, obliged them to recognise the local jurisdiction and laws:—"Standum est consuetudini, et terræ nostræ legi." These German merchants had thus an interest to know these laws; and, to know them, they behoved to translate them into their native language. This appears to explain how a translation into Low-German of the twenty-four articles adopted in the southern Netherlands, under the name of the Judgments of Damme, is found in the manuscript in the Dreyerian Museum of Lubeck; why the manuscripts of Hamburgh contain the same twenty-four articles, followed by the usages of the northern Netherlands; why these Low-German versions, though they quite correspond in the sense, differ in the expressions; and, finally, why these manuscripts are not entitled the Maritime Law of Wisby.

Different causes, all equally probable, could not fail to carry to Wisby a collection of maritime usages which were practised in Flanders and Holland. The Germans settled in Wisby formed, in a manner, a national body; and had even obtained the extraordinary privilege that the senate and the public authorities should be equally divided between them and the natives; and they may have carried thither copies of the translations just referred to. The seafaring people of Flanders and Holland, whose commercial intercourse with Wisby is attested by the Stadt-Lag, and who, in the fourteenth century, having detached themselves from the Hanseatic League, formed a body corporate, the rival of that association, must also, for the decision of their disputes, and the regulation of their private transactions agreeably to the privileges granted them by the sovereigns of these countries, have carried these usages to Wisby in their own language, which differed little from the Low-German.

Some possessor of a manuscript of these maritime usages, perceiving that they had not provided for certain cases regulated by the maxims scattered through the copies of the codes of Lubeck, which were in circulation long before the official compilation of 1586, may have made an extract from these codes for the use of the Germans, and have added this extract to the two series before described.

According to this hypothesis there is no longer any difficulty either in explaining the double use, in the compilation of Wisby, of articles so literally alike that, although consisting of seventy-two articles, it has not in reality more than fifty different from one another, or in reconciling the antinomies. For what would be strange and odd, and a great imperfection, in a single code forming one whole, has nothing extraordinary or absurd in a collection of distinct pieces, independent of each other and composed in different countries.

The most ancient copy that has reached us of this compilation, formed in the manner just described, is the edition published at Copenhagen in 1505, during the first years of the introduction of printing into that country. When or how the compilation, formed in the manner supposed, received the appellation of the Maritime Law of Wisby, it is not easy to determine. What is certain is, that the edition of 1505 bears, as its sole title, Her beghynt dat Hogheste Water-Recht; and that it is only at the end we read, "Hyr eyndet dat Gothlansche Water-Recht, dat de gemeyne Kopmann unn Schippers geordineret unn gemaket hebben to Wisby." The Copenhagen editor may have been the author of this notice or advertisement; and, as it is not easy to see he could have any inducement to give a false title, although such things were frequent in the early times of printing, he may have added this notice in good faith, or ignorance of the real maritime law of Wisby contained in the Stadt-Lag, composed under King Magnus, and in the belief that a series of articles in maritime law coming from Wisby, and composed in a language not less in use at Wisby than the native language, behoved to belong to that city, whose laws, generally, had long enjoyed a high reputation in northern countries. This denomination, whether the result of deception or credulity, may have been easily adopted by those who afterwards made manuscript copies, or printed editions, of the compilation. And the indication of the name of Wisby, originally put by the first printer at the end of the edition, may have been inserted by others in the title itself.

Marquard, in 1662, published a translation of the whole compilation into German, from one of the Dutch versions, in his work De Jure Mercatorum et Commerciorum. Engelbrecht has also given a German translation, in his Corpus Juris Nautici, from the Dutch edition of Verwer. And Hàdorph, in 1689, published a Swedish translation from the edition printed at Copenhagen in 1505. A translation (not literal) or abridgment of these laws has also been published by Cleirac, in his Us et Coutumes de la Mer, in the collection entitled Biblioteca di Gius Nautico, and in the fifth volume of the treatise of Baldasseroni, Delle Assicurazioni Marittime.

Having thus, perhaps, at too great length, accompanied M. Pardessus in his investigation of the compilation so long known by the name of the Laws of Wisby—having been convinced, by his acute critical examination, that the high antiquity claimed for these laws by a long series of northern jurists, historians, and antiquarians, is unwarranted, and even contradicted by the contents of the compilation itself, when accurately and impartially examined—we have only briefly to notice the legal doctrines it propounds.

With respect to property in vessels; joint ownership; preference on the vessel for repairs; hypothec on the vessel, for provisions furnished in a foreign port; relative rights and obligations of the persons employed in the navigation and management of the vessel; general average, or contribution to defray a loss incurred for the good of the vessel and cargo—the laws of Wisby contain detailed regulations, applicable to the state of maritime commerce in those ages, so far identical with and similar in general to what we have seen to be the regulations of the Roles d'Oleron. Further, it has been thought some faint traces may be discovered of a more improved and extended state of the law of maritime commerce in the compilation ascribed to Wisby, than in that of Oleron. Thus M. Emérigon remarks—" In article forty-five of the Ordinance of Wisby, mention is made of the Contrat à la Grosse Avanture, and in article sixty-six, of sureties given for the vessel, Cautions Baillées pour le Navire; from which it is seen that the contract of maritime insurance began to be introduced into commerce under the form and denomination of bail or suretyship, and that the practice of maritime insurance is, therefore, much more ancient than Stypmannus, Giballinus, Ansaldus, and Casaregis have believed." But the texts referred to seem scarcely sufficient to warrant the conclusions thus rather rashly drawn; and it is more safe to rest upon the authentic evidence afforded by the ordinance of the magistrates of Barcelona, in 1435, which establishes that this very important maritime contract had been in use for some time previous to that date.

CHAPTER VI.

OF THE MARITIME AND COMMERCIAL LAW OF THE HANSE TOWNS.

We now proceed with our view of the march of maritime commerce, from the small communities of the south, west, and centre, to those situated in the north of Europe, so far as necessary to trace the effect of such advancement in maritime commerce upon that department of jurisprudence among these northern states.

In the course of the twelfth, thirteenth, and fourteenth centuries, we find assemblages of industrious and active people, in towns situated on the coasts of the North Sea and Baltic, adopting similar schemes of maritime legislation to those we formerly contemplated in the cities situated on the coasts of the Mediterranean. The same causes which gave rise to the codes we have already considered, appear to have operated also in the production of similar bodies of maritime law in the north. Indeed, from the commencement of the period just alluded to, a number of the Hanseatic cities, particularly the maritime cities of northern Germany, had, as we have already seen, established at Wisby a sort of colony, composed almost entirely of their merchants; and this city was a general entrepôt for their commerce with the neighbouring provinces, and with Prussia, Livonia, and Russia. Such a state of civilisation and improvement in navigation and commerce was not, perhaps, sufficient to account for, and we have just seen did not give rise to, the native production of what has erroneously been called the Laws of Wisby; and the absolute identity, in most particulars, and very strong resemblance in almost all, to the earlier compilations of the south and west, distinctly prove that in their maritime legislation the trading cities of the North Sea and of the Baltic profited by the experience of those of the west of France and of the Netherlands, if not also of the Mediterranean. The probability of this conclusion, too, is strengthened by the consideration that, in the twelfth and thirteenth centuries, the great communication between the Baltic and the Mediterranean coasts was opened, the inhabitants of the south having then begun, to a considerable extent, to exchange the more luxurious products of their climate for the coarser but equally useful commodities of the north. Such an intercourse, in which so many different claims and such opposite interests were involved, could not long subsist without recourse to some standard by which commercial and nautical controversies might be adjusted. The salutary effects of the consuetudinary sea laws, already prevalent in the south, must have strongly recommended them to the notice of a rising nation of mariners, comparatively destitute of civil or commercial maxims; and the spirit of universal equity by which the maritime codes of the south and west were characterized, rendered them equally applicable for the decision of nautical questions in the Gulf of Finland as in the Gulf of Venice.

The next general maritime code, in the order of time, is that of the Hanse Towns. The association of these towns appears to have commenced in the earlier part of the thirteenth century, and for more than 300 years it was a most formidable maritime confederacy. This extensive and permanent league of so many independent trading cities, scattered over the distant territories of so many sovereigns, is a singular and interesting phenomenon in the history of modern Europe; but the rise and progress, the prosperity and grandeur, the decline and fall of the Hanseatic Confederacy, may all be traced in the peculiar circumstances in which the nations of the north of Europe were then placed.

After the northern nations, who conquered the provinces of the Western Empire, had settled in these provinces, and, united with the ancient population, presented a warlike barrier sufficiently strong to repel the incursions of succeeding tribes, the latter behoved either to return to their former abodes or to occupy the more northern countries which had been, so far, deserted; and centuries of almost incessant intestine wars and commotions appear to have elapsed before regular, extensive, and strong governments were established. It was only by individuals and families congregating in towns, that a large portion of the population could find any security against the depredations of anarchy, or any alleviation of the rigour of feudal domination. Manufacturing industry in some towns, navigation and trade in others, became the occupation of the inhabitants, and in time enabled them to accumulate wealth sufficient to purchase from their respective—generally distant, and frequently needy—sovereigns, extensive commercial privileges, and the valuable right of being in a great measure governed by themselves. In times when the sea offered little security, when communication by land was exposed to difficulties and dangers of every kind, necessity multiplied the associations of individual merchants and traders for their common defence. The example thus set by individuals appears, in time, to have taught the cities and towns the benefit which they might derive from substituting for the accidental and transient engagements of individuals the permanent union of their collective force as communities. The friendly intercourse consequent upon such associations among these independent states, led them to grant to each other reciprocal commercial advantages, by exemptions or deductions from fiscal duties, and also to communicate to each other the enjoyment of the advantages they obtained in the less civilized countries to which the operations of their commerce extended. It was necessary in such countries to defend each other against pillage, oppressive customs, and vexatious exactions; and whatever particular profit might afterwards accrue from it to individuals, it was the interest of all to act in concert, and mutually to support each other.

From these causes, and in this manner, various successive associations, called Hansen, appear to have been formed among the different cities and towns situated on the coasts of the German Ocean and of the Baltic, in the course of the thirteenth century, embracing, at first, only a few cities and towns, but gradually extending in number and importance, until they were ultimately consolidated into one grand confederacy, under the appellation of the Hanseatic League. At first, the object of the confederacy was not at all warlike, further than self-defence implied and required. In time, however, the confederacy was extended and strengthened. A large mercantile navy afforded the basis, and naturally led to the establishment, of a warlike navy. Their views were no longer confined merely to self-defence; and they perceived that their commercial aggrandisement might be materially promoted by their naval power. Ignorant of the power consequent upon the accumulation of commercial wealth, the great European sovereigns and governments of these ages did not foresee, or were at first indifferent to, the ascendancy which these trading cities gradually acquired in their territories; and they continued, from time to time, to grant them privileges and monopolies, apparently either from the opinion that such commerce could not otherwise be equally well carried on, or from viewing favourably the admission of their subjects into the confederation, in order that, being thereby enriched, they might pay the taxes imposed on them more easily, and increase the prosperity of the country, until at last it became difficult and even dangerous to dispute with these cities the privileges they had thus acquired. In the fifteenth and sixteenth centuries, which may be considered as the period of its glory, the Hanseatic League comprised seventy-two separate states, was divided into four circles or districts, and commanded a sea coast of more than 1200 miles. A regular form of government was established; magistrates and other officers, with their respective tribunals, were appointed; a public treasury was formed; and the union of the whole confederacy was connected by the strongest political obligations. Enjoying such advantages, the League for a long period almost monopolized the trade of the north; and, preserving its treaties and alliances inviolate, it bore a considerable share, and acted a distinguished part, in the public affairs and transactions of Europe.

It is here worth while to stop and remark, with M. Pardessus, how, in situations if not exactly similar, at least analogous, the commercial cities of the north should have presented a spectacle so different from that exhibited by those of the south of Europe. The cities which divided among themselves the commerce of the Mediterranean were in an almost perpetual state of hostility with each other: neither that sea, where they held dominion, nor Asia and Africa, whose commerce they carried on, nor Europe, which they supplied with commodities, sufficed for their avidity of gain and love of domination: each desired to have alone and exclusively the honour and the profit of every great enterprise. On the coasts of the northern seas numerous commercial cities also arose; but no one aspired, at least by force of arms, to pre-eminence over the others; the common interests of navigation, the desire, no doubt immoderate, of domination, in all the countries to which access was open to them, guided and animated them: but no one pretended to destroy the commerce of the other; they considered themselves all as the members of one family, which must be made to triumph in every place, and at any price: but the triumph behoved to be for all; and their union against the common enemy was not disturbed by the pretensions of any one to raise itself upon the ruin of its rivals.

Although powerful for ages, however, the league of so many small and only partially independent states, within the territories of sovereigns and governments, controlling and supported by the great mass of the population of these countries, was an unnatural connection, and could not last longer than the peculiar and extraordinary causes which had given rise to it continued to operate. Composed of a great number of towns, whose limited municipal districts formed the whole territory of the confederation, and which were separated by vast kingdoms, upon which they were so far dependent, the League could not continue permanently to constitute a central authority sufficiently strong to deserve the appellation of a national government. And towards the end of the fifteenth, and still more, in the course of the sixteenth century, circumstances materially changed. Many of the sovereigns of the kingdoms in which the cities of the League were situated became jealous of its prosperity, viewed with dissatisfaction the accession of their cities to the confederation, and came to behold in it an invasion of their own sovereignty, as it was all along the policy of the League to withdraw its members from any jurisdiction which did not emanate from itself. The different nations, to whom the League had for a long time furnished the greatest part of the articles of commerce, began to procure those articles themselves, either by their own manufacturing industry or by importing them in their own vessels. The interests of the relatively foreign or more distant maritime cities, and of the inland cities of the League, came to be so far disunited. The maritime states, by their vessels and their banks, had furnished to the inland cities the means of selling with profit the produce of their industry in the countries to the west, to the north, and to the east of the Baltic. But when the different separate nations came to carry on, in their own vessels, a great part of this commerce, the inland cities had no longer the same interest to remain united with the foreign maritime cities; they found that this union would in future be more burdensome to them than useful; and the greatest part of them renounced it, and determined to pay no further contribution to the confederacy. The great European governments, too, became gradually more enlightened with regard to their own interest and that of their subjects: and, while the principal cities of their dominions withdrew from the League, they excluded the carrying trade, to which the confederacy owed so much of its wealth. In fine, the prosperity of the Hanse Towns had gradually awakened the jealousy and excited the envy of their neighbours; their arrogance, and occasional abuse of power, contributed to inflame it. The result was a combination against them, which gradually effected their ruin; and, in 1630, the members themselves announced the dissolution of the League, by none of the cities sending their representatives to the General Diet which had been convoked at Lubeck, except to notify the resolution which each had taken to abandon it.

This dissolution of the confederacy, however, proved so far beneficial to some of its parts. The cities of Hamburgh and Lubeck, in particular, gained in opulence what they had lost in power. Finding themselves no longer at the head of an ambitious League, which had enabled them to exercise a kind of commercial despotism over their neighbours, they adopted milder maxims of trade; and contenting themselves with the peaceful interchange of commodities, preserved, with a recent temporary interruption, their liberties and political independence.

The association of so many great trading maritime cities, situated in different kingdoms and provinces, which we have just been contemplating, was obviously calculated to lead to the adoption of some common system of maritime jurisprudence. Notwithstanding their very extensive commerce, however, it was not till a late period of the League that the Hanse Towns compiled or promulgated any general code of maritime law. The causes, before alluded to, which ultimately led to the dissolution of the League, account also for the long delay in its maritime and commercial legislation. It was, besides, obviously very difficult to unite, in one single measure, a body composed of so many disparate members. All were united when the object was commerce, by which they subsisted, and which they had all an equal interest in maintaining and extending, as the means of enriching themselves; then the advantages of one uniform direction were duly appreciated; but when success had enfeebled or extinguished that feeling, local self-interested views resumed their influence. The smaller states, led by their interest to form an alliance with the more powerful, but secretly jealous of the preponderance of the latter, were disposed to consider their own independence compromised, if they had abdicated their legislative power by submitting without reserve to laws, in matters of private right, emanating from the assemblies of the confederation, in which the great cities exercised almost the whole authority. And the result was, that, in this department, the acts of the congress were not so much laws as counsels given to each city, to invite it to adopt what had appeared useful or advantageous.

In these circumstances, the first care and chief objects of the administrators of the confederacy were, to give it consistency, to extend its commerce, and to unite, in one and the same interest, the cities already connected with each other by particular association. And, accordingly, its first legislation appears to have regarded the organisation, the political constitution, and government of the League. But any detail on that subject would be foreign to the plan of this historical sketch, although greatly facilitated by the recent history of the League by Sartorius.* And, before proceeding to its individual or private maritime and commercial jurisprudence, we may merely mark the spirit of its public or constitutional legislation.

Every Hanseatic citizen who, being resident in one of the factories abroad, there contracted marriage with a stranger, forfeited his political status as such. No Hanseatic merchant could enter into a commercial copartnership with strangers. In the Hanseatic cities, sales could not take place between two persons of whom neither was a member of the confederation ; which law forced foreigners to employ the latter as intermediate agents in all the pieces of business they had to transact. Grain, coming from the Elbe and the Vistula, could not be transported to other countries if it was not despatched in a vessel cleared out from a Hanseatic city. And there were, also, several maritime regulations dictated by the same spirit of monopoly, and founded on an exclusive commercial system.

Although, however, the political legislation of the confederacy, from the causes before alluded to, preceded much their united legislation in matters of mari-

* Geschichte des Hanseatischen Bundes. 3 vols. 1802–1808.

time commerce, it came, in the course of time, to be felt that, although the greater part of the confederated states had each their peculiar legislation, embracing, of course, maritime and commercial regulations, there would be great expediency in the general adoption, by all the different states, of common and uniform rules in this important department of jurisprudence. And, towards the close of the fourteenth century, the confederated cities appear to have undertaken the task of composing an uniform body of laws; of which their peculiar statutes, especially that which Hamburgh and Lubeck adopted, in almost identical terms, in 1276 and 1299, had laid the foundation. The first Recessus, or ordinance, enacted by the congress on private maritime law, now extant, is not earlier than 1369. But it was chiefly in the fifteenth and sixteenth centuries, and even in the beginning of the seventeenth, that the League was particularly occupied with private maritime legislation, and began to digest it into a body of legal doctrine. A series of short enactments, by the Hanseatic congress, of this description, including that of 1369, and extending to 1591, have been printed by M. Pardessus from manuscripts recently recovered at Hamburgh, by M. Lappenberg, along with the more important ordinances of 1591 and 1614. These two last constitute the great and improved body of Hanseatic maritime legislation. And, in particular, the Recessus of 1614, which was drawn up by the Syndic Domann, who was charged with the task by the congress in 1608, has been, since its date, known and generally cited as the Jus Maritimum Hanseaticum, and was printed in German at Hamburgh in 1657 by Kuricke, with a Latin translation and a commentary, and reprinted in the collection, by Heineccius, entitled Scriptorum de Jure Nautico et Maritimo fasciculus. The matters are there distributed into a great number of articles, classed under fifteen titles or chapters; and, although fundamentally the same, with a few improvements, it is certainly much better arranged and digested than the former compilation.

With regard to the contents of this code, it gives a fuller detail than the Roles d'Oleron, the Judgments of Damme and West Capelle, or the Usages of Amsterdam, or the collection formerly ascribed to Wisby, of the legal and equitable principles which regulate the acquisition and transference of property in vessels, absolute and limited; the mutual interests and duties of part and joint owners; the claims and security arising from the repairs and furnishings made in a home or in a foreign port; the reciprocal duties, powers, and rights of the owners, master, mate, pilot, and crew of the vessel, in relation to navigation, stowage, and wages; the relative rights and obligations of the parties to the contract of affreightment; agreements of reciprocal aid in voyages; the doctrine of damage from collision, of salvage and average, and the doctrine of bottomry and respondentia. But although the contract of bottomry obviously implies an acquaintance with the theory of maritime risks, the contract of marine insurance is not once alluded to. In the words of Kuricke, "Conditores juris maritimi Hanseatici, materiam assecurationis, sicco plane pede, præterierunt." And this renders still more doubtful the conjecture of M. Emérigon, that the caution or security, referred to in the compilation ascribed to Wisby, was the commencement or germ of the contract of insurance. At the same time it is probable that, towards the end of the sixteenth century, and consequently before the promulgation of the Recessus of 1614, this contract was known in those cities of the League where commercial intercourse with the maritime cities of the Mediterranean could scarcely fail to teach them its use. Or, perhaps, as remarked by M. Pardessus, the hazardous character of the contract of insurance did not suit the cautious and plodding spirit which guided the legislation of the League ; and its influential leaders may have seen in the transactions of insurance only a great innovation, of which the advantages were still not sufficiently developed to admit of any attempt to subject them to positive rules, and of which the conditions behoved in each case to be regulated by special contract.

From the time of its formation, the confederacy exerted itself, with great energy, to obtain an abolition of the unjust law which, in almost all the European kingdoms, confiscated shipwrecked goods ; and we find, in some of its Recessus, provisions relative to the aid to be given in cases of shipwreck, relative to the precautions to be taken against pirates, and relative to the recovery of goods captured by the enemy, but no legislation relative to neutrals.

With regard to the transactions of commerce generally, the enactments of the League attest the importance in which it held fidelity in the execution of mercantile engagements, without which there cannot exist any true or genuine credit. He who, having borrowed in one city of the confederacy, did not pay his debt, or who, having lent money upon pledges in security, carried off what his debtor had thus intrusted to him, forfeited the status of a Hanseatic citizen. A debtor, excluded from one of the confederated cities on account of his debts, could not find an asylum in any other of these cities. The bankrupt, whose flight had been advertised, with a description of his person, behoved to be arrested wherever he could be found, and, if fraudulent, exposed in public, loaded with irons, if not punished with death.

The Recessus of the League also contained numerous regulations relative to fidelity in weights and measures, and the quality of different kinds of merchandise ; relative to the capacity and exterior marks of casks in which were contained certain commodities that were purchased and resold by wholesale; and against the debasement of coined money. Some also related to the good order of corporations of tradesmen, to apprenticeships, and to the obligations of agents and commissioners, *præpositi*, to render accounts to their principals or constituents.

It is also rather amusing to find, in the Recessus of the League, special regulations for the commerce of salt, prohibitions against the sale of herrings not yet caught, of grain not yet reaped, and of cloth not yet woven; against the exportation of cloth to be dyed in another place than that in which it was woven; against the exportation of gold and silver to be wrought or manufactured in a foreign country; against selling cloths with a false dye, or perfume of which the quality was adulterated.

There is reason to believe that the contract of exchange was also in practice among the inhabitants of the Hanse Towns, at least in the form in which it exhibits itself in its rude beginning. There occur certainly, towards the end of the fourteenth century, instances of persons selling or disposing in one place of a debt which was to be uplifted in another and distant place; but farther than this the business does not appear to have been carried. Of the strict negotiation and execution, and of the manifold improvements subsequently introduced into this branch of business, they had little or no idea.* In time, however, their communication with the Italian and other states of the Mediterranean placed them in a condition to profit by the use of this commercial arrangement; but the League does not appear to have made any enactments on the subject, as falling within strictly maritime law; and it is late before we find any such rules even in the subsequent particular statutes of the cities of the confederation.

* Sartorius Geschichte des Hanseatischen Bundes, vol. ii., p. 687-8.

CHAPTER VII.

OF THE PROGRESS OF INLAND COMMERCE IN MODERN EUROPE—OF THE LAW OF INLAND COMMERCE—GREAT FAIRS—BILLS OF EXCHANGE.

Having thus concluded our general view of the origin and progress of the commerce of the smaller maritime states—which, after the fall of the Western Empire, arose on the sea coasts of the great European kingdoms, all the way from the Adriatic to the Baltic—and of the special statutes which these small states respectively enacted for their own government, as well as of the general collections of usages which were adopted or followed in these different states, as common or consuetudinary law, without any express legislative sanction—we proceed shortly to notice the progress of the inland as well as maritime commerce of these great kingdoms, and then to consider the different systems of maritime and commercial law which they have respectively established, compiled, or adopted, and the works of their respective authors who have illustrated this branch of jurisprudence.

As formerly observed, the vast inundations of barbarous tribes, which settled in the provinces of the Roman Empire, greatly narrowed and contracted, though they did not extinguish, inland commerce; and ages passed away before it revived to any greater extent than that rude interchange, between the town or village and the adjacent country, of articles of first necessity for consumption or use, without which civil society can scarcely be said to exist. In general, the northern nations, agreeably to their former habits of life, settled in the country, and occupied and divided the lands they had conquered. Instead of taking up their abode in the remains of what had been flourishing towns, the chieftains generally, each according to his ability, constructed for themselves castles or fortresses on the most secure spot of the territories they had acquired, and upheld or extended their power, partly by the support of dependent chieftains who had obtained along with them, or to whom they afterwards gave the possession of, smaller portions of territory, partly by the numerous inferior retainers whom they maintained with the annual produce of their lands. The higher descriptions of magistracy, which had been established by the Romans, were so far destroyed in almost all the countries which fell under the dominion of the northern nations. The governors of Roman provinces were generally replaced by German counts, who exercised, over the German as over the Roman inhabitants, an authority both civil and military. The ancient inhabitants of the inland towns, although reduced in numbers by the ravages of war, still formed a large portion of the population, and were for a time left pretty much to themselves by the invading nations, so far, at least, as regarded their municipal institutions and usages; but being less warlike, they appear, after the conquest, to have fallen very generally under subjection, not merely to the sovereign of the invading nation, but also to the neighbouring chiefs. So far as stripped of the property or interest they had in the adjacent territory, the inhabitants of the towns were in a manner dependent upon the lords and owners of that territory for subsistence; and as the conquering tribes, the new masters of the lands, had not the civilisation, and, of course, not the wants of the former owners, the industry of the townsmen could not, as formerly, by the exchange of manufactured for rude produce, command a supply of subsistence upon a footing of equality. Submission, personal services performed, or taxes paid to the neighbouring lord, were the natural result; and, as there was still less intercourse at first between the conquerors and the ancient population of the towns, than between the former and the ancient population of the country, and, consequently, less opportunity for the growth of personal attachment, the inhabitants of the towns appear in this respect to have been originally in less favourable circumstances than even those of the country.

In time, however, circumstances changed. As the northern nations who settled in the provinces had no interest, so they do not appear to have ever entertained any desire or design to exterminate the Roman population, or to convert them to their own habits and customs, as is incontestably proved by the ascendancy obtained by the Latin language, and the preservation and increased prevalence of the civil law of the Romans. The judicial institutions of the Roman cities, too, admitted of easy adaptation to those of the northern nations. For a long period, indeed, the invading population, partial to and resident in the country, remained strangers to the communities of the towns; but as they increased in numbers, and came more frequently to reside in towns, they concentrated themselves there, and formed with each other communities similar to those of the Roman population; and, at a later period, they united themselves with the Roman population; and, although composed of two distinct elements, ultimately formed only one great community.

In the progress of time, also, the great landed proprietors acquired new wants. The industry of the inhabitants of the towns, requisite for the supply of these wants, became of greater value and importance in the society. The accumulation of wealth, to a certain extent, was the result of habits of industry and economy. The principal inhabitants of the towns rose in rank above the mere tenants and cultivators of the soil. The prospect of attaining greater wealth and consequence attracted a large portion of the labouring population from the country to the ancient towns. New villages were gradually formed; older villages expanded into towns. The personal services of the inhabitants of towns came to be converted into a sum of money: the territorial tax payable by each individual citizen to the sovereign, or the chief of the district, came to be farmed by the principal inhabitants, who became responsible for the rent. A sort of corporation was thus created; and from merely farming the territorial tax payable by the town, the members of the corporation came to aspire to other objects; such as, exemption from the restrictions to which they had formerly been subjected, freedom of trade, and exclusive privileges of trade and manufacture. These pretensions their growing comparative wealth enabled them to bring forward with effect, and gradually to realize; and the jealousy and opposition of the two great powers in the European kingdoms still further promoted their rise and aggrandizement. The monarch had, in general, but too much reason to be jealous of and to dread the power of his nobles—the landed aristocracy, who often defied his government, set at nought the general laws of the realm, and obstructed the regular administration of justice. But the monarch had no reason to be jealous of or to dread the comparatively humble inhabitants of the towns. On the contrary, he found them disposed, by their contributions, to relieve him from those state necessities in which his wars involved him, and inclined, from a regard to their own interest, to support order and the due execution of the laws. He found in them a counterpoise to the power of the landed aristocracy; and he discovered that the most effectual method for reducing the overgrown power of that aristocracy, and for strengthening his own government, was the erection within his territories of a number of free corporate towns, who, in return for the right of governing themselves, and the exclusive privileges of trade and manufacture, might not only contribute to the pecuniary wants of the sovereign, but supply for his support a numerous militia.

These corporate powers and privileges, we have already seen, were obtained first, and perhaps to the greatest extent, by the maritime cities and towns of the European kingdoms from the Adriatic to the Baltic. A similar process, though not in the same degree or to the same extent, took place with regard to the inland cities and towns; and the rise and establishment of such inland corporate towns or burghs may be viewed as another grand era in the commercial history of modern times.

Nor was the rise and comparative independence of the towns productive only of advantage to themselves. The interests of all the members of the same civil society are linked together by indissoluble ties; and, as Dr Adam Smith has ably observed, the increase and riches of the maritime commercial and manufacturing towns contributed, in different ways, to the advancement in civilisation of the nations to which they belonged. By affording a great and ready market for the rude produce of the country, they gave encourgement to its cultivation and further improvement. The inhabitants of the towns, too, came, in time, to employ the wealth they had accumulated in the purchase of lands, of which a great proportion was frequently unimproved. And from their larger capital, and superior habits of skill, industry, and economy, they generally proved more successful cultivators than the old landed proprietors. Further, by enabling and inducing the great landed proprietors to spend their revenues, not, as formerly, in the rude maintenance of idle retainers, but in personal and domestic comforts, conveniences, and luxuries, the commerce and manufactures of the towns gradually introduced order and good government, and with them the liberty and security of individuals among the inhabitants of the country, who had previously lived in a state of almost continual hostility with their neighbours, and of servile dependence upon their superiors. Thus the advancement of the towns, and the progress of commerce and manufactures, were the causes of the fall of the great landed aristocracy in modern times, and of the consolidation of the different and formerly detached independent parts of the European kingdoms, under a comparatively regular and strong government. And, on the other hand, the establishment of a regular government, and of a more efficient and correct administration of justice throughout the territories of these different kingdoms, contributed, in its turn, to the still further extension and improvement of commerce and manufactures, by facilitating the intercourse of individuals of the same or different countries, and by increasing the security of mercantile dealings, and promoting mercantile credit.

The change, however, which we have been contemplating, took place only gradually, and in the course of ages. While Europe was divided, not merely into kingdoms or great states, but each kingdom or great state was subdivided into so many separate and detached independent provinces and principalities, jealous of each other's power and almost perpetually at war with each other, the great obstacles to inland or domestic commerce may be easily imagined. And these obstacles continued for a considerable time even after the Crusades had roused to adventure the spirit of the European nations, and brought them more into intercourse and acquaintance with each other. The non-existence of posts did not permit any regular correspondence. Fatigues, hardships, and vexations of various descriptions, added to the frequent hostile attacks of the natives, rendered the roads difficult and unsafe, either for travelling or for the conveyance of merchandise. Unless in virtue of particular privileges, or special stipulations in treaties, trade was the reverse of free to foreigners. And the miserable state of the laws, and of the administration of justice, over all the countries of Europe, rendered it extremely difficult for the domestic, and still more for the foreign merchant, who in the course of his business behoved to move about with his merchandise, to enforce their rights at a distance; while that rapid execution, those expeditious legal remedies, which are so necessary for the security and support of mercantile credit, were almost entirely unknown.

But these very obstacles and difficulties appear to have been the principal causes which, in time, led to the general introduction of markets or fairs; the object of which was to bring a number of sellers and purchasers together, and thereby to facilitate the conclusion of mercantile contracts: and the same causes account also for the uniformity that prevails in the privileges that were usually granted by sovereigns for holding such markets or fairs, whether at short intervals, for small dealings and retail trade, or at greater intervals, for large and wholesale transactions. Of these privileges the principal were the following:—1. Liberty for strangers to frequent with their wares and merchandise the fairs or markets appointed to be held at stated times. 2. Safe passage for the merchants and dealers and their wares, both in travelling to and from the fairs; and freedom from arrest until the time fixed for the payment of fair or market debts. 3. Freedom from certain duties or customs, and ascertainment of the duties which goods brought to the market behoved to pay. 4. The appointment of a particular judge or court for the decision of all disputes or lawsuits arising from transactions at the fair, under the name of Conservator nundinarum, Maitre, or Conservateur des foires. 5. The regulation, that in all affairs connected with or arising out of contracts entered into at the fair, while all formalities were dispensed with, the most expeditious execution of the law should take place.

In the twelfth, thirteenth, and fourteenth centuries, we find that the institution of such fairs at stated times, and of fixed pay-days at these fairs, was general over Italy, France, and Germany, as well as England; and, as the trading people of these days were comparatively little acquainted with the art of writing, the interest of the seller or creditor was secured by the contract being reduced into writing by the clerk of the fair, under the public authority and under the seal of the fair. These contracts, or *lettres des foires*, as they were called, thus came to form authentic and authoritative documents of actual debt, of which, according to the peculiar, and, in these days, very important privileges bestowed on fairs, payment could be enforced by summary personal execution, in virtue of a *mandement de foire*, or warrant for that purpose.

Indeed, with respect to all debts contracted and payable at the fair, this rapid legal execution was founded so far on the mode of dealing, seeing strangers and foreigners met at the fair only for a short time; and, accordingly, whoever did not pay on the fixed pay-days, not only lost his credit, but, at the first suspicion of departure, was liable to have his person arrested.*

Such appears to have been the mode in which inland commerce first came to be carried on to any extent in modern times, under the protection of the great European governments, in towns and at fairs, established

* Versuch des Wahren Ursprungs des Wechselrechts. Von Martens, 1797.

for the purpose, with extraordinary privileges, and a peculiar jurisdiction. And in tracing the progress of this mode of conducting business, we gradually arrive at those approved arrangements and expedients by which, for upwards of two centuries, commerce and the interchange of commodities have been so much extended and facilitated.

The obstacles to the extension of maritime commerce, during the ages we are now contemplating, appear to have been about as great as the obstacles to inland commerce, in consequence not merely of the perils of the sea, but also of the risk of capture by national enemies or pirates. But here also, as in inland commerce, even the trading maritime independent states into which Italy was parcelled out, although engaged in almost constant hostilities, came to a mutual understanding in matters of traffic, and agreed upon what may be denominated commercial truces, and the establishment of places of safety for free trade, where individuals, to whatever nation or country they belonged, might meet, and purchase or sell their respective commodities.

As the small maritime communities, however, which were not independent states, were, of course, situated within the territories of separate nations, and were the subjects of different sovereigns, there existed the further obstacle of the particular description of money or coin of one independent kingdom or state not being available or current in other independent states. In rude times, the transactions of trade might be so far conducted by barter, or the simple exchange of commodities; but in a multiplicity of cases this would not suit the wants and wishes of parties. And the remedy was sought, and so far found, in the precious metals, which possessed an intrinsic value over the whole globe, and, being susceptible of indefinite division, were well adapted for a common medium of exchange.

In the conveyance, however, of these metals, as ingots or in the shape of bullion, the proprietor incurred nearly the same risks, by land or by sea, as in the conveyance of the actual commodities which were to be purchased or sold. The value of the precious metals, too, depends upon their purity, or freedom from alloy; and this degree of purity cannot be detected or ascertained by simple and transient inspection or weighing. To obviate the latter difficulty, the sovereigns of states resorted to the expedient of impressing marks upon pieces of these metals of which the purity had been ascertained, so as to bear a definite value in the transactions of business. But the metal thus stamped or coined could have no marketable value beyond the territories of the state that issued it, or beyond its own intrinsic value. And when a number of independent kingdoms or states, in commercial intercourse with each other, had issued different coins, it became necessary to compare these coins, and to ascertain their market value in reference to each other: in other words, to convert the money of one country into that of another. The division of Europe into so great a number of kingdoms, principalities, and independent states, all having different coins, increased this difficulty, and created an additional impediment to commerce; and the transportation of the requisite coin by land, from the residence of the merchant to the city or other place where the great fair was to be held, or by sea from one maritime state to another, was attended with almost the same risks as the similar transportation of bullion.

From the operation of the causes just alluded to, we find, from the writers of the middle ages, collected by Muratori and others, that in the course of the twelfth, thirteenth, and fourteenth centuries, a new set of dealers arose throughout the different countries of Europe, namely, dealers in money, who were generally called *campsores*, or money-changers, and appear to have originally proceeded from the more cultivated maritime states of Italy.

At first, and indeed for a long time, these money-dealers, however necessary and useful, appear to have been held in low estimation. From narrow and limited views of morality and general expediency, it was reckoned unjust to reap any profit from the loan of money. From a misunderstanding and misapplication of a passage in Scripture, this opinion came to be strengthened by religious prejudice, and was sanctioned by the authority of the Catholic Church, as well as of many of the European monarchs. In such circumstances, dealings in money were almost necessarily carried on in a great measure by the Jews scattered over the different countries of Christendom. In time, however, the folly of this prejudice became apparent; more enlightened notions of religion and morality were gradually introduced. It began to be perceived that there was no greater impropriety in deriving income from the loan of money, by means of which the borrower is enabled, in trade, to realize a profit, than from the lease of land, by which, through his industry, the lessee is enabled to subsist himself and his family, as well as to pay rent to his landlord. The great utility of the precious metals in facilitating the mutually advantageous exchanges of commodities, came to be more and more felt; and in proportion as the money-dealer became of greater importance in mercantile transactions, his profession rose in respectability.

Along with the dealers in other merchandise, the money-dealer repaired with his commodity to the stated fairs established over Europe; and, as his commodity was in constant and universal demand, he became a person of consequence at the fair. As his money-table was necessary for the accommodation of all the other dealers, he had a peculiar claim to the protection of the government under whose authority the fair was held. Like the other merchants who disposed of their goods, he was equally if not more entitled to obtain a document of the debt contracted to him, under the seal of the fair, and clothed with all the privileges enjoyed by the creditor under its peculiar jurisdiction. For the money so advanced by him, it generally suited the merchant whom he accommodated to give or transfer to the money-dealer some of these documents of debt which he had received from other merchants for the goods he had brought to and sold at the fair. To the money-dealer this was also desirable, as affording a double security for the money he advanced and the credit he gave; and the document of debt thus transferred, for a certain sum advanced in cash by a money-dealer at a fair, specifying a particular pay-day at a subsequent fair, to be kept either in the same or in a distant town, and under the peculiar jurisdiction of the fair, containing a warrant for arresting the person of the debtor who should fail in making payment, combines all the essentials, and obviously presents the model, of our modern bill of exchange.

The precise era of that most useful invention does not appear to have been exactly ascertained; but that it originated, in the manner we have just seen, in the usages and customs observed and in the regulations adopted at fairs, from considerations of general security and convenience, there is every reason to believe. And after it was once established upon a small scale, the utility and convenience of the invention behoved gradually to lead to its more extensive adoption, particularly in foreign and maritime commerce. Indeed, it seems probable that bills of exchange, such, or nearly such, as we have at present, first came into general use in the course of the extended commerce carried on by the maritime cities of Italy, and of the south of France and Spain, under their comparatively free and well administered governments. Weber, in his Ricerche sull' Origine e sulla Natura del Contratto di Cambio, published at Venice in 1810, states positively that such documents were in use at Venice in 1171; and a law of Venice, of 1272, clearly designates Bills of Exchange.* The unpublished statute of Avignon, of 1243, contains a paragraph entitled De Litteris Cambii; a statute of Marseilles, dated 1253,† presents evident traces of them; and a transaction of this description is attested by a document of 1256 relative to England.‡ Farther, in his Colleccion Diplomatica,§ Don Antonio Capmany has discovered and recorded, in the middle of a public authentic instrument, the following copy of a bill of exchange, dated 28th April, 1404, drawn by a merchant in Bruges upon a mercantile company in Barcelona, which approaches pretty much to the present form, and shews that such negotiable documents were then in frequent use:—"Al nome di Dio, Amen. A di Aprile XXVIII, 1404.—Pagate per questa prima di camb. à usanza, à Pietro Gilberto e Pietro Olivo, scuti mille, a sold. X. Barcelonesi per scuto: e quali scuti mille sono per cambio che con Giovanni Colombo, a Gressi XXII. de gresso per scuto, et Pon. a nostro conto; et Christo vi guardi. (Subtus vero erat scriptum.) Antonio quart. Sab. di Brugis."

Upon the whole, it does not appear we can approximate nearer to the date of this useful invention, or discover the name of the inventor or inventors. The great difficulties and risks which we have seen merchants experienced in transporting bullion, or specie, or

* Marin. Storia, &c., tome v., p. 296.
† Lib. i., chap. 27.
‡ Pardessus Collect., tome ii., p. CXII.
§ Tome ii., No. cxxi., p. 203.

coin, from one country to another, created a strong necessity for and an urgent inducement to devise some expedient by which these difficulties and risks might be avoided. In a rude or little extended state of commerce between different countries or nations, or even between different parts of the same kingdom or state, such an expedient could scarcely be found. Until commerce, or the reciprocal exchange of commodities between two countries, became extensive, there was no sufficient *concursus debiti et crediti*, such as to admit of the reciprocal claims and debts being set off against each other in the shape of the current coin of the different countries, or otherwise. It was only when these reciprocal debits and credits became pretty extensive, that the use of bullion or coin having intrinsic value could be dispensed with. Farther, as when the exchange of commodities does not take place between individuals *de præsenti*, credit is given, a considerable degree of confidence behoved to precede the recourse to bills of exchange; and the courts of law of these different countries must have attained such a degree of improvement in the administration of justice, as to afford a remedy which could be relied on in giving speedy execution against the person and estate of the debtor.

When these improvements had taken place, in the natural course of events, men of skill perceived that there was a profit to be realized, whether in receiving the funds which a merchant might have to recover or might deposit with them, and in undertaking to discharge, according as they should receive orders, the debts which the party depositing wished to pay, or in giving to a merchant, who intrusted to them his money, letters or drafts addressed to their correspondents in the city or place to which he was going to repair, to advance the funds which he might there require; and such was manifestly the origin of what we now call bills of exchange.

It seems idle, therefore, to look for the origin of these negotiable documents in any particular event, occurring in any particular country; as Montesquieu seems to have done in the expulsion of the Jews from France, in 1181, by Philip Augustus, according to the story first told, it is believed, by Cleirac, in his Us et Coutumes de la Mer. It is, no doubt, true, as observed by M. Nouguier, the latest French writer on the subject, (1839,) that there is a distinction between the cause or occasion, and the fact or event, of the invention of bills of exchange; that if we inquire what cause has led to the invention, the true answer is, the necessities of commerce; but that if we inquire who were the inventors, in what position, and by whom these necessities were most strongly felt, and what person or persons, experiencing the urgency of these necessities in the most lively manner, produced the thing invented, it would be absurd to call the extension of commerce the inventor; for this would be to confound the mover (*moteur*) with the agent. It is also highly probable that the Jews, being in these ages, as we have seen, the chief *campsores* or money-lenders, persecuted from mistaken religious views, and on account of their alleged pecuniary extortions, scattered over the European kingdoms, yet in a manner forced to keep up a pretty constant communication with each other, clever and acute naturally, and comparatively skilful in such business, from having been trained to it for generations, were really the first inventors of bills of exchange in a rude state. But that they made the discovery or invention at the precise time, and solely in consequence of their expulsion from the kingdom of France by Philip Augustus, is not very likely in the circumstances, does not appear to be proved by any contemporary, or nearly contemporary, authority or document, or by any other authority than the statement of Cleirac, in 1661, made nearly five hundred years after the alleged event, and which seems to have been repeated by subsequent French writers without much further investigation. And it is abundantly manifest that bills of exchange could not have attained the degree of perfection they have reached in the course of the last two centuries, until the interchange of commodities among the European nations, and among the distant inhabitants of the same empire or kingdom, had increased to such an extent as to create a large and permanent amount of reciprocal debit and credit among those different nations, or distantly located subjects of the same government, to be set off against each other in detail by means of these negotiable documents. Indeed the accumulation of moveable capital in banks, whether under the direct authority of the state or not, appears to have been, if not the necessary precursor, at least the requisite accompaniment of such operations of exchange.

PART IV.

OF THE MARITIME AND COMMERCIAL LAW OF THE MODERN EUROPEAN NATIONS.

PART IV.

OF THE MARITIME AND COMMERCIAL LAW OF THE MODERN EUROPEAN NATIONS.

Having taken this very cursory view of the general progress of inland commerce throughout the different kingdoms of modern Europe, as connected with maritime and mercantile legislation, we proceed to consider, at some length, the different systems of maritime and commercial law which the modern European governments have respectively established, whether in the shape of statutes or legislative enactments by the sovereign power of the state, or in the shape of common or consuetudinary law and usage as recorded in the judicial determinations of their tribunals, or in the institutional works or particular treatises of their respective writers who have expounded or illustrated this branch ofjurisprudence. In prosecuting this inquiry we shall adopt the following order, as suggested by the relative position of the countries and the series of historical events:—

In the *first* place, So far as not already done, we shall notice the maritime and commercial laws of the Italian states, statutory and consuetudinary, including Venice and the maritime dominions of Austria; Pisa and Florence, or Tuscany; Genoa; the Papal States; the kingdom of Naples or the Two Sicilies; and Sardinia.

In the *second* place, The maritime laws of Spain and Portugal.

In the *third* place, The maritime laws of Flanders, the southern Netherlands, now the kingdom of Belgium, and of the northern Netherlands, or late United Provinces, now the kingdom of Holland.

In the *fourth* place, The maritime and commercial law of France, down to the present time.

In the *fifth* place, The maritime laws of the northern kingdoms, including Denmark, Sweden, Prussia, and Russia.

And, *lastly*, The maritime laws of England and Ireland, of Scotland, and of the United States of America.

CHAPTER I.

OF THE MARITIME AND COMMERCIAL LAW OF THE ITALIAN STATES.

WITH regard to the modern maritime laws of the Italian states, we have anticipated a good deal, in our historical review of the commercial Republics which, after the fall of the Western Empire, arose on the coasts of the Mediterranean. We traced the early statutes respectively enacted by Venice, by Pisa and Florence, and by Genoa, by which these different states so far embodied and gave a legislative sanction to previous usages. We found these statutes, besides being limited in point of authority to the states which enacted them, were comparatively imperfect, and by no means amounted to what could be called complete bodies of maritime law; and we found reason to believe that these defects were so far supplied, if not by the written, at least by the traditionary remains of that part of the Roman law which related to such matters. We found, too, that, in the progress of time and experience in navigation and maritime trade, various additional rules came to be generally adopted in practice, as recommended and sanctioned by the opinions of persons of skill in such matters, by the decisions of local judges, and by the awards of arbiters; and we found that, after the lapse of two or three centuries of experience, the greatest part of these rules came to be collected in one compilation, called the Consolato del Mare; and that, although to all appearance not framed by the direction, nor sanctioned by the legislative or sovereign authority, of any nation, the doctrines of this compilation were found so equitable and just, so convenient and generally expedient, as to lead to its almost universal adoption as common law by the Italian states. In these states, too, including not merely the trading Republics before mentioned, but also the several kingdoms, dukedoms, and principalities successively formed in that country, the Consolato del Mare appears to have been found adequate to all the exigencies of commerce, and to have contained principles sufficient for the determination of all maritime and mercantile disputes for centuries after its compilation and general adoption; and none of these states seem to have established any peculiar maritime and mercantile legislative code, suited to their own situation and local customs, till a comparatively late period. We have here, therefore, chiefly to refer to the Consolato del Mare, of which we have already given a sufficiently ample account, and which may be now consulted in the editions of Casaregis in 1740, and of Capmany in 1791, and in the still more correct edition of Pardessus in 1831: and what chiefly remains to be done with reference to the Italian states, is to inquire, *first*, what more modern improved codes, if any, have been established by legislative sanction, and what their collections of judicial determinations; and, *secondly*, who are the principal writers who have expounded their local statutes, or the common and general doctrines of the Consolato.

Section I.

Of the Maritime and Commercial Law of Venice, and the Maritime Dominions of Austria.

In Venice we formerly marked the progress of maritime law as consisting of the statute of 1255 and a few subsequent statutes, and of traditionary maritime usages, down to the adoption in practice of the Consolato del Mare, apparently in the course of the century which succeeded the promulgation of the maritime statutory regulations revived and sanctioned, in 1347, by the Doge Andrea Dandolo. The Consolato was translated from the original Catalan into Italian apparently by Giovan Battista Pedrezano, and was printed at Venice in the year 1539; and so completely does that compilation appear to have provided for the maritime questions of these times, that from 1347 we do not find any national general maritime code established by the Venetians, but merely a series of statutes, passed at considerable intervals in the course of the fifteenth, sixteenth, and seventeenth centuries, limited to special objects, such as shipwrecks, the inspection of vessels, the prevention of the overloading of vessels, and quarantine; and particularly the statutes of 1468, 1586, 1602, 1622, and 1624, relative to marine insurances; which most important subject, we have seen, was not embraced by the Consolato.

It was not till towards the close of the eighteenth century, and within a short time of the termination of their existence as a separate independent state, that the Venetians resolved to establish a complete maritime code for themselves, adapted to their own peculiar local situation, usages, and views. This great work, however, they at last accomplished in the year 1786. The code having been sanctioned in all its parts by the sovereign authority and decree of the senate, was promulgated, in September, 1786, by the Magistracy de Cinque Savi alla Mercanzia, under the title of Codice per la Veneta Mercantile Marina. The arrangement of the matters is distinct, the doctrines equitable and generally expedient, and the work is interesting, as one of the later monuments of modern maritime legislation. But, not many years afterwards, the Venetians, like many other nations, were compelled to yield to the victorious arms and ambitious views of Napoleon, and ceased to be an independent state. The French Code de Commerce was promulgated in Italy in 1808; and although Venice and its former territories were, by the treaties of peace concluded in 1815, placed under the dominion of the Emperor of Austria, as part of the Lombard Venetian kingdom, it is not known to us whether the Venetians continue to adopt the French code or have resumed their native maritime and commercial legislation.

Of late years, too, the ancient maritime commerce of Venice appears to have passed almost entirely to the Austrian port of Trieste, which, from the time of its being declared a free port in 1719, has gradually increased in prosperity and risen to importance. At first the inhabitants of Trieste, if they did not borrow the Venetian jurisprudence, must have been guided very much by the maritime usages of the Adriatic, and by the Consolato del Mare. In 1774, the Empress Maria Theresa promulgated an edict, which forms a tolerably extensive maritime code; and, in 1816, there was published at Venice, Editto Politico di Navigazione Mercantile Austriaca, in one vol. quarto.

SECTION II.

Of the Maritime and Commercial Laws of Tuscany, Pisa, Florence, Leghorn.

When formerly contemplating the rise, after the subversion of the Western Empire, of the commercial Republics on the coasts of the Mediterranean, during the middle ages, we traced the early maritime and commercial law of Pisa till that Republic became subject to Florence, and we now mark from that time the progress of the maritime and commercial law of these two cities and of Leghorn, as constituting the maritime law of Tuscany.

Political events, as formerly noticed, did not permit the Pisans, as an independent state, to add to their positive maritime law written regulations on insurances, as they were compelled, in the year 1406, to submit to the dominion of Florence. But Florence, having become a maritime power by the acquisition of Pisa, and more lately of Leghorn, established regulations for insurances, in the years 1522 and 1528, which thus became the completion of the maritime law of Pisa. The preamble bears that the government of the Republic being convinced, upon the representation of prudent and experienced merchants, of what importance it was, for the benefit of both natives and foreigners, to improve and complete the law of insurances, and to reform the abuses which had been introduced into it, instituted a Magistracy of five persons to digest the necessary regulations, and to determine all disputes; and the laws thus enacted are to be found in the Biblioteca di Gius Nautico, printed at Florence in 1785,* and in

* Vol. i., p. 35.

the Italian collection of laws on insurance, by Ascanio Baldasseroni,* printed in 1804.

With regard to the other branches of maritime law, it is clear, from the Discursus Legales of Casaregis, that the Consolato del Mare, which we have considered at such length, was held as common law at Florence, Pisa, and Leghorn, and was amplified by the collection of the decisions of the Rota Florentina. In the course of last century, too, the Tuscan maritime code appears to have been revised, and to have been considerably improved, particularly in point of arrangement. In the year 1748, a concise edict was promulgated at Florence upon commerce and mercantile marine. To this edict additions were made in 1787; and in 1798 there was published in quarto, Collezione dei Statuti di Mercanzia di Firenze e di Livorno. But the French Code de Commerce was introduced into Tuscany under the conquest of that country by the Emperor Napoleon; and although, at the general peace, the Grand Duchy was restored to its former sovereign, that code, it is believed, has remained in force, in consequence of a law passed in November, 1814.

Section III.

Of the Maritime and Commercial Law of Piedmont, including Genoa.

When tracing the rise of the commercial Republics on the coasts of the Mediterranean during the middle ages, we noticed the early maritime legislation of Genoa, till towards the close of the sixteenth century. In 1588 the Genoese undertook the composition of a new civil statute. Some chapters were inserted in it

* Vol. v., p. 233.

relative to jetson and insurances. But from the silence of this code on other maritime matters, we may conclude that the principal regulations of the Statuta Gazariæ, relative to the police of navigation and seafaring people, so far as they had not become useless, or fallen into desuetude, from more enlarged experience and the changes of circumstances, continued to be observed by the magistracy, conservators of the sea. The necessity, however, of establishing more precise rules, of such a nature as to prevent frauds and other abuses relative to loans of money on marine risk, appears to have been felt and recognised. The conservators of the sea made a proposal on this subject, in 1644, to the legislative council of the Republic: a statute on the subject was enacted, if not immediately, at least in 1688, and it was renewed in 1707.

Although, however, the different statutes, now and formerly noticed as published by M. Pardessus, contain a great number of regulations in detail, they present great gaps and deficiencies in the system of maritime law; and there can be no doubt that the Roman law, and particularly the Consolato del Mare, formed the principal basis of the maritime jurisprudence of the Genoese. Indeed this is proved by the celebrated collection of the judgments of the supreme civil tribunal of Genoa, entitled, Decisiones Rotae Genuensis, published in 1582, and republished, first in 1622, and afterwards at Amsterdam, in folio, in 1669; and these decisions themselves constitute a body of judicial determinations, unfolding the rules of the common law, perhaps as valuable as any legislative code of these times.

At Genoa, as well as at Florence, Pisa, and Leghorn, the French Code de Commerce was introduced under the imperial government of Napoleon: and the sovereign of Piedmont has adopted and confirmed it, as the maritime and commercial law of his subjects.

Section IV.

Of the Maritime and Commercial Law of the Papal States.—Ancona.

Of the maritime cities in the Pontifical States, Ancona chiefly deserves attention. After the invasions of the northern nations had ceased, Ancona, from the operation of the causes formerly mentioned, became a Republic; and, in the middle ages, its success and prosperity in navigation and commerce were such as to render it for a time the rival of Venice. Its primitive maritime law appears, like that of Venice, to have been derived from the Roman law and the Basilica, and to have been modified, as in the other cities of Italy, by subsequent general usages and special local statutes. And we should have naturally concluded that the defects in these statutes were, as in the other Italian cities, supplied by the subsequent adoption of the doctrines of the Consolato del Mare, had not the indefatigable researches of M. Pardessus lately led to the discovery at Ancona of a statute, or rather body of maritime laws, consisting of ninety-seven chapters, which may well bear a comparison with the Consolato itself. It appears to have been compiled, in the common language then in use, prior to the year 1397; was, during that year, inserted in a register by the Chancellor Sylvestre; was copied, in 1457, by Benincosa; and is referred to in the subsequent revision and compilation of the general common law of Ancona, then governed as a Republic, written in Latin, finished about 1458, and printed in 1513 and 1576.

As the early maritime laws of Venice, Pisa, and Genoa were composed in Latin, and as at Pisa and Genoa, we have seen, the notaries or clerks of the commercial courts were directed to translate these laws into the vulgar tongue for the use of seafaring people, we might with much probability infer that the compilation we are now considering was a translation from a Latin text; but, on perusal, we are assured that, even with a slight knowledge of the Italian language as spoken in the fourteenth and fifteenth centuries, it is easy to perceive that this compilation is original, and not a mere translation of a document composed in Latin. The elements of this compilation, however, may probably have been borrowed from more ancient statutes, which may have been composed in Latin like the Statuta Navium of Venice, in 1255, and may have been enacted when Ancona carried on a prosperous commerce with Constantinople; and, upon perusal, it appears to be not so much a work begun and completed all at one time, as a collection, in an order not very methodical, of distinct statutes, made at different times on matters of maritime right.

The maritime statutes of Venice, Pisa, Genoa, and Marseilles, which we formerly considered, exhibited the great care which the composers had bestowed in regulating, with an exactness rather too minute, all the cases which could furnish matter for dispute; but a regard to truth renders it necessary to admit that the statute of Ancona is very superior to them in the unity, integrity as a whole, and exactness of its composition. Its excellence is so great, that were it not proved to have existed, in the state in which it has reached us, at the end of the fourteenth century, one would have been inclined to ascribe to it a more recent date. Indeed, on comparing it with the Consolato del Mare, it is impossible not to recognise between those two documents a resemblance so striking, as to induce a belief that the compiler of the one had the other under his eye. The title, too, of the statute of Ancona, is Capituli overo Statuti del Mare; and the title of the Consolato, in the manuscript in the Royal Library of France, is Capitulo de Mar; but that circumstance certainly is too feeble to be held to amount to a proof that the one of these documents has been framed in imitation of, or in the knowledge of, the other. If similar wants, arising in the course of navigation, especially on the same sea coasts, may and must have dictated, in several different states, regulations almost identical, these collections of rules or decisions may also have been designated by a similar name.

The maritime jurisprudence which served as a basis for the compilers of the Consolato, had existed for a long time in Catalonia, the native country of that document, and in the other dependencies of Aragon. Customs or usages are in practice and in tradition, from age to age, long before they are committed to writing, or digested. The seafaring people of Ancona, experienced and skilful observers, may, in frequenting the Spanish ports, have become acquainted with the jurisprudence of the consular tribunals established in Barcelona at the end of the thirteenth and beginning of the fourteenth century; and although at that period the Consolato del Mare, in all probability, did not yet exist in the state in which we have it, there can be no doubt that a very extensive part of the maritime usages of which it presents a compilation had already been committed to writing; but if the inhabitants of Ancona may have thus early become acquainted with the usages of Aragon, it is not more improbable that the seafaring people of the latter country may have become acquainted with the usages of Ancona—a city which had made such progress in early times in navigation and commerce. The resemblance, then, between the two compilations may be very well explained without recourse to the hypothesis that the statute of Ancona served as a model for the Consolato, or the latter document as a model for that statute. It is highly improbable, from the circumstances formerly stated, that the Consolato, even supposing it to have been then digested into the shape in which it has reached us, was known in the ports of the Adriatic in the fourteenth century. Besides, the points of resemblance between the statute of Ancona and the Consolato exist, in general, only in what may be called common law—the law which the same local circumstances, and the same wants, must have caused to be expressed in the same manner, and almost in identical terms, in languages which have so very great an affinity. But when we come to what may be called peculiar positive law, to the points in which the maritime statutes of the middle ages present a great variety, and even direct opposition, there is no longer any resemblance between the statute of Ancona and the Consolato. This dissimilarity is particularly remarkable in the contribution for average losses at sea, and in the allowance to sailors of a certain tonnage for the conveyance of goods, as a part of their wages. It is also plain that the work of the compilers of the statute of Ancona, remarkable though it be, would have been much more complete if they had had the Consolato under their eye. The statute has not provided for a great number of cases, particularly as to the building and repairing of vessels, which the Consolato has treated at length. On the other hand, the statute treats of other questions which are not at all mentioned in the Consolato, and of which, probably, the compilers of that document would have treated if they had been acquainted with the legislation of Ancona.

In 1532, Ancona passed under the sovereignty of the Pope; but, while it underwent some political changes, it preserved its former private law or jurisprudence; as appears from the general civil statute, which recognised the previous maritime statute, having been printed in 1569 and 1579, with the approbation of the Papal government. About the same time the Consolato became known in Italy—was translated and printed at Venice—and was generally adopted by almost all the maritime states of the Mediterranean. At Ancona, also, a similar adoption seems to have taken place, for Benevuto Straccha, a patrician and jurisconsult of Ancona, refers to the Consolato, and not to the statutes of his own native city.

Of all the statutes established by the different maritime states of the Mediterranean, those of Ancona treat most largely of the means of securing to its native citizens the right of having the disputes between them in foreign countries decided by their own judges, and according to their own laws.

The statute of Ancona treats also at length of the measures to be taken for the preservation of the effects of its citizens who have died abroad. But it contains nothing of insurances, although they must have been in practice at Ancona in the sixteenth, and even at the end of the fifteenth century, as the coasts of the Adriatic are mentioned in the ordinance of Florence on insurances, in 1523. The only document on this subject belonging to Ancona is the form of a policy, dated 1567, which served as a text for the treatise of Straccha de Assecurationibus.

The Pontifical States are now governed in matters of private maritime and commercial right by an edict promulgated on the 1st June, 1821, under the title of Regolamento Provisorio di Commercio, which maintains the ancient laws, so far as not inconsistent with it. And this Regolamento is, with some slight modifications, a translation of the Code de Commerce of France.

Section V.

Of the Maritime and Commercial Law of the Kingdom of Naples and Sicily.

After the subversion of the Western Empire, the eastern part of Italy continued for a considerable period (till the ninth century) to be subject to the Emperor of Constantinople. But after the capture of Ravenna, the political connection between Italy and the Eastern Empire became gradually weaker; and, in the eleventh century, the cities of Naples, Amalfi, Salerno, and Gaeta appear to have established their almost complete independence, and to have been governed by magistrates of their own choice. After various vicissitudes, however, these cities were conquered and subjugated by the Norman Princes, and became, at the commencement of the twelfth century, integral parts of the kingdom of Naples; thus losing their political independence, but preserving their civil liberty and their municipal privileges, among which was the right of making treaties of commerce.

That these cities had laws, or at least usages, according to which their magistrates administered justice, there can be no doubt; and while they continued under subjection, more or less strict, to the Western, and afterwards to the Eastern Empire, it is evident those laws must have been the Roman law, as contained in the compilations of Justinian, and afterwards transferred into the compilations of the later Eastern Emperors, under the title of Basilica. But the cities of Venice and Ancona, we have seen, while they retained in substance the ancient maritime law of the Romans, introduced into it certain modifications and additions, the result of new circumstances and events, of new wants, and of more enlarged experience; and there is reason to believe that these modifications commenced in the city of Trani, situated on the Adriatic, and dependent on the kingdom of Naples.

In perusing the copy of the statutes of Fermo, a city in the Pontifical States, on the coast of the Adriatic, extant in the Royal Library of France, printed at Venice in 1507, and reprinted at Fermo in 1589, M. Pardessus found, in an appendix, a document entitled, Ordinamenta et Consuetudo Maris, edita per Consules Civitatis Trani, bearing date 1063. This date is anterior by a century to that of the Constitutum Usus of Pisa, the most ancient maritime law belonging to modern Italy; and M. Pardessus made every exertion to ascertain whether the original, or any copy of this document, existed at Trani. But the result of his inquiries was, that the archives of Trani had fallen a prey to the flames, during the fire which took place in 1799, when the French entered that city, and that no such document could be found; and nothing farther could be ascertained than that there exists at Fermo a copy in parchment of the Statuta Firmanorum, printed in 1507, and of the Ordinamenta of Trani, dated 1063. The farther discussions of M. Pardessus support the belief that this date is correct, and that the document is written in the Italian language, as spoken at that time. And from the copy now published by M. Pardessus, his observations appear to be just—namely, that it exhibits a character of generality, which the Venetian statute of 1255 does not present: that the authors understood well the task they had undertaken: that they did not compose a law for the port of Trani alone, but ascertained the usages then observed on the coasts of the Adriatic, different in some respects from the Roman law, but on that account the more interesting and curious.

Passing from the Adriatic to the other maritime cities of the kingdom of Naples, we should have something definite, if it were possible to discover a document which several writers have ascribed to the city of Amalfi, and have denominated Tabula Amalfitana. But concurring in the critical investigation of M. Pardessus, in the first volume of his Collection, we come to the conclusion, not only that the body of laws described by Freccia under that denomination has not been discovered, and is not extant, but that the account given of it by Freccia is a mere fiction, resting entirely upon his gratuitous and groundless assertion. In the fifth volume of his Collection, M. Pardessus reviews and enlarges his former argument, in consequence of this fiction having been adopted by so many recent writers; and he assuredly places the matter beyond dispute. Indeed, it is surprising that such intelligent historians as Giannone and Sismondi should, without investigation, have sanctioned a story which is shewn to be so inconsistent with historical truth.

The cities of Naples and Salerno do not appear to present any ancient maritime statutes or usages of importance, or different from the doctrines of the Roman law. But M. Pardessus has found a printed work, entitled, Statuta, Privilegia, Consuetudines, Civitatis Gaietæ, which refers to various statutes in the course of the thirteenth and fourteenth centuries, modifying more ancient statutes, enacted apparently when Gaeta enjoyed a sort of independence, and was governed by consuls; and this statute of Gaeta appears to contain a more full development than the statutes either of Marseilles or Ancona, not only with regard to the jurisdiction which the consuls sent by one nation into a foreign country had a right to exercise over their fellow-countrymen, but also of the usages followed in one city with regard to consuls sent to it by a foreign city, for the purpose of recognising and guaranteeing the independent exercise of their jurisdiction over their own countrymen.

Sicily.

The other part of the Neapolitan kingdom, Sicily, appears to have been partially occupied, first by the Phœnicians, and afterwards by the Greeks, and to have derived from these nations the ancient maritime law which Rome afterwards borrowed from the Rhodians; and when it became a Roman province it retained its former maritime law, as having flowed from the same source from which its conquerors derived theirs. On the fall of the Western Empire, it was temporarily occupied by the Goths, was reconquered by the Emperors of Constantinople, and was occupied by the Saracens in 635. During its occupation by the Saracens, its inhabitants appear to have been allowed to retain, and to have been governed by, their ancient laws in all matters of private right. Towards the middle of the eleventh century, the Norman adventurers who had settled in the south of Italy invaded Sicily, and expelled the Saracens; the change of government, which restored to the Sicilians their ancient usages and religion, behoved to contribute still more to the maintenance of the Roman law, which the Norman Princes had no interest to replace by a new legislation, even if such a measure had been within their power; and one of their Princes, Roger, in 1128, established at Messina, under the name of Consuls, magistrates charged with the administration of justice to merchants. After passing successively under the dominion of the Houses of Suabia and Anjou, and of the Kings of Aragon, Sicily came to be united with the kingdom of Naples, under the House of Austria, and continued to be so till the eighteenth century. But the laws established by these successive sovereigns, relative to maritime commerce, are almost all local, or of little importance. And the pre-existing common law appears to have been enlarged during that period by the adoption of the Consolato del Mare, not only from the favourable reception with which that compilation could not fail to meet in a country governed by the Princes of Aragon, but also from the Neapolitan jurisconsults, while they quoted the Roman law as direct authority, likewise founding upon the Consolato in all questions which that law had not expressly decided, and even in those in which usage had introduced modifications; and, ultimately, from the edict of 1797 having placed that compilation in the first rank of written authorities, agreeably to which the judges of commerce are directed to pronounce their decisions.

In the course of last century, the Princes of the House of Bourbon, at intervals, promulgated several regulations (*pragmatiques*) relative to maritime commerce. And, in 1779, King Ferdinand IV. conceived the project of giving to his states a complete maritime code. For the preparation of this great work, his minister, Acton, selected Michel de Jorio, who had devoted a great part of his life to the study of commercial law. And if this learned Neapolitan lawyer had properly understood, or confined himself to, the task assigned him, it is probable the code would have received the royal sanction. But, unfortunately, he availed himself of the opportunity thus afforded him to compose a long theory of commerce and navigation, and of the laws of peace and of war, as well as to write a history of legislative statutes, and of the writings of private authors relative to maritime law. These immense accessories eclipsed what in the work was good, and adapted for the formation of a code: the draft, or projet, printed only to the number of twenty-five copies, for distribution among the counsellors of the Crown, was forgotten. The kingdom of Naples was thus deprived of a code which might have done it honour in the eyes of Europe; and the result has been, that the French Code de Commerce was there adopted, in March, 1819, with some useful modifications.

Section VI.

Of the Maritime or Commercial Law of Sardinia.

When they found, in the decline of their national prosperity, their eastern commerce occupied by the Greeks, and their western in the hands of the Carthaginians, the Phœnicians appear to have recognised the importance of Sardinia; and, by a treaty of navigation between the Roman Republic and the Carthaginians, it is proved that, about 500 years before the Christian era, the latter had establishments in that island. It was conquered by the Romans in the course of the third century before that era, and remained under their dominion till the fall of the Western Empire. Like Sicily, accordingly, the maritime law of Sardinia appears to have been originally what the Phœnicians had taught the Greeks and Carthaginians, and what the Romans borrowed from the Rhodians, and preserved or established in all the countries subject to their sway.

In the year 435 of the Christian era, Sardinia was invaded by the Vandals; was recovered, in 468, by the Emperor Leo; was conquered and possessed for a short time by the Goths; and was again brought under the Roman government of Justinian by the victories of Belisarius. After some ages of repose, it was occupied by the Saracens about the beginning of the eighth century; but, either by the Lombard Kings, or their conqueror Charlemagne, or his successors, the Saracens were forced to abandon their conquest until the commencement of the eleventh century, when they again obtained possession of the island, but were soon after expelled by the united efforts of the Pisans and Genoese.

During such a long series of conquests and reconquests, the ancient maritime law, in all probability, continued to be observed. The conquerors had not leisure to think of establishing new laws for the island; and, although they had done so, the Sardinians, when delivered from their yoke, would have resumed their ancient customs. Although the Sardinians were greatly indebted to the Pisans and Genoese for their delivery from the Saracens, neither of these commercial Republics, perhaps from jealousy of each other, ever acquired the sovereignty of the whole interior of the island. But, from the twelfth century, they long possessed great influence, and had extensive factories and commercial establishments—the Genoese in the northern, and the Pisans in the southern, parts of the island. As the statutes, however, of these Republics had, as we have seen, preserved the ancient law, and been confined to the improvement and completion of its regulations in certain departments, their introduction into Sardinia does not appear to have occasioned any great alteration in the maritime law, which had been observed from the time of the Roman conquest; and they seem to have been adopted, without any express legislative act, from the tendency which people generally have, in a country whose commerce is passive, to imitate the foreigners who come to trade with them.

It is not known whether the Genoese Republic enacted any statute for the government of its subjects who inhabited the northern part of Sardinia, and its consuls there probably conformed to the statutes of the metropolis. But the city of Sassari, situated in the north of the island, had a legislation of its own, dated 1316, containing some regulations in maritime law, of which M. Pardessus has published an extract. And in the southern part of the island the Pisans had very anciently, and long preserved at Cagliari and in some neighbouring towns, factories or mercantile establishments, in which governors, consuls, and judges of their nation exercised their functions, without any other appeal than to the government and tribunals of Pisa. With the view of reforming the abuses which had been introduced into this factory, and of reconciling the interests of the Republic with those of the inhabitants of Sardinia, the government of Pisa, in 1314, sent commissioners to Cagliari to inquire into the conduct of the managers of the factory; and the result of this inquiry appears to have been the composition and enactment, in 1319, of the Breve portus Kallaritani, which exists in manuscript in the archives of the House of Roncioni of Pisa, and has been published by M. Pardessus.

After a succession of wars against the Pisans, the Genoese, and the local chiefs who occupied the interior of the island, the Kings of Aragon at last, in the latter part of the fifteenth century, succeeded in completely establishing their power in Sardinia; and soon afterwards, not merely the general civil privileges and constitution, but the maritime regulations and usages of Barcelona, appear to have been communicated to, and established in observance at Sassari and Cagliari.

In the year 1819, the King of Sardinia authorized a reform of the civil code generally; but this was opposed by the Senate of Turin; and we do not know whether a separate commercial code was enacted, or the French Code de Commerce adopted, as in Piedmont, or whether the foreign jurisprudence still prevails.

Section VII.

Of the Works of Italian Jurisconsults, on Maritime and Commercial Law.

But in order to become acquainted with the details of the maritime and mercantile jurisprudence of modern Italy, it is necessary, in addition to the regular codes promulgated under the public and express authority of the state, and the more ancient compilations by individuals of usages and customs adopted generally from their intrinsic excellence, without any legislative enactment, to consult also the valuable writings of the Italian lawyers, who, whenever their own positive enactments have proved deficient, have proceeded upon, and followed out, the equitable principles of the Roman law, and of the Consolato del Mare; and, recording the decisions of their respective commercial courts, have handed down to posterity a body of juridical wisdom, derived from, and founded on, experience. To enumerate all the modern Italian writers on maritime and commercial law is beyond the limits of the information we possess; but it will be sufficient to notice the principal and most useful authors.

A considerable number of Italian lawyers wrote treatises on different branches of mercantile and maritime jurisprudence in the course of the fifteenth and sixteenth centuries, and towards the beginning of the seventeenth century. Of these treatises, and also of several treatises by the mercantile lawyers of other nations, a collection was made in a large folio volume, and printed, along with the Decisiones Rotæ Genuæ, at Cologne in 1622, and afterwards at Amsterdam in 1669. The volume commences with the Decisiones Rotæ Genuæ de

Mercatura et rebus ad eam pertinentibus, to the number of CCXV. Next follow the treatises of Benevuto Straccha, a patrician and eminent lawyer of Ancona, which were written about the year 1570, and are entitled De Mercatura seu Mercatore; De Contractibus et Causis Mercatorum; De Nautis, Navibus, et Navigatione; De Decoctoribus—namely, concerning debtors, insolvent or bankrupt, and their creditors; and at the end of the volume, De Assecurationibus et Proxeneticis—namely, on insurances, and agents, or brokers; all truly excellent. This collection also contains the treatises of Joannes Nider, De Contractibus Mercatorum; of Baldus de Ubaldis, De Perusio, De Constituto, et De Carceribus; of Hyppolitus de Marsiliis, Bononiensis, De Fidejussoribus; of Jacobus de Arena, De excussione Bonorum, De Sequestrationibus, et De Cessione Actionum; of Benedictus De Plumbino, De Discussionibus; of J. B. Caccialupus, De Debitore suspecto et fugitivo; of Franciscus Cartius, Papiensis, De Sequestris; of Joannes de Grassis, De Cessione Juris; of Jacobus Butrigarius, Bononiensis, De Renuntiationibus Juris; and of Matthæus Brunus, De Cessione Bonorum.

In the year 1547, Julius Ferrotus de Ravenna wrote a treatise de Jure Navali. But this work was not published till 1579, when the author's son had it printed in quarto at Venice, and dedicated the book, although by no means of superior merit, to no less a personage than the Emperor Charles V.

In the year 1618, or 1620, Sigismundus Scaccia, a celebrated lawyer of modern Rome, published, in folio, a long and learned treatise, De Commerciis et Cambio, on commercial dealings in general, and particularly on exchange of money. And this work was reprinted at Frankfort in 1648.

About the year 1655, Roccus, an eminent Neapolitan advocate and civil judge, published two concise and neat treatises, the one, De Navibus et Naulo, concerning vessels and freights, the other, De Assecurationibus, on insurance. These works were reprinted in octavo at Amsterdam, in 1708. And, at this day, Roccus is frequently referred to as an authority by English lawyers.

Towards the close, also, of the seventeenth century, Ansaldus de Ansaldis, a patrician of Florence, and advocate in the courts of Rome, published, in folio at Rome, in 1689, his Discursus Legales de Commercio et Mercatura, to the number of CI. And in 1689-95, Cardinal di Luca published his voluminous work entitled Theatrum Veritatis et Justitiae, in which there are several valuable treatises on commercial subjects, such as De Creditis.

About the end of the seventeenth century, (1692,) or the beginning of last century, Carlo Targa, a very learned Genoese lawyer, published in Italian his Ponderazioni sopra la Contrattazioni Marittime; a work comparatively well arranged, and devoted exclusively to the illustration of strictly maritime law. The principles laid down in this work are, in most respects, conformable to the maxims and usages prescribed in the Consolato del Mare. In his Droit Maritime de l'Europe, published in the year 1805, Azuni informs us the treatise of Targa was still of great authority in the Genoese tribunals of commerce. And the edition we possess was published, in 1805, at Trieste.

But of all the Italian writers on general maritime and commercial law, Casaregis, a noble Genoese advocate, and counsellor of justice to the Grand Duke of Tuscany, while he is one of the latest, is also beyond dispute the best. He taught as a professor of law, and wrote and practised, both as a lawyer and as a judge, from about the close of the seventeenth till towards the middle of last century, having died in the year 1738.

His works, printed at first only partially during his life, were reprinted, a short time after his death, under the inspection of his brother, with such additions as the author had made, in the year 1740, in three volumes folio. Of this last edition, the first two volumes were entirely occupied with the Discursus Legales de Commercio, or treatises on the different branches of maritime and commercial law; namely, Navis, Naula et Naulizationes, Jactus, Averiæ, seu Contributiones, Assecurationes, Cambia Nundinaria et Maritima, Societates et Decoctiones, Accommendæ et Implicitæ, Giratæ, Literarum Cambii. The third volume contains a corrected edition of the Consolato del Mare, with a Commentary by Casaregis; and also a treatise, in Italian, entitled Il Cambista Istruito, on the laws of exchange and banking.

After Casaregis, the next Italian author on maritime and mercantile jurisprudence appears to be Ascanio Baldasseroni, a learned advocate, who, in 1786, published at Florence a treatise, entitled, Delli Assecurazioni Marittime, in three volumes quarto; and a second edition in 1801-1804, in five volumes quarto. Of the second edition of this work, the first two volumes are devoted to the contract of insurance; the third volume is devoted to Cambio Marittimo, or bottomry and respondentia, with a collection of the recent decisions of the Rota Romana, of the Rota Civile de Genova, of the Consoli di Mare di Pisa, and of the Rota Fiorentina; the fourth volume is devoted to jetson, averages, and contributions, with a collection of the opinions of lawyers, and of decisions of the different courts before mentioned; and the fifth volume contains a Collezione delle Leggi, Constituzioni ed Usi, delle Principali Piazze di Commercio d'Europa. In this Baldasseroni displays both acuteness and learning. He was acquainted with the latest English and French authorities at the time he wrote; his arrangement is good; and, upon the whole, the work is well worth the perusal of the British student of law.

About the same time, the Conte Pompeio Baldasseroni, a Tuscan lawyer, published Trattato sulle Lettere di Cambio, entitled, Leggi e Costumi del Cambio; and a third edition, in 1805, at Modena. This work is also very learned; is well arranged; and though prolix, like the work last mentioned, is well worth the perusal of the British student.

In the latter part of the eighteenth century, likewise, Michele de Jorio, a Neapolitan advocate, raised himself, by his talents and learning, to great eminence as a mercantile lawyer. As we have seen, he was employed by King Ferdinand to compose for the kingdom of Naples and Sicily a code of maritime and commercial law; and he actually prepared such a draft, under the appellation of Codice Fernando. But as only twenty-five copies of this work were printed, for the use of the counsellors of state, it is not to be purchased, and has never, it is believed, been brought to Britain; and we know its contents partially only, from the information of M. Pardessus, who had got a present of a copy, that Chapter IV. of the Italian work—published by Azuni in 1795, under the title of Sistema Universale dei Principii del Diritto Marittimo dell' Europa, which occupies one hundred and sixty pages of the French translation of that work, reprinted by the author in 1810, under the title of Origine et Progrès du Droit Maritime—is a literal and textual copy of part of the work of Jorio. This part of the draft of the Codice Fernando, which Azuni ought unquestionably to have acknowledged, and which has reached us in this rather singular manner, indicates great historical research. And we likewise find great learning and legal acuteness and arrangement in the subsequent work, which Jorio published in

November, 1799, in four volumes, and dedicated to King Ferdinand IV., under the title of La Giurisprudenza del Commercio.

The last-mentioned work is apparently unfinished, inasmuch as the author proposes to treat, in two parts, of commerce by land and of commerce by sea; and merely completes the first part: but, in this first part, although he does not treat specially of vessels, mariners, affreightment, or insurance, he embraces a great many of the doctrines of the law of maritime commerce, national and international. The first book, consisting of fifteen titles, treats of the persons engaged in or connected with commerce. The second book, consisting of twenty-six titles, treats of the subjects of commerce, or commodities, and their exportation or importation. The third book, consisting of nineteen titles, treats of property in merchandise. The fourth book, consisting of fifty-six titles, treats of mercantile obligations and actions. The fifth book, consisting of forty-seven titles, treats of obligations and actions which arise from mercantile insolvency and failures. The sixth book, consisting of thirteen titles, treats of mercantile exceptions. The seventh book, consisting of thirty-four titles, treats of mercantile judicial procedures. The eighth book, consisting of forty titles, treats of mercantile books, of operations in books of commerce, and of mercantile letters and correspondence.

Among the Italian writers on maritime law, at the close of the last and commencement of the present century, we may also rank M. D. A. Azuni, who was judge in the maritime and commercial court of Nice, and whose work on maritime law, although subsequently translated into French, and enlarged by the author, was originally composed in Italian. The second volume of his revised and enlarged work, Droit Maritime de l'Europe, treats of maritime international law chiefly in time of war, which does not fall within the range of our present inquiries. The merit of the first volume, republished in 1810, is chiefly historical, as giving a brief account of the private maritime law of ancient and modern nations; and, according to M. Pardessus, the most valuable part of it was derived from the unpublished work of Jorio, before mentioned.

About the commencement of the present century, too, Luigi Piantanida, a Milanese advocate, published a treatise Della Giurisprudenza Maritima Commerciale, Antica e Moderna, in four volumes, quarto, and dedicated his work to the Emperor Napoleon, for whom he professed the highest admiration. The first two volumes, which appeared in 1806, embrace the different subjects of private maritime law; the other two volumes, which appeared in 1807 and 1808, relate almost entirely to international maritime law, and do not fall within the range of this historical sketch. After an historico-political introductory dissertation, the first volume commences with an account of the Consolato del Mare, in which, however, the author does not shew much critical acumen. He next, rather prematurely, passes to risks, adverse events at sea, and their consequences. He next treats, in several titles, of consuls, in the modern sense of that term, namely, commercial consuls resident in foreign countries; of the office and powers of the high admirals of the modern European kingdoms; of maritime jurisdiction generally, political and judicial; and of maritime and commercial judicial tribunals. He then treats, in separate titles, in rather an inverted order, of the captain, of the crew of mariners, and of the vessel itself. In the second volume, the author treats in separate titles of shipwrecks, of the stranding, collision, and burning of vessels; of abandonment, of recovery and salvage; of the unseaworthiness, or innavigability of the vessel; of jetson and contribution, of averages, of maritime exchange, of policies of marine insurance, and of the Actio Exercitoria. In these two volumes the author shews a great deal of learning, classical, middle age, and modern; and the work is certainly worthy of the perusal of the student of maritime and commercial law. At the same time, it is prolix, is loaded with rather extraneous matter, and, from the preceding recital of the titles, is obviously very defective in arrangement.

CHAPTER II.

OF THE MARITIME AND COMMERCIAL LAW OF SPAIN AND PORTUGAL.

Section I.

Spain.

According to the order formerly proposed, we proceed to notice the maritime and mercantile laws of Spain and Portugal; and here, according to Capmany, that excellent modern Spanish writer on the commercial history of his country, with the exception of the Consolato del Mare, we find no general code or body of maritime legislation or jurisprudence established for, or observed throughout, the whole of these kingdoms. In Spain, in particular, almost every province, commercial city, and seaport, was governed by its own local practice, and the general usages of trade; and the principal object of inquiry, accordingly, after the full account already given of the Consolato del Mare, is these separate collections of maritime laws, which were subsequently, at different times, established in the different provinces and states by their respective governments or commercial courts.

Of all these provinces and states, Catalonia and Barcelona, we have already seen, made the earliest progress in general civilisation, and particularly in trade and navigation. Originally compiled at Barcelona, the Consolato del Mare was, from the excellence of its doctrines, immediately adopted, not only in that city, but likewise on all the coasts of the Mediterranean dependent on Spain. And of this compilation, the Barcelonese afterwards supplied the deficiencies, and made various additions, suited to the advancing circumstances of the times, by particular ordinances drawn up under the direction of their municipal magistracy and ancient consulado, or commercial court, and occasionally confirmed by royal authority.

In the year 1343, the municipal magistracy of Barcelona, as we formerly noticed, published an ordinance fixing the rules to be observed in contracts for voyages, namely, contracts of affreightment or charterparty between the owners and masters of vessels, and merchants shipping their goods on board such vessels; and, in the year 1373, a regulation was made fixing the premium or rate of interest to be paid for the exchanges or advances in cash made to those persons who fitted out vessels, and made investments for the Low Countries.

In the year 1394, the magistrates of Barcelona made regulations for rendering the use of bills of exchange more safe and expeditious. The drawer was ordained either to accept the draft, or to declare that he was not to do so, within twenty-four hours after it was presented; and if he did not intimate his intention not to accept the bill within that short period, he was held to have accepted it.

In the year 1401, a bank of exchange and of common and safe deposit was established at Barcelona, also under the authority of the municipal magistracy. And this appears to have been the earliest establishment of the kind in Europe, as the Bank of St George at Genoa was only established in the year 1407. In this money table or common bank at Barcelona, according to the primitive form and method of its institution, was kept and secured, without any premium or interest, all the cash of communities and individuals, in whatever species of current coin; credit being given according to the intrinsic value. And, notwithstanding no interest was given for the money lodged, this establishment afforded great facility to mercantiledealings. In it payments and deposits were made by every description of persons; its being under the authority of the state rendered the security undoubted; and the authentic forms which were observed in it, and the regular mode in which the business was conducted, obtained the confidence of individuals, and promoted mercantile credit. The regulations, too, which were established in this bank tended to secure the moderation of interest and of the premium of exchange, as appears from a document preserved by Capmany, and dated in the year 1404, in which it is stated to be the practice at Barcelona to pay bills of exchange with bank paper, in which the value in exchange could be obtained at much less expense than by the purchase of the actual specie. And, with regard to the era of the introduction of bills of exchange in modern Europe, it may be observed that the document published by Capmany, to which reference has just been made, and which, in a letter from the burgomasters of Bruges, in Flanders, to the municipal magistracy of Barcelona, on the subject of the mode of exchange and payment, contains copies of two bills, drawn in April and May, 1404, by merchants in Bruges upon merchants in Barcelona, which are written in the short form at present in use, and from which it appears that usance, or a fixed time for drawing, was then in practice—that it was then customary to draw first and second bills—and that, when bills were not accepted, it was customary to protest them.

But not only did the municipal magistracy of Barcelona promote commerce and navigation, by establishing a proper police for their harbours—by permanent armaments for scouring the sea of pirates—by treaties with foreign states—by establishing a bank—and by regulations relative to bills of exchange; in no particular did they manifest greater sagacity and spirit of improvement, according to the experience of these times, than in the provisions they made for giving a regular form to marine insurances. Among the different commercial nations of Europe, we have not found, in past ages, any early monument or record which preserves the memory, or marks the precise era, of the introduction and original or primitive practice of this important branch of trade. And until some more ancient monuments be produced than those which we formerly mentioned, and which we may here again notice, Spain is entitled to be considered as the first state in Europe in which this new species of trade was known and carried on. At Barcelona, marine insurance, as we have seen, may be traced back to the commencement of the fifteenth century; and, to prevent the frauds and other abuses which even then had become frequent, certain municipal ordinances were promulgated in the year 1435. These are still in preservation, and consist of twenty chapters; and they relate chiefly to the articles upon which, and the extent to which, natives and foreigners might be insured; to the form and solemnities of the written documents by which the relative obligations and responsibilities of the insurer and the insured were to be ascertained; to the term of payment of the premiums; to the mode of adjusting losses in general, and particularly average losses; and to various other such matters, of which the Consulado del Mar, the maritime commercial court, had an exclusive jurisdiction.

But while by this public document, the earliest of the kind in Europe, it is placed beyond doubt that marine insurance was in practice at Barcelona early in the fifteenth century, it does not appear, on the other hand, that it was in general use in Spain in the year 1401. In that year the King of Aragon granted a charter to the Barcelonese, which has been preserved by Capmany, and in which that monarch confirmed former privileges, and extended the jurisdiction of the Consulado, or commercial tribunal of Barcelona, to all civil causes arising from mercantile contracts, whether mercantile or not. In that charter, questions of copartnership, of exchange, and other such contracts, are specially noticed; but no mention whatever is made of insurance. Indeed, from the preamble of the Ordinance of 1435, it appears that the business of insurance was first carried on under the public authority. And from the precautions which appear, from the contents of the Ordinance, to have been taken in relation to those enterprises—the care with which the benefit of insurance was confined solely to such articles as were objects of commerce to the people itself—and from the restrictions to which the parties to the contract were subjected by government with regard to the value of the things insured, the persons entitled to insure, the distance of the voyage, the production and destination of the commodities—it is manifest that the insurances of those days were the first essays in that line of business, the rude beginnings of what was afterwards to form a great branch of mercantile speculation.

The ordinances just referred to, however, were altered by others, promulgated in 1458 and 1461, in consequence of experience having shewn, in the vicissitudes of times, the necessity of correction and reform; and by these the powers of the insurer and of the insured were enlarged, and various restrictions, both as to the vessel and voyage, removed. Farther, in the year 1484, the municipal magistracy of Barcelona promulgated another ordinance on insurance, which repealed, or rather recast, all the former tentative or experimental ordinances, which is arranged in twenty-five chapters, and the object of which was to give greater security and facility to commerce, and to render more expeditious and general that branch of business. And in these later ordinances we discover greater enlargement of view, and greater freedom from constraint, than in the earlier ones, according as trade was extended, and governments and individuals became more enlightened from experience.

As Spain was thus unquestionably the country in which the most ancient known laws of the middle ages upon maritime insurance were established, we may here, perhaps, with some propriety, recapitulate the historical notices by M. Pardessus of this interesting contract.

It is beyond dispute that neither the laws of the ancient nations who preceded the Romans, nor the body of law digested by the order of Justinian in the sixth century, nor even the compilation of the Basilica, made towards the tenth century, contained regulations upon marine insurance. It is not, certainly, that the jurisconsults, whose works have made us acquainted with the maritime legislation of ancient nations, were ignorant of the chances or risks of losses at sea, or of the accidents to which vessels and their cargoes were exposed. Several texts of the Digest, transferred into the Basilica, prove that these chances or risks were often casual and contingent conditions in other principal contracts.

Nay, as we have seen, we find the entire formula of a contract of bottomry or respondentia, or of loan of money upon marine risk, in the pleadings of Demosthenes. The compilations of Justinian, and the Basilica, too, contain pretty extensive titles on that contract; and every one knows that the rules relative to maritime risks are the same in the contract of insurance and in that of loan on bottomry or respondentia. This is what modern legislators have recognised and established; as may be seen in Article 5th of Title VI. of Book III. of the Ordinance of France, of 1681. It is also the result of the perusal of the first law on insurance digested in Europe, in the fifteenth century.

It is manifest from the later Greek compilation, falsely called Jus Navale Rhodiorum, that the practice of a sort of mutual insurance against the principal accidents of navigation, among the owners or charterers of the vessel and the different shippers of the cargo, was introduced in the course of the twelfth century in some maritime districts, particularly in the maritime cities situated on the Adriatic. But this mutual insurance, which may, perhaps, have subsequently suggested the idea of insurance for a premium, differs from it too essentially to admit of the two being confounded.

At the time Pegoletti wrote, namely, in the year 1330, conventions appear to have been entered into against the Rischio di Mare, e di Genti, at Florence. The text of this author is not explicit; but as he speaks of the salaries of or allowances to brokers, for those pieces of business, at so much per cent. upon the sums agreed upon, M. Pardessus thinks we may infer the existence of contracts of insurance for a premium; that is to say, contracts by which one person undertakes, in consideration of a certain sum, the risk of a commodity or article which belongs to another. The most ancient law of Florence, indeed, which we know upon insurances, is from 1522 to 1523. But anterior laws appear to have existed; and usages are often observed for a long time before they are converted into laws. It is admitted, however, on all hands, that there does not exist the least evidence that insurances were known in Europe prior to the year 1300; and, in point of historical fact, while the practice of insurance for a premium may be inferred to have existed at Florence from the commencement of the fourteenth, perhaps, even at the end of the thirteenth century, the legislation of Barcelona is the first in which this species of business is presented in a distinct manner.

In endeavouring to explain or account for the absence of the contract of insurance among the ancients, and its late introduction in modern Europe, M. Pardessus justly observes, "The sciences in the domain of logic and philosophy," (apparently meaning, by the latter term, the intellectual or mental and moral sciences,) "made, at Rome, much greater progress than the exact sciences. The ancients had some able mathematicians; but we do not find, so far as appears in their works still extant, or in what we know of those which have disappeared, any proof that they had directed their studies to the calculation of chances or probabilities. The Digest, l. xxxv. tit. ii., p. 68, presents a text, in which are established different calculations as to the probable duration of life; but they are only simple approximations, without any exact basis. As little do we know whether, when in the course of the fourteenth and fifteenth centuries adventurous speculators undertook to insure against the risks of navigation, they had any basis founded on mathematical combinations; and it rather appears that time and experience alone have produced the modern theories."

Nor were the Barcelonese more attentive to the enactment of good laws on maritime and mercantile affairs, than to the establishment of a good commercial tribunal for the enforcement of these laws. The jurisdiction of the consular court was at first confined to questions of maritime contracts only. But this jurisdiction, as already noticed, was afterwards extended by royal charter, in 1401, so as to embrace all civil causes arising from any mercantile act or contract whatever, whether by sea or land. And, at the end of the Consolato del Mare, there have been preserved and published thirty-five chapters, which compose the legal constitution of the Consulado, or maritime and commercial court of Barcelona. The constitution of this court served as a model for the other maritime and mercantile tribunals which were erected in Spain, and also in various other parts of Europe, so far as was compatible with the political and local circumstances of these countries. The form of procedure prescribed in these regulations is well adapted for the expeditious determination of mercantile causes. And from this early work of the Barcelonese, some practical hints might be derived and adopted with advantage in the judicial legislation of even these comparatively more enlightened times.

So much for the maritime laws of Barcelona, on which we have formerly, and now again, been led to enlarge, as forming an interesting branch of the history of the commercial law of Europe. In the course of the fifteenth and sixteenth centuries, we also find various particular regulations, relative to maritime and commercial transactions, established in the other kingdoms and cities of Spain; particularly the Ordinances of Burgos and of Seville.

From the middle of the fifteenth century, Burgos was a place of considerable trade; had a Casa de Contratacion, or mercantile corporation, a consular or peculiar commercial jurisdiction, and factories in a number of the ports of the different kingdoms of Europe. The Ordinances of Burgos were collected and formally promulgated in the year 1563, under the sanction of Charles V.; and they treat not only of the fitting out and loading of vessels, but also of the forms of letters, or bills of exchange, and of marine insurance. The last thirty-three chapters relate entirely to insurance, presuppose other regulations on the subject more ancient, and seem to imply that this kind of business was practised in that state from an early period.

In the year 1543, at the request of the merchants and traders to the Indies, a court or council, with a peculiar jurisdiction, was established at Seville, for the regulation and determination of all matters relative to that important branch of Spanish commerce. Soon afterwards, in the year 1556, a long ordinance, consisting of a great many chapters, was promulgated by King Philip II., for regulating the insurance of ships and cargoes to and from the Indies. And in 1678, there were published, in quarto, Ordenanzas para il Prior y Consules de la Universidad de los Mercadores de la Ciudad de Sevilla.

Such maritime and commercial regulations as those we have been considering, behoved, of course, to be of great utility in the different provinces for which they were framed, and in which they were established. But, as Capmany informs us, the utility of these commercial laws was, in a great degree, limited and circumscribed by the state of disunion in which the kingdoms of Spain continued long after they came to acknowledge one sovereign, in the person of Charles V. After the crowns of Castile and Aragon were united in the same monarch, it was to have been expected that the two kingdoms would gradually have been consolidated into one state and people, so as to be productive of new advantages to the subjects of each; but this was by no means the case. The narrow policy of these times either had not the wisdom, or, from fear and distrust, had not the wish, to combine the interests of the different provinces, in order to benefit them as far as the discordance of their customs and constitutions of government would permit; and, under the different Princes of the House of Austria, the two kingdoms continued to look upon each other rather as foreign nations, and had no other connection than the dependence which arose from this subjection to a common sovereign. Indeed the political separation, or disunion of the monarchy, continued, in a great measure, till the family of Bourbon occupied the throne of Spain. After that event, the government became more enlightened; and, in order to increase the power of the monarch, endeavoured to incorporate and unite the detached parts of which the nation was composed. In the course of last century various important measures were suggested by enlightened individuals, and adopted by government, in order to recover the manufacturing and the inland and maritime commerce of Spain from the state of decay into which they had fallen. Of these measures, however, the success was only partial; and, so far as regards our subject, no attempt was made to establish a general code of maritime and commercial law for the united kingdoms and their vast colonies. The old plan of local and particular legislation was adhered to; and to the more ancient compilations already noticed, we have to add the improved Ordinances of Bilboa and St Sebastian, the works of the eighteenth century.

The Ordinances of Bilboa were compiled and revised, and were approved by the King, in 1737; and they were afterwards ratified in 1774. They relate chiefly to averages, to bottomry and insurances, and to bills of exchange; with regard to which last the law is detailed at great length. And by these ordinances chiefly are maritime affairs regulated on the coasts bordering upon the Atlantic Ocean.

The ordinances of the Consulado of San Sebastian were reformed and approved by the royal council of Castile in the year 1766; and in these, along with other commercial subjects, the law of bills of exchange is also fully treated.

Such are, in general, the particular and local codes, of which, till very lately, the maritime and commercial law of Spain was chiefly composed. As already noticed, there was no general national code. The only completely general laws, relative to commerce and navigation, appear to have been those contained in some titles of the fifth book of the Leyes de Partidas, which treat of ships and merchants, and in some pragmatic sanctions in the Curia Philipica, and in the Recopilacion de las Leyes del Regno de Espana. And most of these regulations, of which a considerable portion are of more use in tracing the history of commerce than in directing the administration of justice, Capmany informs us, were not accommodated to the times in which he wrote—viz. the eighteenth century—were not applicable to the then state of the monarchy, and did not by any means constitute a body of maritime legislation.

As already noticed, the relations and intercourse with the Indies were regulated by the laws and usages of the Consulado of Seville, established in 1636, and by those of the Consulado of Cadiz, established in 1680, except in so far as they were derogated from by the pragmatic sanctions of the royal council of the Indies. In short, since the discovery of America, and especially in still later times, Spain has had no commerce or navigation except with the Indies. And, accordingly, that kingdom has comparatively produced few writers on commerce and navigation; and the few authors whom it has produced write almost only in relation to that particular trade.

Of these authors the principal seem to be the following :—

Jouan de Hevia, Bolanos, who, in 1619, published a work entitled Laberinto del Commercio Terrestre y Maritimo.

Veitia Lonano, or Vestia Linange, who, in 1672, wrote a work entitled Norte de la Contratacion de las Indias Occidentales, or Guide to the Commerce of the West Indies, in folio.

El Caballero Abreu, the Chevalier d'Abreu, who, in 1746, published a work entitled Tratado Juridico Politico, sobre las Presas Maritimas, a Juridical and Political Treatise on Maritime Prizes, embracing some of the leading questions of maritime international law. This work was translated into French in 1802.

Suarez, who, towards the end of last century, namely, after the year 1774, published a work entitled Tratado Legal, Teorico y Practico, de Literas de Cam bio, a Treatise, Theoretical and Practical, on the Law of Bills of Exchange. From the quotations from this work, it appears to be of considerable excellence; but the author of this sketch has not succeeded in procuring a copy of it.

Lastly, Don Antonio de Capmany, whom we have so often mentioned, who was some years ago one of the ablest members of the Cortez of Spain, and who, besides his history of the commerce of Barcelona, published in the year 1791, also published a new edition of the Consulado del Mar, under the title of Libro des Costumbres Maritimas, accompanied with learned annotations and commentaries, as well as with more recent pieces of Spanish maritime legislation.

Such seems to have been the state of the maritime and commercial law of Spain at the close of the last, and even for a considerable part of the present, century. The principal commercial cities of the kingdom continued almost all to have their own peculiar laws, although, from the end of the last century, the Ordinance of Bilboa, published in 1737, having been several times revised, and lastly in 1819, had come to predominate. From this state of matters there had resulted great confusion, and a great deal of uncertainty in commercial law, and in the forms to be observed for rendering such operations and transactions secure; and it was to remedy this evil that the Sovereign, in January, 1828, appointed a commission of seven members to prepare the projet or draft of a code, to be binding upon the whole kingdom. This draft was not approved by the King, who directed one of the members of this commission, Don Pedro Sainz de Andino, to prepare a new draft. This new projet was composed of two distinct parts. The first, composed of 1219 articles, under the title of Code de Commerce, treats of commercial matters and contracts, viewed under their general relations, as well as in their different specialties; of factories and bankruptcies; of the organization and competence of commercial jurisdictions. The second part, composed of 462 articles, under the title of the Law of Procedure in Commercial Affairs and Causes, determines the different proceedings to be followed before the commercial tribunals, according to the nature and importance of the action to be instituted. Both these parts of the new projet received the royal sanction without any comment, and were promulgated, the first in May, 1829, and the second in July, 1830.

With regard to the first and rejected projet, M. Victor Foucher, avocat-general du Roi, in his Collection des Lois Civiles et Criminelles des Etats Modernes, 1838, informs us, that, on comparing it with the promulgated law, if the general principles were often similar, there was a difference in their application, as well as in the consequences deduced from them, and that the compilers had viewed the duty of the legislator under different aspects. The authors of the first projet in general confined themselves to laying down definite principles upon each subject of the code, leaving it to the judges, as the administrators of the law, to deduce their legal consequences. In this respect they approached to the form of the French code; from which, however, they kept at a greater distance, in point of principles, than the compiler of the projet which was ultimately sanctioned did. The latter, on the contrary, has, in a manner, followed step by step the parent ideas of the French code, adding all the developments of which they appeared to have been susceptible, and has thus decided legislatively many of the questions, resolved differently in jurisprudence, by the determination of courts of law. The Spanish commercial code may, therefore, be considered as a commentary on the French code, but it is a beautiful commentary; while its author, availing himself of the various sources of the Spanish commercial law, has known how to introduce some happy modifications into the system which served him as a basis.

M. Foucher farther informs us that the principal alterations made upon the French law by the Spanish commercial code are already duly appreciated in France by intelligent men; and that M. d'Andino admits he derived the elements of his work from the clear and precise doctrine of M. Pardessus. "But," continues M. Foucher, "if the Spanish code of commerce be truly a legislative model, notwithstanding some imperfections which may be here and there discovered, it is not so with the Spanish law of judicial procedure." And he goes on to point out various defects in the latter:—such as the excessive number of auxiliary agents and inferior officers in the courts, by which the expense of lawsuits is greatly increased; the necessity imposed on each party of obtaining an order of court for most of the notices they have occasion to give to the opposite party; and the multiplicity of Instances, or of appeals from court to court.

Section II.

Portugal.

In this cursory view of the history of maritime and commercial law in modern Europe, we have classed Portugal along with Spain; and, in fact, the maritime laws of Portugal were nearly the same as those of Seville, as long as the two kingdoms were united. The Portuguese, however, had several peculiar ordinances of their own ancient Sovereigns relative to maritime affairs, which were collected, confirmed, and augmented, in the year 1643, by John of Braganza. Since that period, ordinances relative to trade and navigation have, from time to time, continued to be framed and promulgated by the Portuguese government; and of these ordinances, ancient and modern, collections were published in the years 1747, 1752, 1767, and 1774, under the titles of Ordinaçoes et Leys de Reyno de Portugal, and Colleccão des Leys Decretos e Alvaras.

Portugal has also produced several writers of eminence on the law of maritime commerce, of whom the following are the principal:—Perez, in his Commentary on the Code of Justinian at the title De Naufragiis; Roderigo Zuarïo, De usu Maris, de Navibus Transvehendis, et Mercibus Exportandis; Pedro Santerna, de Assecurationibus, et Sponsionibus Mercatorum.

Of the two last-mentioned authors, the treatises are contained in the collection to which we formerly referred, when noticing the Italian writers, entitled De

Mercatura, Decisiones, et Tractatus varii, in folio published, first, in the year 1608, and afterwards at Amsterdam in 1669. To these may be added Estevan Freitas, De Jure et Imperio Lusitanorum Asiatico.

Finally, although the work does not appear to have reached this country, we find, from the late M. Martens, of the University of Göttingen, that, in 1794, there was published at Lisbon, in quarto, a work entitled Freirii Institutiones Juris Civilis Lusitani, cum Publici, tum Privati, of which the eighth title treats de commerciis.

In the course of the present century, the attention of the government has been directed to the establishment of an improved commercial as well as general civil code. And in 1838, M. Victor Foucher announced a French edition of the Code de Commerce de Portugal.

CHAPTER III.

OF THE MARITIME AND COMMERCIAL LAW OF THE NETHERLANDS, SOUTHERN AND NORTHERN.

Section I.

Southern Netherlands.

From Spain and Portugal, we proceed, according to the order of events in the commercial history of Europe, to consider the laws of the Low Countries, or Netherlands, Southern and Northern; of Flanders, now the kingdom of Belgium; and of the United Provinces, now the kingdom of Holland.

In the course of the thirteenth, fourteenth, and fifteenth centuries, various circumstances, we have already seen, had concurred to render the inhabitants of Flanders and Brabant a trading and manufacturing people. From their geographical position, these provinces were calculated to become a sort of *entrepot* for the commodities of different nations, and to form a point of union and connection between the trade of the south and the trade of the north of Europe. The immediate sovereigns of these countries, the Counts of Flanders and the Dukes of Burgundy, were sufficiently powerful to resist all attacks from the neighbouring nations. They shewed more wisdom and policy than the greater potentates of Europe in these days, in the free reception which they gave to all foreigners who came to trade with their subjects. And in the towns of these provinces there was, from early times, a considerable degree of liberty and independence, at once the cause and the effect of the growth of commercial and manufacturing industry.*

Farther, in the comparatively very imperfect state of the art of navigation in the ages to which we have alluded, a voyage from the Baltic to the Mediterranean could with difficulty be accomplished in one season. It was therefore deemed necessary to divide the distance, by establishing, in the middle of the passage, a common market or emporium between the maritime nations of the north and south; and Bruges was chosen as one of the places most convenient for such trade.

This city, indeed, came in time to be the universal magazine or place of deposit for the wools and other raw produce of England; for the cloths and other manufactures of the Low Countries, in which the Flemings were soon able, from the comparative cheapness of labour, to undersell their instructors, the Italians; and for

---

* Capmany, Mem. Hist. vol. i., part ii., p. 126. Rymer, Fœd. tome iii., part iii., p. 92.

the naval stores and other produce of the north;—and, on the other hand, for all the articles which were exported from the Mediterranean, whether the precious commodities of India, or the natural and artificial productions of the different provinces of Italy, France, and Spain. And thus these commodities, of which the production, the exchange, and the carriage, constituted and supported the active traffic of the Italians, the Provençals, and the Catalonians, were again loaded at Bruges, in the vessels of the Hanseatic States, to be distributed through Germany and the northern kingdoms.

The result of this flux and reflux of commodities, and of all this mercantile industry, was the accumulation of comparatively great riches in the Netherlands. In the fourteenth century, such was the population, greatness, and splendour of Bruges, that it reckoned within its boundaries seventeen separate commercial establishments, all belonging to so many different foreign nations and states. And when, towards the end of the fifteenth century, Bruges, from internal causes which it is unnecessary here to notice, began to decline, Antwerp succeeded as the greatest emporium of Europe, and derived an accession of commerce and wealth from the Portuguese trade with India, to which that nation had recently discovered the passage by the Cape of Good Hope.

Such progress in commerce and navigation naturally required and led to a corresponding progress in maritime and commercial jurisprudence. We have already traced the early maritime usages of the Southern and Northern Netherlands—usages which Quinten Weitsen, in his Treatise on Averages, published in 1565, denominated Gemeene Costume. And we found it clearly established by M. Pardessus, that the first twenty-four articles of maritime usages, which were long observed in the southern Low Countries, under the name of the Judgments of Damme and the Laws of West Capelle, were merely a translation of the first twenty-four articles of the Roles d'Oleron, with an additional article in the latter. We found also that the mercantile and seafaring people of the northern Low Countries, without the interference of public or sovereign authority, and of consent among themselves, adopted, in the course of the fourteenth century, and collected, a number of maritime usages, under the title of the Ordinances of Amsterdam, vulgarly, Ordinantie; and that in this compilation they borrowed, by way of West Capelle, the primitive articles of the Roles d'Oleron, with the additional article in the collection of that city, and likewise borrowed from the statutes of Hamburgh and Lubeck. We found it also established by M. Pardessus, that the Judgments of Damme and the Ordinances of Amsterdam or Holland, with some articles borrowed from the statutes of Lubeck, were employed to form, and actually constituted, the compilation long known by the title of the Laws of Wisby. And, in the formation of these different compilations, we found that the respect entertained for usages, ancient and sanctioned by long practice, did not admit of the idea of recasting or new-moulding the two documents, in order to exclude from the one the articles which it had literally borrowed from the other, or to reconcile certain texts which seemed to exhibit antinomies. The one was transcribed at the end of, and immediately following, the other; and care was taken to preserve each document in its identity, and with its proper title. For an account of the manuscripts still extant of the maritime usages of Holland, commonly called Ordinantie, to the number of ten, and of the three printed editions of that compilation, by Van Leuwen, by Vagenaar, and by Verwer, we must refer to M. Pardessus, and particularly to the edition published by himself in 1837.

In following the progress of the maritime law of the Low Countries, we find that, next to the early usages we have just been considering, the placards or edicts promulgated by the Sovereigns of the House of Austria served as a second branch of that law. These edicts, with a very few exceptions, preceded the compilation of the local municipal customs in which are found rules of maritime law. They have been the foundation of the ordinances which a great number of the cities of the United Provinces established, after they obtained their independence: they have preserved their authority there; and this authority continued to the time when, in our days, the French codes were there introduced.

The earliest of these edicts, or placaats, was promulgated by the Emperor Charles V., who, by marriage, had become Sovereign of the Netherlands, in March 1537 for Brabant: it relates both to bills of exchange and insurances; but the regulations relative to each of these subjects are short and unimportant. They serve more to ascertain that these contracts were then in use than to regulate such transactions. With regard to insurances, this edict places beyond doubt that letters of insurance (the name then given to what we now call policies) were in practice among merchants. Indeed, the preamble of an ordinance of Philip Duke of Burgundy, in 1458, transcribed into that of the Ordinance of 1537, makes mention of the insurances which merchants effect with each other, of marine adventures and perils, and of bottomry or loan upon the body of the vessel. And these documents appear to be the most ancient, in the Low Countries, which treat of insurance. They presuppose also the previous existence and practice of such transactions; but the Chronicle of Flanders cannot be admitted as affording satisfactory evidence that the Count, in 1310, established a Chamber of Insurance at Bruges. The Ordinance of 1537 was succeeded by that of 1549; but the latter relates more to maritime police, the state of maritime commerce at that time, and the increasing number of accidents and losses at sea, than to private maritime law. And, for remedying such evils and abuses, the Ordinance directs how vessels must be fitted out, what must be their reach or burden, and what the number of the crew, and of guns, according to the countries for which they were destined, and the description of merchandise with which they were to be loaded; enjoins the master to enter into agreements for mutual assistance and defence; provides for the inspection of vessels before they sail, to ascertain they are seaworthy, and to prevent overloading; regulates contracts of affreightment between the shippers and captains; admits the intervention of the officers of the port to reconcile their differences; prohibits the loading in foreign ships when native ships can be procured; prohibits borrowing on bottomry, except in some cases; recognises insurances; treats of the prohibition of commerce with the enemy, of letters of marque, and privateering; recognises the rights of natives to reclaim the property of goods taken by pirates; and prohibits captains from allowing their ships to be boarded except by friends.

This Ordinance of 1549 was replaced by another of 1551, compiled by the Chancellor Viglius, and divided into two parts: the first reproducing the Ordinance of of 1549 with some variations; and the second devoted to private maritime law, and published at length by M. Pardessus. In the reign of Philip II., King of Spain, who succeeded to his father, the Emperor Charles V., as Sovereign of the Netherlands, and whom the recent discoveries of Columbus, and Vasco de Gama, contributed to render the most powerful monarch in Europe, the

Ordinance of 1551, was replaced in its turn by that of 1563, likewise compiled by the Chancellor Viglius. The first title contains, with some additions and variations, the first part of the Ordinance of 1551. The following titles reproduce, with additions and changes, the second part of the Ordinance of 1551; embracing the legal doctrines relative to shipwrecks, average losses, damage done in the course of navigation, the legal obligations of the masters of vessels and mariners, and, particularly, in more full development, the law of marine insurances, which were then practised more at Antwerp than in almost any other city of Europe.

The more the business of marine insurance was extended, the more was the necessity felt of improving the law applicable to such transactions. It may easily be believed that great abuses must have taken place, when, by an edict in 1568, Philip II. prohibited all kinds of insurance. But he revoked that edict in 1569; and a new and special ordinance on that subject was, in 1570, promulgated by the Duke of Alba in the name of the King.

Section II.

Northern Netherlands.

Soon after the promulgation of the general maritime and commercial legislation of the Emperor Charles V., and of Philip II. of Spain, as Sovereigns of the Netherlands, the seven Northern Provinces threw off the yoke of the House of Austria, and established their political independence. The Southern Provinces which remained under their former sovereigns, of course, continued to observe the maritime and commercial law which, we have just seen, the sovereigns had established, with occasional modifications from particular local usages. By the revolution which established the independence of the

United Provinces, the commercial and maritime greatness of Bruges and Antwerp was, to a great extent, transferred to the Hague, Utrecht, Amsterdam, Rotterdam, and Middleburgh. And the trade and naval power of the Dutch, which were so immense, compared with the extent of their territory, and which embraced in its range almost every quarter of the globe, could not fail to lead to the establishment of laws for regulating the various branches of which their domestic and foreign commerce was composed.

At the same time, although maritime commerce, from the date of the independence of the United Provinces as a Republic, except during their late temporary subjugation by the French, all along formed the principal occupation of the people, it does not appear the Dutch, till very recently, digested and enacted, by the supreme authority of the state, any general national code of maritime and mercantile law. And this may have arisen from the nature of their political organization, when they succeeded in establishing their independence, by which the country was divided into so many separate and independent provinces, each of which, and, indeed, each of the cities of which, had peculiar usages and interests—interests often opposite to each other, so as to render it difficult to effect a general legislative concurrence in such matters of private law. Accordingly, the Dutch appear to have continued to observe the early usages of the Netherlands, borrowed chiefly from the Roles d'Oleron, known under the titles of the Judgments of Damme, or Laws of West Capelle, and Laws of Amsterdam ; to have preserved, at the time of their separation from the Southern Provinces, the improved legislative enactments of Charles V. and Philip II. ; and, since that time till very recently, to have rested satisfied with modifying that general legislation, and supplying its defects by particular local or municipal statutes.

These local statutes, or municipal usages, subsequent to the legislation of Charles V. and Philip II., may be viewed as constituting a third branch of the private maritime and commercial law, both of the Southern and of the Northern Provinces of the Netherlands. And they have been carefully collected by M. Pardessus, and arranged, first geographically, and next chronologically. In the Southern Provinces we find the Custom of Antwerp of 1582, relative to insurances, against wager-policies, &c., and the Custom of Ostend of 1610, relative to the conveyance of goods in vessels. But the most important of these municipal ordinances are by the different cities of the United Provinces. Thus we find the statute of Amsterdam of 1527, on bottomry; the Ordinance of Amsterdam of 1598, on insurances and averages, and on the commercial court for the decision of such questions; the Ordinances of Amsterdam of 1606, 1607, 1610, 1614, 1620, 1621, and 1626, relative to insurances, averages, payment of premiums, bankruptcy of underwriters, and the summary mode of procedure for the settlement of such disputes; the Ordinances of Amsterdam of 1682, 1687, 1688, 1693, and 1699, relative to consignments of goods, bills of exchange, bills of lading, sale of vessels by part owners, and specification in the policy of insurance. And the Ordinance of 1598 was renewed, and still farther improved and augmented, particularly in the years 1744 and 1745, as collected by Magens, and as still more lately reported by Ricard, in his Traitè de Commerce d'Amsterdam, Part II., Book III., Art. 2. Again we have the Ordinance of Rotterdam of 1604, renewed in 1635, relative to insurances, averages, insurance brokers, commissioners for the trial of such questions, and another Ordinance, in the year 1655, relative to maritime affairs in general. And both these ordinances were renewed and enlarged in the year

1721. This last ordinance is comprehensive, and pretty well arranged; and treats not merely of averages and insurances, but also of the reciprocal duties of masters and mariners, owners and freighters. Again, we have the Ordinance of Middleburgh of 1600, on averages, insurances, and summary procedure in commercial tribunals, and this ordinance was afterwards renewed and improved in 1689 and in 1726.

Section III.

Dutch and Flemish writers on Maritime and Commercial Law.

So much for their state regulations in maritime and commercial law. The writers of the Dutch, and of the Flemings or Belgians, on this subject, are neither so numerous nor so voluminous as might have been expected from their laborious industry in other branches of learning and legal knowledge.

Their principal early authors, Peckius and Vinnius, content themselves with writing commentaries on, and illustrating, the titles of the Roman law relative to maritime affairs, and reconciling the rules of that system with the usages of their own Republic. Early in the seventeenth century, Peckius published his Commentarii in Titulos Digestorum et Codicis ad rem Nauticam pertinentes. And, in 1647, Vinnius published this work with notes and observations, which were reprinted at Amsterdam in 1668.

About the beginning, also, of the seventeenth century, Quinten Weitsen, Counsellor of the Court of Holland, published a valuable little treatise De Avariis, on averages. And this work was republished towards the end of that century, with notes and observations by Simon Van Leuwen and Matthew de Vicq, and again, in an improved order, by Casaregis in 1740.

In 1678, Simon Van Leuwen also published his work entitled Censura Forensis, seu totius Juris Civilis Romani, Recepti, et Practici, Methodica Collatio; in which, to a certain extent, the maritime, and to a much greater extent, the commercial law of Holland are ably treated; and in 1698 and 1704, John Voet published his Commentarius ad Pandectas, in two vols. folio; in which he incidentally treats of the maritime and, particularly, of the commercial law of Holland.

About the beginning, also, of the seventeenth century, namely, in 1609, Grotius published his treatise entitled Mare Liberum. In 1652, Graswinckel published his treatise entitled Vindiciæ Maris Liberi. And, in 1655, there was published a Collection der See Rechten, namely, of the Laws of the Sea.

At the close of the seventeenth, and during the early part of the eighteenth, century, Gerard Noodt, besides his various valuable works on the Roman law, published his De Fœnere et Usuris Libri tres, a work more nearly connected with mercantile law; and, during the early part also of the eighteenth century, the able Cornelius Van Bynkershoek published not only his Dissertatio de Dominio Maris, and his Treatise de Lege Rhodia de Jactu, which we formerly had occasion to commend when examining the authenticity of the work called Jus Navale Rhodiorum, but also various valuable works on the Roman law, on international law, in his Quæstiones Juris Publici, and in his treatise on the Competent Judge of Ambassadors, and likewise on the private commercial law of Holland in his Quæstionum Juris Privati Libri Quatuor.

Finally, in 1716, Verwers published a work entitled Nederlands Zee Regeln, or Loix Maritimes des Pays Bas;

and, in 1757, Wedderhopp published his useful work entitled Introductio ad Jus Nauticum.

During the occupation of the Netherlands by the French, under the Emperor Napoleon, the French Code de Commerce was, of course, established in that country. After the union, at the general pacification of 1815, of the Netherlands, Southern and Northern, into one kingdom, the government proposed, in 1819, several new codes, or parts of a new civil code: but these were not adopted by the states-general; and the result was, a resolution in 1821, merely to make such ameliorations of the existing laws as might be suggested by the ablest lawyers of the kingdom.

In the course of the years 1824 and 1825, it appears that, not only a civil code, but also a commercial code had been composed. As none of these codes, however, were to be carried into execution as law till the whole were finished, we have not learned that this Code de Commerce became law throughout the kingdom of the Netherlands, before its separation in the year 1830 into the kingdoms of Holland and Belgium. Since that separation, it rather appears that the kingdoms of Holland and Belgium have each established commercial codes for themselves; for, in the year 1839, M. Victor Foucher published, as the seventh Livraison of his Collection des Lois Civiles et Criminelles des Etats Modernes, the Code de Commerce du Royaume de Hollande, translated by M. Willem Wintgens.

CHAPTER IV.

OF THE MARITIME AND COMMERCIAL LAW OF FRANCE.

HAVING finished our cursory sketch of the maritime and commercial law of the Netherlands, Southern and Northern, we proceed to take an historical view of the maritime and commercial legislation of France, and of the works of the lawyers of that country who have written on that branch of jurisprudence.

SECTION I.

Southern Provinces, Provence, Languedoc, Marseilles, Narbonne, &c.

In considering Marseilles as one of the maritime Republics which arose in the middle ages on the northern coasts of the Mediterranean, we have in part anticipated the maritime law of the south of France; and, as centuries elapsed before the different provinces of that kingdom were united under one national, strong, and central government, we may first shortly notice a little further the progress of maritime law in those separate provinces which bordered upon the Mediterranean and the Atlantic.

Provence, with the exception of the Republic of Marseilles and its territory, had, of course, been subject to the legislation of Rome. After the fall of the Western Empire, Arles, the metropolis of that part of Gaul, became ultimately the seat of an independent kingdom; and, during the period of its freedom, it promulgated several statutes, in the course of the eleventh and twelfth centuries, particularly that of 1150, which is still extant in manuscript. But the object of these statutes was not so much to combine in one single body all their civil legislation, as to regulate the points for which the Roman law, still in observance, could no longer provide, in consequence of the change which had taken place in customs and in institutions.

When the province of Languedoc ceased to form a part of, or to be dependent upon, the Roman Empire in the west, and had been conquered by the Visigoths, their chief bodies of law appear to have been the Theodosian code, and the Breviarium of Alaric II.; but the habit of being so long governed by the Roman laws soon disposed the inhabitants of that country to adopt, in place of these imperfect and insufficient compilations, the system of law digested by direction of the Emperor Justinian, of which the study was introduced into France in the twelfth century; and Languedoc was accordingly one of these provinces, which were all along governed by the Roman law as their principal or fundamental law, with such modifications as local statutes or judicial determinations had introduced into it. In addition to the maritime law of the Romans, the inhabitants of Languedoc appear also to have adopted and been guided by the usages collected in the Consolato del Mare, from their communication and intercourse with Catalonia, in which that compilation had its origin. Indeed, Montpellier, one of the most commercial cities of Languedoc, appears, from the commencement of the thirteenth century, to have held a charter from its overlords, Princes of the House of Aragon, and to have had a judge named by them, called Bayle, for the determination of maritime disputes, who, of course, would conform to the jurisprudence followed in the other dominions of the King of Aragon. And the adoption of this jurisprudence was expressly recognised when Louis XI., by an Ordonnance of September 1463, conferred judicial functions upon the Consuls de Mer of Montpellier.

Like Montpellier, Narbonne appears also to have had considerable maritime commerce, not only with Barcelona, Marseilles, and the Italian cities, but likewise with the coasts of Asia and Africa; and, in the administration of justice in maritime affairs, the Roman law and the usages collected in the Consolato del Mare, appear to have served as guides.

Section II.

Western Provinces, Guienne, Roles d' Oleron.

With regard to the ancient maritime law of the provinces situated on the Atlantic Ocean, Aquitania, being almost entirely subdued by the Romans, naturally followed the fate of the provinces situated upon the Mediterranean; and maritime usages in that country could not differ much from those of Narbonne and Languedoc. But, whatever may have been the progress of the Roman arms in Brittany, Neustria, and the countries bordering on the Channel, it is doubtful whether the legislation of the conquerors was imposed upon the vanquished. The maritime usages, however, which were followed in these countries, could not differ materially from those which the Roman jurisprudence had introduced in the south; especially seeing maritime law, as we have often remarked, from its peculiar nature, admits of but little variety in its fundamental principles.

Nor did this state of things undergo much alteration from the invasion of Gaul by the German nations. Each conquering tribe or nation had its own peculiar law, and generally allowed the vanquished the use of their laws; and, accordingly, we look in vain for any texts of maritime law in the Salic, Ripuarian, or other codes of the nations who issued from Germany. Charlemagne and his successors, incessantly harassed by the invasions of pirates from the north, undertook and continued measures for the protection of the coasts, as appears from the Capitularies de Littorum Custodia still in preservation. But none of these documents contain any private maritime law. Although, however, neither the laws of the German nations who took possession of Gaul, and there founded the empire of the Franks, nor the capitularies of the second race, present any proper texts of positive maritime legislation, we must not from thençe conclude, either that the provinces situated upon the ocean carried on no maritime commerce, or that they had no rules for the regulation of mercantile contracts, or for the decision of disputes resulting from commerce. It appears from the Collection of Capitularies, that the Counts charged with the protection of the coasts decided, with the assistance of certain discreet men, (*prud'hommes,*) or Scabini, the disputes to which maritime affairs gave rise.

Section III.

Admirals of France.

When, in the progress of the feudal governments, the functions of governors and judges, which the great lords exercised as delegates of the King, became hereditary, and their patrimony, those who, like the Dukes of Aquitaine, Brittany, and Normandy, and the Counts of Thoulouse and Provence, had become masters of the sea-coast, were under the necessity of watching over the safety of these maritime districts, and of granting to seafaring people a protection, without which the latter would not have frequented their ports. The exercise of this superintendence, and the levying of the regal duties, *droits*, which, in usurpation of the sovereignty, these great lords claimed and exacted, required the institution or rather the preservation of officers of the description of the custodes maritimi, of which the capitularies prove the existence under the second race. It is probable that the connection of the superintendence with which these officers were charged, with the private interests involved in it, bearing reference to navigation, led to their being applied to for, or invested with, the determination of disputes. And there was thus established, or rather continued, as one of the consequences of the peculiar nature of the feudal government, a jurisdiction which ultimately assumed the name of Admiralty, when the word admiral had been admitted into the language to designate the grand officer who presided over navigation, and the maritime power and interests of the nation.

This mode of administering justice, however, was not uniform. Some maritime cities, of which the great lords had deemed it for their interest to respect the liberty and to preserve or extend the privileges, and others, who by means of enfranchisement, or the formation of communities or incorporations, had the right of managing their own affairs, enjoyed also that of administering justice within their own territory by their own magistrates. Experience soon convinced them how advantageous it was to choose, for the determination of their maritime disputes, men accustomed to commerce, under the name of Jurés de la Mer; and in the south, we have seen, this description of municipal jurisdiction received the appellation of Councils of *Prud'hommes*.

The officers of the King, or of the great lords, the

arbiters or judges of the cities, do not appear at first to have had any positive law to serve as a guide for their decisions; they pronounced according to equity or their conscience; but, the recurrence of the same questions, and the renewal of similar decisions, which they could not fail to remember, or to be reminded of, in time, formed insensibly a body of jurisprudence preserved by tradition.

In proportion as the Kings of the third race, among whom Louis XI. in this respect distinguished himself, succeeded in uniting the great fiefs to the Crown, they confirmed the jurisdiction which had belonged to the great feudatory princes upon the admiral of France; or, if they found it expedient, to respect the rights of some great lords, or of some cities, they established an appeal from the tribunals of the latter to the royal courts.

This was effected by the Ordonnance of 1350 for Normandy, and generally by the Ordonnance of Charles V. of 1373, usually designated as of the date 1400. The jurisdiction of the admiralty received a farther extension, by empowering it to judge in all the causes, although not commercial, of the foreign merchants who, in the course of the thirteenth and following centuries, were not only permitted, but encouraged by great privileges, to settle in France; and this jurisdiction of the admiralty was recognised and confirmed by the subsequent Ordonnances of Charles VIII., in 1490; of Louis XII., in 1508 and 1511; of Francis I., in 1517 and 1543; and of Henry II., in 1555.

Section IV.

Tribunals of Commerce.

But the execution of these laws frequently, and for a long time, experienced serious obstructions. They were too much of a political character, and the fiscal exactions excited the complaints of seafaring people. The usual and most grave complaint against them was, that they bestowed the judgment of private disputes upon judges deputed by the admiral to the prejudice of the local jurisdictions; and the difficulties were increased by the laws, which, during the reigns of Henry II. and Charles IX., created consular jurisdictions, or special tribunals of commerce. The interposition of the sovereign authority became necessary; and the Edict of Henry III., of March 1584, remodelled the former laws, and recast them into one entire body, which maintained its authority until the promulgation of the celebrated Ordonnance of 1681.

The admiral came thus to be invested with a dignified office, which conferred upon him, in certain respects, the exercise of part of the royal authority:—Justice was administered in his name; he levied the fines which regularly belonged to the royal treasury: the ordinances relative to the marine could not be executed without a mandate signed by him. As he thus combined an authority at least equal to that of the parliaments, the laws concerning his functions, and those of the officers who acted in his name, had no occasion for registration in these courts to acquire an obligatory character.

No sooner was Henry IV. in the peaceable possession of a throne—which he had attained as much by the attraction of his virtues as by the force of his arms—than he thought of procuring for his subjects, among other advantages, the benefits of an extended commerce; but the sudden death of that great Prince snatched him from the midst of his labours for the accomplishment of that and other useful projects. His successor, Louis XIII., was too much occupied with other matters, during the first years of his reign, to be able to resume, or to prosecute steadily, this important work; and it was only under the administration of Cardinal Richelieu that any considerable progress was made. In the Ordonnance of 1629, of which Marillac was the author, various articles were inserted, tending at once to establish order in the royal military marine and a good police in mercantile navigation, also settling some points previously undecided; and, under the direction of the same able minister, there were afterwards prepared drafts of different edicts and regulations relative to these subjects, which, although not promulgated, served nevertheless to contribute towards the subsequent legislation.

From the leading objects of the different ordonnances before mentioned, it was not to be expected they should contain almost any rules for the guidance of individuals in their business transactions, or of judges in their decisions of litigated questions. And the Edict of 1584 and the Ordonnance of 1629 are the only ones which contain any articles on private maritime law; but these rare and brief regulations evidently presuppose the existence of a common law preserved by tradition, by local statutes, and by judicial determinations; and it cannot be doubted that, in the provinces of France situated upon the ocean, the law consisted in what we call the Roles d'Oleron.

Section V.

Roles d' Oleron.

This remarkable document, originating in the western provinces of France, we have already seen, from the sole consideration of the wisdom of the rules it contains, was adopted in Castile, in England, in Flanders, in the Northern Netherlands, by the most commercial cities of the Baltic, and even in the kingdoms of the north of Europe; and we may only here recapitulate that this compilation, whatever may be its merit and the generality of its adoption, was not composed by the authority of sovereigns, or of magistrates exercising the right of promulgating laws or statutes; that, although it bears the name of Oleron, because, it appears, one of the copies which has the most served to promote its circulation was certified by a greffier, or notary, of that city, in 1266, it has nothing in common with the genuine and actual local Coutume of the Isle of Oleron, in which are also found several regulations on maritime law; and that it appears to have been composed prior to 1266, since the copy certified of that date contains explanations and articles which are not found in other copies in a more ancient language.

Guidon de la Mer.

But the common law contained in the Roles d'Oleron in time required supplements, especially in consequence of the introduction of the contract of insurance, which, according to an Edict of 1556, appears to have taken place in the French commerce upon the ocean, at the commencement of the sixteenth century. And there was compiled at Rouen, under the title of Guidon de la Mer, a body of maritime usages chiefly applicable to insurance and bottomry.

There is no occasion to inquire whether or not the Guidon de la Mer is to be considered as a law, or even as a coutume, compiled through the intervention, or with the approbation, of public authority. What is obscure in this respect, with reference to the Roles d'Oleron, is indisputable with regard to the Guidon de la Mer, which has evidently been composed by a private individual. It is to be regretted the name of the author has not been transmitted to us, as he merited an honourable place among those men who have the most contributed to the improvement and diffusion of the knowledge of maritime law. The supposition of Valin, in ascribing the compilation to Cleirac, appears to be quite erroneous. It is incontestable that the Guidon de la Mer was composed and published in France; the advertisement which precedes it, and the title which it bears, in all the editions, place the fact beyond doubt. The time of the compilation is not so well known; but it could not be posterior to 1607, since the dedication of the edition of that year announces that the work was printed of new; and, from a comparison of different documents, M. Pardessus concludes it may have been composed during the last years of the sixteenth century.

From the Guidon it appears that, at its date, the practice of marine insurance was general in France, Spain, Italy, Flanders, and England; and although at this period no ordinance or edict had in France established any regulations for this branch of business, it appears from Dumoulin de Usuris, and from the Edict of Charles IX., of 1556, establishing the consular jurisdiction at Rouen, that insurance was in use in the west and north of France in the earlier part of the sixteenth century. Nay, it is probable that, from the introduction of this kind of business at Rouen, some time before 1556, the Guidon de la Mer was there composed, to serve as a manual for the consular jurisdiction established by the edict of that year. And, from the vicinity and intercourse with Barcelona, it is also probable insurance was practised at a still earlier period in Marseilles, and the other cities of the south of France.

Farther, while the Guidon unfolds at greater length the doctrines of insurance, it treats also of almost all the other maritime contracts. In Chapter V., it enters into details on averages, not merely to determine the relations between the underwriters and the assured, but also between the shippers of goods and the owners and master of the vessel; and particularly the contribution to average losses, which is treated in so obscure and incomplete a manner in the Consolato. Chapters VI., X., and XI. treat of prizes and ransoms, of reprisals and letters of marque. Chapter XVIII. treats of loans on bottomry, of which the Consolato takes so little notice. Chapter XIX. treats of associations for building and fitting out vessels, and of the different obligations of the part-owners and master.

But the Guidon never acquired such authority in foreign countries as the Roles d'Oleron; and the reason is obvious. The Roles d'Oleron, as the first monument of maritime law in that part of Europe, was borrowed from France by the neighbouring less advanced nations as a set of rules to guide them in their nautical operations and transactions. When the Guidon was compiled, all the neighbouring commercial countries had laws and customs pretty fully developed; the Guidon merely collected these regulations, and, in particular, is only a commentary on those established in the Low Countries in 1551 and 1563 relative to insurance, and never had any authority out of France.

Mornac, Cleirac, &c.

Besides the anonymous author of the Guidon de la Mer, a few other writers in the earlier part of the seventeenth century contributed their aid in France towards the elucidation of the law of maritime commerce. About the beginning of that century, Mornac wrote a commentary on the title of the Roman Digest ad Legem Rhodiam. In 1656 and 1663, Giballinus, a jesuit of Lyons, published, in two volumes folio, a work entitled De Universa Negotiatione, which contains a treatise De Usurio et Commerciis. In 1661, Cleirac, who was an advocate in the Court of Admiralty at Bourdeaux, published his collection, entitled Us et Coutumes de la Mer. This compilation consists of three parts. The first part contains the Roles d'Oleron, which had been previously edited by Garcie, with a Commentary by Cleirac; the laws of Wisby, and the laws of the Hanse Towns; all of which codes we have already considered. The third part is a compilation of the ancient Ordonnances of the French kings, which relate to the marine, and which we have also already noticed. The second part contains the Guidon de la Mer, in which we have just seen the usages and customs concerning maritime contracts are pretty well unfolded.

From the preceding detail, we perceive what was the state of the maritime and commercial law of France at the commencement, and during the early part, of the seventeenth century. There were no general maritime statutes or legislative acts except the Ordonnance of 1400, the Edicts of 1549 and 1584, and the Ordonnance of 1619, of which the regulations related more to the police of navigation and to maritime captures than to maritime contracts and transactions; but which, so far as concerned jurisdiction and superintendence on the part of government, were less imperfect than in the other branches of maritime law just alluded to. The most important part of the maritime law of France, that which regulated contracts and directed the adjudication of contested cases, consisted solely of the traditionary Roman law and of local statutes and usages, such as those of Marseilles, Montpellier, and Narbonne in the south, extended and improved by the adoption of the Consolato del Mare; and in the western and northern provinces, likewise of local usages, particularly the Roles d'Oleron and the principles of the Roman law, traditionary or as derived from the compilations of Justinian, as, in a manner, forming the common law of the kingdom in the matter of contracts. But, in the lapse of time, many of those local statutes and usages had ceased to be sufficient or even applicable; and the extension of navigation and commerce, and the introduction of new arrangements and species of business, required new and additional regulations, founded upon more enlarged experience.

Section VI.

Ordonnance du Commerce—Ordonnance de la Marine, 1681.

Such was the imperfect state of the maritime and commercial law of France prior to the reign of Louis XIV. The ambition of that monarch, and the eminent talents of his minister, Colbert, effected a wonderful change in that as in various other departments of government. After having almost created a navy, and raised it to a state of splendour corresponding to the extent of his power, after having formed various establishments for the protection and encouragement of the national commerce and manufactures, and of the navigation and maritime commerce of his subjects, it only remained for Louis to confirm and regulate that internal and maritime commerce by a system of laws adapted to the circumstances of the times.

The task was undertaken and accomplished through the influence of Colbert. The Ordonnance du Commerce, and, a few years afterwards, the Ordonnance de la Marine appeared; and the success of the legislation corresponded to the ambitious wishes of the monarch.

The Ordonnance du Commerce of 1673 is calculated to regulate the operations of commerce generally. It treats of merchants, dealers, and merchandise in general; of bankers, agents, and brokers; of the books of these persons; of bills of exchange; of companies; of personal and real execution; and of failure and bankruptcies. In the compilation of this work Colbert availed himself of the assistance of M. Savary, a name familiar to every intelligent merchant. Savary, according to Voltaire, was the first person in France who wrote on commerce. His Parfait Negotiant and the Dictionnaire du Commerce, the work of himself and his brother, were enterprises equally useful as new. He had been a practical merchant for a long time; was consulted by the Council of State, when deliberating upon the Ordonnance of 1673, in everything that regarded trade, and digested almost all the articles of that ordonnance, which is, upon the whole, well arranged.

But the Ordonnance de la Marine surpassed in excellence the Ordonnance du Commerce. It was reserved for the genius of Colbert to perceive the advantage of collecting and arranging all the materials of maritime law before enumerated, and of forming out of them a code which might complete the laws already in existence, and, at the same time, reconcile and digest the variety of ancient usages into one consistent and uniform body of positive legislation. This was accomplished, under his care, by the Ordonnance of 1681. And, as M. Pardessus truly observes, it is well known with what admiration, and almost enthusiasm, it was received in Europe, even by the states the most jealous of the glory with which Louis XIV. was then surrounded.

The eulogium pronounced by Valin upon this "chef-d'œuvre in legislation," as he calls it, is perhaps rather overcharged, from a very excusable patriotic partiality; but, with due allowance in this respect, it is worthy of notice as the criticism of one of the ablest writers of any nation on maritime law:—"Universal admiration," he says, "was excited by the appearance of an Ordonnance so beautiful in its economical distribution, so wise in its general and particular policy, so correct and exact in its divisions, and so learned, that it presents as many abridged treatises of jurisprudence as there are subjects which it embraces."

"Indeed," continues the same author, "so complete is this work, that, considering the little attention which had previously been paid in France to maritime law, it is astonishing that lawyers should all at once have been found able to form a body of doctrine so connected, so precise, and so luminous, and at the same time so profound.

"The ancient Ordonnances contained only a small number of regulations on maritime police, which were scarcely sufficient for the maintenance of good order. It was necessary, therefore, to supply their limited extent by new regulations, and, while throwing away what was defective in the ancient regulations, to improve and render more complete what was really useful in them.

"The part of the Ordonnance relating to jurisprudence was still more difficult of execution. The ancient Ordonnances had almost totally neglected that department; and when the maritime laws of the ancients did not afford assistance, the compilers of the Ordonnance of 1681 were reduced to the necessity of investigating the maritime usages established among different nations; and to do so with advantage they behoved to select their course amidst the contrariety of these usages; to cut off and throw aside what was insufficient and useless to elucidate what was obscure; to adapt to the manners of their own country what was good; and to add what had escaped the foresight of the original founders of maritime law."

With regard to the history of the composition of this excellent work, the information transmitted is very imperfect. The Procés Verbaux of the discussion and compilation of the Ordonnance de la Marine of 1681, have not been preserved like those of the Ordonnances of 1667 and 1670 on civil and criminal procedure. Nay, the superior merit of their work, Valin observes, has not been able even to save the names of the framers of the Ordonnance sur la Marine from oblivion. It is, indeed, almost incredible, and affords a striking instance of the fragile nature of human glory, that the authors of so valuable a work, which was first given to the world at so late a period as 1681, and in comparatively so enlightened a country as France, should have been almost entirely unknown when Valin wrote in 1766; and we can only, therefore, notice the indirect and inferential, if not conjectural information, which M. Valin, and, more recently, M. Pardessus, have collected on the subject.

In the preface to his able Commentary on the Ordonnance, M. Valin states that, among the manuscripts in the Library of the Duc de Penthiévre, admiral of France, he found a large and curious collection of the ancient maritime laws, viz. of the Roman and Rhodian laws of the Consolato, and of the Uses et Coutumes de la Mer, of the Ordinances of the Emperors Charles V. and Philip II. of Spain, of the Roles d'Oleron, of the Ordinances of Wisby, and of the Hanseatic League, of the statutes on insurances, of Antwerp and Amsterdam, of the Guidon de la Mer, of the drafts of edicts prepared by order of Cardinal de Richelieu, and of the French Ordonnances down to 1660. And although M. Pardessus was not able in 1837 to discover this collection, he agrees with M. Valin in thinking that, if not the sole, it must have been one of the preparatory labours destined for the composition of the Ordonnance, especially as M. Valin, in different places, found several passages rejected, with this remark, "Not of a nature to enter into an ordonnance, and to form the subject of it."

It would thus appear that the compilers of the Ordonnance made use only of documents that are well known, and which have been all inserted in the recent collection of M. Pardessus, from better original texts than those of the editions which had been published in the sixteenth and seventeenth centuries, besides a great number of valuable documents, some printed, others not previously published, which had not been consulted by the framers of the Ordonnance. But the works with which they appear to have been occupied, undoubtedly presented, upon a great number of important points, rules and decisions entirely opposite to each other. The compilers consequently behoved to make a choice; and the loss of the Procés Verbal of their conferences is to be regretted, as it might have informed us of the reasons and grounds upon which they decided.

With regard to the names of the individuals who compiled the Ordonnance, M. Valin mentions a mission given by Louis XIV. to M. Lambert d'Herbigny, Marquis de Thibouville, to inquire into the administration of the ports and harbours, and the distribution of justice, and also to collect all documents and information proper for preparing the composition of a maritime code; and M. Pardessus found still extant, and quotes, the commission and instructions, dated January 1671, which, besides the correction of abuses in the admiralties, and other objects, embraces also the composition of a body of ordonnances for establishing a system of jurisprudence for these courts, by which merchants and seafaring people might be supported in their rights and privileges, and assured of having justice rendered to them in all their concerns.

But, considering the mission of M. d'Herbigny, merely as connected with the compilation of the Ordonnance sur la Marine, it is manifest, as observed by M. Pardessus, that this magistrate could not be required to combine and arrange the numerous materials destined for so great a work; and that, in fact, he merely transmitted them to Colbert, who was the soul of all the projects of Louis XIV. That author has, farther, found in the Royal Library, and quotes, a manuscript by Colbert, entitled "Instructions pour Mon Fils," from which it appears that his son, M. de Seignelay, was conjoined in the labours of the Minister of Marine; and that his Majesty had established commissioners at Paris—of whom the chief was M. de Morangis, or Barillon—to receive and deliberate upon all the documents which should be sent by M. d'Herbigny, and commence the composition of the body of ordonnances. It thus appears that even this magistrate was merely the head of a commission, who must have admitted or employed compilers versed in the knowledge and the language of the law. Accordingly, Valin, in 1766, records the tradition at Paris that the author of the work was an advocate, whom Louis XIV. rewarded by giving him the office of Maitre des Requetes, but who was obliged to resign it—his means not enabling him to support such a rank. And Verwer, a Dutch merchant, informs us, in his Tractact van Bodemereyen, published about the beginning of last century, that he contributed his aid in 1679, when he resided at Rotterdam, to the compilation of the Ordonnance de la Marine of France, published in 1681, at the request of M. Legras, who had been sent into that country for that purpose. Bretonnier, also, one of the most learned jurisconsults at the bar of Paris, mentions that his contemporary, Le Vayer de Boutigny, for a long time an advocate, and whom his Report of the Judgment of the Conseil du Roi of the 13th April, 1679, in the contest for jurisdiction between the Juges Consuls, under the recent Edict de Commerce and the ancient Admiralties, proves to have been profoundly skilled in maritime matters, was, in his professional capacity, employed to labour in the compilation of the Ordonnance de la Marine; and, as the instructions of Colbert to his son mention his assisting at the conferences to be held in the house of M. de Morangis, there must have been several joint-labourers in this great work.

Of all the enactments of the French Kings, relative to maritime law, this Ordonnance is the most important. The plan is methodical. It is divided into five books. The first treats of the admiral, of his droits, powers, and rights; of all the institutions having for their object the police and the protection of maritime commerce, and of the jurisdiction which was then vested in the office of admiral: the second, of persons employed in maritime commerce, and of property in vessels: the third, of maritime contracts of every kind: the fourth, of the police of the harbours and sea coasts: the fifth, of marine varech, sea weed, sea wreck.

The second and third books are obviously those more immediately connected with the private law of maritime commerce. But M. Pardessus observes he would have been justly reproached for splitting into pieces this fair monument of legislation, and he therefore resolved to republish it whole and entire, noticing the French laws at present in force, which have renewed or modified its regulations, particularly the Code de Commerce of 1807.

It has been objected to the authors of this Ordonnance, that their decisions were too laconic, and that they had not sufficiently foreseen the cases likely to occur in future. But the first objection, Valin justly observes, since it does not imply any want of clearness, is precisely their eulogy; for, next to its equity, the greatest merit of a law consists in the perspicuity yet brevity of expression. And for the second objection there appears to be no better foundation. What is required in any legislative enactment, in which points of law or jurisprudence are treated, is, that the great principles should be there presented, accompanied with cardinal decisions, from which may be drawn the solution of the greatest number of particular cases, and that this excellence cannot be denied to belong to the Ordonnance de la Marine is proved by the fact, that although maritime commerce, which had been vastly augmented since that time, had given rise to a great number of particular questions, it had for more than two thirds of a century, in order to decide these questions, been found necessary only to make a just application of the general rules contained in the Ordonnance, without there having been any occasion for new laws. For Valin informs us that, of the different changes which were made in the Ordonnance down to the time he wrote, there was not one which did not belong to the department of police —a matter from its nature subject to variation according to circumstances; and that there was not one which belonged to the department of jurisprudence; clearly shewing that the stability of a body of law depends on the justice, correctness, and fertility of the principles which it has recognised and sanctioned. And, in confirmation of these observations of Valin, it may be remarked, that even the learned and able personages whom Napoleon employed to frame a new commercial code for his transitory empire, although abundantly disposed to change, yet, after the experience of nearly a century and a half, found but very little to alter and not much to add; and held out to the public, as a recommendation of the result of their labours, that the Imperial Code de Commerce was substantially the same as the Ordonnance de Commerce and the Ordonnance de la Marine of Louis XIV.

We have been led into these details relative to the French Ordonnances of 1673 and 1681, from their being confessedly the most complete pieces of maritime and commercial legislation which any nation had then produced. And, we trust, we need make no apology for these details, when it is known that Lord Mansfield, when Chief Justice of the Court of King's Bench, did not disdain or hesitate to derive from this foreign source many of those enlarged and enlightened views of equity and expediency which, in all matters connected with commerce, characterised the judgments of that court during the long period his Lordship presided in it.

Section VII.

Subsequent Ordonnances.

We proceed now to trace the history of the maritime and commercial law of France subsequent to the Ordonnance de Commerce of 1673 and the Ordonnance dela Marine of 1681. These two important enactments, as was to be expected, continued to form the basis of all the succeeding legislation of the monarchy in relation to these subjects. From time to time, indeed, various ordonnances, edicts, declarations, arrets du conseil, and reglemens, were established and promulgated, which made changes in a variety of matters embraced by, or connected with, the original codes of Louis XIV. But many of these arose merely from the urgent wants of the state on different occasions; many of them were called for by particular circumstances, and ceased with these circumstances, either suddenly or by degrees, after different modifications; and many of them were merely individual regulations of a temporary and transient nature. As already noticed, too, the great proportion of these subsequent royal enactments regarded naval police, not maritime jurisprudence; and the leading principles of maritime and commercial law established in the original compilations remained entire and unaltered. Accordingly, the great object of the French maritime and commercial lawyers, in the earlier part of the eighteenth century, was to write commentaries on the Ordonnances of 1673 and 1681.

In 1714, Marville wrote a commentary on the Ordonnance de la Marine; but, although it went through no fewer than six editions, this was a work of little merit or use. In 1761, M. Jousse, a councillor in the Presidial Court of Orleans, published a commentary of some value on the Ordonnance de Commerce. Jousseau, an advocate of Marseilles, likewise wrote a commentary on the Ordonnance de la Marine, which is of some value, and contains some notes relative to the particular usages of that ancient commercial city.

Valin, Pothier, Emerigon.

But of all the commentaries, that of M. Valin, advocate and King's counsel in the Court of Admiralty of Rochelle, is incomparably the best. That work consists of two volumes quarto; and was published first in 1760, and afterwards in 1766. In this work, Valin illustrates the text of the Ordonnance de la Marine with judicious observations and with learned information, derived from almost every source, ancient and modern, native or foreign. And of the excellent mode in which he has executed this task, some idea may be formed from the following quotations from the author's preface :—

"It is now essentially necessary," says he, "not merely to be acquainted with the Ordonnance de la Marine of 1681, but also to have a thorough knowledge of the ordannances, edicts, declarations, arrets du conseil, and reglemens, which have intervened since the date of that Ordonnance. And as the anterior almost always serve to make the later regulations better understood, I have paid particular attention to this matter. I have not, indeed, made a complete collection at length of every one of our maritime laws, ancient and modern; for by doing so I should merely have multiplied my volumes, and presented to the public a dry and uninviting compilation, instead of a work of real utility. But I have thought it my duty to humour the scrupulous delicacy of those readers who, always suspicious of the good faith and correctness of authors, refuse to give them any credit upon their bare assertion in matters of fact that are susceptible of proof. I have therefore endeavoured to satisfy that class of readers, by furnishing them with my proofs; but I have done so with selection and reserve. I have contented myself with giving, at the suitable places, copies of the essential pieces, viz., of the ordonnances and reglemens which constitute the law at this day; and, with regard to all the rest, I have merely pointed out, in a summary and analytical notice, the anterior or intermediate regulations, with the different changes they have undergone, tracing back and ascending to the source, as far as has been practicable."

Again, "That very fertility in principles, which constitutes the excellence of the Ordonnance, increases the difficulties of a commentary, of which the object is to give everywhere the reason of the law; and to indicate, as far as possible, without affectation, however, and without prolixity, the consequences which ought naturally to result from it. For that purpose, it is necessary to comprehend thoroughly the sense and spirit of the law, and especially to seize correctly the principles of each subject, in order to guide one's self from consequences to consequences, by means of this assistant thread; and such is the labyrinth of difficulties, which I did not foresee till it was too late. It is, perhaps, because others have perceived them sooner, that we have hitherto been deprived of a commentary which has now become too necessary not to be eagerly desired."

In short, Valin's work has justly met with universal approbation. "M. Valin," says Emerigon, his liberal competitor in this branch of jurisprudence, "is the only person who has executed the bold project of writing a commentary on the Ordonnance de la Marine. Success has justified his enterprise. He has opened the way: he has removed and smoothed a thousand difficulties; and, by his collection of edicts, declarations, and reglemens, which have intervened since the date of the Ordonnance, and which, without the aid of this author, would have remained buried in the dust of the public registers, he rendered to the public the same service which Cnæus Flavius rendered to the Roman people by divulging the Fasti and the Formulæ. And if M. Valin has not given to that part of his work which concerns maritime contracts all the interest of which it appears susceptible, it is because his design was confined to explaining each article of the Ordonnance without stopping to give dissertations, which can only be properly introduced into particular treatises."

Contemporary with the learned and highly estimable Valin, was the celebrated Pothier, Judge of the Presidial Court and Professor of the French Law in the University of Orleans. He died in 1772. He was no less distinguished for the extent and profundity of his learning than for the acuteness and the soundness of his judgment; and he is unquestionably the greatest of the French modern civilians. His comprehensive and active mind embraced every department of law. By an arrangement founded on principle, by the introduction of order and method, he has justly entitled himself to the honourable appellation of Restorer of the Roman Pandects. But his most generally useful work is his series of Treatises on Obligations and Contracts, in which he has adapted the reason and the equity of Roman jurisprudence to the circumstances and the practice of modern times. And in this work there are valuable treatises on the contract of affreightment, on the hiring and wages of seamen, on averages, on insurance, on bills of exchange, on copartnership.

When alluding to these treatises of Pothier, in his elegant work on the Law of Bailments, the late very learned and amiable Sir William Jones hesitated not to express his admiration in the following strong language:—"I seize with pleasure an opportunity of recommending these treatises to the English lawyer; exhorting him to read them again and again: for, if his great master, Littleton, has given him, as it must be presumed, a taste for luminous method, apposite examples, and a clear manly style, in which nothing is redundant, nothing deficient, he will surely be delighted with works in which all those advantages are combined, and the greatest portion of which is law at Westminster, as well as at Orleans. For my own part, I am so charmed with them, that, if my undissembled fondness for the study of jurisprudence were never to produce any greater benefit to the public than barely the introduction of Pothier to the acquaintance of my countrymen, I should think that I had, in some measure, discharged the debt which every man, according to Lord Coke, owes to his profession."

Contemporary also with Valin, but a little younger, was the equally learned and able M. Emerigon, advocate in the Parliament of Provence, and judge in the Court of Admiralty of Marseilles. Of the character of this estimable lawyer some idea may be formed from an interesting anecdote given by Valin. After noticing the very indifferent translations into French of the Consolato del Mare, Valin proceeds thus:—" I know, however, a celebrated lawyer, who has commenced a new translation of the Consolato, enriched with notes for the understanding of the text, and with observations relative to the provisions of our Ordonnance, and the present usages of commerce. It is M. Emerigon, that generous, learned man, with whom chance made me acquainted, and who was no sooner informed that I was engaged in composing a commentary on our Ordonnance, than he offered me, with a cordiality and a disinterestedness perhaps without example, the whole collection of decisions and authorities relative to that object, which he had made in the course of his assiduous and judiciously directed studies. It may easily be believed I hesitated long about accepting an offer of this description. I at last determined to do so, only because he had the secret of persuading me that it was merely for his own particular use that he had made this rich collection. He then sent me a copy of it, of which I made such use, that almost everything good to be found in this commentary, in the department of jurisprudence, is in some measure as much his work as mine."

The translation by Emerigon of the Consolato del Mare, here alluded to by Valin, we are informed by M. Pardessus, was relinquished before it was finished, and was never given to the public. But, about twenty years after the publication of Valin's Commentary, viz., in 1783, Emerigon published, at Marseilles, his excellent Traité des Assurances et des Contrats à la Grosse, in two volumes quarto, to which the English writers, Mr Justice Park and Mr Sergeant Marshall, appear to be considerably indebted. This book is ostensibly merely a treatise on the law of marine insurance, respondentia, and bottomry. But, in the course of it, he very frequently stops either to treat incidental questions, or to develope different points relative to those which form the principal object of his work. And in this way he embraces a great part of the maritime ordonnance, and discusses a vast number of subjects connected with the law of mercantile navigation and commerce in general.

In addition to the works of these three great maritime and commercial lawyers, Pothier, Valin, and Emerigon, it only remains to notice the treatises of Dupuy de la Serra, and of Senebier. The treatise of Dupuy de la Serra is entitled "The Art of Letters or Bills of Exchange, according to the usage of the most celebrated commercial places of Europe, and according to the jurisprudence of the French kingdom." It is not only very learned, but lays down and applies the leading principles of the law distinctly and methodically, and contains a great deal of practical information. When the work was first published we have not been able exactly to ascertain; but a new edition was published at Geneva in 1789; and to it is added a collection of ordinances, edicts, and decisions relative to commerce.

The work of Senebier is entitled "A Treatise on Exchanges and Arbitrations;" and, besides a great deal of practical detail, it also explains methodically the general principles of jurisprudence applicable to the commerce of money, viz., to exchanges and bills of exchange. The edition which we have was published at Lausanne, in 1797; but the work was originally published at an earlier period.

As the Ordonnance de Commerce was very inferior to the Ordonnance de la Marine, it appears to have been the intention of the unfortunate Louis XVI. to remedy this defect, and to improve still further the commercial legislation of his kingdom. And, in 1786, M. Pardessus informs us, a commission appointed by him had actually prepared and caused to be printed a Projet de Revision de l'Edit du Mois de Mars 1673, appellé communèment Ordonnance de Commerce. But the establishment and promulgation of this improved Ordonnance de Commerce appears to have been prevented by the unhappy events which soon after followed.

Section VIII.

Code de Commerce.

During the period of what may be termed the Revolutionary Government of France, it is scarcely necessary to observe, the maritime and commercial law of that country received no improvements. The old system was shaken, if not overturned; no certain, consistent, or permanent code was established in its place; and the most violent and unnatural regulations were made and enforced for a time, and then recalled, and new ones equally unreasonable substituted. At last, the consular government, more steady in its plans and more vigorous in its means of execution than any of the preceding governments, conceived the project of a reform in the maritime and commercial law of France. In the year 1800, a commission was established, under the Minister of the Interior, composed of seven members, lawyers and merchants, and charged with the task of compiling and digesting a projet of a code of commerce and marine. In 1802, this work was finished and published by order of the consuls. But this work was still merely the combined opinions of a small number of men. The First Consul wished for farther information. He was desirous to collect the general opinion of merchants and traders, as well as of the commercial courts. And, by the consular authority, this projet of the code was directed to be transmitted to all the mercantile tribunals and to all the chambers of commerce throughout the country, with an invitation to them to give their observations on it within a limited time. From these tribunals and chambers, and also from several distinguished lawyers and merchants, the commission received a variety of scientific and practical observations. Of the collection of observations, which the publication of the projets of the code had thus procured, three members of the commission, Gorneau, Legras, and Vital Roux, made an Analyse Raisonnèe, and proposed corrections and improvements, which the additional information so procured had suggested as necessary or expedient. The code then underwent a new discussion and general revision in the council of the Emperor. And, in September, 1807, under the title of Code de Commerce, it was approved of by the legislative body, was enacted as law, and was ordered to be printed and published.

When they presented this code to the legislative body, the leading members of the commission, the orators of government, in a series of preliminary discourses addressed to that body, explained the reasons (motifs) by which they had been directed in their labours; and it may not be altogether uninteresting to extract from the first of these discourses the account which the orators of Napoleon give of his views in framing this code.

After admitting that France will always reckon

among the fairest monuments of her legislation the Ordonnance de Commerce and the Ordonnance de la Marine, promulgated under the influence of the genius of Colbert, the orators of Napoleon, with more vanity than is quite excusable, and with the spirit of hostility to Great Britain then prevalent, proceed to shew that these laws are no longer suitable to, nor sufficient for, the commerce of the French Empire.

"Since the publication of these laws," say the orators, "the territory of France has been almost doubled; whole states in the south, vast provinces in the north, have added to the extent of her maritime frontiers, to the number of her rivers and navigable canals, to the immense variety of her agricultural productions, to the always increasing diversity of her manufactures.

"On the other hand, at first under thereigns of the last Kings, then during the interregnum, which has been called the Revolution, and, finally, under the dynasty which rises to efface all the glory, and to repair all the misfortunes, of these later times, the morals of the nation in general, and commercial morality in particular, have undergone great changes, and are not yet fixed. And it is of great importance to seize them in this moment of oscillation, to strengthen and confirm them into good and honourable habits, to direct them, or, let us dare to say so, to bring them back to that loyalty and that good faith of which our great commercial cities were formerly the nursery, and of which they still preserve noble examples. It is of high importance to mould into one common system the usages and jurisprudence of the mother country and of the united territories; to put an end to the regulations framed by the provincial parliaments, which formed a sort of secondary legislation in the bosom of the primary legislation; to efface all traces of the rules established by local customs, by municipal laws, the first benefit and the last inconvenience of our ancient civil legislation."

"It is of high importance," continue the orators, "that the commercial laws of France should suit equally the commerce of consumption of great cities, the speculative commerce of great entrepots, the industrious commerce of great manufacturing towns, the immense navigation of great seaports, the active coasting trade of the smallest harbours.

"Finally, it is of high importance that the commercial code of the French Empire should be founded upon, and digested into, principles which may prepare for it an universal influence—principles which may be adopted by all commercial nations—principles which may be in harmony with those great commercial habits and usages which embrace and bind together the old and the new world."

Such are the rather pompous terms in which the orators of the French Emperor, in Autumn, 1807, ushered into the world his Code de Commerce. How far, in his subsequent political conduct, he acted up to or accomplished these views and objects, the then existing generation of the continental nations felt, and history will record.

With regard to the contents of the Imperial Code de Commerce, it consists of four books. The first contains the laws which regulate commerce in general; the second contains the laws peculiar to maritime commerce; the third treats of failures and bankruptcies; and the fourth treats of the competency of the tribunals for commercial affairs, and of the mode of judicial procedure in different cases.

Of this celebrated code, of which the influence was once so extensively diffused, we shall only remark that, in point of arrangement and otherwise, it has certainly great merit, but that its greatest merit consists in being substantially the same with the commercial and maritime ordonnances of Louis XIV., as explained and unfolded in the writings of Valin, Pothier, and Emerigon.

Subsequent writers, Pardessus, Boulay-Paty.

It only remains to notice the French writers on maritime and commercial law since the period of the Revolution, besides those engaged in the compilation of the Code de Commerce.

In 1801, M. Boucher, Professor of Commercial and Maritime Law in the Academy of Legislation of Paris, published a work, entitled Institutions Commerciales, in quarto, in which he treats at length of mercantile jurisprudence, and of the usages of trade; and, in 1803, he published his Institutions au Droit Maritime, also in quarto, which he announces as a complete work on maritime legislation, having for its basis the Ordonnance of 1681, to which he had adapted the subsequent particular laws, both of the ancient and new regime. But neither of these works appear to be of much value; and the introductory dissertation which M. Boucher prefixed to his edition of the Consolato del Mare, in 1808, as well as the translation by him of that celebrated compilation, M. Pardessus appears to consider as derogatory to the juridical criticism and literature of France.

In 1805, M. Azuni, formerly judge of the Maritime and Commercial Court of Nice, and afterwards member of the Academy of Legislation of Paris, published, in two volumes octavo, an improved edition of a work, formerly published by him in Italian, under the title of Droit Maritime de l'Europe. But this work relates more to maritime international law, properly so called, than to private maritime jurisprudence; and the most valuable part of it, containing an historical account of the maritime laws of ancient and modern nations,

M. Pardessus assures us, is merely a copy of part of the unpublished draft of the Codice Fernando, prepared by Jorio for the kingdom of Naples.

The next eminent French writer on the law of maritime commerce is M. Pardessus himself, who published the first edition of his excellent Cours de Droit Commercial in 1816, and a second edition, in 1821, in four vols. octavo; and who, in 1828, and during the intermediate period, has likewise published, in five vols. quarto, with the announcement of a sixth and concluding volume, his Collection de Lois Maritimes anterieures au XVIII. Siecle, accompanied with learned dissertations and notes, exhibiting together the result of his indefatigable antiquarian researches, and the exercise of an acute, judicious, and impartial criticism.

In 1822 and 1823, M. Boulay-Paty published, in four volumes octavo, his learned Cours de Droit Commercial Maritime d'apres les Principes et suivant l'ordre du Code de Commerce.

In 1829, there was published, under the direction of M. Dupin Ainé, a posthumous work by M. Gautier, entitled Etudes de Jurisprudence Commerciale, containing a well-arranged and useful collection of texts from works of authority, illustrating the principal doctrines of mercantile law.

In 1833, M. Frémery published a valuable work, at once philosophical and practical, under a title descriptive of its nature—Etudes de Droit Commercial, ou Droit fondé sur la Coutume Universelle des Commerçans.

CHAPTER V.

OF THE MARITIME AND COMMERCIAL LAW OF THE FREE CITIES OF GERMANY.

Proceeding northward from France and the Netherlands, we are next to notice the maritime and commercial laws of the trading cities of Germany, and the writers on this subject whom they have produced. These states, after the dissolution of the Hanseatic League, which we have already considered, while they continued so far to observe the maritime laws sanctioned by that once formidable power, appear also, as they did prior to that singular confederacy, to have framed each for themselves particular ordinances, either by adapting that system to their own peculiar circumstances, or by supplying its defects and extending its rules so as to embrace the new transactions to which the general advancement of commerce could not fail to give rise.

Section I.

Hamburgh.

There can be no doubt that, before the city of Hamburgh received its charter of legislation from the Count of Holstein, in 1292, its mercantile and seafaring inhabitants had agreed among themselves upon certain customary rules for the regulation of their transactions, and to serve as a guide for the judges of their disputes; and, from documents discovered by M. Lappenberg, and printed by M. Pardessus, it appears that, from 1256, or, at the latest, 1261, commerce was regulated at Hamburgh by maxims, which we again find in the codes that were afterwards compiled. The most ancient monument, however, of the laws of Hamburgh which is known, is a series of twenty-eight articles, to which it is generally agreed to give the date of 1270. Of these articles, some appear to have been composed for the commercial factories which Hamburgh had established in Flanders; but the greater part present rules applicable to commerce in all the places to which the navigation of Hamburgh extended. It must, however, be always borne in mind that the greatest part of these primitive regulations, and even the statutes, which in the sequel unfolded maritime law still farther, were not intended to form complete bodies of legislation. There evidently existed general and common usages, arising in the earliest times in which navigation had acquired any importance, and preserved by tradition. The subsequent written regulations which presuppose them, had for their object either to rectify these usages agreeably to experience, or to modify them agreeably to some particular necessities, or to render more certain some points upon which people had not agreed or been at one. And this, while it explains, at the same time, affords an excuse for, their insufficiency and imperfection, sometimes also their obscurity; because allusion is there made to matters of which there is no longer a distinct conception or knowledge.

This series of articles of 1270 is annexed to almost all the copies of the most ancient civil statutes of Hamburgh, and is also found in the manuscript bearing the date of 1292, which, under the date of 1306, contains five additional articles of maritime law, of which one corrects or rather replaces article fourteenth of the preceding series.

When, in 1497, the city of Hamburgh compiled and digested of new its civil statute, a special title was devoted to maritime law. The articles of 1270 and of 1306 were then recast in a new order, and with additions which, notwithstanding the numerous matters borrowed from the former statute, formed a new work. The compilation of Wisby, or at least the second and third parts, borrowed from the southern and northern Low Countries, appear to have previously served at Hamburgh as a kind of subsidiary law; and the compilers of the maritime statute have borrowed much from these different documents.

In 1603, Hamburgh again revised its civil legislation; and the thirteenth title of the second part of the statute of that date is allotted to maritime law, and has been reprinted in an official edition in 1771, and specially commented upon by Langenbeck, in his Anmerkungen über das Hamburg-Schiff-und-Seerecht, 1774, in quarto. The statute of 1603 makes no mention of insurances; but these were very probably by that time known to, and practised by, the merchants of Hamburgh, who seem then to have followed, in this department of business, the jurisprudence of the Netherlands, their policies being framed according to the custom of the Bourse of Antwerp. In 1630, Roulandus published a Dissertation on the Law of Hamburgh respecting Insurances; and, subsequently, the merchants engaged in this branch of business compiled successively, in the years 1677, 1683, 1687, 1693, 1697, and 1704, rules, which became the basis of an Ordinance which the Senate of Hamburgh promulgated in 1731.

Since the promulgation of that ordinance, the merchants of Hamburgh, interested in insurances, have established among themselves regulations to supply the insufficiency of the law, either founded upon their own experience or agreeable to the statutes and jurisprudence of foreign countries. And the Senate of Hamburgh is stated to have been lately occupied in digesting a new statute, if it has not already completed its labours. The treatise on insurance by M. Benecke, published in 1810, entitled System des Assecuranz und Bodmereiwesens aus den Gesetzen und Gebräuchen Hamburgs und den verzüglichsten Handelnden Nationen Europens, so wie aus der Natur des Gegenstandes entwickelt, is one of the most recent and best works on the subject. Farther, the laws of Hamburgh, respecting bills of exchange, were translated into English in 1799; and reference may be made to the work of Spangenberg in 1814, entitled Ideen über Nothwendigkeit und Organisation eines Handelgerichts in Hamburg.

Section II.

Bremen.

The position of Bremen was favourable for maritime commerce; and, although its earliest civil code of 1303, and even the revised code of 1433, contain only three articles relative to maritime commerce, there can be no doubt that, in such matters, its inhabitants must have been guided by that common and customary maritime law which is followed almost everywhere, without our being able to indicate the monuments that ascertain and record it, and the existence of which must have preceded the compilations of customs and usages, while it is presupposed by the small number of those very consuetudinary rules which have been committed to writing.

It farther appears, that the citizens of Bremen borrowed from Hamburgh, so far as suited them, the series of articles of 1270 before mentioned, which are annexed to the manuscript, if not of the statute of 1303, at least of the statute of 1433.

A state which has not yet established positive laws upon matters of such a description as to give rise to daily business transactions, of which the fulfilment and execution must be enforced, is naturally led to borrow the usages of a neighbouring people with whom it has frequent commercial intercourse. The want, however, of a more complete legislation being felt at Bremen, the senate, in 1606, prepared a new compilation, which would probably have contained a more extensive title on maritime law than the previous statutes. But the citizens refused to adopt this compilation; and the senate, in this department, appears to have merely enforced among the citizens the obligation of conforming to the ordinances of the Hanseatic League, particularly the Ordinance of 1614; and actually passed an order to that effect in 1687. The compilation of Wisby also, when the manuscript copies and prints of it were more extensively circulated, may probably have formed, at Bremen, a subsidiary law; and, when the contract of insurance became known in the navigation of the Baltic, Bremen, following the example of Hamburgh, conformed itself to the ordinances which Charles V. and Philip II. had promulgated on that subject in the Low Countries.

The statutes of Bremen give no distinct information as to the manner in which maritime disputes were adjudicated in that city. It is probable the very general practice of such questions being decided by arbiters, may have prevailed in early times, while the tribunals pronounced upon appeal from the decisions of these arbiters. And there do not appear to have been any special and extraordinary jurisdictions for the trial of maritime and commercial causes, which seem to have been subjected only to the summary procedure of ordinary tribunals.

Reference may be here made to Post De Cura Civitatis Bremensis circa Rem Nauticam, 1780; and to Focke adumbratio Juris Mercatorii Privati Reipublicæ Bremensis, 1797.

Section III.

Lubeck.

Before the conquests of the German Princes over the people who inhabited the southern coasts of the Baltic had given rise to the foundation of the great number of maritime cities and towns which afterwards formed the Hanseatic Confederacy, these countries appear to have carried on a pretty active commerce, which, though circumscribed by the shores of the Baltic, and harassed by an habitual state of warfare, was necessarily subject to certain rules, or, at least, usages. The German colonies which, in the twelfth century, replaced the Vandal Cities, in all probability preserved this more ancient maritime law, although very imperfect, or merely local. In the course of time, enlightened by experience, they substituted for it usages more complete and more general, to be found chiefly in the statutes of Lubeck. And these usages, again, received development, corresponding to the rise of new wants and the extension of navigation, in the ordinances of the Hanseatic League. The most respectable authors have pronounced an eulogium on the maritime laws of Lubeck: have ascribed to that city the glory of having furnished models of legislation to Livonia, Pomerania, Mecklenburg, Holstein, and Lower Saxony; and add that, in all the cases in which the positive laws of the neighbouring states did not decide a contested question, recourse was had to the laws of Lubeck, as to written reason.

Founded in 1140 by Adolphus of Holstein, Lubeck, in 1158, obtained from its Sovereign, Henry the Lion, the confirmation of a statute which became the basis of those it afterwards enacted, when it obtained the right of self-government. And the Emperor Frederick Barbarossa, in 1188, granted and guaranteed to the inhabitants of Lubeck, both the maintenance of their laws and the right of reforming them, by a statute which Frederick II. renewed in 1226. The early statute of 1158, so far as it consisted of ordinary civil law, was probably, as well as the municipal constitution, of Saxon origin, and so far borrowed from Soest, a city of Westphalia, which, though inland, already carried on a pretty considerable commerce. But such an inland town could not furnish materials for composing a body of maritime law; and the regulations relative to navigation, in this early statute, are so few in number, that we must either suppose Lubeck could succeed to the commerce of the Vandal Cities, and carry on that commerce without laws or rules, which would be absurd; or we must hold that, until it inserted in its statutes rules of maritime law, sufficiently developed, Lubeck was governed by the customs of the more ancient seafaring people, whose territory it occupied and whose commerce it continued. But the magistracy of Lubeck did not delay the exercise of the privilege, granted them in 1188, of revising and improving their legislation; and a statute was enacted in 1240, which contains twelve articles on maritime law, and of which various copies appear to have been made towards the close of that century. About the middle of the same century, having entered into an alliance and copartnership with Hamburgh, for the prosecution of trade with Flanders, Lubeck adopted, with some modifications and additions, the series of articles of maritime law, for the mercantile establishments in that country before noticed. And the code of 1240 appears to have been revised and digested of new in 1348, containing eleven articles on maritime law.

From 1348 to 1582, the city of Lubeck does not appear to have revised its general civil code under legislative authority: but various copies of the former code appear to have been made, with additions by private individuals, and to have been communicated to the neighbouring maritime cities of the Baltic; and, in 1530, this city established a special ordinance on maritime law, which, having been adopted by the Hanseatic League, formed a part of the statutes of that Confederacy. At last, in 1582, the inconveniences resulting from the circulation of copies of the collections of civil laws differing from each other and unauthenticated, induced the senate of Lubeck to employ commissioners to draw up a regular digest. This work, promulgated in 1586, is divided into six books, of which the last relates to maritime law, and its regulations, derived, in general, from the more ancient compilations, are still in force. In the course of the sixteenth century also, not merely the ancient statute of Wisby, known under the name of Stadtlagh, but also the more recent compilation of Wisby, which was printed in 1505, and of which there previously existed copies at Lubeck, appear to have had, in that state, the authority of subsidiary law.

Subsequent to the statute of 1586, there was enacted at Lubeck, in 1655, an ordinance on the manner of adjudicating maritime disputes. And Lange ascribes to the corporation of shipowners of Lubeck a series of forty-eight articles upon the police of mariners; but which appears to have been composed for navigation in general, without its being known where it was compiled. The maritime codes of Lubeck, even that of 1586, contain no regulations upon insurance. In this department, Lubeck appears to have followed the example of Hamburgh, and ultimately adopted the Ordinance of Hamburgh of 1731 on that subject. Reference may also be here made to Lübeckische und diver Städte Holstein Gebräuchliche, See und Andere-Rechte, published at Leipsic in 1707, in quarto.

Having thus briefly traced, historically, the maritime legislation of three of the principal free-trading cities of Germany, we may now notice the statutes of one or two of the less prominent trading cities, and a few of the writers in this department of jurisprudence whom the more commercial districts of Germany have produced.

In the year 1669, the city of Dantzic, and, about the year 1730, the city of Königsberg, established and promulgated their respective statutes relative to the laws of navigation and maritime commerce. In 1661, Stypmannus published, at Stralsund, his work entitled Jus Maritimum; reprinted in 1740 by Heineccius in his Fasciculus Scriptorum de Jure Nautico, in quarto. In 1662, Marquhardus published, at Frankfort, in two vols. folio, a work entitled De Jure Mercatorum et Commerciorum singulari. In 1686, Leickherius published a treatise De Dominio Maritimo. In 1668, there appeared the treatise by Strykius, De Navibus; and in 1710, his treatise De Cambialium Literarum, Acceptatione. In 1698, there appeared a treatise by Groningius, De Navigatione Libera. In 1719, Lubeck published a work De Jure Averiæ. In 1726, Heineccius published his works entitled Elementa Juris Cambialis and De Vitiis Negotiationis Collibisticæ. And the work of Phoonsen, on the laws and usages of exchange in the principal places of trade in Europe, was republished by Lelong, at Rotterdam, in 1755, and had been translated into French by Ricard in 1715.

With regard to the law of the Inland commerce of Germany, there may be consulted the following works:—Thema, De Nundinis, 1650; Lyser, De Jure Nundinarum,

1654; Rhetius, De Nundinis Solemnibus, 1661; Horix, De Jure Instituendi Nundinas in Imperio Romano, et Germanico, 1752; Lubeck, De Jure Stapulæ, 1711; Bunau, De Jure circa Rem Monetariam in Germania, 1716; Boehme, De Commerciorum apud Germanos Initiis, 1751; Schott, Incrementa et Jura Mercaturæ in Germania, 1763; Raumburger, Grundsaetze des Heil. Rem Reichs, und anderer Konigreichs und Staaten, Rechte und Gewohnheiten in Wechsel und Commercion Sachen nebst einem Appendice, von Assecuranz und Sec-affairen Francfort, 1723, und Erneueste. u. verm. Ordn. in Wechsel u. anderer Handelsgeschäften a Kaiserl. freyer Reichs-stadt Francfort a Mein, 1800. And with regard to the law of workmen, or manufacturing industry in Germany, there may be consulted Struve, Systema Jurisprudentiae Opificiariae in formam Artis Redactum, 1738, three vols. quarto.

CHAPTER VI.

OF THE MARITIME AND COMMERCIAL LAW OF NORWAY AND ICELAND.

From the principal free maritime cities of Germany, we proceed, geographically, to consider the maritime commercial law of the northern kingdoms of Norway, Sweden, and Denmark. We have already had occasion to trace the origin and very extensive influence, not merely in the Baltic, but in all the northern seas of Europe, of the maritime laws of the Hanse Towns; and when, in the natural course of events, that once formidable trading Confederacy came to be broken asunder, its excellent legislation in maritime affairs commanded the respect of its conquerors; and was, in fact, in a great measure, adopted by those very nations by whom its power was subverted. The great tract of country which is bounded on the west by the North Sea, on the east by the Baltic, and extends, from south to north, from the Elbe to the Frozen Ocean, appears to have been almost unknown to the ancients; but came, in the course of the middle ages, and in more modern times, after a great number of revolutions, to form the kingdoms of Norway, Sweden, and Denmark. These kingdoms, although very frequently in a state of warfare with each other, have been sometimes united for a period, in whole or in part, under one and the same government; and we, accordingly, find a great similitude in their legislation, particularly in the department of maritime law.

Section I.

Norway.

The ancient chronicles of Norway inform us that the barrenness of the soil and the scarcity of grain forced the inhabitants to seek their subsistence by fishing, which the extent of sea coasts, and the vicinity of the northern seas, frequented by the whale, herring, and other species of fish, rendered easy and abundant. The nature of the country, too, intersected by arms of the sea, bays, rivers, and lakes, rendered navigation indispensable, not merely for fishing, but for the communication requisite for procuring and exchanging the necessaries of life. And the habit of living upon the sea thus became a part of the character of the Norwegians, and led them soon to profit by the superiority which it gave them upon that element.

For a long time, also, the country was divided into a number of tribes or small states, independent of each other, and incessantly engaged in hostilities; each contending for a more favourable station, or a more fertile portion of territory, and endeavouring to appropriate its produce. And not only had each small tribe to defend itself against its immediate neighbours; it was necessary, also, they should be prepared to repel the people who inhabited the coasts of the Baltic, and who, being equally barbarous, and not less enterprising than the Norwegians, committed upon the coasts of the latter the same hostile depredations as they experienced from the former. Thus piracy became the habit and practice of the whole nation, and the object of all the ambitious; and it is not till a later period, when the north, ceasing to send forth, periodically, swarms of barbarians upon the southern countries, began to feel the benefit and value of civilisation, which the Christian religion promoted and extended, that we find in Norway, if not the first monuments, at least the remembrance and oral tradition of some laws worthy of that appellation.

About the middle of the ninth century, Halfdan, Sovereign of the south part of Norway, afterwards known by the name of Ædcivie, we are informed, caused the traditionary customs of their forefathers to be collected into a code, which historians designate by the title of Leges Ædcivences. But this code, if it ever existed, which is not very probable, and if it was written, which is much less probable, must have been merged in the later codes, of which the revision and improvement became necessary, in proportion as civilisation made progress, and it became requisite to accommodate legislation to new manners and customs.

In the following century, (the tenth,) Harold succeeded in subjecting progressively the chiefs of all the small states into which Norway had been formerly divided, and formed of it really one kingdom. To insure respect for property, one of his first measures was to enact the punishment of exile against any Norwegian who committed piracy against a fellow-countryman. And among the first delinquents to whom this law was applied, was Rollo, who, notwithstanding his high birth, being thus forced to quit his native country, ravaged France, and ultimately obtained the sovereignty of the province since known under the name of Normandy.

The union thus accomplished, and the formation of one people out of so many separate tribes incessantly at war with each other, could not fail to promote commerce; and we find the Norwegians now frequenting the ports of Jutland, Holstein, and Saxony, and even advancing westward in their voyages to the Orkneys, Scotland, Ireland, and Wales. From this time, the Kings of Norway appear to have made, in succession, various attempts to render their legislation more uniform; and the chronicles attest that, in 1039, a general code, known by the name of Gragas, was compiled under the direction of Magnus the son of Olaus. But the only one of these early codes, mentioned in the chronicles, which has reached us, is the Gulaping of Haco, which bears the date of 940, but probably contains the additions made by subsequent kings. To the twelfth century we may ascribe, if not the compilation, at least the publication, of a collection of customs known under the name of Biarkeyer-Rett, or municipal law, a sort of common law for the different cities and towns. which served as a basis for the particular statutes which they were authorized to enact. In the thirteenth century, Magnus the son of Haco became not only the pacificator, but the legislator of his country, and received the surname of Lagabacher, or reformer of laws. The anterior civil laws were revised and corrected, in order to form a code for the whole kingdom; and the compilation having been approved by a national assembly, held in the Isle of Gulay, received the title of Gulaping of 1274, from the name of the place where the assembly met, afterwards transferred to Bergen. The reputation of this code for wisdom was so great, that William the Conqueror is said to have borrowed some of its regulations for England, and it continued to be the common or general law of Norway in the sixteenth century.

But the regulations relative to maritime commerce, contained in the early compilations just mentioned, although carefully selected and published by M. Pardessus, are few in number. Indeed, Norway does not appear to have had any proper legislative code of maritime law till that promulgated by Christian V. in 1687. And in the intervening periods, the Norwegians appear to have been guided in their maritime and commercial transactions by the usages of the inhabitants of the neighbouring cities of Germany. These foreigners, profiting by the ignorance of the sovereigns, or, perhaps, by the venality of their councillors, went so far as to engross almost all the advantages of commerce. At first they confined themselves to the demand of being admitted or tolerated; but, very soon obtaining renewals and extensions of privileges, sometimes by address, sometimes by violence, they succeeded in founding a sort of independent colony at Bergen. In such circumstances, it is easy to see what was then the maritime law observed in Norway. As the citizens of the Hanseatic Confederacy were authorized to have their disputes adjudicated agreeably to their own proper laws, and by the judges whom they established, without any concurrence on the part of the local government, and as they were the sole masters of commerce, their commercial usages, their weights and measures, their laws, of which we have already given an account, obtained a preponderance, which did not, indeed, annihilate the former laws of Norway, but could not fail to weaken and limit their operation. And when this yoke, equally humiliating as ruinous, ceased, and the Norwegian commerce assumed its natural course, the ancient laws, compiled at a period when navigation was little advanced, even though modified by the influence of the institutions which time had introduced, were found insufficient, and the usages imported by the Hanseatic confederates in all probability continued to be observed.

The inconvenience of this defective state of the national law came in time to be strongly felt. In 1557, Christian III., King of Denmark and Norway, commenced measures for remedying the evil; and, in 1604, Christian IV. finished the work. But these attempts at legislation were not successful; and it was reserved for Christian V. to accomplish the compilation of a general code for both nations, which was promulgated in 1683 in Denmark, and in 1687 in Norway; and which may be therefore more properly noticed under the laws of Denmark.

Section II.

Iceland.

As, in a manner, a colony and province of Norway, we notice the ancient maritime law of Iceland. In the latter part of the ninth century Iceland was found deserted; but when Harold rendered himself master of the whole of Norway, many of the petty chiefs, who had previously participated in the sovereignty, not choosing to submit to the humiliation of a subordinate station, and even a number of families of considerable power and comparative civilisation, passed over into

Iceland; and, so great was the emigration, that, in sixty years, the island was pretty well peopled. These emigrant Norwegians carried with them their customs and usages. The chiefs and more wealthy families were followed by a multitude of other inhabitants, attached to them as dependants or servants. To the latter the former gave grants of land, upon condition of recognising their civil power, and of accompanying and assisting them, when it should be necessary to take up arms for defence or offence. And there was thus formed a vassalage and patrimonial jurisdiction such as, from similar causes, were introduced in the more southern countries of Europe. But these local chiefs, supreme judges of all those who were subject to their authority, had neither one common law, nor a power which could enforce agreement or obedience when they were divided among themselves. Recourse to arms alone terminated their contests, if they had not the wisdom to agree upon a reference to arbiters. And Iceland was thus incessantly menaced, until Uffliot, with the consent of his countrymen, went to Norway to instruct himself in the laws of that country; and, on his return, compiled a body of laws which was adopted in 928, and for a long time maintained its authority under the name of Lex Ufflioti. On the introduction, in the year 1000, of Christianity, this code underwent several modifications; and, in 1117, it was revised and reduced into writing by the chief judge, Haflits.

These early codes, M. Pardessus points out to us, contained an important institution for the progressive formation and amelioration of the laws of Iceland, which merits the consideration, if not the imitation, of these more enlightened times. They gave the chief judges the power of supplying the silence of the law, by edicts promulgated for the whole period of their magistracy. In fact, a nation which is advancing in civilisa tion, where new wants and relations create transactions and matters of dispute hitherto unknown, cannot foresee and provide for everything, in the general laws deliberated upon by the assembly of the people. And it is well that experience should prepare and judge of the expediency of the laws before they acquire a character of irrevocability. The power of issuing and establishing edicts conferred on the magistrates, had not in Iceland, any more than in Rome—whence, if the chronology of events permitted, one would say it had been borrowed—any danger for public liberty, because the offices of the judges were elective and temporary. It was surrounded with provisions and guarantees which left few opportunities for abuse: it was made the duty of the chief judge to promulgate his edict: each individual knew from that time the law which was to direct him: this edict could not change the law, but merely supply it. These precautions were even carried further: where a question occurred before a tribunal upon which neither the code nor the edict in force had declared any determination, all the judges of the district, accompanied by select assessors, were convoked: the cause was pleaded before them: the decision was pronounced in a solemn manner: and, for the future, it became a rule to which individuals were bound to conform until a legislative statute enacted otherwise.

If there be no chronological collection of all the documents of which the ancient law of Iceland is composed, time has at least spared one work in which they are all blended together, and united with a good deal of method, viz., the Grágas, cited by a great number of writers, and of which M. Schlegel published an edition in 1828, with a preliminary dissertation, which M. Pardessus describes as a chef-d'œuvre of historical science, and of judicious and luminous criticism. The compiler of this work is unknown, and its date can only be ascertained, by approximation, to have been prior to the union of Iceland with Norway in 1262. It appears to have been originally designated by the expressions Codex Legum Antiquus, Generalis Juris Corpus; and to have afterwards got the vulgar denomination of Gragas, "Greygoose," to distinguish the old law from the codes of Haco and Magnus, which supplanted it. This work M. Pardessus considers as neither properly a statutory or legislative code, nor the mere production of a private individual for facilitating the study and knowledge of the law; but thinks it probable that, for the better discharge of their functions, in supplying the defects of the law, the supreme judges reduced into writing explanations to be transmitted to their successors; at the end of which, each of them mentioned the new laws and decisions relative to cases not foreseen; and that such was the origin of the Gragas. But M. Schlegel is of opinion that, in the Gragas, we have the ancient code of Iceland, such as it was arranged by Haflith, but with additions derived from the more recent laws, and from the edicts of the chief judge, in which he speaks in the first person, like the Roman Prætor, and of explanations given by him and by other distinguished lawyers of the country.

The Gragas is divided into ten sections or books: the seventh, De Commerciis, divided into eighty-five titles, treats of the different kinds of contracts and transactions which may take place between individuals: the tenth, De Re Nautica, divided into four titles, treats of maritime law. Such a body of law was the almost necessary result of the insular position of Iceland, and of its population from and intercourse with Norway. And the maritime regulations just mentioned appear to be one of the most ancient parts of the Icelandic legislation of which the Gragas has preserved the interesting remains.

But there is another monument of Icelandic legislation which presents a title on maritime law. Iceland was, for a pretty long time, a kind of republic; and this was the brightest period of its literary history. The disputes of the chiefs of districts, the influence of the clergy, intimately connected with that of Norway, the expectations of some great proprietors to have more security for their wealth and greater scope for the acquisitions of power under a monarchial government, induced the Icelanders to place themselves under the King of Norway, by the convention of 1261 and 1262. They were promised the preservation of their laws, which, although in a great measure borrowed from those of Norway, had characters of nationality which rendered them dear to them. But this promise was evaded; and, in 1265, Haco made the criminal law in the Gragas much more severe. They are said to have then desired to be placed under the laws which King Magnus established for Norway in 1274. And a new Icelandic Code, compiled by Judge Ion, and, therefore, called Īon's Bog, (John's Book,) was promulgated, after the death of Magnus, by his successor Eric, in 1281, and still governs Iceland. It resembles much the laws which Magnus had given to Norway; in particular, the title on maritime law is almost literally conformable to the similar title in the laws of Bergen, with a good many regulations inserted from the ancient Gragas.

CHAPTER VII.

OF THE MARITIME AND COMMERCIAL LAW OF SWEDEN.

SECTION I.

Ancient Laws.

IN Sweden, as in other countries, the law of maritime commerce originated in urgent wants; was improved, in the progress of time, by experience; and was modified by invasions and changes of government. The ancient monuments of the legislation of Sweden are of two descriptions, the one called Gothic codes, the other called Swedish codes. The first elements of the Gothic codes belong to a period during which the provinces they governed were independent states. Of these codes, the one of which the memory is the most ancient is that of Westro-Gothia, which is said to have been composed before the introduction of Christianity; but which must have been much altered by that and other subsequent events; and which, as still extant, and published by Stiernhielm in 1663, and translated into Latin by Loccenius in 1692, may be ascribed to the twelfth or thirteenth century. The laws of Ostro-Gothia are said to be less ancient and more complete; are said to have been compiled in 1168, 1251, and 1260; and were published at Stockholm in 1607 and 1665. A third Gothic code is that of the Isle of Gothland, which must not be confounded with the municipal statute of Wisby, its principal city; and which, as edited by Hadorph, in 1687, appears to have been compiled in the course of the twelfth century. This island was for a pretty long time independent; till its inhabitants, worn out by their own intestine divisions, placed themselves under the King of Sweden, who there maintained a governor, called Jail. In 1366, Waldemar III. of Denmark invaded the island; but this provoked the vengeance of the Hanseatic Confederacy, and his occupation was short. King Albert of Sweden afterwards impledged the island to the Prussian Knights for a considerable sum, which, in 1408, the celebrated Queen Margaret of Sweden discharged. And Gothland, subject sometimes to Denmark, sometimes to Sweden, was ultimately ceded to the latter power by the treaty of 1644. These three Gothic codes contain nothing concerning maritime affairs except some regulations as to the police of the coasts, and shipwrecked goods, and some traces of commerce with foreigners.

With regard to the Swedish codes, the general opinion is, that the first written laws are those of Upland, compiled in the ninth century anterior to the introduction of Christianity. But these original laws were necessarily revised, and adapted to new habits, customs, and wants, by the Christian Princes; such as, Eric, Canute, Berger, and Magnus Ladislas; and the compilation of the laws of Upland, which has been handed down to the present time, appears to have been made by the order of Berger the son of Magnus, was edited in 1607, and a Latin translation by Loccenius published in 1700. The other Swedish codes are those of Westmania, the next ancient to those of Upland; those of Sudermania, compiled in 1326; those of Haelsinge, which come next; and those of Dalhe, which bear little trace of modern legislation; all published at Stockholm in 1665, 1666, and 1676.

Although, however, each province of Sweden had thus, in former times, its own proper laws, similar in substance, but different in many points, the laws of Upland appear to have had a sort of superiority over the others, inasmuch as, where the latter were silent, recourse was had to the former—the pretty obvious consequence of the Kings of Sweden having fixed their residence at Upsal. When the constantly increasing power of the Kings of Upland had ultimately terminated in placing both the Gothic and the Swedish provinces under one government, the advantages of one uniform code were recognised; and this task was undertaken in 1347, in the reign of Magnus, son of Eric. But, from the resistance of the clergy, the projected code was not carried into execution till 1442, when the different laws before noticed were moulded into one code, which bears that date, promulgated by King Christopher, and of which Archbishop Raguald Ingenmund, in 1481, made a Latin translation, printed in 1614; and even this general code of 1442 was not completely in vigour till, under Charles IX., a rectified text was published in 1608, under the title of Landslagh. From that time, however, being again published in 1663 and 1726, and translated into Latin by Loccenius, it preserved its authority and force till the new code of 1734, of which there are numerous Swedish editions, and a Latin translation by König.

But the particular and also the general laws just noticed had for their object only that department of the civil law of a nation which is common to all situations in life, independently of the professions exercised by individuals, and were chiefly applicable to that portion of the nation which, occupied in agriculture, was scattered over the country. The habits and the interests of the inhabitants of the towns, the manufacturing industry, the commerce, and the navigation, to which they applied themselves, differed too much from the customs, the habits, and the modes of dealing, practised in the rest of the territory, for the common law to suffice for them. Accordingly, in Sweden, as well as in Norway, there existed a special law for the towns, consisting of the privileges which each community derived from the Sovereign, when he erected it into a town corporate, or burgh, and of the municipal statutes which the inhabitants, in concurrence with the magistrates, had the power of enacting.

The only ancient Swedish laws of this description, of which the text has been preserved, appear to be the statute of Birka and the municipal law of Wisby. And the texts which have been preserved of their particular laws, and of the general law of towns corporate, are, properly speaking, the only monuments of the maritime law of Sweden.

Birka, situated on the lake Melar, near where Stockholm now stands, was, from the introduction of Christianity into Sweden, if not before, a place of considerable trade, and appears to have attained such a degree of prosperity as to have had a municipal code. And when Stockholm was founded in a more advantageous situation, this code appears to have been transferred to Stockholm, and granted to that city by Berger in 1254. This statute of Birka has been edited by Hadorph, from the text of 1254, and contains only four chapters relative to maritime law, which appear in the code of the towns to be afterwards noticed.

But the maritime legislation of another city in the kingdom of Sweden, more celebrated in history, requires a little more detail, viz., Wisby, the capital of the Isle of Gothland. Although its situation in this island of the Baltic may in very early times have rendered Wisby suitable and convenient as a central point and entrepot for the commerce which the cities situated on the south and west of that sea might have with Russia, and although this is attested to have been the fact, during the tenth century, by the Norwegian chronicles, it does not appear that any foreign traders had formed any important establishments there before the eleventh century. But the trading town of Vineta, in the Isle of Usedom, having been destroyed in 1043, and the other towns on the south of the Baltic, belonging to the Vandals, having also been destroyed by the Saxon Princes, Gothland became the centre of maritime commerce. And if the city of Wisby did not owe its foundation to these circumstances, it owed at least its increase. It does not appear to have as yet attained great celebrity in the eleventh century, seeing Adam of Bremen does not once mention it. But, besides the causes before alluded to, it must have been enriched by the effect of the disasters which Sleswick in Holstein, and Sigtuna in Sweden, experienced about the middle of the twelfth century; and it is chiefly from that time we are to date its flourishing state, which all the historians of the north so delight to describe.

The city of Wisby was composed partly of natives, partly of Germans, who had there not merely a right to residence and mercantile establishments, but enjoyed all the privileges of the city, and participated in the public functions. Formed especially by and for commerce, it must have soon established laws, and maritime laws could not be omitted. Accordingly, and from other historical documents, it is highly probable that, from the twelfth century, Wisby had written laws—a statute which comprehended both general, civil, and also commercial law. But we now possess or know no other municipal statute of Wisby than the statute which was compiled in the beginning of the fourteenth century, viz., about 1320; and we can merely form conjectures as to the contents of this ancient code. A number of writers have supposed that Wisby owed its laws to the Emperor Lotharius; but, as shewn by M. Pardessus, the charter of Lotharius, referred to in the preamble of the statute, at the beginning of the fourteenth century, no longer exists; and the charter of Henry the Lion, which, according to this preamble, confirmed in 1163 the grant formerly made by his grandfather, contains nothing relative to civil or maritime legislation, but merely certain privileges and guarantees of security to the inhabitants of Gothland. At the same time, the privileges thus granted to Wisby by Lotharius and his successors, prove that that city was of pretty great importance from the twelfth century; and consequently afford a strong presumption that a statute may there have been reduced into writing, of which the wisdom may have led to its adoption by the town of Riga. This statute, however, was not in its ancient form identically the same with that which has reached us; for, Siegel assures us, it was divided into eleven books; whereas the statute of the fourteenth century is divided only into four books, of which the third book is subdivided into three parts, and the fourth into three parts. This last statute is thus not merely a republication of the text of the preceding statute, but a new work; although it is probable it reproduced the principal regulations of the preceding statute, especially in what concerns maritime law.

Beside the statute we have just been considering, viz., the Stadtlagh of Wisby, there is also the more recent compilation, generally known under the title of the Laws of Wisby, or Hogheste Water-Recht, and which we formerly ascertained, through the learned researches and sound criticism of M. Pardessus, to be composed of three fragments; the first part being found literally in the codes of Lubeck, the second part being identical with the twenty-four primitive articles of the Roles d'Oleron, and the third part being conformable to a series of articles known in Holland under the name of the Usages of Amsterdam, Enchuysen, &c. Since the researches of M. Pardessus, the able and learned

M. Schlegel, it appears, has also investigated this subject; and, not having had access to the documents which establish the antiquity of the Roles d'Oleron, he places this compilation, usually ascribed to Wisby, next in point of antiquity to the Consolato del Mare. Agreeing with M. Pardessus that the compilation, Hogheste Water-Recht, is quite different from the maritime law contained in the municipal statute of Wisby, and is not the work of a legislator, or of a magistrate, or judge, M. Schlegel believes that it was composed at Wisby by a corporation of merchants, as a sort of agreement, or consuetudinary statute, which, without giving it the characteristics of law, imparted to it at least the authority recognised in written customs. And as the Isle of Gothland was for a great part of the fourteenth century, and even in 1646, under the Danish dominion, the result of M. Schlegel's reasoning is, that this compilation might be claimed by Denmark. But the previous and the additional investigations and arguments of M. Pardessus, on which we cannot here further enlarge, appear completely to refute the arguments of M. Schlegel, and to prove that this compilation is merely the work of a private individual or individuals, composed of fragments borrowed from different countries, where these fragments had the authority of written customs: a work to which its utility may and must have given great influence; but still the work of a copyist, and consequently posterior to the time when the documents copied already existed in the countries from which they were borrowed.

Section II.

Code of Gustavus Adolphus—Loccenius, Stypmannus.

From the cities of Wisby, and Birka, and Stockholm, having had particular statutes, containing rules of maritime law, the idea naturally occurred of compiling from them the common principles to form a code to which each city would only have to make such additions as its localities required. This seems to have produced in Sweden the Stadtlagh, or code of the cities. And in 1618, Gustavus Adolphus, having caused the most ancient and authentic manuscripts to be collected and carefully compared with each other, ordered the publication of an official and authoritative text of the Stadtlagh, which received the appellation of Legisterium Sueciæ, and contains a pretty extensive title on maritime law.

Upon this collection of the maritime laws of his country, Loccenius wrote an able and learned commentary, in his work entitled De Jure Maritimo et Navali, Libri Tres, published at Stockholm in 1652. In this work, Loccenius treats, not only of property in vessels, of maritime contracts, of bottomry, and of averages, but also of marine insurances, De Aversione Periculi, vulgo, Adsecuratione. About the same time, viz., in 1661, Stypmannus published, at Stralsund, his work entitled De Jure Maritimo et Nautico, in quarto; and, in 1667, Kuricke, the author of the commentary, Ad Jus Hanseaticum, published his Diatriba de Assecurationibus and Quaestiones ad Jus Maritimum Pertinentes; of which three works an edition was published by Heineccius, at Magdeburg, in 1740, under the title of Scriptorum de Jure Nautico et Maritimo Fasciculus.

In about half a century after its promulgation, even the revised code established by Gustavus Adolphus was found by experience to be insufficient; and, in 1667, Charles XI. caused to be digested a special code of maritime law, which still governs Sweden, with the exception of the first part, relative to the crews and police of vessels, modified by the enactment of 1748, and of the sixth part, relative to averages and marine insurances, modified by the enactment of 1750. This code was commented upon at length by Flintberg in 1796, under the title of Schwed Seerecht mit Anmerkk, and extended to a third edition in 1815; was translated into Latin by Loccenius; and was published, in 1834, in Swedish and French, by M. Pardessus. This code, M. Pardessus observes, well merits attention; for, although neither so complete nor so well digested as the Ordonnance of France of 1681, it presents some very wise regulations, which would not have been out of place in that Ordonnance, and from which instruction might have been derived even by the compilers of the French Code de Commerce of 1807, who, probably, had not, any more than those of the Ordonnance of 1681, the Swedish code under their consideration.

CHAPTER VIII.

MARITIME AND COMMERCIAL LAW OF DENMARK.

SECTION I.

Ancient Law.

THE existing monuments of maritime legislation in Denmark are not so ancient as those of Norway. It is difficult, however, to believe that, till the twelfth century, the period at which the documents still in preservation commence, Denmark, whose inhabitants have always been distinguished as active and bold navigators, should have been devoid of rules to guide individuals in their transactions and judges in their decisions. It is to be presumed rules were followed similar to those found in the Norwegian codes. When it is considered that the vast northern territory, designated under the general appellation of Scandinavia, has been inhabited by nations of one common origin, placed in the same situation, and cultivating the same habits of life, it cannot be doubted that their civil legislation has been founded on the same principles; and if this be probable with regard to their general civil legislation, for a much stronger reason might it be so with regard to their maritime legislation.

The most ancient monuments of this description in Denmark are not what, in our present language, can properly be called laws; namely, acts emanating officially from sovereigns, or depositaries of public authority: they consist only of traditional customs and local usages established by common agreement of the citizens, sometimes in an express manner, sometimes by little and little, by a sort of tacit consent; or of the collections of decisions pronounced at first by judges in particular cases, and, afterwards, generalized in such a manner as to admit of their application to all similar questions.

A body of jurisprudence thus formed could, in what concerns maritime law, receive extension and improvement only so far as commerce itself, in its advancement, multiplied the transactions which it was required to regulate, or the disputed questions which judges had to determine. But if, from certain causes, the navigation of a country, whose jurisprudence established itself in this manner, passed into the hands of foreigners, allowed to have their differences decided according to their own proper laws, and by the magistrates or judges of their own nation, the native or local jurisprudence behoved to remain stationary—nay, could not fail insensibly to fall into desuetude, and to give place to that which presided over the business transactions of which the monopoly was in the hands of these foreigners. And in this way, it appears, it may be best explained how it happens that the monuments of maritime legislation in Denmark, anterior to the code promulgated by King Frederick II. in 1561, are so few in number and so little developed.

Maritime commerce first became extensive in this kingdom by the establishments formed there by the German cities, of which the Hanseatic League was afterwards composed; but, as in Norway and Sweden, this extension served only to found and secure the monopoly of the League, at the expense of the native merchants. And this explains why the proper maritime law of Denmark behoved to remain stationary—why, neglected and almost forgotten, during the Hanseatic domination, it remained in a state of such imperfection as forced the country to adopt, if not as an express or positive law, at least as a customary and subsidiary law, the usages of the League. Nay, so accustomed were the natives to conform to these foreign usages, that, when kings, more enlightened as to their interests, or more capable of defending or vindicating them, profited by the divisions and increasing weakness of the League to revive maritime commerce among their subjects, the Hanseatic usages formed the basis of the codes which they prepared and ultimately adopted; and that of 1561 is, in fact, modelled upon the Hanseatic statutes and jurisprudence.

The earliest maritime law of Denmark is to be found in the municipal statutes of the different towns or provinces, and the subsequent usages which were adopted for the purpose of modifying them, and, more frequently, of supplying their defects. The most ancient of these municipal statutes is that of Sleswick, about the beginning of the thirteenth century, which contains only a small number of rules of maritime law; and this statute was adopted by Flensburg in 1284, with some slight changes. About the same time, also, Apenrade adopted the statute of Sleswick; and, in 1292, Hadersleben also enacted a statute, in which a good deal is borrowed from that of Sleswick. In 1240, a civil code was established for Jutland, but did not supersede any previous municipal rules of maritime law, of which there are few traces in this code. In Holstein, the city of Kiel, in 1232, and the town of Plöen in 1236, adopted the law of Lubeck. A collection of decisions, under the title of the Laws of the Province of Scania, appears to have been made in the thirteenth century, but merely contains some regulations as to shipwrecks. There are, likewise, two collections of judicial decisions under the name of the Laws of Iceland, which appear to have been made in the course of the thirteenth and fourteenth centuries, to have been held in estimation, and to have possessed authority for a long time before such usages had been confirmed by the Sovereign. The municipal statute of Copenhagen of 1254 contains nothing relative to maritime law, although the port of that city was by that time much frequented; and the subsequent statute of 1294 contains only four articles of this description, and of no value in general maritime legislation.

But it is not to be supposed that the business transactions to which navigation gave rise occasioned no disputes, or that there were no rules for the decision of these disputes. It is rather to be believed that the principles, though few in number, which are found in the Statute of Sleswick, and in the similar collections of usages in the neighbouring towns and provinces, were followed in the other parts of Denmark. This law, quite imperfect as it was, was perhaps sufficient in the early times, when more regular commerce succeeded piracy; and so much the more so because the foreigners who came into that country had, in all matters in which they were interested, the right of being judged by their own magistrates, according to their own proper laws, and because these foreigners ultimately got possession of all the maritime commerce of Denmark. Their customs, evidently more perfect than those of that country, became, in the necessary course of events, a subsidiary law—not only while they retained great influence and a real monopoly, but also after Denmark had shaken off this onerous and humiliating yoke.

We have no positive proof that the Hanseatic legislation, composed of the statutes, or recessus, served as rules in Denmark for contracts and the decision of disputes relative to maritime commerce among the natives. This may be supposed from reasons of analogy. But it appears much better established, that the celebrated compilation, known by the name of Hogheste Water-Recht, and evidently made, whoever was its author, for the use of the Hanseatic merchants, enjoyed great credit in Denmark. It was there the first edition of it was published, in 1505; the Danish translation of it in 1545 is the most ancient that is known; and the Danish code of 1561 has almost literally adopted its regulations. Even the Compilation of Wisby, as printed in Denmark in 1505, appears to have been found insufficient; and, in 1508, eighteen articles in Danish were added, which resemble the corresponding part of the Stadtlagh of Sweden.

Section II.

Code of Frederick II.—1561.

But, in the course of time, and in the progress of commercial experience, the necessity for more complete, and more definite and fixed, legislation came to be strongly felt; and Frederick II., who holds a distinguished rank among the legislators of Denmark, in 1561, promulgated a maritime code destined for the regulation of all his dominions, including Norway. This code has borrowed a great deal from the Compilation of Wisby, from the Hanseatic Statutes, or recessus, and from the Ordonnance of the Low Countries, of 1551, before noticed; only a small number of its provisions being peculiarly Danish legislation.

Section III.

Code of Christian VI.

The Code of 1561 was followed by special laws on particular points, which had not been foreseen; such as, a law of 1638 cited by Loccenius, De Jure Maritimo, tit. iii., cap. vi., number 4, prohibiting the sale of a vessel for a certain number of years after its construction. But these special enactments, and whatever else composed the maritime law of Denmark, were united and embraced in the fourth book of the code of civil laws which Christian VI. caused to be compiled and promulgated in Denmark in 1683, and in Norway in 1687; which was translated into Latin in 1698, and again in 1710, under the authority of government, and under the title of Leges Danicæ; and which is still in force.

In 1746, Christian VI. granted a charter in favour of the insurance company established at Copenhagen, which contains many salutary regulations, both on the subject of marine insurance and on averages. In 1803, the Danish government promulgated an Ordinance for regulating the conduct and fixing the obligations of its subjects, both merchants and seafaring people, during the time of war, among the other maritime powers. And, in the course of the same year, another Ordinance was published, concerning the salvage of vessels and goods shipwrecked on the coasts of Holstein and the other Danish provinces.

In the course of the last century, too, Denmark produced a few celebrated writers on particular branches of maritime law. M. Hübner, Assessor to the Consistorial Court of his Danish Majesty, in 1759, published a well-known treatise De la Saisie des Batimens Neutres. And M. Schlegel, Professor of Law in the University of Copenhagen, in 1800, published an able treatise on the visitation of neutral vessels under convoy. These works, it is obvious, belong rather to the maritime law of nations, or to that we have seen may be properly termed maritime international law, than to private maritime and commercial jurisprudence, the proper subject of the present sketch. But, in 1776, Mazien published, at Copenhagen, Tableau des Droits et Usages de Commerce. And M. Schlegel has also more lately, in 1827, published an able and learned dissertation on the indigenous autonomy, or, in less pompous language, the native legislation of Denmark.

CHAPTER IX.

OF THE MARITIME AND COMMERCIAL LAW OF PRUSSIA.

SECTION I.

Ancient Laws.

THE position on the Baltic, at the mouths of four great rivers, of some provinces of the Prussian Monarchy, early called the inhabitants of these territories to navigation and maritime commerce. These territories consist of Pomerania, East and West; of part of ancient Poland, including Dantzic; and of ancient Prussia, including Königsberg.

Western Pomerania comprehended, during the middle ages, as principal towns, Gripswald, Stattin, Stralsund, &c. These cities appear, in maritime matters, to have been governed originally by a sort of common law observed by the cities of the Vandals. When they felt the necessity of introducing supplements and modifications into their municipal statutes, these cities, in the course of the thirteenth century, adopted, in preference, the legislation of Lubeck. When they became members of the Hanseatic League, these towns adopted its legislation; and very probably also, at least until that Confederacy had a complete body of maritime law, digested definitively in 1614, they conformed to the Compilation of Wisby, of which there existed an ancient manuscript at Gripswald. In 1667, the former maritime law of these towns appears to have been, if not entirely superseded, so far replaced by the Swedish code of that date. Of the principal towns of Eastern Pomerania, Colberg and Rognewalde, the first appears to have adopted the law of Lubeck in 1255; but, it is probable that, having acceded to the Hanseatic League, they conformed to the maritime law of that Confederacy; and that the Compilation of Wisby, after copies of it were circulated in the countries adjacent to the Baltic, became there a subsidiary law. Farther, there is reason to believe these cities continued to conform to these laws, until the King of Prussia enacted more complete maritime laws for the government of all his states.

Of the maritime territory of ancient Poland bordering upon the Baltic, subsequently acquired by Prussia, the principal cities, Dantzic, Marienburg, Culm, Thorn, Elbing, &c., appear to have been primarily under the dominion of the Grand Masters of the Teutonic order. But it does not appear that the ordinances of the latter contained any special titles on maritime law. And it is probable these cities adopted the statutes of the Hanseatic League. There is also reason to believe that these cities availed themselves of the more recent Compilation of Wisby, conferred upon them by the Grand Masters.

The port of Dantzic was frequented, in the thirteenth century, by the seafaring people of Lubeck, who there obtained privileges in the years 1263 and 1288, and was thus led to adopt the laws of the latter city. In 1455, a statute was enacted, of which maritime law forms a very small part. The defects of this statute, although revised in 1457, required further revision in 1573 or 1579, and again in 1597, published in 1599; and this last revised statute refers to the Hanseatic Ordinance of 1591, and constitutes the Plebiscita Gedanensia, of which Kuricke cites almost all the articles in his commentary on the Hanseatic Ordinances, or Recessus, of 1614. As the monuments of the maritime law of Dantzic were thus so limited, it is very probable that the magistrates conformed in their judgments to the Compilation of Wisby. And such seems to have been the maritime law of Dantzic while it remained a free city, under the protection of Poland, until, in 1793, it passed under the dominion of Prussia.

The maritime provinces which formed what was termed the Duchy of Prussia, were formerly, like those of Poland, under the dominion of the Teutonic Knights. In the early part of the sixteenth century, Königsberg appears to have had a willkür or statute; and the maritime part of the duchy had an official compilation of general customs in 1540: but neither of these compilations appear to have contained any maritime regulations, except with regard to shipwrecks; and, from the very little maritime law included in these compilations, there is reason to believe that, in such matters, recourse was had to the laws of the Hanse Towns and the Compilation of Wisby. In the beginning of the seventeenth century, (1620,) a more extended code was executed, under the direction of the Elector John Sigismond; of which Titles eighteen and nineteen of Book IV. relate to maritime law; and this last Title is a literal copy of a great part of Book VI. of the Statute of Lubeck of 1586. This code of 1620 was revised in 1685; but the portion of maritime law received only two slight additions.

Section II.

Code of 1727, *Code of Frederick II., and of Frederick-William II.*

A desire to complete this department of legislation induced the King of Prussia, in December, 1727, to cause to be promulgated a new code of maritime law, which has been commented on by L'Estocq; and underwent, in 1766, several modifications relative to insurances. The code which Frederick II. caused to be digested by his Chancellor, Cocceii, contains nothing regarding maritime law; and, having recognised the imperfection of this code, as formed too closely upon the model of the Roman law, Frederick afterwards charged Carmer with this laborious task, which produced the code of the Prussian states promulgated by Frederick-William II. in 1794, translated into Latin at Berlin in 1800, and published of new in April, 1803, with additions. On this code, M. Pardessus observes—"In doing justice to the science of the jurisconsults who concurred in the composition of this great work, it is impossible to avoid remarking, that it contains too many details, definitions, interpretations, and doctrines; and that, if other codes err, or are defective, from a brevity which, in fact, leaves blanks in them, the Prussian code has gone into the opposite excess. But it is, nevertheless, one of the most remarkable works, and one of the most useful to jurisconsults, which has been published in our modern times; and it contains numerous and wise enactments relative to maritime law."

CHAPTER X.

OF THE MARITIME AND COMMERCIAL LAW OF RUSSIA.

Section I.

Eastern and Northern Provinces.

The maritime law of the vast Russian Empire may be considered with reference to the different seas by which it is surrounded, the Black Sea and the Caspian, the Frozen Ocean and the Baltic.

It was by the countries bordering on the Euxine and the Caspian that Russia received, in ancient times, the produce and manufactured commodities of Asia, and conveyed them, by inland communications, to Novgorod or to the Northern Ocean. The maritime law observed on the coasts of the Black Sea must have been that which the ancient Greeks, the founders of the first commercial establishments in these regions, had there introduced—a law which experienced no change when these countries passed under the dominion of the Romans, seeing the maritime legislation of that people was conformable to that of the Greeks. After the change in the seat of the Roman Empire, this legislation, as contained in the Digest, and afterwards in the Basilica, became the rule for mercantile transactions on the shores of the Black Sea, including Armenia and Georgia. The Venetians, the Pisans, and the Genoese, next carried their usages into the factories which they established on the coasts of that sea; but their maritime law was, as we have seen, in a great measure a traditionary record of the Greco-Roman law. And when the barbarous inhabitants of Central Asia had destroyed the establishments of these Republics, the commercial towns which they allowed to remain, or which were found under their protection, continued to follow the ancient usages. With regard to the usages which regulated the navigation of the Caspian Sea, nothing is known, except during the period Georgia possessed some ports on that side where the Greco-Roman law may have been observed.

Of the coasts of the Frozen Ocean, the savage and ignorant inhabitants do not appear to have had any maritime laws, or even maritime usages, peculiar to themselves; the Norwegians, who traded there, followed their own usages; and, when the celebrated Republic of Novgorod formed establishments there, its citizens probably carried with them their own usages.

Section II.

Western and Baltic Provinces.

But we possess more satisfactory information regarding the early maritime legislation of the Russian provinces which border on the Baltic; namely, those of Novgorod, of Livonia, including Riga, and of Courland, Esthonia, and Finland.

Novgorod was one of the most ancient cities of Russia. About the commencement of the eleventh century, a general civil code was there promulgated under the title of Pravda Rouskaia, or Pravda Slavian, and was afterwards modified and enlarged; but it contains only one article on maritime law, relative to the illegal and forcible seizure of ships, similar to that of the Byzantine code in the sixth century. Another general Russian code was subsequently compiled in 1498, but was not carried into execution till 1550; and this code was again revised and promulgated in 1649. These general codes, however, which have been printed with a commentary in the course of last century, do not contain any articles on maritime law. Nor is this surprising, as each maritime city had its own peculiar statutes and usages. And, with reference to Novgorod, there exists a compilation of this description under the name of Skraa. Among a number of articles of police and local arrangements, foreign to or unconnected with general maritime law, this compilation presents very important provisions upon the respective obligations of seamen and their employers; upon jetson and sacrifices made for the common safety; upon the obligations of the master, who undertakes the conveyance of merchandise. This document, however, properly speaking, does not belong to Novgorod. It is not the work of magistrates, or of any public authority in that city, which exercised the power of making laws binding on the Russians. The German and Gothland navigators and merchants, in early times, obtained at Novgorod a sort of territorial colony, where they were governed by their own laws, administered by their own magistrates. Previous treaties, or, at least, grants of privileges, emanating from the native Sovereign or local authorities, were necessary to ensure the safe exercise of this franchise. And a previous treaty, and other documents, prove that it was in full activity in 1280, and the following years. The object of the compilation of the Skraa was thus merely to govern a body of mercantile people, strangers to Russia, admitted to reside there, for the purpose of carrying on trade, and is evidently the exclusive work of foreigners to Russia. But it is certain that it was composed for the purpose of receiving its execution within the Russian territory. And, from the character of universality which belongs to maritime law, it is highly probable that the provisions of this compilation served also as rules for such of the native inhabitants of Novgorod as applied themselves to maintain traffic, seeing in that department their own civil law was silent.

With regard to the date of this compilation, it was not the result of a grant of privileges to the Hanseatic League. It belongs to a period anterior to the formation of that general Confederacy, in the fourteenth century, when there were merely associations belonging to different maritime cities; in fact, it only concerned the body of merchants established in the Isle of Gothland and the traders of that isle; and the result of the learned researches of M. Lappenberg, and M. Pardessus, is to hold this document as of the date of 1229, 1231, or, at least, in the earlier part of the thirteenth century.

There exist three manuscripts of the Skraa, two at Lubeck and one at Copenhagen. The first manuscript of Lubeck, evidently the most ancient, includes only a part of what is contained in the second and in that of Copenhagen, viz., the first twenty-seven articles of the two last, and contains nothing which bears any reference to a period subsequent to 1240. This primitive Skraa contains a number of articles of local police, which could only have been framed for the factory of Novgorod, and would otherwise have been of no use; but it also contains a number of articles of a different kind, concerning general private maritime law. And it is a matter of curiosity to ascertain from what source these have been derived. They are not to be found in the first statutes of Sleswick, one of the towns which earliest carried on commerce with Russia, nor in those of Lubeck. Are they, then, the remains of the maritime law followed by the Vandal Cities, and on which a part of the population was mingled with that of the cities of Lower Saxony, which succeeded them? Or are they a fragment of that old maritime law of Wisby, so celebrated in the north, and hitherto generally believed to have been found in the compilation of which M. Pardessus has demonstrated the comparatively recent character? At all events, these articles recognise rules which flow so directly from the essential relations between shipmasters and mariners, that, written or unwritten, whichever it may be, they must have been followed wherever navigation was prosecuted. With regardto the source of the articles added at the time of the second Compilation of the Skraa, nearly the half of them are literally conformable to the Code of Lubeck of 1240. And as the legislation of Lubeck has always been held in high estimation by the German cities adjacent to the Baltic, and it appears, from documents recently published, that those cities had consented to appeals being carried from the court of Novgorod to Lubeck, it is to be inferred that it was not that city which borrowed some articles from the Skraa, but rather that the Germans, accustomed during the thirteenth century to adopt the statutes of Lubeck, inserted a number of the articles of these statutes in the additions which they made to the primitive code of the factory of Novgorod.

Of the Russian Baltic province of Courland, acquired from Poland, the two maritime cities, Windau and

Libau, do not present any statutes containing regulations relative to maritime law, nor any special law; and it is probable that, in early times, they followed the same law as the other maritime cities which, after having been subjected to the Teutonic Knights, were incorporated with Poland.

The Russian Baltic province of Livonia, of which Riga is the principal maritime city, appears in 1254 to have entertained the plan of adopting the law of Lubeck; and probably, also, followed afterwards the maritime law of Sweden of 1667. But Riga, founded in 1192, and which owed its increase, and its great commercial importance, to the merchants of Bremen and Lubeck, appears, according to Siegel, to have derived not merely its primitive laws in maritime matters, but its whole civil law, from the statutes of Wisby, divided into eleven books. On the other hand, Pufendorff has published, as a statute of Riga, a text which bears such a strong resemblance to the most ancient statute of Hamburg, of 1270, that it is scarcely possible not to believe that it was borrowed from the latter city. But if the magistrates of Riga borrowed the statute of Hamburg, they did so with discernment, and modified and adapted it to their own particular circumstances; and they afterwards composed a statute for themselves, towards the end of the fifteenth or beginning of the sixteenth century. After having passed under the dominion of Poland, the city of Riga was conquered from that kingdom by Sweden in 1621. And, while it was under the latter government, it subjected its statutes to a revision, which appears to have been completed in 1672, and the result of which was the code still in force in that city. The maritime laws contained in the fifth book of this statute, are much more extensive than in the preceding statutes; and the regulations are in general borrowed from the statute of Hamburg of 1603, although they contain traces of an existence anterior to the Swedish domination.

With regard to Esthonia, another of the Baltic provinces of the Russian Empire, its principal maritime city, Revel, formed part of the Hanseatic League, and appears, from its foundation in the thirteenth century, to have adopted the law of Lubeck. Nay, it appears even to have continued to conform to the law of the latter city, agreeably to the successive modifications which it underwent. And, at present, the maritime law followed at Revel is the sixth book of the statute of Lubeck, compiled in the thirteenth century, and the Swedish laws, both of which have been already noticed.

Of Finland, now also incorporated as a Baltic province of the Russian Empire, the maritime law, from the long previous dependence of that country upon Sweden, was, of course, until its late incorporation, just the maritime law of that kingdom, of which we have already given some account.

Until the year 1782, the general legislation of the Russian Empire, relative to maritime commerce, thus consisted only of the small number of documents before mentioned, and of usages and some particular laws established in the earlier part of last century. With the exception, indeed, of Novgorod, which was one of the towns united in the once formidable Hanseatic Confederacy, Russia, properly so called, had comparatively little maritime commerce till the reign of Peter the Great. The enterprising genius of that great Prince, it is well known, led him to form the grand design, unknown to his predecessors, of assuming an important rank among the great powers of Europe, although the largest part of his Empire was situated in Asia. And, enlightened by the observations which he made during his travels in Holland and England, as well as by the advice of the persons of merit whom he attracted around him, Peter soon perceived that, to obtain an influence in European affairs, it was necessary to form an outlet in the Baltic for the productions of his vast empire ; and he established, at the same time, a powerful navy, to make himself respected by the other nations of Europe, particularly those of the north. The inconsiderate war which Charles XII. excited against him, furnished the Czar with the means of accomplishing his grand object. He penetrated across Ingria to the Gulf of Finland; and, in 1703, the magnificent city of Petersburgh arose from the marshy ground at the mouth of the Neva, to be the capital of the Empire of all the Russias.

Section III.

Peter the Great—Empress Catherine—New General Code.

But, amidst all his schemes and exertions for promoting the internal and external commerce of his empire, the Czar does not appear to have thought of encouraging the navigation of his subjects by good maritime legislation, and by the establishment of intelligent tribunals, well adapted for the determination of maritime and commercial questions. He did too much, it has been observed, for his naval forces, and not enough for his mercantile marine. If he had employed a part of the sums which his useless gallies and an indifferent fleet cost him in facilitating commerce in the ports of Petersburg, Riga, Revel, and Archangel, the navy of his vast dominions would have reaped the benefit and attained to much greater eminence.

The Empress Catherine II., however, who governed the Russian Empire with so great celebrity, and with such advantage to her subjects, and who, notwithstanding her personal crimes, is entitled to be placed in the rank of great and able sovereigns, soon perceived the urgent expediency of forming for her dominions an uniform code of maritime law. Indeed, from the commencement of her reign, she displayed personally a great genius, as well as taste for legislation in general. Of her exertions in this department, the ukases, and ordinances for the administration of the different governments, the charter granted the nobility, the regulations for the police of the Empire, are monuments. In 1769, she published her own instructions to the commission charged with the preparation of the projet of a new code of laws. And, in 1782, she promulgated the body of mercantile navigation laws, according to which the Senate and the Custom-House Court of St Petersburg were to dispense justice between merchants, traders, and seafaring people, and which is distinguished by the wisdom of its provisions.

Between the years 1780 and 1790, Catherine also promulgated an ukase on the law of privateering, and entered into conventions with other maritime powers for the establishment of a general maritime code, which should ascertain in future the rights of neutrals during war, and should put an end to, or, at least, limit, the exercise of certain powers which other belligerent maritime nations claimed as right. But these matters belong not to private maritime law, but to the public law of nations, or, more appropriately, international law, which we may perhaps have an opportunity of afterwards illustrating. A new general code of private law, however, was promulgated by the government of Russia some years ago, of which a considerable portion is allotted to private maritime and commercial law.

CHAPTER XI.

MARITIME AND COMMERCIAL LAW OF ENGLAND.

Section I.

England—How no systematic Code.

Notwithstanding the great advantages of an insular situation, it was long before England made any considerable advances in maritime commerce; and, consequently, the progress of maritime legislation and jurisprudence could not fail to be proportionally slow.

Nor is this circumstance surprising, when the state of the people and of the country, in more remote periods, is considered. During the Saxon Heptarchy, England was divided into a number of petty kingdoms, the Princes of which, as is usual among rude tribes, were almost perpetually at variance with each other, and engaged in hostilities. The country was exposed to the fierce incursions of northern pirates, the remains of those hordes who had overwhelmed the Roman Empire; and, independently of their ignorance, the people did not enjoy the security requisite for the cultivation of commerce.

Next followed the Norman Conquest, and blasted the fair prospects which the superior genius and comparatively enlightened policy and institutions of Alfred had afforded. And, although the Norman Conqueror has, perhaps, erroneously been represented as having introduced the feudal system, it seems certain that the Conquest was the completion of that system in England, and the establishment of the rigours and other disadvantages of that species of military government. The former great landed proprietors were removed to make way for the retainers of the Conqueror; and the portion of the population likely to engage in commerce and manufactures was still more depressed and degraded.

It has been held out, indeed, by some writers, that England had made great progress in maritime commerce and in naval affairs even so early as the twelfth century; and, in proof of this, reference is made to the laws of Oleron, as a compilation, directed by an English monarch, for regulating the trade and navigation of his subjects. But, as we had formerly occasion to observe, when the matter is impartially considered, and free from the influence of national bias, it must be admitted that the Roles d'Oleron, though afterwards sanctioned and established by the King of England, are the production, not of his *then* comparatively less civilized subjects, but of the more industrious and skilful inhabitants of those continental dominions which he had acquired by right of marriage. The fact seems to be, that these laws were neither framed by nor for the accommodation of the people of England, but were framed by and for the accommodation of the industrious trading and seafaring people of the western coast of France, and, particularly, of the Duchy of Guienne in the Bay of Biscay; and, consequently, they can afford no evidence of the actual state of the maritime and commercial law of England at that time.

Accordingly, even in the reign of Edward III., upwards of a century afterwards, commerce and navigation appear to have been at a low ebb. Scarcely had the nation recovered from the shock of the Norman Conquest when it was engaged in supporting its Monarch's pretensions to the French crown: and it long continued to waste its vigour and its wealth in wild attempts to conquer that country. Next succeeded the destructive civil wars between the Houses of York and Lancaster, which long deluged the kingdom with blood, and to which a period was put only by the union of the different titles to the crown in the person of Henry VIII. Under that Monarch the Reformation took place; and it was not till the reign of Elizabeth that the dissensions, to which such an important event could not fail to give birth, began to subside. The exertions of Edward III. to excite a spirit of industry among his subjects, and the many wise establishments proposed and encouraged by him, had proved, in a great measure, fruitless. But, during the long reign of Elizabeth, and under her wise and prudent administration of government, the nation, no longer harassed by those causes by which it had been formerly distracted, began to perceive its true interests, and so became aware of its own capacity and talents for mercantile and manufacturing enterprise, and of the very advantageous situation of the country for the cultivation both of Inland and foreign commerce. The influence of arts and commerce had begun to produce a favourable change in the condition of the great body of the people. The wealth, and consequent independence and power, thus acquired by the commons, united to the crown, had enabled the latter to reduce the power of the aristocracy, and to establish a more regular administration of justice, and greater security to individuals. The operation of the same causes, during the long and peaceful reign of James I., raised the commons to such a degree of power as to lead them to set at defiance the crown as well as the aristocracy; and the unhappy contest ended in the temporary subversion of the Monarchy. But the intelligent part of the population of the country soon saw the folly, as well as the pernicious consequences, of such proceedings. And the result of the struggle between the crown and aristocracy, and the commons, was the temperate and wise arrangement of 1688, by which a greater portion of civil liberty has been secured to the people of this country, and for a longer period than perhaps ever fell to the lot of any other nation. The grand principles of the political constitution thus established, so far as commerce is concerned, are, on the one hand, the absolute security of property, the complete certainty which the individual possesses that he will reap the fruits of his industry, and, on the other hand, the entire liberty which the individual enjoys of exerting his talents and employing his means in the manner which he conceives to be most conducive to his own interest. And, under this constitution, the people of England, though among the last of the European states in availing themselves of the physical advantages of their situation, have, in more recent times, made ample amends for their long-continued inactivity by the astonishing extension of their trade and navigation, as well as by the excellence of their maritime and commercial jurisprudence.

At the same time, it must be admitted that the improvement in the maritime and commercial law of England has not all along, or altogether, kept pace with the vast extension of commerce, manufactures, and navigation. Even at this day, England cannot, like many of the other European states, boast of having a well-digested and systematic maritime and commercial code. In the Statute Book we find merely detached enactments of the legislature applicable to particular branches of trade and navigation. Parliament has never sanctioned any general systematic compilation of maritime and commercial regulations, such as that executed in France under the auspices of Colbert. The great body of the maritime and commercial law of England must be sought in the decisions of the different courts of justice; and these decisions, of course, being merely the judgments pronounced in particular cases, do not present what can be called an authoritative collection—a digest of general principles.

The want of such a systematic maritime and commercial code in England has excited the surprise of many natives as well as foreigners; and, while we entertain the highest possible respect for, and admiration of, the laws and the lawyers of the sister kingdom, we may be permitted to think that the compilation of a maritime and commercial code, composed on enlightened principles, deduced from the practical experience of maritime and trading states, and particularly from the practical, legislative, and judicial experience of England herself, during the last two centuries, would be a work of great national utility. On the other hand, we are well aware that the want of such an authoritative systematic code is much less felt in England than it would be in most other countries; and this seems to be the reason why the formation of such a code has not engaged the attention of government—not the difficulty of passing an act of Parliament, as has been absurdly enough supposed by Azuni, a recent continental writer. Parliament has so far legislated, with regard to particular branches of trade and navigation; and these enactments have, from time to time, received amendments by the same authority, according to the changing circumstances of the people. And, with regard to those departments of trade and navigation which are left to the regulation of the common or consuetudinary law, a series of able, learned, and independent judges have, since the era of the Revolution of 1688, accumulated a body of equitable and enlightened decisions upon the particular cases which have come before them, at least equal, if not superior, to what the tribunals of any other nation have yet produced.

Section II.

Early Maritime Law—Roles d'Oleron—Black Book of Admiralty.

Having premised these general remarks, we proceed to notice the sources and component parts of the maritime and mercantile law of England.

Although the laws of Oleron were neither framed by, nor directly or chiefly for the use of, the people of England, but by and for the use of the then industrious mercantile and seafaring people of the Duchy of Guienne, this compilation is, no doubt, the source, and came in time to form the basis, of the maritime law of that kingdom. The laws promulgated by William the Conqueror contain a title on jetson and contribution, of which the doctrine resembles the Roles d'Oleron more than the Roman law. That the collection of maritime regulations drawn up by the direction of his mother, Eleanor Duchess of Guienne, under the title of the Roles d'Oleron, was confirmed by King Richard I. on his return from the Holy Land, we have already had occasion to see, from the investigation of M. Pardessus, may not be quite consistent with historic truth. But whether this compilation was made under the direction of Duchess Eleanor, or received the sanction of Richard or not, or whether it was composed under sovereign or municipal authority, or was merely, as M. Pardessus concludes, a compilation, by one or more private individuals, of usages formerly observed, and of previous judicial determinations, there can be no doubt that such a compilation then existed, and that its rules were in observance on the western and northern coasts of France; and, from the intercourse which behoved to subsist, to a certain extent, between the dominions of the same Sovereign, the compilation could not fail to be received with respect in England. In an ordinance of King John, the laws of Oleron appear to have been recognised; and they appear to have served as a rule for maritime transactions towards the end of the reign of Henry III. Prior to the reign of Edward I., the extension of navigation, whether for the purposes of commerce or the defence of the kingdom—the foreign expeditions occasioned by the crusades—the necessity of repressing piracy—the insubordination of sailors and seafaring people, and the great disorders and excesses which appear to have then prevailed among them—had all led to the establishment of the jurisdiction of the Admiralty; and, during that reign, the Admiralty Court appears to have adopted the Roles d'Oleron as rules for the administration and distribution of justice in matters of private maritime right.

Finally, in the celebrated inquest of Queenborough, in the reign of Edward III., (1375,) relative to maritime police and the jurisdiction of the Court of Admiralty, it is expressly declared that the Roles d'Oleron are the law according to which this jurisdiction decides, and shall determine all disputes relative to maritime commerce. And, having thus acquired a kind of indirect legislative authority in England, they continued, with eight additional articles, emanating from the English Admiralty jurisdiction, and relating to cases which had not been previously foreseen or correctly determined, to form a sort of common law for maritime trade and disputes.

The Roles d'Oleron, however, do not appear ever to have been expressly established in England by any direct legislative enactment. They seem to have owed the indirect influence which they acquired in that country chiefly to their own intrinsic excellence. Thus Sir Leoline Jenkins, a great civilian, and Judge of the English High Court of Admiralty, in the reign of Charles II., says:—"I call them the laws of Oleron, not but that they are peculiarly enough English, being long since incorporated into the customs and statutes of our Admiralties, but the equity of them is so great, and the use and reason of them so general, that they are known and received, all the world over, by that rather than by any other name." And, says Molloy:—"The sea laws instituted at Oleron never obtained any other or greater force than those of Rhodes formerly did; that is, they were esteemed for the reason and equity found in them, and applied to the case emergent."

After this early adoption of the laws of Oleron, trade and navigation underwent such great changes, that the subjects of many articles of this code grew entirely obsolete; and rules more conformable to modern customs and usages came, from time to time, to be recognised or established. Notwithstanding the antipathy of the English, in general, to the use of the Roman law, many useful principles came to be adopted from that law into the maritime jurisprudence of England, particularly from the titles of the Digest, "De Nautico Fœnore, de Usuris Maritimis, de Actione Exercitoria;" but only subsidiarily to the customs of Oleron, the basis of the structure. Thus Selden, in his dissertation, Ad Fletam, cap. 8:—"Juris civilis, vel Caesarii, usus, ab antiquis sæculis, etiam nunc, retinetur, in foro maritimo, seu curia Admiralitatis." Many parts, too, of the maritime law of England were, according to the statement of Dr Arthur Duck, in his treatise, "De Usu et Auctoritate Juris Civilis," lib. ii., c. 8, § 25, borrowed from the Consolato del Mare. And this is extremely probable, both from the extensive trade carried on in England, in early times, by the Italians, generally known, in these ages, by the name of Lombards, and from the commercial intercourse which, we have seen, the industrious inhabitants of Barcelona maintained at an early period with the inhabitants of the Netherlands and of England. From the vast influence, also, which the Hanse Towns possessed in England, prior to the reign of Elizabeth, there can be little doubt that the maritime law of England received considerable accessions and improvements from the excellent code promulgated by that once powerful Confederacy; and from the great traffic which subsisted, in early times, between the province of Flanders, particularly the towns of Bruges and Antwerp and Britain, there is reason to believe that the English are indebted to the Flemings for various salutary regulations with regard to trade and navigation.

The Black Book of the Admiralty appears to have been commenced in the reign of Edward III., and to have been continued under Richard II. and Henry IV.; and the object of this compilation was obviously to form a sort of manual or practical collection for the jurisdiction of the Admiralty. The documents which it contains are in the old Norman French language; but were, in the reign of Charles II., translated into English by Thomas Bedford, upon the suggestion of Sir Leoline Jenkins. Of these documents, there are six. The first two relate chiefly to the office and conduct of the admiral, and the rights belonging to him; the third contains the articles of the inquest of 1338, which relate entirely to the repression of crimes and delinquencies on the seas and coasts, to the national navy, and other matters quite unconnected with private maritime law; the fourth is entitled the Laws of Oleron, and contains a series of thirty-five articles, all relative to private maritime law; the fifth is the inquest made in 1375 at Queenborough, by order of King Edward III., before William de Latymer, Chamberlain and Keeper of the Cinque Ports, and William de

Nevyll, High Admiral; and the articles, eighteen in number, have for their object, to determine points which had not been foreseen, either by the primitive Roles d'Oleron, or by the articles which had been added to them in the Black Book; and all, especially and exclusively, relate to private maritime law. After these articles there follows a series of sixty-three regulations, ordering inquiries and prosecutions relative to different crimes and delinquencies committed on the high seas or coasts.

The police and penal regulations, contained in the inquests of 1338 and 1375, were recast and digested into fifty-nine articles in the Latin language, by Roughton; and this document is inserted in the Black Book, at the end of the preceding, and is annexed to the edition of the work of Clerke, entitled, "Praxis Supremæ Curiæ Admiralitatis," published in 1743. The object of Roughton appears to have been to compile and digest all that concerned the powers and rights of the admiral in the department of maritime police, in a language more easy to be understood than the old Norman French; to save the trouble of research; and to form a whole of the regulations upon the same point, which were separated and scattered over the anterior documents. This work is authenticated by the subscription of the Duke of Norfolk, who was High Admiral in the beginning of the reign of Henry VIII.; and it appears to have been afterwards revised and enlarged according as new circumstances arose. An English translation appears to have been made in 1591, in the reign of Elizabeth, when Sir Julius Cæsar was Judge of the Admiralty; and another translation in 1639, in the reign of Charles I. But neither Roughton, nor those who revised or enlarged his work, occupied themselves with the rules in the Black Book relative to private law; and, in the same way, Selden, Exton,

Coke, and Prynne, while they have made numerous citations from the Black Book, in the works which they have published on the rights and jurisdiction of the Admiralty, solely and entirely occupied with that subject, have neglected and omitted the rules of private maritime law which it contains.

Section III.

Progress of Maritime and Commercial Law, Statutory and Common.

Such appear to have been the original and early so far extraneous sources from which the maritime law of England was derived. But, after the English, in later times, became more extensively a seafaring and trading people, the maritime and mercantile law of the country naturally grew up with its commerce. And that body of law may now be considered as composed of two great branches of regulations, which are frequently blended, inasmuch as they are often both applicable to the same subject or department of business, but which are distinguished from each other by the species or description of authority by which they have been, or are, established or enforced. The one of these great branches is the statutory law, relative to trade and navigation, comprehending all the acts of Parliament which have, from time to time, been passed relative to these subjects: the other great branch is the common or consuetudinary law, relative to trade and navigation, comprehending what the English lawyers call the marine law and the law merchant.

Statutory.

With regard to the first of these branches—the statutory law—England, as already noticed, has no general legislative code of maritime and mercantile law, such as France and most of the other European states now possess. The comparatively few acts of Parliament, relative to trade and navigation, which are to be found scattered up and down in the Statute Book, generally embrace only single and detached subjects. They do not lay down or arrange the principles of the law; they usually presume and take for granted the existence of these principles, as already recognised in the common consuetudinary marine law and law merchant. And they have obviously been passed, from time to time, not with the view of laying the foundation, or of forming a part of a systematic whole, but in order to supply occasional defects in the common law, to correct abuses, and to promote grand objects of national policy.

The particular provisions of the acts of Parliament here alluded to, we cannot here consider in detail—we shall merely notice some of the more important departments which are regulated or materially affected by these legislative enactments.

The privileges of British vessels, the description of vessels entitled to these privileges, and the transference of property in British vessels, have all been regulated and ascertained by a series of statutes which have been passed, from time to time, since the middle of the seventeenth century, and are known under the general appellation of the navigation laws; and these statutes, it is well known, originated in state policy; the object of these being to increase British shipping, and to secure, at all times, a supply of seamen for the national navy, the natural bulwark of an insular empire.

The statute 43, Elizabeth, 1601, shews the frequency, at that time, in England, of disputes in the practice of maritime insurance, which had become pretty prevalent in Europe in the course of the fifteenth and sixteenth centuries, and which the English seem to have borrowed immediately from the Low Countries. But this statute merely establishes a Commission and summary mode of trying such questions of marine insurance as had formerly been decided by certain grave and discreet merchants nominated by the Lord Mayor of London, and does not contain any of the doctrines of this branch of law. Nay, even the later statute 17, Charles II., c. 6, contains no rules as to the form or effects of the contract of insurance.

Several statutes were also passed in the course of last century relative to the papers with which a merchant ship ought to be furnished—relative to convoys for merchant vessels in time of war—relative to the responsibility of the owners of merchant vessels—relative to apprentices in the merchant service—relative to agreements between ship-masters and seamen, particularly as to wages and the support of disabled seamen—relative to harbours and pilots—and relative to the impressing of seamen. Farther, the Statute Book exhibits a great number of statutes relative to the importation and exportation of commodities, and the customs and duties payable thereon, and relative to the British plantations and colonies. And it also contains many acts of Parliament relative to the Admiralty Instance Court, which, although they cannot strictly be said to form a part of private maritime law, inasmuch as they do not afford any rules for the decision of causes in that court, go to limit its jurisdiction, or ascertain its boundaries, and to correct excesses or encroachments on the common law courts. Farther still, in the course of last century, several statutes were passed relative to the destruction or molestation of ships, and relative to stranded ships and salvage. And, during the reigns of George II. and George III., some few statutes were passed, to restrain the abuses of insurance; but not one has yet been made either to ascertain an old principle or to sanction any new one in that important department of maritime and commercial law. A few acts, also, in the Statute

Book, passed during the period just alluded to, have reference to bills of exchange and copartnership. But these relate chiefly to promissory notes and inland bills of exchange; while foreign bills of exchange and copartnership, having been introduced by, and grown up under, the customs and usages of merchants, form an important part of the consuetudinary Lex Mercatoria.

In the reign of George IV., the navigation laws, as well as those of customs, or indirect taxation, underwent a thorough revision under the enlightened direction of Mr Huskisson. And the statutes 4, Geo. IV., c. 41, and 6, Geo. IV., c 109, and 6, Geo. IV., c. 110, then passed, while they are more perspicuously expressed and more methodically arranged, solve and settle, in a satisfactory manner, those numerous questions which had occupied the attention of the English courts for a series of years, and had occasioned a considerable litigation in ascertaining and establishing the true construction of the previous statutes relative to property in British vessels; though not more litigation, perhaps, than was to be expected from the difficulties of legislation in such matters. In the reigns of George IV. and William IV., several statutes were also passed, elucidating and fixing various points in the law of banking establishments and joint-stock companies.

Common or Consuetudinary Law.

From this cursory review of the principal enactments of the legislature relative to trade and navigation, it is manifest that the great body of the maritime and mercantile law of England is not statute law, but common or consuetudinary law. And it may, therefore, be proper to notice at greater length the sources from which this consuetudinary maritime and mercantile law is derived, and the authority upon which it rests.

Lex Mercatoria.

Of this branch of the law of England, Mr Justice Blackstone speaks in the following terms :—" To this head (that is, to the second division of the unwritten law of England, consisting of particular customs) may, most properly, be referred a particular system of customs, used only among one set of the King's subjects, or Lex Mercatoria; which, however different from the general rules of the common law, is yet engrafted into it and made a part of it; being allowed, for the benefit of trade, to be of the utmost validity in all commercial transactions."* Again—" The affairs of commerce are regulated by a law of their own, called the law merchant, or Lex Mercatoria, which all nations agree in and take notice of; and, in particular, it is held to be a part of the law of England, which decides the causes of merchants by the general rules which obtain in all commercial countries, and that often even in matters relating to domestic trade; as, for instance, with regard to the drawing, the acceptance, and the transfer of inland bills of exchange."† Farther, in another place, adds the same learned judge and commentator :—" In mercantile questions, such as bills of exchange and the like, in all marine causes, relating to freight, average, demurrage, insurance, bottomry, and others of a similar nature, the law merchant, which is a branch of the law of nations, is regularly and constantly adhered to. So, too, in all disputes relating to prizes, to hostages, and ransom bills, there is no other rule of decision but this great universal law, collected from history and usage, and such writers of all nations and languages as are generally appproved of and allowed."‡

* Com. vol. i., p. 75. † Vol. i., p. 273. ‡ Vol. iv., p. 69.

This account of the maritime and commercial law of England is certainly rather vague, and not very distinct or satisfactory. We have endeavoured to elucidate the subject generally in the first part of this work; and, without presuming to criticise any farther the doctrine of the learned Justice, we may cite the observations thereon of Dr Hoffman, an able and very learned lawyer of the United States of America:*—"Of the Lex Mercatoria. The student, no doubt, will find some difficulty in ascertaining the origin and defining the limits of this system. As a body of law, he will, perhaps, be unable to comprehend why it should be considered as a branch of the law of nations.† So, likewise, he may not agree with the learned commentator who classes it under that part of the English Lex non Scripta, denominated 'Particular Customs.'‡ By some he will find it defined as the 'general usages or customs of merchants in mercantile negotiations;' whilst others would have that to be the law of merchants, in any place, which is the usage of that place. It is not for us, in such a work as the present professes to be, to enter much into legal discussions, or to solve for the student his numerous legal doubts. How far the Lex Mercatoria may be derived from the general usages of merchants of all nations, and thus far claim a place in the law of nations, as being quasi juris publici—how far general use, among the merchants of England, constitutes the Lex Mercatoria of that country, or how the local usage may become law, or the entire system be ranked with particular customs, the inquiring student will, no doubt, inform himself. We would, however, remark, that this general mode of expression, relative to the origin or limits of this system of law, is

* Course of Legal Study, vol. i., p. 415-16.
† Blackstone's Commentaries, iv., 67.
‡ Blackstone's Commentaries, i., 75.

calculated to mislead the student. The Lex Mercatoria of any particular country—as, for example, England—may perhaps be defined a system of principles or rules, peculiarly regulating mercantile transactions, derived principally from the customs of merchants in different nations; from the usages, either general or local, of the merchants of England—which customs or usages of foreign or English merchants have been judicially sanctioned; and, lastly, from express legislative provision. Hence this system, whether we regard its extent or the sources of its origin, cannot, with propriety, be classed with particular customs; for a particular custom affects only the inhabitants of a particular district; whereas the Lex Mercatoria is not restricted within any defined limits, but extends over the whole realm, and operates everywhere over certain transactions. So, likewise, this law need not be specially pleaded, as particular customs must generally be; nor is this law to be tried by a jury, as customs are."

Referring to our elucidation, in the first part of this work, of the peculiar nature and relative position of the law of maritime commerce, we are led to believe that the body of common or consuetudinary legal doctrine, recognised, in England, under the appellations of the Marine Law and the Law Merchant, or Lex Mercatoria, is, according to the most intelligent English lawyers, to be found in and collected from the three following sources:—1*st*, The ordinances of different commercial states; 2*d*, The treatises of learned authors; 3*d*, The decisions of the courts of law in England, and in other countries which follow the general marine law and the law of merchants.

Foreign Ordinances.

Now, with regard to the first of these sources, the ordinances of other countries cannot properly be said to be in force in England; but they are of authority, inasmuch as they express the practice and established usage of other nations in maritime and mercantile contracts and transactions, which are governed by general rules, forming in the aggregate a branch, not, as we have seen, of international law, properly so called, but of internal national law, distinguished from the other branches of the latter, by being similar among and common to most civilized states. Non habent vim legis, sed rationis.

Of the ordinances of other commercial states which thus possess an indirect influence in England, we have already noticed the principal—the laws of Oleron, the laws of Wisby, the laws of the Hanse Towns, and the laws of the Netherlands; and to these we may add the celebrated ordonnance of Louis XIV., of which we have so often spoken, from which Lord Mansfield did not hesitate to derive instruction as to the true principles of maritime and commercial law, and to which reference is so often made in the works of the latest and best English writers in this department of jurisprudence, such as Mr Justice Park, Mr Sergeant Marshall, and Chief Justice Abbott, afterwards Lord Tenterden.

Treatises of Learned Authors.

With respect to the second of the sources before alluded to, the treatises of learned authors, the maritime and commercial law of England seems, till within the last sixty years, to have been more indebted to the labours of foreign than of native writers. Of those foreign writers we have already taken notice when tracing the history of the maritime law of their respective countries. And we may only here refer to the collection of Cleirac, entitled, Us et Coutumes de la Mer, including the Guidon de la Mer, and to the works of

Stypmannus, Loccenius, Roccus, Bynkershoek, Casaregis, Savary, Valin, Emerigon, and Pothier.

Of the earlier English writers on maritime law, the attention appears to have been much occupied with discussions concerning the dominion of the sea, and the nature and limits of Admiralty jurisdiction, as opposed to or distinguished from the jurisdiction of the courts of common law.

In 1615, William Wellwood published a treatise, De Dominio Maris, and, in 1613, an Abridgment of Sea Laws, in quarto, which appears to have been composed chiefly of the laws of Oleron, Wisby, and the Hanse Towns.

In 1622, Gerard Malynes published, and dedicated to King James, his treatise, in folio, entitled, "Consuetudo, vel, Lex Mercatoria, or the ancient law merchant, divided into three parts, according to the essential parts of traffic, viz., commodities, moneys, and exchanges for moneys, by bills of exchange." This is a very learned and valuable work; and, although the style is antiquated, and the book contains a great deal of bad metaphysics and useless erudition, yet, considering the age in which he wrote, the author has great merit. The work embraces all the essential branches of maritime and mercantile law; it shews that insurance and bills of exchange had then been long in common use; and it is still referred to as an authority by the English law writers of the present day. An improved edition of the book, with a collection of sea laws attached to it, was published in 1686.

In the year 1635, the celebrated Selden published, and dedicated to King Charles I., his treatise, entitled, Mare Clausum, seu de Dominio Maris, in which, in opposition to Grotius, he maintains that the sea, as well as the land, is susceptible of appropriation; and that the King of Great Britain is lord of the circumjacent seas, as a perpetual appendage of the British Empire.

In 1661, Godolphin, who was Judge of the Court of Admiralty about the middle of the seventeenth century, published his view of the admiral's jurisdiction.

In 1663, Dr Richard Zouch, commonly called Zoucheius, published, among other works, a treatise entitled Jurisdiction of the Admiralty of England asserted against Sir Edward Coke's Articuli Admiralitatis.

And, in 1664, John Exton, who succeeded Godolphin as Judge of the English Court of Admiralty, published a work entitled "The Maritime Dicacology," or sea jurisdiction of England, set forth in three books.

In the reign of Charles II. Sir Leoline Jenkins, who was Judge of the Court of Admiralty, as well as Ambassador on the Continent, distinguished himself as a great civilian; and was eminent for his skill in admiralty and maritime jurisprudence, as well as in international law. His speeches, letters, and life, were published, in 1724, by Mr William Wynne.

Between 1680 and 1690, Guy Miege published collection of sea laws, which were afterwards attachea to the improved edition of the Lex Mercatoria oı Malynes.

In the year 1692, Charles Molloy, an English barrister, published his well known work, entitled "De Jure Maritimo et Navali," or a treatise of affairs maritime, and of commerce. This book treats of the principal branches, not only of the public maritime law of nations, but also of private maritime and mercantile jurisprudence, such as property in merchant vessels, freight, charter-parties, and demurrage, insurance, and bills of exchange. A new edition of this work was published in 1722 by the author's son, with an addition of modern cases. Another edition, still farther improved, was published so late as the year 1769; and, till the recent publications of Mr Justice Park, of Mr Sergeant Marshall, of Chief Justice Abbott, Lord Tenterden, and of Mr Chitty, the treatise of Molloy, although, it has many defects, continued to be the standard English work of authority on maritime law.

In 1746, there was published, in two vols. 8vo, a collection of the laws, ordinances, and institutions of the Admiralty of Great Britain, civil and military.

In the year 1750, Windham Beawes, who was long British Consul at Seville and St Lucar, published a work, entitled Lex Mercatoria Rediviva, or the merchants' director; in which, along with pretty full details respecting the commerce and manufactures of the times, he conveys a good deal of practical information on the different leading branches of maritime and mercantile law. In 1783, an improved edition of this work was published, in folio, by Thomas Mortimer, British Vice-Consul at Ostend; and, in 1813, a still farther improved edition of this work was published by Mr Chitty, in two vols. quarto.

In the year 1715, Malachy Postlethwayt published, in two vols. folio, his translation of the Universal Dictionary of Trade and Commerce of M. Savary; on which he engrafted a vast deal of valuable matter relative to the trade, commerce, and manufactures of the British kingdoms, and brought down the history of commerce to the middle of the last century. In this work also, which has been improved in subsequent editions, there is to be found a good deal of useful practical information on the different subjects of maritime and commercial law.

In 1775, Mr Magens, a merchant, republished, in two vols. quarto, his Essay on Insurances, which he had previously published, in German, at Hamburgh. The Essay itself is very short. It shews a considerable degree of practical knowledge of insurances, derived form the ordinances of different countries; but, as Mr Marshall observes, the book would have been much more valuable had the author been better acquainted with the general treatises on the subject. The remainder of the work consists of calculations of averages, of letters and state papers relating to commerce, and of a collection of marine and commercial ordinances and treaties of commerce.

In 1775, Mr Thomas Parker, barrister-at-law, published, in quarto, "The Laws of Shipping and Insurance." This work consists chiefly of a collection of the acts of Parliament relative to navigation and insurance, and of a digest of the adjudged cases of the English courts of common law, particularly of those of Lord Mansfield.

In 1783, Mr Weskett, a merchant, published, in octavo, what he calls "A Complete Digest of the Theory, Laws, and Practice of Insurance;" and in this work he has put together, in an alphabetical arrangement, a large quantity of materials on insurance and other branches of maritime jurisprudence.

Still, however, England, from the time of Molloy, had not produced any scientific or systematic treatise, by any eminent lawyer, on any of the branches of maritime and commercial law, till Mr Park, in 1786 or 1788, published his "System of the Law of Marine Insurances." In the composition of this valuable work, Mr Park is understood to have been much indebted to Lord Mansfield and Sir Francis Buller. Independently of Lord Mansfield's judgments in the Court of King's Bench on the contract of insurance, the detail of which occupies a considerable part of the book, Mr Park appears also to have enjoyed the benefit of his Lordship's private conversation on such legal topics, and to have had access to the valuable collection of foreign works in this department of law which his Lordship had made. With such advantages, the work could scarcely fail to be excellent. At the same time, we are inclined to think that, even in the more recent editions of his work, in 1796 and 1817, Sir James Allan Park has been excelled by Mr Sergeant Marshall, in point of lucid order and scientific arrangement In his "Treatise on the Law of Insurance," published in 1802, Mr Marshall has drawn his information from every accessible source, foreign and domestic. In particular, he seems to have profited much by the study of the admirable French treatises of Pothier and Emerigon; and his book is truly a model in this species of composition. Besides these standard works on insurance, by Sir James Allan Park and Mr Marshall, we may only farther notice the still more recent treatises of Mr Burn, Mr Annesley, and Mr Steven, which, though much inferior in merit, may be consulted with advantage.

Nor was England, till lately, more productive of scientific treatises on those other branches of maritime jurisprudence, which are of no less importance than the contract of insurance. It was not till 1792 that Mr Reeves published his useful "History of the Law of Shipping and Navigation." During the whole course of the eighteenth century, so fertile in literature, there was not a single scientific professional writer on property in merchant vessels, on the rights and obligations of the persons employed in the navigation of them, or on the rights and obligations of the persons engaged in the transactions of freight and charter-party, by which vessels are converted to use in the conveyance of commodities. It was not till 1802 that Mr Abbott, afterwards Lord Chief Justice Tenterden, under the patronage and encouragement of Lord Chancellor Eldon, published his excellent treatise on the law relative to merchant ships and seamen; and, in his preface, that author remarks:—" Considering the great importance of every branch of law relating to maritime commerce, it is a matter of surprise that no treatise on the subjects discussed in the following sheets should have been written by any member of the profession of the law for a very long period of years. It is now more than a century since the first publication of the work of Molloy, the only English lawyer who has written on these matters."

With regard, again, to those grand auxiliary contracts of maritime commerce, the contract of bills of exchange, and the contract of copartnership, the work on bills of exchange ascribed to Mr Cunningham, and published in 1759, is but a meagre compilation of adjudged cases, taken from the reports of Strange and others, with very little general information, and still less method. It was not till between the years 1789 and 1800 that the different treatises on the law of bills of exchange, by Bayley, Kyd, and Chitty, or that the treatise by Watson on the law of copartnership, appeared; the last of which writers observes:—"It appears somewhat singular that partnership should never have been treated by any English writer in a systematic form, and that even the rules of authority and practice should have remained scattered in the works of reporters, without any attempt having been made to collect them, prior to the author's first essay at the conclusion of the eighteenth century."

In more recent times, in the course of the present century, the want of methodical treatises on the different departments of private maritime and commercial law, has been so far supplied by the treatises of Lawes, on charter-parties of affreightment and bills of lading, in 1813; and of Holt on the shipping and navigation laws, in 1820; by the digest of the law of partnership, by that able lawyer and amiable individual, Basil Montagu, in 1815; and, in 1824, by the voluminous but pretty well arranged, and, though not profound, useful compilation of

Chitty, on the laws of commerce and manufactures. But, before leaving this branch of the subject, we may repeat a remark which Sir William Grant, the late most able and profound Master of the Rolls, made to the author a good many years ago, that, unfortunately for the illustration and scientific arrangement of the law of England, the ablest and most distinguished lawyers at the bar, from having had either no time or no inclination to write, have left the task of composing legal treatises to members of the profession of inferior talents.

So much for the second source of the maritime and commercial law of England, the treatises of learned authors.

Judicial Determinations.

The third source from which this body of legal doctrine is derived, as formerly noticed, is the decisions of the courts of law in England, and also in other countries which follow the general marine law and the law of merchants. And, from the preceding observations, it may have been anticipated that this is the grand and most fertile source of English maritime and commercial jurisprudence : indeed, in no department is the excellence of the English system of government more conspicuous than in its great judicial establishments. The constitution of these establishments has been generally considered as peculiarly well adapted for the correct distribution of justice among individuals. "It is universally agreed," says Mr Justice Park, "by all writers upon jurisprudence, that nothing tends so much to the elucidation of truth and the detection of fraud as the open *viva voce* examination of witnesses in the presence of all mankind, before judges who, from their knowledge of books and men, acquired by long study and experience, are well qualified to discriminate and decide between right and wrong; and before twelve upright citizens, who have an opportunity of observing the appearance, countenance, inclination, and deportment of those who are thus examined upon oath." Further, what is nearly of as great importance, the judges of England have, since the reign of Queen Elizabeth, been distinguished for their talents and learning And since the Revolution of 1688 particularly—that great event by which the constitution was settled, and the civil rights of the subject were defined and secured—there have presided in the courts of law of that country a more unbroken and continuous series of upright as well as able and enlightened men, than ever graced the tribunals of any other nation. The vast and increasing accession of external and internal trade, consequent upon the establishment of a settled and regular, as well as free and liberal, government, while it occasionally demanded the solicitude of the legislature, behoved greatly to amplify and extend the jurisdiction of the courts; and the luminous arguments and solemn decisions by which the true principles of the law have been unfolded and applied to the commercial transactions and relations of men, as contained in the English books of reports, have come, in the course of the last and of the present century, to form a body of enlightened legal doctrine which cannot be contemplated without respect and admiration.

To give any minute description of the different books of English reports, or to detail the merits of the various eminent judges whose decisions they record, this is not the place. But it may be useful to notice briefly the authority which judicial decisions possess as a part of the maritime and mercantile law of England, and to point out a few of the leading judges who have been the great improvers of that department of the law.

The authority of judicial decisions, in general, as

forming a branch of the common law of England, is thus luminously described by Douglas, Lord Glenbervie, in his book of reports, according to the view suggested more than two centuries ago by Lord Chancellor Bacon: —"The immediate province of the courts of justice is to administer the law in particular cases. But it is equally a branch of their duty, and one of still greater importance to the community, to expound the law they administer, upon such principles of argument and construction as may furnish rules which shall govern in all similar and analogous cases.

"Such are the various modifications of which property is susceptible, so boundless the diversity of relations which may arise in civil life, so infinite the possible combinations of events and circumstances, that they elude the power of enumeration, and are beyond the reach of human foresight. A moment's reflection, therefore, serves to evince that it would be impossible, by positive and direct legislative authority, specially to provide for every particular case which may happen.

"Hence it has been found expedient to intrust to the wisdom and experience of judges the power of deducing from the more general propositions of the law such necessary corollaries as shall appear, though not expressed in words, to be within their intent and meaning.

"Deductions thus formed, and established in the adjudication of particular cases, become, in a manner, part of the text of the law. Succeeding judges receive them as such, and, in general, consider themselves as bound to adhere to them no less strictly than to the express dictates of the legislature."

Farther, Sergeant Marshall observes:*—"With respect to judicial decisions, none are considered as binding authorities in our superior courts but such as have been

* Introduction, p. 23.

there determined, and even these may be reconsidered; and if, upon a full examination, they are found to militate against any clear and indisputable principle of law, they may, as in other cases, be overruled. As to foreign decisions, though they are of no authority in our courts, yet they are of value in order to shew, upon doubtful points, how learned men in other countries have understood the principles of that law which is supposed to be in force in this. Valet pro ratione, non pro introducto jure."

The first grand improvement made in the commercial law of England, by an enlightened train of judicial decisions, appears to have been in the department of equity, and in matters of bankruptcy. Mr Justice Blackstone dates the prevalence of liberality of sentiment, and the adoption of enlightened principles of redress, in the English courts of equity, from the time Lord Nottingham presided there.* But the great promoter of this branch of English jurisprudence was Lord Hardwicke, who presided in the Court of Chancery from the year 1736 to the year 1756.

Nor was the improvement of the commercial law of England, by enlightened judicial decisions, long confined to the provinces of equity and bankruptcy. Mr Justice Blackstone marks, among the leading improvements in the administration of private justice, during the period which had elapsed from the era of the Revolution to the time when he wrote, "the liberality of sentiment which, though late, (says he,) has now taken possession of our courts of common law, and induced them to adopt the same principles of redress as have long prevailed in our courts of equity; namely, the introduction and establishment of paper credit, by indorsement upon bills and notes, shewing the legal possibility and con-

* Volume iv., p. 441.

venience, which our ancestors so long doubted, of assigning a chose in action;" and "the great system of marine jurisprudence, of which the foundations have been laid, by clearly developing the principles on which policies of insurances are founded, and by happily applying those principles to particular cases."

"The period," says Mr Evans, "during which Lord Mansfield presided in the Court of King's Bench, will ever be regarded as an important era in the annals of English jurisprudence. His decisions will be resorted to, not merely as individual precedents in cases having a direct coincidence of circumstances, but as important guides in investigating the grounds and rudiments of the law.

"Possessing a mind in which the most exalted talents were improved by the most extensive cultivation, he regarded jurisprudence as a rational science founded upon the universal principles of moral rectitude, but modified by habit and authority; and was anxious to exert those talents in tracing every question of private right or public justice to its proper source; in marking the extent and limits of positive authority; in extracting from a series of particular decisions those common principles which might afterwards be easily resorted to, and distinctly applied; and in detecting the fallacy of arguments deduced from the literal interpretation of incidental expressions, or from an affinity of circumstances unsupported by a true analogy of character.

"It was his endeavour to render the tribunal where he presided, not only the instrument of immediate justice, but an instructive seminary to such as were engaged in professional studies; and his distinct and accurate investigations have contributed, not less than the excellent commentaries of Sir William Blackstone, to display the title of the English law to the rank of a connected and elegant science."

The spirit with which Lord Mansfield proceeded has been thus also described by his intimate friend, Mr Justice Buller :—" Within thirty years, the commercial law of this country has taken a very different turn from what it did before. Before that period we find that, in courts of law, all the evidence in mercantile cases was thrown together : they were left, generally, to a jury, and produced no established principle. From that time, we all know, the great study has been to find some certain general principles which shall be known to all mankind, not only to rule the particular case then under consideration, but to serve as a guide for the future. Most of us have heard these principles stated, reasoned upon, and explained, till we have been lost in admiration at the strength and stretch of the human understanding."

" After some of the decisions of the courts of Westminster, upon questions of insurance, came to be generally known," says Mr Sergeant Marshall, " the confidence which the justice, impartiality, and ability of these courts inspired throughout Europe, soon induced the merchants of all countries to prefer English insurances to those of any other country. Even our enemies, in time of war, were not afraid to rely on British justice ; and they still continued to cause the greater part of their insurances to be effected in London ; such insurances being, for a long time, tolerated by the British government."

" Upon his succeeding Sir Dudley Ryder in the office of Chief Justice," continues Mr Marshall, " Lord Mansfield soon found a considerable influx of business into the Court of King's Bench, arising, in a great measure, from the celebrity of his own talents. A great increase of insurances, not only upon British commerce, but likewise upon that of other countries, produced, about this time, a number of causes upon this subject, to which it became necessary for him to turn his particular attention; and, indeed, he seems to have taken pleasure in the discussion of questions arising upon this contract, in which, more, perhaps, than upon any other subject, he displayed the powers of his great and comprehensive mind. From the books of the common law, very little could be obtained; but, upon the subject of marine law, and the particular subject of insurances, the foreign authorities were numerous and, in general, satisfactory. From these, and from the information of intelligent merchants, he drew those leading principles, which may be considered as the common law of the sea and the common law of merchants, which he found prevailing throughout the commercial world, and to which almost every question of insurance was easily referable. Hence the great celebrity of his judgments upon such questions, and hence the respect they commanded in foreign countries. 'One cannot but admire,' says the French author, Emerigon, who wrote in 1781, after giving an account of a decision of the Court of King's Bench; 'one cannot but admire this mode of proceeding, however remote from our customs; for the impression which virtue makes upon us is so strong, that we love it even in our enemies. Tanta vis probitatis est, ut eam in hoste etiam diligamus. The judges in England do not consider it enough to decide aright; they give the reasons of their decision, that it may be known the people are subject to the empire of the law rather than to the authority of man.'"

The design and plan which, we have thus seen, was commenced, and was so far happily accomplished, by Lord Mansfield, has been steadily kept in view, and followed out, by the eminent judges who have succeeded him. The state in which the maritime and commercial intercourse of the different European nations was placed, during the two long wars consequent upon the French Revolution, gave rise to a great number and variety of new questions in all the different departments of maritime and commercial law; and, with the solution and determination of these questions, all the different descriptions of English courts were occupied, both during the war and for a considerable time after the restoration of peace. During these periods, the courts of common law, in their decisions on commercial matters, have been successively guided by the practical acuteness and sagacity of Lord Ellenborough, and by the learning and sound views of Lord Tenterden; and the talents of Lord Chief Justice Denman have been universally acknowledged. In the tribunal of last resort, and in the Court of Chancery, it is sufficient to mention the names of Lord Eldon, Sir William Grant, and Lord Brougham. Nor has the improvement of the maritime and commercial law of England, through the medium of judicial decisions, been confined to the Court of Chancery and to the courts of common law. It has been equally conspicuous in the admirable administration of the law in the High Court of Appeals from the Colonies, in the Court of ppeals in Prize Causes, in the Court of the Judges Delegate in Causes Civil and Maritime, and in the High Court of Admiralty of England. In these courts, we have only to recall to memory the names of Sir William Grant, Master of the Rolls, and of Sir William Scott, afterwards Lord Stowell, Judge of the Court of Admiralty. In profound knowledge of the law, in soundness and acuteness of judgment, in integrity and freedom from bias, in the laborious discharge of his duty, and in the expeditious dispatch of business, Sir William Grant is universally admitted to have been the complete model of a judge, not only in his own proper Court of Equity, but in the Court of Appeals from the Colonies, and in the Court of Appeals in Prize Causes. And it is equally admitted on all hands that, not only in his own proper court, the High Court of Admiralty, but also in the other high courts of appeals, Lord Stowell happily combined, in his judicial character, the learning and talents of the profound lawyer, the extensive erudition and refined taste of the accomplished scholar, and the enlarged views of the enlightened statesman. His appointment as judge took place in the year 1798, and yet he lived to verify the prediction of Dr Arthur Browne of Dublin, in 1802, that the "numerous great and able decisions of the eminent judge who now presides in the English High Court of Admiralty promise to raise as splendid and as consistent a system of jurisprudence—in a court the importance of whose decisions has, in our days, interested all Europe—as was erected in the province of equity by Lord Hardwicke, or by Lord Mansfield in the sphere of the common law."

Such being now the advanced state of maritime and commercial law in England, accomplished almost entirely through the medium of judicial determinations, the inquiry occurs, what farther can be done to perpetuate the improvements thus attained without impeding future progress, and to facilitate the due administration of the body of jurisprudence thus evolved and recorded. And, although it may be vain to attempt or expect to establish a perfect system, either in the internal private law of a state or in any other department of social arrangement, it by no means follows that a nation should not aim at all the improvement of which this very important branch of its law is susceptible. Now, there is reason to believe that very considerable advantage would arise from the occasional interposition of the legislature in expressly recognising, by an induction from particular cases, those general rules which the experience of our tribunals have sanctioned, in arranging those great practical principles and leading decisions from which may be derived the solution of a great proportion of the individual questions likely to occur in future, and in laying down, as clearly as practicable, the law, in that great multiplicity of instances in which, in point of justice, it is of little consequence whether the rule be fixed in the one way or the other, provided it be known and established. Indeed, as we have seen, this has been so far accomplished in practice, not merely in ancient times, but also by many nations of modern Europe, and apparently with beneficial effects. We have already had occasion to notice the authoritative compilations of this description which were made during the earlier periods of the history of several of the modern European nations, and also during the last and present century. At present, we may only again allude, in particular, to that excellent piece of legislation which was composed under the administration of the great Colbert, the celebrated Ordonnance de la Marine of Louis XIV., of which that Monarch was so justly proud; from which Lord Mansfield, when called upon to expound the maritime and commercial law of England, did not disdain to derive information and instruction; and which formed the basis and the model of the Code de Commerce of Napoleon. Such was the excellence of the jurisprudential part of this code, that its very able and learned commentator, M. Valin, assures us, as formerly noticed, the principles therein laid down had been found to embrace all the new cases which had occurred during a period of upwards of eighty years subsequent to its promulgation. M. Professor Bravard Veyrieres farther assures us, that this excellent piece of legislation had, in the department of jurisprudence, required no material change, even down to the year 1838, a century and a half from the date of its composition.* And if a

* Revue de Legislation, vol. viii., p. 130.

portion of that judicial talent and wisdom, which have so eminently distinguished England for a century past, were employed in digesting and directing the formation of such a code, there can be no doubt the result would be still more beneficial. The English nation has now attained a higher degree of advancement in commerce and navigation than any other nation ever did before. A great part of the field of commercial legislation has been actually travelled over and surveyed. The collection of reported judicial determinations is unequalled in any age or nation. They present a mass of invaluable materials, derived from practical experience, for the formation of such a code. By means of the mere process of analysis, such a body of general rules may be deduced from this multitude of particular cases as may meet and provide for, at least, the majority of cases which are now likely to arise. The general rules of investigation, by which the other arts and sciences have been so much improved, may, with great advantage, be also applied to this department of legislation. And if the work were conducted under the auspices of minds such as those which have, for the last century, presided over the English courts—stored with literature, extensive and profound; guided by enlightened views of commercial expediency; and, at the same time, matured and disciplined by sober and cautious procedure, by long judicial experience in the detail of actual business—we might expect a monument of legislation unrivalled in the annals of mankind.

That such a work may be accomplished at no very distant period, we may be permitted to hope. In the meantime, the want of such a complete authoritative code, it is manifest, can only be supplied, and that only in some measure, by the labour of private individuals, in digesting, in methodical treatises, the different departments of maritime and commercial jurisprudence, and arranging the particular cases under the general provisions of the statute law, and under the general rules of the common law which the judgments of the tribunals have expounded and recognised.

CHAPTER XII.

MARITIME AND COMMERCIAL LAW OF SCOTLAND.

Section I.

Obstacles to Commercial Advancement, Permanent and Occasional.

Although possessing the local advantages of a maritime situation, it was long before the Scottish nation devoted themselves, in any considerable degree, to the pursuits of trade and navigation. According to the earliest authentic accounts, we find the population of Scotland, as among most rude nations, consisting of a number of separate and almost independent tribes, and the territory divided among a number of great chiefs, the military leaders and, at the same time, the civil magistrates of the population of their respective districts. In tracing the history of the Scottish people from this rude state, so far as can be collected from authentic documents, we observe the origin, progress, and decline of the feudal government and institutions, similar to what took place in the other kingdoms of modern Europe, only varied by certain peculiar circumstances and events. The formal feudal subordination of the great military proprietors to the King, appears to have been completed in the reign of Malcolm III., in the course of the eleventh century. But various peculiar causes contributed, in Scotland, to continue, to a comparatively late period, the power, or, at least, the turbulence of the feudal aristocracy, to prevent the successful union of the crown with the commons against the nobles, and to retard the rise of the commons to wealth and power, and the consequent establishment of a more regular government.

Of these causes, some appear to have been permanent, others of an occasional and temporary nature. Of the former class, the most obvious is the physical construction of the country, as intersected by chains of mountains, and thereby divided into separate districts; and the operation of this cause is thus perspicuously explained by the late able and ingenious Professor Millar: —"The nature of the country, rugged mountains, and, in many parts, hardly passable, produced a number of separate districts, in which particular barons were enabled to establish and maintain an independent authority. Within these natural barriers, which divided one territory from another, a great lord easily reduced all the small proprietors into subjection; at the same time, residing in the midst of his retainers and followers, he was, in a good measure, secured from any foreign invasion. Landed property was thus quickly accumulated by a few great nobles, whose power over their inferiors, and whose influence in the government, became proportionally extensive. While they lived at home in rustic state and magnificence, they had little temptation to court the favour of the crown, and still less to purchase it by a surrender of their privileges; nor did the sovereign often find it advisable, however they might incur his displeasure, to run the hazard of marching against them, in their fortresses, and of endeavouring by force to subdue them. In this situation, they continued for many centuries to suffer little degradation, either from the immediate power of the most warlike, or from the secret intrigues of the most artful and politic princes."*

But while the effects of the mountainous nature of the country on the progress of society in Scotland must be acknowledged, it ought, at the same time, to be kept in view, that the operation of this cause consisted not so much in giving the Scottish nobles any pre-eminent political power beyond what the nobles of the other European kingdoms possessed, while acting in concert either against the crown or the lower classes of the community, according to what seems to have been the opinion of some of our historians,† as in continuing to a later period the insubordination of the military chiefs, and thereby retarding the establishment of an efficient civil government throughout the nation. In the absence of such an efficient government, individuals behoved to protect themselves, and entered into leagues and bands, or associations, for the purposes of defence or attack.‡ Men of power and station engaged in such associations in order to increase the number of their dependents, and to sustain and promote their influence; inferior men, in order to obtain countenance and support in return for their individual services.§ Tribes, clans, and even families, carried on hostilities against each other, and the prerogative of private war continued to deform society down to the reigns of the Stuarts.||

Another obvious permanent cause of the slow progress of trade and manufactures in Scotland, is the nature of the soil and climate; and its effects are thus

* Historical View of the English Government, vol. iii., p. 32.

† Dr Robertson's History of Scotland, vol. i., p. 19, 20, &c.

‡ Statute 1444, cap. 30.

§ Craig Jus Feud, lib. ii. dieg. xi.

|| Statutes 1424, c. 2; 1429, c. 129; 1449, c. 12; 1476, c. 70; 1567, c. 21. Gilbert Stuart, Public Law of Scotland. Notes 14, 15.

illustrated by the same philosophic author :—" In Scotland, the barrenness of the soil and coldness of the climate obstructed the progress of agriculture, and, of course, chilled the growth of manufactures. The necessaries of life must be had in plenty before there can be a general demand for its conveniences. Accordingly, though villages and towns, employed in some branches of traffic, arose in different parts of the country, and though these, in conformity to the practice of other European kingdoms, were incorporated by the King, and endowed with various exclusive privileges, yet, in spite of every encouragement, they continued poor, and were for a long time unable, as political auxiliaries of the crown, to perform any important service."*

It has been maintained, indeed, by an ingenious historian, that, in the history of the different feudal kingdoms of Europe, the original condition of the inhabitants of towns was a state of political freedom and importance : that, during the decline and consequent confusions of the feudal system, the towns were subjected to various oppressions exercised by the Sovereign and the nobles; and that, by the charters of community subsequently granted by the Sovereign to the towns, the liberties of the latter were merely revived. Nay, the same eloquent author maintains an ingenious argument to shew that the burghs of Scotland were represented in Parliament at a very early period.† But, for the adoption of such an opinion, the historic documents extant do not appear to afford any sufficient grounds; and, in afterwards noticing the slow progress and limited political influence of the towns of Scotland, we shall be led to an opposite conclusion.

---

* Historical View of English Government, by Professor Millar, vol. iii., p. 34.

† Gilbert Stuart, Public Law of Scotland. Notes 27, 28.

Along with the leading and permanent causes just alluded to, various occasional events concurred to retard the advancement of the Scottish nation in arts and commerce. From the accession of Malcolm III., about the middle of the eleventh century, when the authentic annals of Scotland may be said to commence, to the termination of the reign of Alexander III., towards the close of the thirteenth century, a considerable intercourse appears to have taken place between the English and Scottish nations, as well as their respective princes. In particular, during the reigns of Alexander II. and Alexander III., the two British nations appear to have been on a very friendlyfooting. At this early period, too, the public institutions and customs of the two kingdoms appear to have borne a strong resemblance to each other; and the general similarity of laws, originating in similarity of circumstances and situation, in long amicable intercourse, and in the natural adoption, by the less advanced, of the views and usages of the more cultivated people, may be found in the more ancient English statutes, and in the treatise ascribed to Chief Justice de Glanville, compared with the compilations in the Scotch collection by Skene, which passes under the title of Regiam Majestatem. But this early amicable intercourse did not last long. By the death of Alexander III., and of his grandaughter, the Maiden of Norway, towards the close of the thirteenth century, the nation was exposed to all the evils of a disputed succession to the crown, internal discord, and foreign invasion. After Wallace had gloriously withstood, and Robert Bruce had successfully repelled, the invader, and maintained the integrity and independence of the kingdom, the great defect of the government, the insubordination and turbulence of the nobles, still continued unabated. Of this defect the successive monarchs appear to have been aware, but were unable to apply any effectual remedy. It was in vain that James I. endeavoured to introduce among his subjects the polity of a more civilized people. And the eagerness, and various attempts of the Princes of the house of Stuart, to undermine and destroy the exorbitant power of the aristocracy, were merely productive of disasters to themselves, and of a series of disorders in the country.

The only other classes of the community to whom the monarch could have recourse for assistance against the hereditary nobles and great proprietors of land, were the clergy and the commons, including the small landed proprietors and the more wealthy inhabitants of the towns. As the ecclesiastical profession required labour and study, which the ignorant and barbarous nobles of the middle ages disdained, the church was then the principal road by which men of talent and learning in the inferior ranks of society raised themselves to comparatively high stations, and acquired influence in the state. But, although they had more intelligence and address, and were sufficiently devoted to the crown, the dignified clergy of Scotland, in Roman Catholic times, were by no means able to contend with the military power and brute force of the feudal chieftains. And just when James V. had commenced the experiment, by employing the dignitaries of the church in all the more important offices of the state, to the exclusion of the lay nobility, the scheme was frustrated by the Reformation.

With respect to the smaller landed proprietors, a great many of them appear, from affection, from interest, or from fear, to have attached themselves to the nobles or great proprietors in their neighbourhood, and to have lent their services in support of the power of these chiefs; while, in general, they seem, from the expense or inconvenience attending it, to have declined the exercise of their right of sitting and voting in Parliament.

It was to no purpose that James I. attempted, by an act of the legislature, to enforce the attendance of these lesser vassals. And when another statute was soon afterwards passed, excusing the small vassals from that duty, but requiring them, as in England, to send representatives to Parliament, they availed themselves of the dispensation, but neglected to fulfil the condition; so that, before the reign of James VI., the attendance of the knights of shires had not been made effectual. And when, at last, the burghs, particularly those on the eastern coasts of the kingdom, came to make some progress in commerce, and to carry on some trade with Flanders and France—when the principal burgesses thereby acquired comparative wealth, and, consequently, comparatively greater power—when they came to be favoured by the crown, as having an interest opposite to the nobles, and even after they came to be consulted and to have a seat in the legislature, in consequence of their contribution towards the expenses of government—still their political influence and importance in the state was in a great measure lost, by their sitting in one house, and by their voices and votes being mingled with those of the great military nobles and dignified clergy.

SECTION II.

Maritime and Commercial Law prior to the Union of the Crowns.

Such continued to be the condition of the mercantile and manufacturing classes of the nation down to the reign of James VI.; that is, almost as long as Scotland remained a separate kingdom. In such a state of affairs, great improvement in the law of maritime commerce was not to be expected; and, accordingly, during this period of its history, the monuments of the national jurisprudence in this department are but scanty.

In the Leges Burgorum, or Laws of the Burghs, which are referred to in the statute 1474, c. 53, as forming a part of the law of the land, we find not only rules for government of the burghs, but also a good many regulations relative to the exercise of crafts, and relative to foreign commerce. In the statutes, too, which were passed during the reigns of the five Jameses, in the reign of Queen Mary, and in the reign of James VI., prior to his accession to the throne of England, we find a considerable number of regulations, not only with regard to the trade of the royal and free burghs, but also with regard to trade in general, the exportation and importation of commodities, staple goods, and bullion. A considerable commercial intercourse appears to have been carried on, not only with England, when the political relations of the countries permitted, but also and particularly with the Low Countries and France. Many of the dignified clergy, who were more intelligent, and had a greater relish for the conveniences and elegancies of refined life, than the military nobility, were not merely the patrons of navigation, but actual traders on their own account. In the reign of James IV., especially, Scotland appears to have attained a higher degree of civilisation than during any period prior to the eighteenth century.

Although the alliance and intercourse which the Princes of the house of Stuart maintained with France was a system of policy perhaps not even expedient at the time, and of which the union of the two sister kingdoms happily superseded the necessity, it was, nevertheless, productive of some advantages to Scotland. During such an intercourse, the more civilized behoved to impart some of its improvements to the less civilized people. And, in particular, the Scotch people appear not only to have imitated the French in the constitution of their courts of justice, in the education of their lawyers, and in their forensic eloquence, but also to have adopted from them various regulations relative to maritime commerce.

The first treatise or special collection of regulations on this subject which Scotland produced, is that of Sir James Balfour, who was Lord Clerk Registrar, and President of the Court of Session, in the reign of Queen Mary; and who, about the year 1579, composed his work, entitled "Practics; or, A System of the more Ancient Law of Scotland."

In that work, Sir James digested, in treatises on separate subjects, *first*, the legislative enactments of the Scotch Parliament, including the more ancient statutes, as well as those of James I. and his successors; *secondly*, the consuetudinary law of the country as contained in the books of the Regiam Majestatem, in the Quoniam Attachiamenta or Leges Baronum, and in the Leges Burgorum; *thirdly*, the Decisions of the Court of Session or Supreme Civil Court down to the times in which he wrote, both prior and subsequent to the more regular constitution of that Court by King James V.

Of these treatises, two are entitled "Burrow Lawis" and "Gild Lawis," which contain a great deal of curious information as to the comparatively rude arts and manufactures and limited commerce of these times. But the treatise most intimately connected with our present subject is the one entitled "Sea Lawis." In that treatise, Sir James not only shews his acquaintance with the maritime laws of other nations, but affords a proof that, long before his time, the Scotch had adopted, as part of their maritime law, those regulations which experience had pointed out to the earlier seafaring nations on the western and northern coasts of Europe.

The materials of which the treatise is composed, appears from its title:—"The Sea Lawes, collectet furth of the Acts of Parliament, the Practiques, the Lawes of Oleron, and the Lawes of Wisbie, and the Constitution of François, King of France, annis 1543 and 1557."

From such materials, which we have already had occasion to consider at length, Sir James, who was a man of acknowledged talent, could not fail to compose a work of considerable value. And some notion may be formed of its contents from the following general titles into which it is divided :—

"Of the masters and shipmen.
"Anent fraughting of shippis.
"Anent ladening of shippis.
"Anent making of sail.
"Anent casting of güdes and sea-wrack.
"Anent arriving, discharging, and lousing of shippis.
"Anent hurt or harm done by ane ship to ane uther.
"Anent the flude mark.
"Anent letter of mark.
"Anent actionis and pleyis of shipmen.
"Anent the Conservatour.
"Anent the Admiral, his office, and jurisdictions."

Such is the earliest monument of Scotch maritime law; and we may consider it as affording a pretty correct representation of the progress of the nation in that branch of jurisprudence towards the close of the sixteenth century; for, although the treatise of Sir James Balfour was not printed till more than a century and a half after the date of its composition, it was all along accessible, in manuscript, to the lawyers of Scotland; and numerous transcripts, we are informed, were made from it. By this time, also, through the connection of the nation with the Continent, particularly with France, the lawyers of Scotland had begun to study with zeal the comprehensive code of Roman jurisprudence; and, in determining the few questions which, from time to time, arose out of mercantile and maritime contracts, transactions, and relations, the supreme courts had begun to derive the principles of their decision from that valuable digest of legal science.

Section III.

Maritime and Commercial Law from the Union of the Crowns to the Legislative Union of the Kingdoms.

So much for the history of the maritime and commercial law of Scotland prior to the accession of James VI. to the throne of England. That event, and the still more important event, the reformation of religion, behoved to have, and actually had, a great influence upon the state of the Scottish people; and this influence may be traced in the slow progress which was made, for a long period thereafter, in arts and commerce, and in mercantile and maritime law.

The union of the crowns of England and Scotland was so far favourable to the latter country, inasmuch as it prevented the recurrence of those hostilities in which the two nations had been engaged for ages; but, in other respects, the union of the crowns was unfavourable to the immediate progress of arts and commerce, and to the rise of the commons in Scotland. Beside the consequent reduction of the country to the situation of a distant province, and the bad effects of this change upon the administration of the Government, the removal of the Sovereign and of his court to the southern part of the island obviously withdrew the great inducement to the cultivation of those elegant arts which are the natural offspring of luxury and refinement. But this was not all. The removal of the royal residence was followed by a correspondent migration of the Scottish nobility and gentry, who naturally resorted to the new seat of government, partly in quest of amusement, but chiefly with the view of preferment. By this desertion of the great landed proprietors, Scotland lost, of course, the market which had formerly arisen from supplying them with the necessaries and conveniences of life. A great part of the revenue of these proprietors, the free produce of the land, was carried to and spent in a comparatively foreign country, instead of giving employment to native industry; and the middle and lower ranks of the people were thus not only greatly discouraged in the improvement of manufactures, and in the prosecution of mercantile adventure, but were also deprived of those means of doing so which would otherwise have resulted from the accumulation of the surplus produce of the land, in the shape of manufacturing and commercial capital.

Farther, by his accession to the throne of England, the King of Scotland was placed above all contest with those nobles to whom he had formerly been frequently obliged to yield, and whose power had always been so formidable. He had, therefore, no longer any occasion to have recourse to the inhabitants of the boroughs, or to the smaller landed proprietors, as a counterpoise against the aristocracy. The aids and contributions of the boroughs were now of much less consequence to the crown; and, although they continued to be favoured by the monarch, they did not attain to any great political importance or influence in the state.

The other great event to which we alluded, the Reformation, although of the highest importance and advantage to the country, not only in a religious, but in a political and civil point of view, whatever effect it may have had ultimately, had no direct or immediate tendency to promote manufactures, navigation, and commerce. The Reformation in Scotland, it is well known, was begun, not by the King, as in England, but by the great body of the people, in opposition to the wishes of the Monarch and his ministers; and, in this way, the leaders of the Reformation were induced to carry matters a greater length than they otherwise might have done—to recede farther from the ancient hierarchy, and to establish a completely popular system of ecclesiastical government. In the progress of this struggle for religious liberty, the middle and lower classes of the people acquired an importance in the state which they did not before possess; and, in the pursuit of religious freedom, they certainly acquired more just and liberal notions of civil liberty and political independence. This very pursuit, however, by engrossing their attention so much, rather tended, in the meantime, to divert these classes from commercial enterprise. Unfortunately, also, the reformation in the religious establishment by no means tended to remedy the great defect in the Scottish government, the overgrown power of the aristocracy. The nobles, at first, joined with the middle and lower orders in promoting the Reformation, chiefly that they might appropriate to themselves the benefices and the spoils of the dignified clergy. From the same interested motives, they concurred in supporting the Presbyterian establishment, that they might not be deprived of the estates they had thus obtained. Instead, therefore, of being diminished, the power and wealth of the nobles were rather increased by the Reformation; and the intestine disputes and civil wars which broke out in the reign of Charles I., and continued till the Restoration, checked every effort of peaceful industry. The ill-advised measure of the government, in afterwards attempting the re-establishment of Episcopacy against the wishes of the nation, protracted the religious struggle down to the period of the Revolution; and it was not till the close of the seventeenth century that the people of Scotland began again to enjoy internal tranquillity, and to shew any decided inclination for nautical and commercial adventure.

Correspondent to the state of the nation during the seventeenth century was its progress in maritime and commercial law. In the early part of that century, several useful statutes were passed, particularly with regard to the public records of land rights. But almost the only one of these statutes at all connected with commercial law, is the act 1621, for preventing fraudulent alienations by bankrupts. From the year 1621 to the year 1642, Sir Alexander Gibson of Durie compiled his Reports of the Decisions of the Court of Session during that period; but in very few of the cases was it requisite to apply the principles of commercial law. About the same time, Sir Thomas Hope of Craighall, advocate to King Charles I., composed his "Minor Practicks; or, Treatise of the Scottish Law." But almost the whole of this work relates to feudal rights. In the reign of Charles II., Sir George Mackenzie, advocate to that Monarch, composed his small treatise, entitled "Institutions of the Law of Scotland;" but only a small part of it relates to contracts and obligations; and exhibits little else than a meagre abstract of the Roman law relative to such matters. Before this time, however, the leading Scottish lawyers had cultivated successfully the study of that system of jurisprudence, and had begun to apply to practice those equitable views which the study of such a system is calculated to inspire. And it has been truly observed that the law of Scotland, in matters of contract, is a scion of the Roman law. In earlier times, this study was, of course, promoted by the classical habits of the clerical members of the Court of Session, as established by James V. And, in the course of the seventeenth century, it had become the fashion for Scotch lawyers—generally small landed proprietors, or the younger sons of great landed proprietors—to prosecute, or, at least, to finish their study of the Roman law in the universities on the Continent. In France, in particular, they were accustomed to pass some part of their youth, and to attend the sittings of the Parliament of Paris, after the model of which the Court of the Lords of Council and Session was formed.

In the comparatively more tranquil reigns of Charles II. and William III., as already noticed, the people of Scotland had some cessation from the struggle for religious liberty, and began to direct their attention to commerce. The magnificent scheme of an establishment in the Isthmus of Darien, though unfortunate, and, perhaps, premature, affords a proof, from the great encouragement it met with from the people of Scotland, of the progress they had recently made, not merely in the spirit for commercial enterprise, but also in their enlarged views of commercial aggrandisement. In consequence of this advancement, the laws of trade naturally became of greater importance towards the end of the seventeenth and in the beginning of the eighteenth century. And in the decisions of the Court of Session, which Lord Fountainhall ably reported from 1678 to 1712, commercial questions, though still rare, are more frequent than formerly. But it was reserved for Lord Stair, the great master in the law of Scotland, after the lapse of a century from the death of Sir James Balfour, to effect the next great improvements on the commercial jurisprudence of the nation. The advantages which the law of Scotland derived from the professional labours and exertions of this truly able man, are many and great. He reported the decisions of the Court of Session, in his own time, for a long period, and in a style far superior to that of any of his predecessors. He suggested and was the means of inducing the Scottish legislature to pass many important statutes founded on correct and enlightened views of commercial expediency. And, in his Institutions, we have various profound and scientific treatises on different branches of mercantile law. Besides general remarks on property in vessels, we have separate titles, not only on sale, but on mandate or commission, on bills of exchange, and on copartnership. The contract of insurance, too, is mentioned as one of those agreements which may occur, but is not frequent in business intercourse. And the title on Reprisals and Prizes shews that, in those times, the Scotch were not far behind their southern neighbours, or even the continental nations, in unfolding the doctrines of maritime international law.

Such progress, towards the close of the seventeenth and the beginning of the eighteenth century, augured a continued advancement in the cultivation of commerce and commercial law; the more especially as Scotland, after the Revolution of 1688, and particularly after the legislative union of the kingdoms, began to enjoy a government superior to any it had formerly possessed. But this was by no means the case. With the unhappy frustration of the Darien scheme, the national spirit for commercial enterprise seemed, if not to expire, at least, for a time, to slumber; and, from the time of Lord Stair, little progress was made in commercial law for nearly two-thirds of a century.

Section IV.

Maritime and Commercial Law subsequent to the Union of the Kingdoms.

The union of the kingdoms, though calculated and

destined, in time, to be of solid and permanent advantage to the Scottish nation, was not immediately productive of such beneficial consequences. The removal from Scotland of even the Court of the Viceroy, though, perhaps, ultimately useful, tended, in the meantime, to do away still more any inducement which the nobles and great landed proprietors had to remain at home; and, of course, to withdraw more completely the encouragement afforded, by their residence, to the industry of the lower orders of the people. The measure of the union itself was, at the time, productive of internal divisions. And the attachment of some of the nobles, and of the less civilized but more warlike part of the nation, to the lineal representative of the ancient Royal Family, involved the country in two successive rebellions, which, while they wasted the blood of brave men, who would have been better employed in the defence of their country against external foes, diminished the security of the inhabitants of the Lowlands and more cultivated districts, and distractedthe attention of the nation from trade and the pursuits of peaceful industry.

The influence of those national calamities and intestine divisions upon the progress of commercial law was abundantly obvious. The middle orders did not rise so soon to wealth and importance as they otherwise would have done. The limited trade and commerce of thenation presented comparatively few questions for the determination of the courts of law. The attention of the judges and lawyers was engrossed by the discussion of the numerous and important questions of feudal law and of landed right, to which the forfeitures consequent upon the two rebellions gave rise. And, while the principles of the old feudal system of landed property were thus elucidated and determined, the rules of commercial law were almost entirely neglected. It was not till some time after the second Rebellion of 1745, and the abolition of local hereditary jurisdictions in 1748, that the middle classes and the great body of the people came to devote themselves steadily and exclusively to industrious pursuits. And it is within the last eighty years that the Scottish nation entered upon its present grand course of improvement in manufactures, commerce, and navigation.

From the time of Lord Stair, the only writer on commercial law whom Scotland produced, in the early part of last century, is Mr Forbes, advocate, Professor of Law in the University of Glasgow, who composed a learned and pretty well arranged treatise on bills of exchange; a work which, in the absence of more profound and scientific treatises, must have been found very useful. Towards the middle of the century, Lord Kames and Lord Kilkerran composed their very valuable collections of decisions; but the judgments in questions of commercial law form but a small portion of these collections.

About the middle of last century, Mr Erskine, Professor of Scotch Law in the University of Edinburgh, composed his learned, judicious, and very useful works, the "Principles and the Institutes of the Law of Scotland;" but neither of these works contain much doctrine or discussion on the subjects of commercial law.

In his different works, Lord Kames happily illustrated the doctrine of equity, and the history and principles of general jurisprudence; and in the latter department he was ably followed up by Professor Millar of the University of Glasgow, in his ingenious and philosophical courses of lectures on the civil or Roman law; but neither of these eminent men directed their attention particularly to commercial legislation. And, so unaccustomed, as Mr Bell observes, were the lawyers of Scotland to the views which merchants entertain, or so lost to all concern in what related to trade, that the first bankrupt sequestration statute, passed so late as the year 1772, for the purpose of accomplishing one of the most useful changes upon the ancient law, was opposed in a report of the Faculty of Advocates.

Nay, even in the admirable course of judicious practical lectures, for which the bar was so much indebted to the late Professor of Scotch Law in the University of Edinburgh, afterwards Baron Hume, the doctrines of maritime and mercantile jurisprudence occupied only a very small space. In short, it was only towards the close of the last and in the course of the present century, that Scotland has produced professed writers of eminence in maritime and commercial law.

In 1787, Mr Millar, son of Professor Millar, published his elements of the law relative to Insurances; in which, in a methodical arrangement, he unfolded the principles of equity and expediency by which that important contract is regulated; and, with the few decided cases on that subject, which the courts of Scotland then supplied, combined the more copious doctrine afforded by the judicial experience of England and other nations.

About the commencement of the present century, Mr Bell, now Professor of Scotch Law in the University of Edinburgh, first gave to the public his excellent treatise on the law of bankruptcy; and, having afterwards extended his views and enlarged his work into commentaries on mercantile jurisprudence, he had the great merit of rendering the student of Scottish law acquainted with the judicial determinations of the English tribunals in this department; and made a valuable present, not merely to his brethren of the bar, and to the other members of the profession, but to the whole commercial interest of Scotland.

In the course of the present century also, Mr M. Brown, in addition to his other contributions towards the advancement of the law of Scotland, published an able treatise on the contract of sale; and Mr Robert Thomson, a learned treatise on bills of exchange.

SECTION V.

Component Parts of Maritime and Commercial Law of Scotland.

From the preceding observations, some notion may be formed of the progress, historically, of the maritime and commercial law of Scotland; and we may only notice briefly the sources and component parts of that law.

Statutes.

The first great source and component part of the maritime and commercial law of Scotland is, of course, the legislative enactments by Parliament relative to such matters, including the Scotch statutes still in observance; such of the English statutes as relate to trade, it being provided, by the act of union of the kingdoms, that, in this department, the law should be the same in Scotland as in England; and such of the British statutes, passed since the Union, as are applicable to Scotland.

Common Law.

The second great source and component part of the national maritime and commercial jurisprudence, is the common or consuetudinary law; those usages and rules of practice which, whether native and indigenous, or spontaneously borrowed and adopted from other nations, have grown up with the people, and been established and enforced by their judicial tribunals. Of the extraneous sources here alluded to, the chief is certainly those parts of the civil law of the Romans which relate to maritime commerce.

Sources.—Roman Law.

From a very early period, the judges and lawyers of Scotland were accustomed, like those of the continental nations, to search in the Roman Digest and Code for precedents; and, if these could not be found, for equitable views and principles, by which they might regulate their judgments, or support and illustrate their arguments. And, since the Pandects contain a record of a great proportion of the ordinary transactions which constitute what is termed the business of human life, such as they actually occurred during the advancement and the decline of one of the most distinguished nations that ever ran the course of civilisation, and also a record of the judicial wisdom of a series of as acute and profound jurisconsults as ever adorned any nation, applied in determining the questions to which those transactions gave rise, there is no room for doubt that the Scotch judges and lawyers must have profited much by the study of the Roman law, and improved the early jurisprudence of the kingdom, by the extended experience of a more enlightened people.

To certain political doctrines, introduced into the imperial compilations after Rome had lost her free constitution, the lawyers of England have objected, and with justice, as being inconsistent with national liberty and the principles of a representative government. But these exceptionable doctrines, introduced at a less happy period of Roman history, every student of the jurisprudence of that nation must be fully aware, do not pervade the great mass of judicial experience in matters of private right contained in the Pandects, or at all taint or affect the fair and equitable principles by which the decisions recorded in that work are governed; and if the admiration expressed for the Roman system of jurisprudence, by the profoundly learned and accomplished Sir William Jones, be deemed too high, we must, on the other hand, in impartiality, maintain that this body of laws has been so far groundlessly censured and greatly undervalued by that able metaphysician and historian, instructor of the Prince of Parma, the Abbé de Condillac,* and by that ingenious speculative lawyer, Mr Bentham,† whether we consider the internal excellence of the work as a code of private civil right, or its influence in meliorating, during the middle ages, the otherwise rude jurisprudence of modern Europe.

It is, no doubt, the fashion of this comparatively enlightened age to despise authority and usage, and to hold that, in legal discussions, they are nothing, and principle everything; and, certainly, we have no inclination to support the almost absurd degree of veneration in which the Roman law, and the almost innumerable commentators on it, were once held among the European nations. But, on the other hand, it does not appear that the disposition of the day to reject entirely all authority and usage on matters of law, and to be regulated merely by what is called principle, is quite consistent with absolute wisdom. Man is obviously, in a great measure, the creature of experience; and although, from the eminence he has now attained in the march of civilisation, he may look back with congratulation upon the inferiority of former ages in intellectual attainments, it does not appear that the slightest change has taken place in the faculties or susceptibilities of his nature, or that he is to advance in a different, or in any other manner, or by any other means, than those by which he

---

* Cours d'Etude, vol. viii., p. 45–56, and vol. x., p. 90.

† Traités de Legislation Prelim., vol. i., p. 22, 168, 289, and vol. ii., p. 11, &c.

has arrived at his present state of improvement in art and science. Indeed, in no department of art or science does it appear more necessary to proceed with patient observation of the phenomena of matter and of mind, and strict analysis of facts and events, and with a cautious deduction from the experience thus acquired, than in matters of legislation, whether involving public or private right. General utility, the greatest good for each individual which is attainable in the circumstances in which mankind are placed on this globe, is, no doubt, the grand and only justifiable object of all coercive legislation. But in following this principle as a guide, it is necessary to proceed with circumspection. The all-wise Author of Nature has not seen fit to give to man the power of perceiving *a priori*, or intuitively, what is universally or even generally expedient in all cases, and, least of all, in complicated cases. For this imperfection of intellect, however, which appears necessarily incident to the nature of limited, created beings, the bountiful Creator of the universe has so far provided a remedy by endowing man with certain feelings and emotions, which arise almost instantaneously in certain circumstances, and which produce nearly the same course of action as if he had been influenced by extended views of general expediency. In all human legislation, therefore, it seems indispensably necessary to take into consideration these universal feelings and emotions, these laws of our common nature, and to guard against the adoption of any abstract opinions of general expediency, formed without a due regard to the constitution and situation of the being whose conduct it is proposed to regulate. To ascertain whether the proposed arrangement be agreeable to this principle, we must trace the consequences of former events or arrangement, similar or different; in other words, we must have recourse to experience. Nor has this recourse to the experience of former ages and other countries become less necessary or expedient from the events of the last sixty years. Many individuals, observing how little practical good has arisen in legislation from abstract theories, deem it dangerous and presumptuous, even amid the boasted illumination of this age, to embark on the wide ocean of general utility; and many others, forming, perhaps, a more correct estimate of what man is capable of doing, with the limited faculties with which his Creator has endowed him, and in the limited circumstances in which he is placed, conceive that the general good is, upon the whole, more effectually promoted, and with less risk of evil, by gradually, from time to time, modifying or abolishing those particular arrangements which have grown up in the progress of society, by which the interests of particular classes have been injured, and by adopting such arrangements, in the different departments of legislation and government, as have been ascertained to be of practical benefit to a definite extent, without proving injurious to any class of the community.

Without sacrificing, therefore, any of the advantages to be derived from what has been deemed the more philosophic mode of investigation, it seems wiser, in the general doctrines of legislation, as well as in the more minute details of jurisprudence, to abide and to steer by the landmarks of experience, and to bring the views of abstract principle, not merely in statutory *a priori* legislation, but in the more minute development and exposition of the common law, to the test of a comparison with the institutions and usages of other nations and other ages. And, as the Scottish judges and lawyers appear, from an early period, to have looked abroad for instruction and illustration in evolving the doctrines of maritime and commercial law, it seems expedient they should still continue to do so. Distinguishing and setting aside those branches of the

Roman Digest which had no application to the circumstances of the Scottish nation, these judges and lawyers selected and adopted, and wisely adopted, the Roman doctrines of contracts and *quasi* contracts, as containing rules well adapted for the determination of such questions as the business transactions of a people advancing in civilisation usually give rise to. And in that Digest, they found, and also wisely adopted, what appears to be the only genuine remains of the Rhodian laws, of the laws of this insular people, who appear to have attained to as great an extension, and to as high a degree of improvement, in maritime commerce, as any nation of antiquity; and who alone, of all the nations of antiquity that cultivated navigation and commerce as a national object, have transmitted, through the Roman jurisconsult, to modern times, any fragments of original legislation in this department of jurisprudence.

Foreign Maritime and Commercial Law.

Pursuing the same plan and practice of deriving instruction from the legislation and judicial experience of other nations, the Scotch judges and lawyers appear, next to the Roman Digest, to have studied the compilations of maritime law formed, from time to time, by those states of modern Europe who preceded Great Britain in the career of commerce and navigation. The statutes of King James IV. and King James V. shew that the attention of the national council was then beginning to be directed to those interesting objects; and, although it does not appear that the Consolato del Mare—the code of maritime law universally observed by the trading states of the Mediterranean—was early known in Scotland, the compilation of Sir James Balfour, the Chancellor of Queen Mary, on sea laws, shews that the Scottish lawyers, availing themselves of the intimate intercourse which then subsisted between the government of that country and of France—at that time a comparatively much more refined nation—sought practical instruction for the decision of maritime and mercantile cases, not merely in the Laws of Wisby, but in the Laws of Oleron and in the Ordonnance of King Francis, as subsequently inserted in the Collection by Cleirac of the Us et Coutumes de la Mer.

Writings of Foreign Lawyers.

After the connection of Scotland with France ceased, and England and Scotland were so far united by the accession of James VI. to the throne of the former kingdom, it might have been expected that the example of England would have acquired considerable influence in the gradual formation of the Scottish common law. But, whether from remaining national jealousy, or other causes, this does not appear, for a long period, to have taken place to any sensible or material extent or degree. And, during the seventeenth century, we find the Scottish lawyers still studying, chiefly as the sources of their maritime and commercial law, the commentators on the Roman Digest, and the laws of the seafaring states in the centre and north of Europe—namely, the Collection usually known as the Laws of Wisby, the enlarged and improved compilation made under the authority of the Hanse Towns, and the laws of the commercial cities of the Netherlands, including both Flanders and Holland, with which enterprising states Scotland appears then to have carried on a more extended commerce than with England. Nay, even during the greater part of the eighteenth century, we find the Scotch lawyers referring for illustration, and supporting their arguments and opinions on mercantile and maritime jurisprudence, not so much by the judgments of English courts and the works of English lawyers, as by the laws of the trading states of the Continent, and by the able commentaries on these laws as well as on the Roman Digest, such as Voet, Vinnius, Van Lewen, Stypmannus, Loccennius, Ansaldus, Straccha, and Bynkershoek. In fact, although the eminent talents and knowledge of Sir Leoline Jenkins, in matters of admiralty jurisdiction, and the excellence of the work of Molloy, De Jure Maritimo et Navali, must be universally admitted, England herself did not, till the last century, begin to possess any great body of judicial determinations in the multifarious transactions of maritime commerce; and, of course, did not present any very superior model for the imitation of other nations. Scotland was a great many years behind in the march of commercial improvement; and, till the close of last century, the Scotch courts were chiefly occupied with the discussion and exposition of the doctrines of land rights, which, from the then great diversity in the circumstances of the two nations, did not admit of much assimilation to the law of England, supposing such an assimilation to have been expedient or desirable. But, from the days of Lord Hardwicke and Lord Mansfield, the commercial and maritime law of England, we have seen, has advanced with a celerity and to an extent unprecedented in any other nation; and, outstripping Scotland in its judicial career, now presents, for imitation and adoption, a much more comprehensive collection of adjudged cases on maritime and commercial jurisprudence, a more complete body of practical judicial wisdom, than ever adorned the annals of any other country. Of the value of the present which England has thus unintentionally and incidentally made, the judges and lawyers of Scotland are now aware. The influence which the judicial determinations of England have had in improving the views of the principles of maritime and commercial law entertained by the Scotch judges and lawyers in the course of the last sixty years, is now abundantly obvious; and there is a prospect of the assimilation ofthe jurisprudence of the two countries, in matters of navigation and commerce, to as great an extent as is desirable.

Judicial Decisions of England.

That we should thus express any doubt of the expediency of an immediate and complete assimilation of the laws of the two countries on such matters, may excite surprise; and had England every practical excellence to impart, and Scotland nothing superior to retain, the advantage of a complete assimilation, so far as practicable, would be beyond dispute. But, although we entertain the most unfeigned admiration of, and veneration for, the maritime and commercial jurisprudence of England, as matured, in the course of the last and present century, by the varied talents of a Hardwicke, a Mansfield, a Thurlow, a Rosslyn, an Ellenborough, an Eldon, a Grant, and a Stowell, we may, on the other hand, be permitted, with deference, to question the expediency of some of the rules which have obtained a place in the English system of common law. We may be permitted, also, with deference, to think that some of the rules which have grown up among the Scotch, congenial to the spirit of their own system, are, if not superior, at least not inferior, in extent and liberality of view, in point of commercial expediency and otherwise; and, as the judicial determinations of England have, of course, no direct, imperative, or obligatory force in Scotland, the inhabitants of the latter country may be permitted to profit by the experience of England, and to improve their own jurisprudence, by selecting only what is excellent, and setting aside whatever may have been founded on less extended views, or may have been ascertained, by experience, to be less practically useful.

Of the truth of the preceding observation, various

illustrations might be adduced. At present we may merely allude to what had grown up, quite independently of statute, to be strictly and properly a rule of the common law of England—namely, that a mercantile agent or factor cannot pledge. This rule, however proper at an early stage of commercial advancement, appears to be ill adapted even to the comparatively less advanced state of commercial enterprise at which Scotland has now arrived. Accordingly, this rule seems, in more recent times, to have been enforced by the English courts more upon the authority of precedents of former judgments, pronounced when views of commercial law were less extended and enlightened, than from a conviction of its being founded on sound legal principles.* And it has lately been deemed necessary to pass a statute for the express purpose of altering this rule of the common law of England, and of assimilating it, in this respect, to the common law of Scotland. Various similar instances might be found, upon investigation, and also instances of superiority in the usages and institutions of Scotland; such as the late statutory abolition in England of the mesne process of imprisonment, which was never known in Scotland, and the recent statutory adoption, in England, of certain regulations in the law of bankruptcy, similar to what had previously existed in Scotland. In this point of view, an impartial exposition and comparison of the systems of the two sister kingdoms might not be altogether without its use. For it thus appears, that a nation more advanced in commerce and civilisation, generally, may derive instruction and benefit from the usages and institutions of another intelligent people, though less advanced in the career of improvement.

From the preceding deduction it appears that, while

---

* Martini *v.* Coles, 15th February, 1813, M. and S. Rep. vol. i., p. 140.

the maritime and commercial law of Scotland is contained in the Scotch and British legislative enactments applicable to Scotland, in the reports of the judicial determinations of its tribunals, and in the works of its eminent lawyers, arranging the doctrines thus established, it has, for a long period, received, and is likely to continue to receive, extension and improvement from extraneous sources, either foreign, strictly so called, or which, though not native, can now be scarcely considered as foreign.

With regard to the first of these sources—the maritime and commercial ordinances of foreign nations—the recorded decisions of the maritime and mercantile tribunals of those nations, and the works of their learned lawyers in this department of jurisprudence, have, of course, no positive or binding force in Scotland. But, as the recorded practical wisdom, founded upon the experience of those other nations which have preceded the Scotch in the cultivation of the useful arts and sciences, or are running along with them the career of civiliastion, they are entitled to great deference and respect. They will, in general, be found to furnish valuable precedents and principles for regulating the determination of the multifarious cases which are daily occurring. And of these foreign authorities we have already given a pretty full account.

The other great class of extraneous legal authorities, which, although not native, or positively imperative, can scarcely be considered as foreign, is the admirable body of practical doctrine contained in the reported judgments of the English courts of equity and common law since the Revolution of 1688. And there can be no doubt of the expediency and propriety of Scottish judges and lawyers endeavouring to supply deficiencies in their own system, and to enrich the comparatively scanty judicial annals of Scotland, with the abundant harvest of English judicial experience. But this study of what must so far be considered the law of a foreign country, is attended with inconvenience, inasmuch as it is by no means clear to what extent that law ought to be pleaded in the Scottish courts; and not unfrequently have the rules of the English law, and the judgments of the English courts, been urged as authorities, when they were by no means applicable. It is sufficiently obvious, in general, that, when the rules of the English law proceed or are founded upon any peculiar positive statutory enactment confined in its operation to England, or any peculiar positive institution or usage in internal, political, or judicial arrangement, or otherwise, they cannot be pleaded as in any way illustrative of the law of Scotland. But to ascertain in detail what are the cases in which the judgments of the English courts are admissible, and may be relied on as authorities, and to draw exactly the line of demarcation, is a task of difficulty, requiring a good deal of experience, practical skill, and discernment; and this illustration from abroad must be made with due selection and discretion. In particular, due care must be taken to distinguish different classes of English judicial determinations as entitled to different degrees of authority in Scotland. Of one class of these judicial determinations, the object has been to fix the import and application of British statutes relative to matters of trade and navigation; and these are obviously entitled to almost as much authority and obligatory form in Scotland as the judgments of the Scottish courts. Another class of English judicial decisions, being founded on general principles, not influenced by any peculiarity in the law of England, and proceeding on extended views of commercial usage and expediency, are also entitled, even in Scotland, to all the authority which reason, and the experience of one of the most enlightened nations in the world, can bestow. Another class of English judicial decisions are founded chiefly on peculiar legislative enactments, institutions, and local customs and usages of perhaps doubtful expediency—such, for instance, as distinctions between the jurisdiction of the common law courts and of the Admiralty Court of England; and these, of course, can have no claim to authority in Scotland, and can afford no proper illustration of its laws.

CHAPTER XIII.

OF THE MARITIME AND COMMERCIAL LAW OF THE UNITED STATES OF AMERICA.

WE cannot close this historical sketch without noticing the progress which the great North American nation has, since the establishment of its independence, made in the cultivation of the law of maritime commerce. Of this, as of the other departments of their jurisprudence, the Americans were naturally led, from their origin, to assume the laws of England as the basis. But these laws they appear partly to have reliquished, as no longer applicable to the different or altered circumstances in which they are placed; partly to have modified and adapted to their new situation; and partly to have enlarged and amplified.

From the great similarity in the proceedings and transactions of maritime commerce, and the consequent similar, common, and general, or almost universal nature of the rules by which it is regulated, this branch of the commercial jurisprudence of the United States may have deviated less than the other branches from the law of England; but to some extent it appears to have done so;

and partly from the more free adoption of improvements suggested by the experience of other nations. "We border," says the very learned, intelligent, and unassuming Dr Hoffman; "we border on the ocean more extensively than any other nation of ancient or modern times; our internal resources are greater; the means of transporting the products of agriculture and of manufactures, from remote interior places to the ocean, are vastly beyond anything hitherto known; from all of which we infer that maritime jurisprudence, if not already so, is destined to become, in our country, a much more extended and perfected system than yet exists. These views we cannot regard as merely prospective and anticipative. We have already done, in this country, more to fashion the elements of this branch of jurisprudence into a systematical whole than any other nation. It is true, indeed, that we have had the learned labours of the whole world at our command; but it is equally true that the nations of Europe have not reciprocally profited by what has been respectively effected by each. The United States, on the contrary, in their legislation, their judicial investigations and decisions, and in the researches of their jurisconsults, have sought for light and improvements from every source exempt from narrow jealousies, and untrammelled by the customs or by the binding force of the decisions of former days. Were the maritime or admiralty law of this country, practical as well as theoretical, carefully collected and digested, it would form, as we think, a code more free from incongruities or defects than could be extracted from the like sources of any other country."*

Whether the estimate which this truly useful and estimable lawyer has thus formed of the maritime and

* Course of Legal Study, by Dr Hoffman, 1836, vol. ii., p. 463, 464.

commercial law of his country may not be too favourable, we do not presume to say; but the predominance of English maritime and commercial jurisprudence in the United States is sufficiently apparent, from the number of English reports of judicial determinations, compilations, and treatises, which he enumerates and cites as authorities in his very complete and valuable course of legal study.

The navigation laws of the United States, and the other maritime and commercial legislative enactments by the Congress, which are binding on the whole of the confederated states, and peculiar to the nation, do not fall within the scope of this historical sketch of the private law of maritime commerce, any more than the peculiar laws of England or of France, relative to maritime courts and admiralty jurisdiction. And the chief improvement or enlargement which the Americans have made, in this department of jurisprudence, appears to be found in a series of judicial determinations, since the era of the national independence, by the supreme court of the United States, and the district admiralty courts. These judgments of the supreme court, in matters of maritime and commercial law, are contained in the successive reports by Cranch, Wheaton, and Peters. And the judgments of the district admiralty courts are contained in the reports by Gallison, Mason, Wheaton, and Peters.

The maritime and commercial law of the United States appears also to have been amplified and improved by the labours of distinguished lawyers; partly in giving enlarged editions of English and other treatises; partly in more original treatises of their own composition. Thus there is an edition, by Mr Justice Story, of the treatise by Abbott, Lord Tenterden, on the law of merchant ships and seamen; an edition, by Smith, of Chitty's treatise on bills of exchange; and a translation by Mr William Frick, of Jacobsen's Laws of the Sea, with reference to maritime commerce. There are, also, the more original and very valuable commentaries of Mr Justice Story on the law of bailments and on the conflict of laws, as well as on equity jurisdiction and on the American constitution. There are, likewise, the very valuable commentaries of Mr Chancellor Kent on American law generally, of which the second volume treats of personal rights and property, and embraces many of the doctrines of commercial law; and particularly his commentaries on maritime and commercial law. There are Johnson's Chancery Reports, containing the decisions of Mr Chancellor Kent, than which, Dr Hoffman assures us, he knows of no other body of equity law at once so learned and elementary. There are Wheaton's Admiralty Practics, in his appendix to his Reports of Cases in the Supreme Courts of the United States, and his Digest of the Laws of Maritime Captures and Prizes; which last, however, belongs more to international law than to the private national law of maritime commerce. There are, also, the learned opinions of Judge Ware and of Dr Cooper on private maritime law and admiralty jurisdiction.

CHAP. XIV.

MARITIME LAW OF ASIATIC NATIONS.

Before closing this historical sketch, we may also refer, by way of appendix, to some accounts which have more recently appeared of the maritime and commercial law of the inhabitants of Hindostan, and of the eastern coasts of Asia, and the adjacent islands in the Pacific Ocean.

We had, near the commencement of this sketch, occasion to remark, so far as appeared from ancient history, the little disposition evinced by the Indians for, and the little progress made by them in, navigation and commerce. From the Digest of Hindu Laws, however, translated from the Sanscrit, and published by Mr Colebrooke in 1801, it is ascertained that, at an early period, the Indians had fixed, and so far developed, laws on contracts generally. And from the Institutes of Hindu Law, translated from the Sanscrit by Sir William Jones, and published in 1796, it is established that the Ordinances of Menu recognised the maritime contract of Fœnus Nauticum, or loan of money upon marine risk.

On the eastern side of Asia, again, it appears that, so early as the thirteenth century of the Christian era, the inhabitants of Malacca had not only an inland, but also a maritime code. This maritime code was translated by the late Sir Stamford Raffles: and for a perusal of this translation, which appeared in the twelfth volume of the "Asiatic Researches," the author is indebted to his early, intimate, and inestimable friend, William Erskine, Esq., the highly valued friend of the late Sir James Mackintosh and Sir John Malcolm, a gentleman pre-eminent in profound knowledge of eastern languages, literature, and science; and who, it is hoped, will live to make, from original and native sources, another valuable addition to the history of India.

After a general account of the Malaya nation, Sir Stamford gives a translation of their maritime institutions, and prefixes the following contents:—

"CONTENTS.

"CHAP. I.—Authority of the Code—Description of persons on board a prahu—Of the officers and crew, their authority, duties, and the nature of their engagements—Of the kiwis, or traders.

"Chap. II.—Of the divisions of a prahu—Regulations for the safety of a prahu while at sea—Of fire—Of throwing cargo overboard—Of prahus running foul of each other—Of putting into ports, and the mode of trading—Of detentions—Of persons quitting a prahu.

"Chap. III.—Of persons who may be in distress, or who have been wrecked at sea—Of troves—Of carrying off slaves from another country.

"Chap. IV.—Of crimes and punishments on board a prahu—Of disrespectful and contumacious conduct towards the nakhodah—Of adultery, and criminal connection with women on board a prahu—Of quarrels and dissentions—Of theft."

Sir Stamford next prefixes the following explanation:—

"In the following sketch, which defines the laws and usages of the Malays at sea, the Malacca code has been selected for the text, as well on account of the admitted superiority of that once flourishing kingdom among the Malaya states in general, as from the circumstance of this code having, with but slight modifications, been adopted by several of the ancient and powerful states in the island of Celebes, and still continuing in force among many of the Bugis and Macassar traders from that island. The Bugis and Macassar states, which are nations radically distinct from the Malays, possess a maritime code of still greater antiquity; but, in later times, they appear to have, in many instances, adopted the sea laws of Malacca, nearly in the same manner as the Romans adopted the celebrated Rhodian code."

"The Malacca code appears to have been compiled during the reign of Sultan Muhammed Shah, the first sovereign of Malacca recorded in the Malaya annals to have embraced the Muhammedan faith. This circumstance is understood to have taken place about the year of the Christian era 1276. The origin of the

Malaya code may therefore be considered as nearly coeval with the first establishment of Islamism among the Malays. The authority of the code is thus stated in the preamble:"—

"These are the laws to be enforced in ships, junks, and prahus:—

"First of all, Pati Harun and Pati Elias assembled Nakhodah Jenal, and Nakhodah Dewa, and Nakhodah Is-hak, for the purpose of consulting and advising relative to the usages at sea, and of compiling, in conformity thereto, a code of Undang Undang, or institutions. After they had consulted together, and collected the laws, they presented them to Datu Bendahara Sri Maharaja, in the kingdom of Malacca, who laid them at the feet of the illustrious Muhammed Shah; whereupon that Prince said—'I grant the request of the Bendahara, and establish these laws and institutions for your government and that of your posterity. When you administer these laws at sea, they shall not be afterwards interfered with on shore. Henceforth let the laws of the sea be carried into effect at sea, in like manner as those of the land are carried into effect on land; and let them not interfere with each other; for you' (addressing himself to the nakhodahs) 'are as rajas at sea, and I confer authority on you accordingly.'

"The several nakhodahs who had framed the code were then honoured with titles. Nakhodah Jenal received the title of Sang Yahi de Raja, Nakhodah Dewa that of Sang Utama de Raja, and Nakhodah Is-hak that of Sang Setia de Raja.

"In such manner were the laws established and made known during the times when the kingdom of Malacca was tranquil and prosperous, during the reign of Sultan Muhammed Shah, and when Sri Nara de Raja was Bendahara, and governed that country.

"Therefore, as the laws of the sea are established

as well as the laws of the land, let them be observed, in order that whatever is undertaken may be properly regulated. Let these laws be followed towards all countries, inasmuch as the laws of the sea which relate to the sea only, and the laws of the land which relate to the land only, are defined; because those of the sea cannot interfere with those established on shore.

"According to these institutions let the law be administered at sea, that no disputes and quarrels may take place. Let them be known, and descend to posterity, that men may not act according to their own will and inclination, but that order and regularity may prevail on board vessels as well during prosperity as adversity. Let not what is established be done away, nor these laws be resisted or disobeyed.

"If these laws are attended to, no one can question the authority of the nakhodah; for, as the rajah is on shore, so is the nakhodah at sea. This authority has been conferred by the sultans of the land upon all nakhodahs, in order that they may administer the laws on board their respective vessels. Whoever does not admit this authority, offends against the law."

From the contents, a pretty accurate notion may be formed of the code. And the following enactments only may be quoted as more curious or extraordinary:—

"*Of the Kiwis or Traders.*

"This is the law relating to the kiwis: They shall pay for the tonnage they require, unless they have assisted the nakhodah, in his trading concerns, to the extent of three or four tahils—(twenty-four or thirty-two dollars;) in which case the nakhodah shall give them two or three coyens of tonnage, or one division of the hold; it being considered that the profit on the three or four tahils is an adequate compensation.

"The mala kiwi shall be entitled to half of the division of the hold, in which the rice or provisions are stowed—(petah gandung;) because he is the pung'hulu, or head man of all the kiwis."

"*The Laws respecting Throwing Cargo Overboard.*

"When there is a violent storm, and it may be necessary to throw overboard a part of the cargo for the safety of the prahu, a general consultation shall be held with respect to the property in the prahu; and those who have much and those who have little must agree to throw overboard in proportion.

"If the nakhodah omits to assemble all those who are interested, and the cargo is thrown overboard indiscriminately, the fault shall be on the nakhodah of the prahu; for such is not the custom."

"*Of Detention.*

"The law is, that, when the season is nearly over, (musim kassis,) and the nakhodah of the prahu omits to sail, the kiwi shall wait, on his account, for seven days; after which, if the nakhodah does not proceed, and the season is over, the price paid for the divisions of the hold shall be returned to the kiwis.

"If the kiwis are the cause of the delay, and the season is nearly over, the nakhodah shall detain the prahu seven days on their account, after which he is authorized to sail without them, if they are not ready; and no more shall be paid or done relating thereto."

"*Of Troves.*

"Whatever is found on the sea, whoever may discover it, is the property of the nakhodah of the prahu, who may give what he thinks proper to the persons who found it."

"Whatever may be found on shore by persons belonging to the prahu, at the time when they are not acting under the nakhodah's orders, nor performing the duty of the prahu, even if the parties are kiwis or turun menugen, the trove shall be divided into three parts, and one-third shall appertain to the finder, and the remaining two parts become the property of the nakhodah."

In perusing this eastern code of laws, one cannot fail to remark the striking similarity to some of the early and rude usages of the maritime states of the Mediterranean, as recorded in the Consolato del Mare.

The Bugis, too, (it appears, from Lieutenant Newbold's Political and Statistical Account of the British Settlements in the Straits of Malacca, published in 1840,) have codes of law similar, in many respects, to the Malayan compilations. "The maritime code of the Bugis has been translated by the Rev. Mr Thomson of Singapore. It is a very brief and unsatisfactory compilation, but resembles the maritime code of the Malays in some of its more important provisions. The nakhodah, or captain, has absolute power while at sea, controlled only by the unanimous voice of his two chief officers, the Jummudi and Jurabattu, and the whole crew. It is divided into fourteen sections. The first five are on freights and passage-money; the remaining sections, up to the 13th, treat partly of freight, passage-money, &c., and contain rules for partnership in trade, &c.; the 14th section defines the power of the captain and of his officers while at sea, leaves the trials for criminal offences to their decision, and gives them "the power of life and death."*

In endeavouring to ascertain whether the early jurisprudence of the eastern nations afforded any illustration of the history of bills of exchange, the author applied to his friend, Mr Erskine; and he is indebted to

---

* Vol. ii., p. 229.

that gentleman for pointing out the following passages, which, although they relate not so much to bills of exchange as to other artificial circulating media of little or no intrinsic value, are curious as shewing that a state paper currency had been tried in China, on one occasion, with success; but generally the reverse; and that the eastern sovereigns had early debased the coin of their realms, and endeavoured to force a compulsory state paper currency long before the Revolutionary government of France had issued their assignats, or the governments of Great Britain and of the United States of America had suspended cash payments by the national banks.

" *Of the kind of Paper Money Issued by the Grand Khan, and made to Pass Current throughout his Dominions.*

" In this city of Kanbalu is the residence of the Grand Khan, who may truly be said to possess the secret of the alchymist, as he has the art of producing money by the following process:—He causes the bark to be stripped from these mulberry trees, the leaves of which are used for feeding silk worms, and takes from it that thin inner rind which lies between the coarser bark and the wood of the tree. This being steeped and afterwards pounded in a mortar until reduced to a pulp, is made into paper, resembling, in substance, that which is manufactured from cotton, but quite black. When ready for use, he has it cut into pieces of money of different sizes, nearly square, but somewhat longer than they are wide. Of these the smallest pass for a denier tournois; the next size for a Venetian silver groat; others for two, five, and ten groats; others for one, two, three, and as far as ten bezants of gold. The coinage of this paper money is authenticated with as much form and ceremony as if it were actually of pure gold and silver; for, to each note, a number of officers, specially appointed, not only subscribe their names, but affix their signets also; and, when this has been regularly done by the whole of them, the principal officer, deputed by his Majesty, having dipped into vermilion the royal seal committed to his custody, stamps with it the piece of paper, so that the form of the seal, tinged with the vermilion, remains impressed upon it, by which it receives its full authenticity as public money; and the act of counterfeiting it is punished as a capital offence. When thus coined in large quantities this paper currency is circulated in every part of his Majesty's dominions; nor dares any person, at the peril of his life, refuse to accept it in payment. All his subjects receive it without hesitation; because, wherever their business may call them, they can dispose of it again in the purchase of merchandise they may have occasion for; such as pearls, jewels, gold, or silver. With it, in short, every article may be procured.

"Several times in the course of the year, large caravans of merchants arrive with such articles as have just been mentioned, together with gold tissues, which they lay before his Majesty. He, thereupon, calls together twelve experienced and skilful persons, selected for this purpose, whom he commands to examine the articles with great care, and to fix the value at which they should be purchased. Upon the sum at which they have been thus conscientiously appraised he allows a reasonable profit, and immediately pays for them with this paper, to which the owners can have no objection; because, as has been observed, it answers the purposes of their own disbursements; and, even though they should be inhabitants of a country where this kind of money is not current, they invest the amount in other articles of merchandise suited to their own markets. When any persons happen to be possessed of paper money which, from long use, has become damaged, they carry it to the Mint, where, upon the payment of only three per cent., they may receive fresh notes in exchange. Should any be desirous of procuring gold or silver for the purposes of manufacture, such as of drinking cups, girdles, or other articles, wrought of those metals, they, in like manner, apply at the Mint, and, for the paper, obtain the bullion they require. All his Majesty's armies are paid with this currency, which is to them of the same value as if it were gold or silver. Upon these grounds it may certainly be affirmed that the Great Khan has a more extensive command of treasure than any other sovereign in the universe."*

According to P. Gaubil, paper money had already been current at Pekin under the Grand Khan Oktaï, who himself only imitated what had been practised by the dynasty that preceded the Yuen or family of Jenghis Khan.—C'est cette annee 1234, qu'on fit la monnoie de papier ; les billets s'appelloient tchao. Le sceau du pon-tchm-se, ou tresorier general de la province etoit empreint dessus, et il y en avoit de tout valeur. Cette monnoie avoit déjà couru sous les princes de kin.† By Du Halde we are informed that its establishment was attempted also by the first princes of the dynasty that succeeded the Mongals.‡

In Miles' Shajrat ul Atrak,§ it is said, "Gunjatoo Khan, (son of Abukai, son of Hulako, &c.,) was a very liberal Chinese prince, so much so, that the revenue of his kingdom could scarcely supply his expenses. In the year 693 Hejira, the use of jad, or stamped paper, to serve as current money, was introduced, in commercial transactions, into Persia, by the advice of Az-ud-din Mozef-

---

* Marsden's Translation of the Travels of Marco Polo, p. 553–5.
† Observ. Chronol., p. 192.
‡ Note 677, p. 559.
§ Pages 266–7.

fer. These notes, which were called jad in Persia, were long slips of paper, stamped on both sides with the arms or seal of the prince; and, on both sides, also, the profession of faith, or the names of two witnesses; and, between these, the words, in the Khutaie language and character, Nokta Aburnucheen Noorcheen—the name of the kaan of Khutaie, and called by the Moghuls the 'King of Kings.' By the introduction of these jad or bank-notes, however, the resort of merchants to Persia was interrupted or abandoned, and the purchase and sale of all merchandise entirely stopped. The usurers, therefore, assembled, and represented these circumstances to Gunjatoo Khan, and he ordered his stamped paper regulations to be abolished."*

The effects of tampering with the coin may be seen also in the reign of Mahomed Toghlak in India. He was extravagant, and lavished vast sums on his pleasures and favourites; he levied heavy duties on the necessaries of life; the country was involved in distress; farmers fled to the woods; land was left uncultivated; famine ensued. "The copper money," says Ferishta,† "for want of proper regulations, was productive of evils equal to those already specified. The King, unfortunately for his people, adopted his ideas upon currency from a Chinese custom of using paper on the Emperor's credit, with the royal seal appended, in lieu of ready money. Mahomed Toghlak, instead of stamped paper, struck a copper coin, which he issued at an imaginary value, and caused it to pass current, by a decree, throughout Hindostan. The Mint was under bad regulation. Bankers acquired large fortunes by coinage. Foreign merchants made their payments in copper to the home manufacturers, though they themselves received, for the articles they sold, silver and gold in

* Marco Polo, 359.

† Briggs' Translation, vol. i., p. 414.

foreign markets. There was so much corruption practised in the Mint, that, for a premium to those persons who had the management of it, merchants had their coin struck considerably below the legal value; and these abuses were connived at by the government. The great calamity, however, consequent upon this debasement of the coin, arose from the known instability of the government. Public credit could not long subsist in a state so liable to revolutions as Hindostan; for how could the people in the remote provinces receive for money the bare representative of a treasury that so often changed its master? From these evils the discontent became universal; and the King was, at length, obliged to call in the copper money. Such abuses had occurred in the Mint, however, that, after the treasury was emptied, there still remained a heavy demand. This debt the King struck off, and thousands were ruined. The state, so far from gaining by this crude scheme, had exhausted its treasury; and the bankers and some merchants alone accumulated fortunes at the expense of their sovereign and the people."* The tankas of silver, it seems, had amalgamated in them a great deal of alloy, so that each tanka only exchanged for sixteen copper pice; making, as Briggs remarks, "a tanka worth only about fourpence, instead of two shillings."†

In farther illustration, if not of the maritime, at least of the commercial law of the Hindus, both in the early ages, when the Code of Menu was composed, supposed to be about 900 years before the Christian era, and also in later times, the author is happy to add the following extracts from the recently published admirable History of India by the Hon. Mountstuart Elphinstone:—

* Briggs' Translation, p. 44–5.

† Ibid., p. 410.

* "The following statement of the principal titles of law, in the Code of Menu, implies an advanced stage of civilisation :—

"1st, Debt on loans for consumption. 2d, Deposits and loans for use. 3d, Sale without ownership. 4th, Concerns among partners. 5th, Subtraction of what has been given. 6th, Non-payment of wages or hire. 7th, Non-performance of agreements. 8th, Rescission of sale and purchase.

"Some of these heads are treated of in a full and satisfactory manner, while the rules in others are meagre, and such as to shew that the transactions they relate to were still in a simple state."

"A creditor is authorized, before complaining to the court, to recover his property by any means in his power, resorting even to force, within certain bounds. This law still operates so strongly in some Hindu states, that a creditor imprisons his debtor in his private house ; and even keeps him, for a period, without food, and exposed to the sun, to compel him to produce the money he owes."

"Interest varies from two per cent. per mensem for a Bramin, to five per cent. for a Sudra. It is reduced to one-half when there is a pledge, and ceases altogether if the pledge can be used for the profit of the lender. There are rules regarding interest on money lent on bottomry *for sea voyages*, and on similar risk by land ; and others for preventing the accumulation of interest on money above the original amount of the principal.

"Various rules regarding sureties for personal appearance and pecuniary payments, as well as regarding contracts, are introduced under this head—(Contracts.)

"Fraudulent contracts and contracts entered into for illegal purposes are null. A contract made, even by a slave, for the support of the family of his absent master, is binding on the master.

* Vol. i., p. 61–63.

"A sale by a person not the owner is void, unless made in the open market; in that case it is valid if the purchaser can produce the seller; otherwise the right owner may take the property on paying half the value.

"A trader breaking his promise is to be fined; or, if it was made on oath, to be banished.

"A sale may be unsettled by either party within ten days after it is made, but not later.

* "The Code of Menu is still the basis of the Hindu jurisprudence; and the principal features remain unaltered to the present day. The various works of other inspired writers, however, and the numerous commentaries by persons of less authority, together with the additions rendered necessary by the course of time, have introduced many changes into the written law, and have led to the formation of several schools, the various opinions of which are followed respectively in different parts of India.

"In all of these, Menu is the text book; but is received according to the interpretations and modifications of approved commentators; and the great body of law thus formed has again been reduced to digests, each of authority within the limits of particular schools. The law now goes much more into particulars on all subjects than in Menu's time. Attornies or pleaders are allowed, and rules of pleading are prescribed.

"Different modes of arbitration are provided; and, although many of the rudest parts of the old fabric remain, yet the law bears clear marks of its more recent date, in the greater experience it evinces in the modes of proceeding, and in the signs of a more complicated society than existed in the time of the first code."

"The improvements, however, in the written law, bear no proportion to the excellence of the original sketch;

---

* Vol. i., p. 156–159.

and the existing code of the Hindus has no longer that superiority to those of other Asiatic nations which, in its early stage, it was entitled to claim over all its contemporaries."

"Many great changes have been silently wrought without any alteration in the letter of the law. The regular administration of justice by permanent courts, which is provided for in Menu, and of which the tribunals, with their several powers, are recorded by later writers, is hardly observed by any Hindu government. The place of those tribunals is, in part, taken by commissions appointed, in a summary way, by the Prince, generally granted from motives of court favour, and often composed of persons suited to the object of the protecting courtier. In part, the courts are replaced by bodies of arbitrators, called Panchayets, who sometimes act under the authority of the government, and sometimes settle disputes by the mere consent of the parties. The efficiency of these tribunals is, in some measure, kept up, notwithstanding the neglect of the government, by the power given by Menu to a creditor over his debtor, which still subsists, and affords a motive to the person withholding payment to consent to an inquiry into the claim."

PRINTED BY PETER BROWN, ST JAMES' SQUARE, EDINBURGH.

Printed in Dunstable, United Kingdom

91220117R00288